A Most Indispensable Art

Edited by James B. Petersen

A Most Indispensable Art

Native Fiber
Industries from
Eastern North America

The University of Tennessee Press / Knoxville

Library of Congress Cataloging in Publication Data

A most indispensable art : native fiber industries from eastern North
America / edited by James B. Petersen.—1st ed.
        p.   cm.
    Includes bibliographical references and index.
    ISBN 0-87049-915-7 (cloth: alk. pa.)
    1. Indian textile fabrics—East (U.S.) 2. Indian baskets—East (U.S.)
    3. Indians of North America—East (U.S.)—Antiquities. 4. Woodland
    culture. 5. East (U.S.)—Antiquities. I. Petersen, James B.
E98.T35M67   1996
746.41'0974—dc20   95-4405
                                                     CIP

To R. L. Andrews, 1953–1990

Contents

Illustrations

MAPS

TABLES

J. M. Adovasio

Foreword:

A Note about R. L. Andrews

Rhonda Lynette Andrews was recognized by several of her contemporaries as one of the three truly great perishables analysts of the twentieth century, an assessment that is fully supported by her published works and one with which I heartily concur.

Born in Groves, Texas, in 1953, Rhonda displayed an intense interest in the physical world around her from a very early age. Not only the familiar household pets like cats and dogs but also the myriad backyard animal life of the Texas Gulf Coast became regular objects of her childhood fascination. Nurtured by her parents, this keen interest in "things living," as she put it, persisted and was amplified in her early education. It blossomed and expanded during her high school years in England at the American School of London. During her secondary education, Rhonda was an avid reader of a broad array of subjects, not the least of which were popular and more technical treatments of history and archaeology. She also traveled extensively during that period, visiting such exotic locations as Crete and Tanzania.

Upon graduating from high school in 1972, Rhonda returned to the United States to pursue a degree in anthropology. Her choice of anthropology as a career was based on a belief that it was far and away the most eclectic of the sciences, and that its breadth and numerous possibilities for interaction with other fields like biology, geology, and history most closely paralleled her own catholic scholarly interests.

Literally from the outset of her undergraduate education, Rhonda showed the same intense interest in a variety of natural and physical sciences that she had as a child. She enrolled initially at the University of Pittsburgh in an experimental undergraduate program that encouraged students to pursue a self-designed course of study that included hands-on laboratory work, and she became involved in a series of projects, first in physical anthropology and then in archaeology, that cemented her interest in the field and shaped her subsequent educational and professional career.

In 1974, Rhonda enrolled in the University of Pittsburgh Summer Field Training Program in Archaeology, which at that time was beginning a second season of excavations at the now internationally known Meadowcroft Rockshelter site. During her first field season she displayed an acute awareness and developed a great mastery of the many nuances of archaeological fieldwork and the subtleties of closed-site excavation. Almost from the outset, she showed an ability to make and operationalize suggestions for improving the nature and quality of data retrieval, a propensity which both Joel Gunn and myself encouraged to the great benefit of this singular project.

Upon completion of her first season at Meadowcroft, Rhonda had her first exposure to perishables analysis as an assistant—and very soon after that as a full-fledged analyst—in the Basketry Analysis Facility at the University of Pittsburgh. Her initial research involved the vast collection of fiber artifacts from Dirty Shame Rockshelter in Oregon, a project that she pursued relentlessly until its completion and publication 12 years later.

Rhonda's interest in perishables seems to have developed or, more accurately, to have crystallized at the same instant she first saw and handled an ancient basketry fragment. Her awareness that these fragile items contained a wealth of information about the individuals and societies which produced them was immediately fueled and quite literally burned through the remainder of her unfortunately short but brilliant professional career.

Since, at that time, a significant number of basketry and related items excavated anywhere in the Americas passed through the Basketry Analysis Facility of the University of Pittsburgh, Rhonda had more than ample opportunity to process, analyze, interpret, and write up a startlingly diverse array of perishable products. In so doing, she continuously refined her analytical methodology to extract, within the limits of the art, the last and finest increment of information contained within these sometimes breathtakingly beautiful but far more often fairly unlovely items.

Shortly after she initiated work on the Dirty Shame material, Rhonda also began her involvement with the analysis of the even more massive corpus of perishable data from Antelope House in Canyon de Chelly, Arizona. Like the Dirty Shame perishables analysis, this project would also take more than a decade to complete.

In rapid and overlapping succession, there followed a long series of other projects, including the analysis of textiles from the Bronze Age site of Bab edh-Dhra in Jordan; textile impressions from Jarmo in Iran; basketry and related objects from Hinds Cave in Texas; Archaic cordage from Squaw Rockshelter in Ohio; carbonized perishable remains from Meadowcroft Rockshelter in Pennsylvania; baskets and miscellaneous perishables from Walpi Pueblo in Arizona; musk-ox-hair cordage from Avayalik Island in Labrador, Canada; Fremont basketry from cave sites in Idaho; a late Pleistocene/early Holocene hunting net from Sheep Mountain in Wyoming; basketry and related perishables from Lakeside, Floating Island, and Danger caves in Utah; basketry and textiles from Tin Cave in Arizona; and other smaller projects too numerous to enumerate. Most recently, she had taken on the spectacular waterlogged collection from the Archaic Windover Bog Cemetery site in Florida. While working on all of these projects, she completed her first degree in anthropology, graduating summa cum laude, and was designated a University Scholar.

Though her involvement with perishable analysis projects dominated her professional time, she nonetheless continued her interests in other areas. She participated in the Meadowcroft excavations yearly until their completion in 1978, and thereafter she engaged in fieldwork at a wide variety of other sites in Pennsylvania and surrounding states, most notably in the re-excavation of the portal deposits at Danger Cave in Utah. In order to better understand the prehistoric stage upon which the actors of antiquity performed, she received a second degree in geology, again graduating summa cum laude and becoming a University Scholar for a second time.

Throughout her involvement with the Meadowcroft project and other field activities, Rhonda assisted in the development of improved field recordation and documentation methods, and she was in charge of the computerization of the data base from Meadowcroft and a number of other sites. Though space precludes any elaboration of her contributions in this area, I offer to say her improvements contributed immensely to the precision of the many University of Pittsburgh field projects conducted in the 1970s and 1980s.

Rhonda was active in a variety of professional organizations, including the Society for American Archaeology, at whose meetings she invariably presented papers on a yearly basis, as well as the Great Basin Anthropological Conference. She also took quiet pride in her membership in Sigma Xi and Phi Beta Kappa.

Throughout her highly productive and multifaceted career, Rhonda was also a gifted draftsperson and artifact illustrator—a substantial number of reports, monographs, and publications produced by both the University of Pittsburgh's Cultural Resource Management Program and the Basketry Analysis Facility were enhanced by her graphic-art skills. Particularly notable in this regard were her illustrations for *Basketry Technology* (Adovasio 1977), "The Antelope House Basketry Industry" (Adovasio and Gunn 1986), *Basketry and Miscellaneous Perishable Artifacts from Walpi Pueblo, Arizona* (Adovasio and Andrews 1985), and, of course, *Perishable Industries from Dirty Shame Rockshelter Malheur County, Oregon* (Andrews, Adovasio, and Carlisle 1986).

In all of her diverse research activities, many of which were collaborative enterprises with myself and others, Rhonda exhibited a singular constellation of characteristics I have never encountered before and certainly never will again. She was incredibly thorough and precise to the point of being a genuine perfectionist, a trait which is evident in all of her writing. Her background and expertise in research was exhaustive, and no remotely applicable comparative reference escaped her eye. Her analytical and synthetic skills, fortified by a mastery of computers and statistical manipulation, elevated her research to an entirely different plane of interpretation.

Rhonda never missed the opportunity to ask new questions about the objects she examined, and it was always her desire to render the execution of each new project better than the last. And here, she always succeeded. Her major works, notably the Hinds Cave, Dirty Shame, Antelope House, and Walpi projects, were all unanimously hailed as permanent contributions to the field of basketry and textile studies specifically and to material culture studies generally.

In these and all of her other publications, the reader is continuously reminded not only of the breadth and depth of her interest but also of her clear realization that the objects she so carefully described were the products of *living* humans in vibrant societies. As they *should* be, artifacts for her were not to be studied simply as artifacts *per se*, but rather as documents of complex human behaviors. As such, she "read" those documents like no one else I have ever known.

At the time of her death, Rhonda was characteristically involved in a wide range of projects. These included the final preparation of the Windover Bog Cemetery textile report, the publication of the Nan Ranch Mogollon collections from New Mexico, the publication of the Lakeside and re-excavated Danger Cave portal material from Utah, the final write up of the Bronze Age Bab edh-Dhra material from Jordan, and a host of smaller enterprises. All of these projects will be completed in the analytical facility which she was to direct and which now bears her name at the Mercyhurst Archaeological Institute of Mercyhurst College in Erie, Pennsylvania. This facility, the R. L. Andrews Center for Perishable Analysis, is the direct descendant of the Basketry Analysis Facility that she developed and directed at the University of Pittsburgh and, along with her contribution to this volume and her other published works, will allow her name and signal accomplishments to be perpetuated for future generations of perishables analysts.

Though I am obviously biased, I believe Rhonda's contributions and, thereby, her meteoric career, will stand and be recognized as long as there are archaeologists who concern themselves with the most perishable of human products. To borrow, paraphrase, and personalize a refrain from a recent song, we'll never see the likes of her again.

R. L. Andrews, 1953–1990.

Preface

From the tree where the bark grows, they make several sorts of baskets, great and small. Some will hold four bushels, or more; and so downward, to a pint. In their baskets they put their provisions. Some of their baskets are made of rushes; some of bents; others, of maize husks; others, of a kind of silk grass; others, of a kind of wild hemp; and some, of barks of trees; many of them, very neat and artificial, with the portraitures of birds, beasts, fishes and flowers, upon them in colours. Also they make mats of several sorts for covering their houses and doors, and to sleep and sit upon. The baskets and mats are always made by their women. . . .

—Daniel Gookin 1674 (1792:11)

The textile art dates back to the very inception of culture, and its practice is next to universal among living peoples. . . . At all periods of cultural development it has been a most indispensable art, and with some peoples it has reached a marvelous perfection, both technically and aesthetically.

—William H. Holmes (1896:10)

Material culture has been a significant component of anthropological research since the founding of the discipline of anthropology in the nineteenth century. Research questions about technology, subsistence adaptations, and social identity and interaction, among others, have been long studied by anthropologists through the analysis of material culture. Few, if any, other categories of material culture in the archaeological and ethnographic records preserve as many clues about these research questions as do fiber industries, and yet they remain incompletely studied in most continents and culture areas. In particular, the study of native fiber industries from eastern North America has been underemphasized.

Fiber industries, or "perishables," including but not limited to basketry, other fabrics, cordage, netting, and complex cordage constructions, have an ancient tenure among native aboriginal populations in eastern North America, likely spanning over 11,000 years. These industries certainly served economic, social, ceremonial, and even symbolic functions among native cultures over this long temporal span, and thus they are material manifestations of prehistoric and historic aboriginal lifeways. Why then have fiber perishables been generally ignored by anthropologists working in the East?

With regard to the archaeological record, this situation can be partially explained by biases against fiber industries due to their typically fragile character and a corresponding lack of familiarity with systematic methods for their analysis among regional researchers. Comparable biases in the ethnographic record are attributable to similar factors, as well as to the destructive nature of early culture contact and culture change among native populations after the arrival of Europeans, Africans, and others in eastern North America. A deficit of chronological and contextual information about native fiber industries is thus typical all across the broad region.

This volume has been compiled to address this notable deficit. Many of the papers were presented in a symposium at the forty-ninth annual meeting of the Society for American Archaeology (SAA) in Portland, Oregon. This SAA symposium provided the genesis of the present volume in 1984, but its compilation has included the addition of several chapters to provide broader coverage, the loss of several potentially valuable contributions, and, most unfortunately, the loss of several participants. The late Kate Peck Kent, a longtime analyst of southwestern fiber perishables, originally planned to contribute a chapter, and, more recently, the untimely death of Rhonda Andrews made revision of her co-authored chapter difficult. As an important contributor to the field and an avid student of fiber perishables wherever they occur, Rhonda was an enthusiastic supporter of this project from its inception. Consequently, the volume editor ultimately solicited a dedicatory foreword in her memory from her co-author and husband, James Adovasio. Most recently, we are saddened to learn of the death of Lucy Sibley, another volume contributor, as this volume goes to press.

The scope of the volume is broad in its geographic and conceptual dimensions. The geographic scope of the chapters ranges from local studies in the Midwest, Southeast, Mid-Atlantic, New England, and Upper Great Lakes to broader regional syntheses for large portions of eastern North America. While archaeological specimens are emphasized, the methods, results, and interpretations can be more or less equally applied to ethnographic collections as well. Specific contributions range from a historical overview of archaeological and ethnographic studies of eastern fiber industries by the editor, documentation of the earliest known samples in the region, ca. 9000–1000 B.C., by Andrews and Adovasio, and several analyses of more localized fiber industries in specific spatial and temporal dimensions. Gardner's plea for appropriate conservation and curation of fiber industries may represent the most critical contribution in the collection, however.

While not all of the potential research topics inherent in fiber perishables are represented, this collection includes a representative sample of established and innovative approaches to such analyses. Particular emphasis has been given to differentiation of social groups through perceived differences in fiber industries by several researchers, including Hamilton and others and Maslowski, Johnson, and the editor. The potential for reconstruction of fiber artifacts using negative impressions is also stressed by these researchers and by Kuttruff and Kuttruff. Site-specific analyses of actual fiber artifacts by Heckenberger, Sibley, and their various colleagues document the potential complexity and richness of fiber perishables, in spite of their restricted contexts and obviously incomplete preservation. Finally, Catherine Fowler provides a comparative perspective about the entire collection of essays from the standpoint of western North America, where such studies have a longer tenure and a more complete development.

A great deal remains to be done to develop fully the study of fiber industries in eastern North America and elsewhere. Nonetheless, all of us hope that this collection will stimulate additional appropriate analyses of extant and reconstructed fiber industries that are systematic, descriptive, and exhaustive. If nothing else, we hope it will encourage more interest in fiber perishables as an important component of the anthropological record wherever they occur.

REFERENCES CITED

Gookin, Daniel
1792 *Historical Collections of the Indians in New England.* Belknap and Hall, Boston.
Holmes, William H.
1896 Prehistoric Textile Art of the Eastern United States. In *Annual Report of the Bureau of American Ethnology, 1891–1892,* pp. 3–46. Smithsonian Institution, Washington, D.C.

Acknowledgments

Although acknowledgments are scattered through the volume in conjunction with individual chapters, the volume editor owes thanks to various people who have helped along the way. At the UMF Archaeology Research Center, Belinda Cox and William Crandall provided invaluable assistance with many of the drafted graphics and tables, respectively. Fred Dearnley in the UMF Instructional Media Center also provided important assistance for the volume illustrations. In particular, Shirley Thompson patiently and expertly provided critical word-processing support throughout the many later drafts of the entire volume, waiting on the volume editor and, in some cases, the individual authors alike.

At the University of Tennessee Press, Kimberly Scarbrough, Stan Ivester, Scot Danforth, and other staff provided encouragement and support over a lengthy period. Their patience is much appreciated.

A number of people provided useful comments about the individual volume contributions, but Dale Croes, Mary Elizabeth King (Black), and Dwight Wallace all read the entire draft manuscript and offered useful comments and criticisms. In addition, King (Black) was also the discussant for the SAA symposium at which many of the papers were first presented.

Several journals and institutions allowed figures and maps to be reprinted with their permission, including the Carnegie Museum of Natural History for Figures 3.2A, 3.3, 3.4, 3.5A, 3.7, 3.9, and 3.10 and Maps 3.1 and 3.2; the Museum of Anthropology, University of Michigan for Figure 7.1; and *Mississippi Archaeology* for Figures 9.1–9.4 and Maps 9.1 and 9.2. Adovasio's dedicatory foreword about R. L. Andrews and the photograph of her were previously published in *American Antiquity*, the journal of the Society for American Archaeology. We are grateful for permission to reprint all of these materials.

Finally, the individual authors are owed a particular note of thanks for their patience and forbearance with this volume. A very lengthy period of time transpired from inception of the project to its completion, and it may have been tempting for some (or all) of the contributors to abandon it at one point or another. That they did not do so is a testimonial to their spirit of cooperation and to their belief that this project is an important one. We all hope that the reader feels the same way, too. As is customary, the volume editor accepts responsibility for any errors or omissions herein.

1

James B. Petersen

The Study of Native Fiber Industries
from Eastern North America:
Resume and Prospect

As noted in a review of *Prehistoric Textiles of the Southwest* by the late Kate Peck Kent, "contemporary anthropological archaeology does not emphasize either through training, practice or publication, the analysis and interpretation of material culture. . . . This is particularly true in the area of so-called 'perishable' artifacts" (Adovasio 1984:179). Unfortunately, Adovasio's comment is applicable all across North America and elsewhere too. It has become unfashionable among some anthropologists to labor over archaeological and ethnographic artifacts, unless perhaps they can be used to address one or another problem of pressing processual concern (MacKenzie 1991:22–23; Stott and Reynolds 1987). Consequently, many contemporary anthropologists have incompletely developed or abandoned their appreciation for material culture in general, in spite of the fact that artifacts remain the most tangible manifestation of human culture.

Analysts of fiber artifacts still continue to study this often mundane form of material culture. Their labors are rewarded by typically intriguing glimpses of culturally sensitive, if fragile, artifacts, even when they are fragmentary archaeological specimens. Fiber artifacts, or "textiles," as they are sometimes called, do not necessarily provide major insights into fashionable issues in every analysis, but they often provide substantive clues about the relative technological and aesthetic achievements of particular cultures, whether extinct or extant.

Even when fragmentary, this information can be more than a descriptive catalogue when samples are substantial and/or taken in conjunction with samples from comparable temporal and spatial contexts. For example, studies of fiber industries from western North America have demonstrated the utility of archaeological and ethnographic specimens alike in the reconstruction of various aspects of culture history, including culture continuity and change, social complexity and interaction, among others (e.g., Adovasio 1985, 1986; Adovasio and Andrews 1985; Adovasio and Gunn

1986; Bernick 1987; Croes 1989a, 1989b, 1992; Croes and Blinman 1980; Fowler and Matley 1979; Kent 1983a, 1983b; Magers 1986; Turnbaugh and Turnbaugh 1986; Whiteford 1988).

In contrast, archaeological fiber industries from eastern North America have received considerably less attention than their counterparts in the West due, in large part, to less favorable conditions of preservation. The same general situation pertains to many ethnographic specimens from eastern North America as well, as described more fully below.

Using a broad definition of the East as the region from the Rockies eastward to the Atlantic Ocean, only rare circumstances allow the preservation of prehistoric fiber specimens in this large area. Favorable conditions of preservation include localized aridity in caves and rockshelters, complete saturation in water, carbonization, replacement by metallic salts, and/or biotic sterilization; all have occasionally enabled preservation of actual prehistoric fiber industries in the East (e.g., Andrews and Adovasio this volume; Duggan and Riggs 1991; Epstein 1963; Gilliland 1975; Jones 1936a; Sibley and Jakes 1982; Wedel 1961; Wright 1987).

More commonly, evidence of prehistoric fiber artifacts is preserved as negative impressions on aboriginal ceramics and other more rare substances across the region (e.g., Drooker 1990, 1992; Holmes 1884; Maslowski 1984). Unfortunately, this evidence has received relatively little attention as a separate technological class, beyond simple mention of its presence on ceramics, for example. Even where studied and reported, evidence of fiber perishables preserved as negative impressions is somewhat limited by the fact that all relevant structural details may not be visible, and it is difficult, if not impossible, to identify the nature of the raw materials beyond very general characteristics (King 1978:90–91).

Historic ethnographic fiber industries from the East have been more thoroughly studied than their prehistoric antecedents. However, even these artifacts are less well known than their western counterparts because of the early and often completely destructive nature of culture contact between Native American and Euroamerican populations in the East. For example, only a single type of basketry, plaiting, is reported as "common" among aboriginal populations in eastern North America in Driver's monumental survey of Native American cultures (1975:Maps 24 and 25), but this perspective is certainly biased. As should be obvious, fiber artifacts remain incompletely known in the East for both the prehistoric and historic periods.

This chapter summarizes past studies of aboriginal fiber industries from the East to partially mitigate the long-term biases against them, as poorly preserved and typically overlooked in material analyses. As used here, fiber artifacts are one major category of "perishables," or those traditional industries which are manufactured predominantly from organic materials such as wood, bone, antler, and other organic materials. The term "perishables" is used sometimes to describe all of these industries collectively because they do not typically survive as archaeological or ethnographic specimens without being kept from the elements.

Fiber industries are constructed from vegetal or other fibers of some sort, notably including but not limited to basketry, other fabrics, netting, cordage, and complex cordage constructions. Some or all of these industries are variously called "textiles" by various researchers (e.g., Drooker 1992; Holmes 1896; King 1979, 1986), although this latter term is often reserved for "cloth" or fabric structures, as discussed at greater length in a subsequent section of this review.

It is assumed here and elsewhere in this volume that considerable information about fiber industries can be obtained from the East in spite of obvious obstacles, and that such evidence is generally of great consequence wherever it occurs. Besides a brief discussion of past studies, consideration is also given to methodological issues, classification alternatives, relevant theory, and possible future directions in the study of fiber industries.

HISTORY OF PAST RESEARCH

As with many other aspects of North American anthropology, the study of fiber industries in its early stages was undertaken by personnel associated with the Smithsonian Institution Bureau of American Ethnology and other museums, such as the Peabody Museum at Harvard (Willoughby 1905, 1935; see also Fang and Binder 1990). William H. Holmes (e.g., 1884, 1888, 1896) and Otis T. Mason (e.g., 1885, 1901, 1904) provided exemplary studies of the diversity of North American textiles in general and basketry in particular. These two scholars recognized the distinctiveness of the various fiber technologies employed by prehistoric and ethnographic aboriginal craftsmen, and Holmes, in particular, was explicit in his use of ethnographic data to reconstruct the functional contexts in which these technologies may have been used. Holmes (1884) apparently was the first anywhere to emphasize the potential of reconstructing fiber industries from their negative impressions preserved on aboriginal ceramics (Figure 1.1) and may have been the first to study archaeological specimens (King 1975:10).

Mason (1904) published the first attempt to apply a broad system of classification to North American aboriginal basketry. His work is still an important document of regional differences between cultural groups in terms of basketry, specifically including discussion of archaeological and ethnographic specimens from the East (Mason 1885:305–306, 1904:372–391). Unfortunately, these early studies and other more recent examples were hampered by a poor understanding of the antiquity of these industries (Drooker 1992:9–11). Early claims for the great antiquity of some specimens were the source of considerable debate (e.g., Wilson 1889, but see Andrews and Adovasio this volume; Andrews et al. 1988; Petersen et al. 1984; Stile 1982).

The increased excavation of archaeological sites of a ceremonial nature during the late nineteenth century and early portion of the twentieth century, particularly in the Midwest and Southeast, provided various samples of partially preserved prehistoric fiber industries (e.g., Fowke and Moorehead 1894; Mills 1907, 1909, 1922; Shetrone 1931; Willoughby 1932). However, these finds were not fully reported and today can be used only when they are illustrated.

Charles C. Willoughby (1938) used some of these fiber specimens in his classification of textile variation among the products of nonloom manufacture, as he recognized them. Willoughby's work still offers useful descriptive information about the nature of Hopewellian fiber industries, ca. 200 B.C. to A.D. 300. More recent analyses have expanded the formal and social aspects of these industries, which are better known than most due to their typical association with native copper artifacts and corresponding preservation (e.g., Carr and Hinkle 1984; Church 1983, 1984).

Other early cemetery and/or ceremonial site excavations across the region also occasionally produced fiber specimens which are suggestive of technological complexity (e.g., Carey 1941a, 1941b; Gilliland 1975; Webb 1941; Willoughby 1924), but in the absence of comparative materials, all of these samples were too limited to discern clear patterns. Perhaps the most intriguing and unique samples of fiber industries known from anywhere in eastern North America were recovered from Spiro (Craig) Mound during the 1930s by looters (Hamilton 1952). Although still not exhaustively published, fiber specimens from Spiro (Craig) Mound, including dyed designs, feather or fur wrapping and spun wild turkey down elements, document the considerable complexity of late prehistoric fabrics and basketry (e.g., King and Gardner 1981; Kuttruff 1988, 1993; Trowbridge 1938; Willoughby 1952). Contemporaneous specimens from the Etowah site were also early recognized as being complex and very sophisticated (e.g., Willoughby 1932; see also Sibley and Jakes 1989; Sibley et al. this volume).

Excavation of both open and cave or rockshelter habitation sites during this same period provided other extant and reconstructed samples of fiber artifacts from the East, but usually from contexts of imprecise antiquity (e.g., Dellinger 1936; Funkhouser and Webb 1929, 1930; Harrington 1924; Orchard 1920; Over 1936; Scholtz 1975; Smith 1910; Watson 1969, 1974a; Webb and Funkhouser 1936; Wintemberg 1946). Cross-dating was therefore hampered. Nonetheless, some of these samples were combined with others from more strictly ceremonial contexts, again largely burials, to characterize prehistoric fiber industries for specific temporal periods. Examples include the Early Woodland period

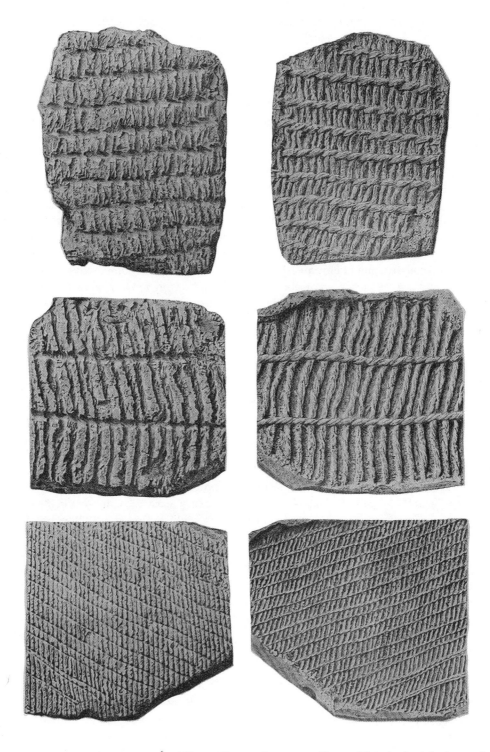

Figure 1.1. Early illustration of positive casts of fiber artifacts and corresponding prehistoric aboriginal ceramics. (From Holmes 1884.)

Adena "culture" and various Mississippian period "cultures," among others (e.g., Webb and Funkhouser 1931; Webb and Snow 1945). Support of salvage archaeology and other projects by the Federal W.P.A. during the 1930s produced still other samples of actual fiber specimens and negative impressions thereof from both habitation and ceremonial contexts (e.g., Griffin 1938, 1939; Haag 1942; Lewis and Kneberg 1946; Munger and Adams 1941; Webb 1938, 1939; Webb and DeJarnette 1942). During this same era, some researchers began to argue for more thorough and systematic analysis of fiber industries, specifically including specimens from the East (e.g., Miner 1936; Weltfish 1930a). Likewise, research efforts were directed towards identification of specific vegetal sources of raw materials employed in producing archaeological and ethnographic examples (e.g., Bell and King 1944; Jones 1936a; Whitford 1941). This important work continues today (Jakes et al. 1994).

Research in the second half of the twentieth century has seen more emphasis given to prehistoric and ethnographic fiber industries, but again few broad-scale systematic analyses have been published using samples from the East. As with prior analyses, very few archaeological specimens have been reported in detail. Most have received little more attention than brief mention of their recovery, including various extant specimens (e.g., Bell and Baerreis 1951; Fowler 1966; Hadlock 1947; Harper 1956; Husted 1969; Jeppson 1964; Jones 1966; Kidd 1953; Kraft 1976; Lehmer 1954; Miller 1960; Ritchie 1955, 1965; Christopher Turnbull 1976; Walthall 1980; Wedel 1961; Wood 1976).

In particular, samples of fiber industries from research and salvage projects in the Lower Pecos region on the margin of the Desert West have been relatively common. These permit reconstruction of what is undoubtedly the longest and best known sequence of fiber artifact manufacture in the East[1] and adjoining areas. It spans a period over 9000 years in duration, ca. 7500 B.C.–A.D. 1700 (e.g., Adovasio 1970, 1974; Alexander 1970; Andrews and Adovasio 1980; Epstein 1963; McGregor 1992; Weir 1983; Word and Douglas 1970; see Taylor 1966, 1988). In this region and elsewhere in the

East, some analysts have begun to record cordage twist, twined weft slant, and other construction details over the past few decades, but details of classification have been often idiosyncratic, without usage of metrics and/or full description (e.g., Bower 1980; Conway and Moser 1967; Cowan 1979; Dragoo 1963; Epstein 1963; Henning 1966; King 1974; Shippee 1966; Trubowitz 1983; Watson 1969, 1974a, 1974b).

Negative impressions of fiber artifacts have also been increasingly studied over this period, typically as preserved on ceramics but also including clay hearths and other contexts. Positive casts are often made to facilitate reconstruction of the original structure, but even then it is sometimes difficult to fully and accurately identify all structural types and other attributes, given the indirect and one-sided nature of the evidence. Fiber raw materials are rarely identifiable from casts, for example. Nonetheless, analysts have given attention to cordage twist and/or weft slant, to other attributes, and to the difficulties in trying to separate cordage from fabrics on the basis of such impressions (e.g., Browning 1974; Doyle et al. 1982; Drooker 1990, 1991, 1992; Falk 1983; Johnson 1978, 1982, 1991; Kellar 1967; Kuttruff 1980; Kuttruff and Kuttruff 1992, and this volume; Logan 1952; Maslowski 1973, 1984; Quimby 1961; Rachlin 1955, 1958, 1960; Railey 1984; Wilder 1951; Winfree 1972). Although many of these analyses include only select details, the inclusion of data on cordage twist and other structural attributes is exemplary.

Examination of the extensive archaeological literature on aboriginal ceramics in the East quickly reveals that the large majority of analyses briefly mention the presence of "cord-marking" or "cord-paddling," "fabric-marking," "net-marking," etc., used as surface finish and/or decoration. However, these designations are often loosely applied, and few, if any, other details are typically reported for the fiber industries, even when they constitute the predominant mode of ceramic finish and/or decoration (e.g., C. Chapman 1980; J. Chapman 1985; Coe 1964; DePratter 1979; Evans 1955; Jenkins 1981; Kehoe 1973; Lehmer 1954; Lewis and Kneberg 1958; Logan 1976; McPherron 1967; Neumann 1978;

Ritchie and MacNeish 1949; Sears and Griffin 1950; Walthall 1980; Wood 1976). Clearly, these and numerous other samples represent a monumental data base for the study of fiber industries in the East given future analysis, a point previously emphasized by William Hurley (1979; see also 1974, 1975), among others.

Detailed analysis of archaeological fiber industries has been rarely undertaken anywhere in the East. Some of the exemplary studies mentioned above might be included in this category, but none offer exhaustive details about their respective assemblages. Only a few exhaustive studies have been undertaken in the past decade or two (e.g., Adovasio 1982; Adovasio and Andrews [with Carlisle] 1980; Andrews and Adovasio 1980; Andrews et al. 1988; Bird 1960; Chapman and Adovasio 1977; Drooker 1990, 1991, 1992; King 1968; Kuttruff 1987, 1988; McGregor 1992; Petersen and Adovasio 1990; Petersen et al. 1987; Stile 1982). Unfortunately, most of these recent analyses document small, relatively limited samples (but see Andrews and Adovasio 1980; McGregor 1992; Drooker 1992).

Exhaustive, systematic analyses of fiber industries have been more common to date in western North America, and some of these represent sizeable samples (e.g., Adovasio 1970; Adovasio and Andrews 1985; Adovasio and Gunn 1986; Andrews et al. 1986; Croes 1980, 1989a, 1989b; Croes and Blinman 1980; Hewitt 1980; Loud and Harrington 1929; Magers 1986; Morris and Burgh 1941; Rozaire 1974; see Fowler this volume). Other exemplary analyses have been done elsewhere in the New World (e.g., Adovasio and Maslowski 1980; Bird and Hyslop 1985; Doyon-Bernard 1990; Dransart 1992; King 1979, 1986; MacNeish et al. 1967; O'Neale 1945, 1948; Rodman 1992; Wallace 1979). Although less emphasized here, various Old World studies are also important (e.g., Adovasio 1975–1977; Adovasio and Andrews 1976; Adovasio and Maslowski 1988; Barber 1991; Bar-Yosef and Schick 1989; Bender Jorgensen 1992; Hald 1980; Walton 1989).

It should be quite apparent that additional analyses of archaeological fiber industries from eastern North America (and elsewhere) are sorely needed. Comparable analyses of ethnographic fiber industries from the East are more difficult to summarize because they have been undertaken by an even more diverse group of analysts, many of whom exhibit an art history perspective, rather than an anthropological interest. However, the work of the indefatigable ethnographer Frank Speck included study of fiber industries from the Southeast and Northeast, among other areas (e.g., Speck 1911, 1914, 1920; see Duggan and Riggs 1991).

In New England, Fanny Eckstorm (1932) and Speck (1940) documented ethnographic remnants of what were once almost assuredly more complicated fiber industries (see Bower 1980; Gookin 1792; Willoughby 1905). More recent reports on early historic samples from this area and the adjacent Canadian Maritime Provinces have further documented the diversity of traditional industries in the far Northeast, including quill, bark, and various other vegetal fiber products (Figure 1.2).[2] (See, e.g., Fang and Binder 1990; Harper 1956; McMullen 1992; Turnbaugh and Turnbaugh 1987; Whitehead 1980, 1982, 1987, n.d.)

Figure 1.2. Old (nineteenth-century?) Micmac birch-bark and porcupine-quill box with dyed elements, probably from the Canadian Maritime provinces.

Considerable debate has followed Brasser's suggestion that the well-known plaited "woodsplint" basketry of this region was a European introduction (Figures 1.3–1.5) (Brasser 1975; see also Bardwell 1986; Lester 1987; McMullen 1992; McMullen and Handsman 1987; M. Schneider 1984; Turnbaugh and Turnbaugh 1986). Regardless of this issue, various summaries of northeastern ethnographic fiber industries document the social contexts of production and distribution, but offer only limited description of the specimens themselves or systematic documentation of comparative attributes (e.g., Flannery 1939; Lismer 1941; McBride 1990; McMullen and Handsman 1987; Pelletier 1977, 1982; Turnbaugh and Turnbaugh 1986). The correlation of prehistoric and historic fiber industries remains a vexing problem in the Northeast.

Figure 1.4. Passamaquoddy basketmaker Clara Keezer at the Maine Indian Basketmakers Alliance Gathering at the College of the Atlantic, Bar Harbor, Maine, July 1994.

Figure 1.3. Recent Passamaquoddy split ash basket, with dyed elements, from eastern Maine, USA. Made by Clara Keezer, 1986.

Figure 1.5. Micmac basketmaker Frank Hannan at the Maine Indian Basketmakers Alliance Gathering at the College of the Atlantic, Bar Harbor, Maine, July 1994. Note members of the California Indian Basketweaver's Association looking on.

A similar situation prevails in other portions of the East as well. In the Great Lakes area, some details are available to describe ethnographic fiber industries that survived into near modern or modern times (e.g., Fang and Binder 1990; Jones 1935, 1936b, 1946; Lauersons 1984; Lismer 1941; K. Petersen 1963; Ritzenthaler and Ritzenthaler 1970; Skinner 1921; Turnbaugh and Turnbaugh 1986), but precious few extant specimens are known that can be clearly attributed to the early historic period (e.g., Jones 1966; Kenyon 1982; Kidd 1953; Phillips 1987).

Likewise, some information is available for the ethnographic Plains region (e.g., Brasser 1987; Gilmore 1925; M. Schneider 1984; Turnbaugh and Turnbaugh 1986; Weltfish 1930b), as well as the Southeast (e.g., Burt and Ferguson 1973; Duggan and Riggs 1991; Fang and Binder 1990; Goggin 1939, 1949; Green 1992; Speck 1920; Turnbaugh and Turnbaugh 1986). However, the articulation of these industries with those of the late prehistoric and early historic periods remains little known in most areas, with a few exceptions (e.g., M. Schneider 1984; Scholtz 1975). As is the case in the Northeast, broad-scale detailed comparative analyses of ethnographic fiber industries from these areas await further research.

METHODS AND CLASSIFICATION SYSTEMS

Methods for analysis of diverse fiber industries vary in accord with the goals of the analysis. Likewise, the classification system employed in any one analysis may vary to some degree with the particular goals. Of course, the nature of a specific sample and the constituent forms of fiber industries also structure the analytical methods and classification system to be employed. To date, researchers have not agreed upon one mutually exclusive classification system for fiber industries, due, in part, to the intergrade between certain forms, such as basketry and "cloth," for example (Dransart 1992:133).

The full range of fiber industries manufactured by aboriginal populations in the East during a tenure of at least 11,000 years remains unknown, but it is likely staggering (for detailed discussion of the antiquity of different technologies, see Adovasio

1974, 1982; Andrews and Adovasio this volume). Any basic descriptive system should recognize some combination of raw materials, technology, morphology, and decoration to systematically reduce the variation in a sample to a manageable and meaningful level. All of these modes (Rouse 1960) have been employed by analysts of fiber industries in the past with varying results. Simply stated, previous analyses have been variably successful depending on the classification systems they employed.

Any sample of fiber artifacts most often can be conveniently classified primarily on the basis of the manufacture techniques and/or its finished forms. Of course, the former may work better for fragmentary archaeological specimens, while the latter may be used most effectively for more complete ethnographic specimens.

In the broadest sense, fabric can be defined as the "generic term for all fibrous constructions," typically including multiple elements in the construction, whereas textile refers "specifically to woven (i.e. interlaced warp-weft) fabrics" (Emery 1980:xvi; see Burnham 1980). Thus, fabrics may include a wide variety of constructions, but textiles are more limited in scope in many scenarios (but see King 1979:265, for example, where "textiles" apparently include "cordage, basketry, and fabric specimens").

Still more specifically, the term basketry can be used to label baskets, bags, and matting, all of which represent a continuum from three-dimensional to two-dimensional fabrics (or textiles). Basketry is distinguished by some analysts (e.g., Adovasio 1977; Andrews and Adovasio 1980) as being manually woven without a frame or loom in contrast to loom-woven specimens, which are sometimes labeled as "textiles" or "fabrics" in what is a more restricted use of these terms.

The framework suggested by Adovasio (1977) was especially designed for North American archaeological basketry specimens, i.e., fiber artifacts which often are incompletely preserved. In this case, basketry technology is subdivided into three categories: twining, plaiting, and coiling. Other distinctive technologies in Adovasio's analytical framework include cordage, netting (including knotted and knotless categories), and miscellaneous constructions of various sorts (e.g., Andrews and Adovasio 1980; Andrews et al. 1986; McGregor 1992). Adovasio's approach can be directly or indirectly criticized on various grounds (e.g., Emery 1980:60, 68; King, personal communication 1992; Newton 1987:137–138; Wendrich 1991:2–3), most notably because critics believe it lumps and therefore overly simplifies some construction techniques (e.g., plaiting, which is used for various woven and interlaced constructions in Emery's [1980] terms).

In contrast, the broad, systematic, and very specific classification employed by Irene Emery (1980) is best applied to largely whole or complete specimens in some aspects. For example, "warp-faced" and "weft-faced weaves" are differentiated by Emery on the basis of "longitudinal" and "transverse" orientation, respectively; "warp-twining" and "weft-twining" are similarly differentiated. Thus, these distinctions often can be made only when selvages and other finishing details are evident (Emery 1980:75–77, 196–201), making them difficult to recognize for many archaeological specimens and impossible for most specimens preserved as negative impressions (e.g., Kuttruff and Kuttruff this volume). Consequently, this classification system is overly specific in these cases and a more basic system might be more broadly useful, at least for archaeological analyses.

To date, there is still little consensus in devising a basic classification system for basketry and other fiber industries, although Adovasio's and Emery's systems, among others, have been widely applied (also see Balfet 1957; Seiler-Baldinger 1994). For example, in another scheme (D'Harcourt 1962), plaiting and braiding are not classified as woven, but rather as a separate technology, as is twining in a variation of this scheme (Engel 1963).

Usage of one or another of these classificatory schemes certainly structures the course of an analysis by restricting the range of variation in a sample (Wendrich 1991). This matter may not be as critical as advocates of the different schemes sometimes maintain, as long as the categories are systematic, mutually exclusive internally, and well described

and illustrated. Nonetheless, the general lack of agreement on analytical attribute sets and the definition of key attributes such as "spin," "ply," "compound" and "simple," "warp," and "weft," among others, do sometimes pose very significant problems in the comparison of different researchers' results.

The exact analytical methods employed in the study of fiber industries seem less controversial than the different classification schemes (e.g., King 1978; Wendrich 1991). Adequate techniques of recovery, cleaning, and conservation are critical prior to the initiation of any archaeological analysis and many others, too (e.g., Adovasio 1977; Gardner 1980, 1988, this volume; Walton 1989; Wendrich 1991). Beyond technological classification, Adovasio (1977) presents a useful discussion of the methods for analysis of basketry, and Hurley (1979) does the same for the analysis of cordage; Hurley provides an extensive inventory of cordage structures and composite structures.

A comprehensive analysis of basketry, cordage, and other fiber artifacts might well include, for example, consideration of the number of specimens versus the number of represented individual forms, the types of specimens represented, including selvages and/or other structural details, such as the number of plies (or yarns), as well as inferred form and function. Still other concerns in a comprehensive analysis might include wear patterns, raw material identification, metrics for various attributes, and provenience information, among other data. Parenthetically, it should be noted that Hurley's (1979) technological inventory is based almost entirely upon negative impressions from ceramics, a few of which may have been misinterpreted because structural elements applied as decoration (largely cordage and complex cordage constructions) were not differentiated from underlying elements applied in the prior application of surface finish (largely fabrics) on the ceramics (Hurley 1974, 1975, 1979; cf. Rachlin 1955).

Few other accounts offer comprehensive discussion of appropriate methods for the analysis of fiber industries, except those summarized in the introductory sections of several published analyses (e.g., Adovasio and Andrews [with Carlisle] 1980;

Andrews and Adovasio 1980; see Wendrich 1991; Wild 1988). More explicit discussions of suggested analytical procedures for loom-woven and nonloom-woven fabrics besides basketry, cordage constructions of various sorts, and other miscellaneous fiber industries will be useful contributions to the field in the future.

TOWARD THEORY AND THE ANTHROPOLOGICAL SIGNIFICANCE OF FIBER INDUSTRIES

The analysis and publication of data about fiber industries from eastern North America may be construed as an end in and of itself. These technologies certainly formed an important component of the material-culture inventory of aboriginal populations over much, if not all, of their long span of occupation, as emerging evidence has begun to suggest. A descriptive, technological, documentation approach, with its emphasis on artifact form by choice or necessity, certainly has continuing importance and will contribute to regional and broader-scale culture historical research, as reflected elsewhere (e.g., Moore and Romney 1994; Welsch et al. 1992). However, the study of fiber industries can also serve the goals of anthropology beyond material-culture description, including elucidation of the social function and/or symbolic meaning of artifacts (MacKenzie 1991; Stott and Reynolds 1987). Thus, such analyses can potentially address form, function, and meaning in fiber industries.

McMullen and Handsman (1987:25) have recently noted, for example, that various forms of information can be encoded in material culture "about how people lived, organized themselves and their work, and thought about their world and how it was changing." They argue that static material culture, specifically baskets, can be used to "translate" dynamic cultural processes, such as social interaction, economic exchange, cultural isolation, work organization, and social relations of the makers, as well as other dimensions of resistance and communication.

As has been long noted, fiber industries and other forms of material culture potentially serve social functions as critical markers of cultural identity, or "ethnicity," and social interaction in both spatial and temporal dimensions (e.g., Church 1984; Davidson 1936; Holmes 1896; King 1975; Miner 1936; J. Schneider 1987; Sibley and Jakes 1989; Turnbaugh and Turnbaugh 1986; Weltfish 1932). Adovasio (1977:4), in speaking specifically of basketry, explains:

In point of fact, no class of artifacts available to the archeologist possesses a greater number of culturally bound and still visible attributes. No two populations appear to have ever manufactured basketry in precisely the same fashion, whether their products were coiled, twined or plaited, flexible, semi-rigid or rigid. This situation is demonstrable ethnographically and seems to be valid archeologically as well.

Although many of the technical attributes by which specimens of basketry may be distinguished are minor and seemingly inconsequential, it is precisely these details that are important because they tend to be more localized, conservative and culturally determined. A considerable amount of data can be extracted even from very small and poorly preserved remnants. The tiniest portion of a mat, bag or basket may possess many diagnostic attributes that can be isolated and compared to those from other fragments. Unfortunately, archeologists generally ignore such remains because they are unfamiliar with the potentialities inherent in their identification.

Turnbaugh and Turnbaugh (1986:66) echo this perspective about basketry: "All North American Indian basketry varies regionally and culturally, in terms of its technology. No two peoples created baskets that are just alike, even though their vessels often resemble each other's. Manufacturing and decorative methods, basket forms and functions, and materials used always differ in identifiable ways from people to people and from region to region."

Mary E. King (1975:11–12) applies this same perspective more broadly to archaeological "textiles," again apparently broadly referring to cordage, basketry, and fabrics. She says: "I have come to regard [archaeological textiles] as perhaps the most culturally revealing of all categories of artifacts. . . . While textiles can serve [various] purposes, most of their uses are highly personal. . . . Clothing becomes an extension of one's body and personality. . . . Consequently, archaeological textiles could and should tell us a great deal about the behavior of people in the past." King's (e.g., 1978, 1979, 1992) other publications echo this same perspective, although she is critical of some related assumptions, as discussed further below.

Numerous other examples of the culturally distinctive nature of basketry and other fiber industries can be cited (e.g., Haberlin et al. 1928; Kroeber 1922; Mason 1904; Weber 1986). This same distinctiveness is rightly recognizable for many other fiber artifacts, including but not limited to hammocks, garments, and other types of loom and nonloom fabrics, netting, and even simpler constructions, such as cordage (e.g., Adovasio 1982, 1985, 1986; Crawford 1916; Fry and Adovasio 1970; King 1975, 1978; Maslowski 1984, 1985; Newton 1974, 1987; Rachlin 1960; Rowe 1981; J. Schneider 1987; Taylor 1967:154–161; Walton 1989). The most optimistic of analysts maintain that cultural meaning of cognitive conceptual sorts, including iconography or color symbolism in some cases, can be derived from the study of material culture (e.g., Dwyer 1979; King 1975:11–12; McMullen and Handsman 1987; Ribeiro 1987c; Taylor 1967; see McGregor 1992:11).

Criticisms of the materialist approach in general have an equally long tenure in anthropology (e.g., O'Connell et al. 1982; see Taylor 1967:154), but many of the points of contention are subjective and therefore beyond detailed examination here. Consideration of cultural factors beyond technology clearly seems to be an appropriate consequence of the study of material culture, whether the samples be of archaeological or ethnographic origin. Evidence for various culture-historical circumstances, including cultural continuity, change, and social relations, is preserved in some forms of material culture more than others, and, as suggested above, few, if any, materials surpass fiber industries in this regard.

Examination of a few examples—even such simple constructions as cordage and composite cordage structures—from the ethnographic record document the "culturally charged" nature of fiber industries. Gender roles and other social relations, economic exchange, and a myriad of related cultural behaviors often incorporate fiber artifacts. For example, among the Mehinaku and other native peoples of the Upper Xingu in the Brazilian Amazon, a simple fiber cordage and small bark strip construction, the "inija" woman's belt (Figure 1.6), as it is known to the Mehinaku, serves as a very important symbol of adult femininity. More commonly reported as the "uluri," this vaginal ornament is uniquely distinctive of the Upper Xingu region, crosscutting various language families, where 10 or so Xinguano cultures share its usage (Gregor 1977:Figure 18, 1985:Figure 5; Levi-Strauss 1948:Figure 33). This scanty garment is an important component of many rituals among the Mehinaku and other Xinguanos as a symbol of sexuality (Gregor 1985:47–49).

Among the Yanomamo in the Amazon and Orinoco drainages, a woman's "apron" or "pesimak," constructed of spun, plied, and twisted cotton and other fiber cordage (Figure 1.7), is worn daily as a reflection of female modesty. However, decorated specimens, seemingly reflective of individuality in their details, are more typically worn on special occasions (Couture-Brunette 1986:66–75). Women in the Trobriand Islands and elsewhere in Oceania use simple vegetal fiber "skirts" or "sepewana," along with baskets and simple bundles of little modified fibers, as mortuary goods. In particular, the fiber skirts are culturally meaningful in terms of manufacture, use, and economic distribution, with broad-scale social importance (Weiner 1976:91–103, 1989).

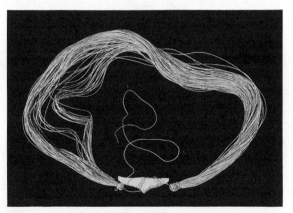

Figure 1.6. Recent Mehinaku *inija* woman's belt from the Upper Xingu River area, Mato Grosso, Brazil.

Figure 1.7. Recent Yanomamo *pesimak* woman's apron with feather decoration from the Catrimani River area, Roraima, Brazil.

Figure 1.8. Recent Arnhem Land Aboriginal knotless netting bag with ocher decoration, Northern Territory, Australia.

Other comparable fiber constructions in the ethnographic record amplify the potential uses of such artifacts. In Arnhem Land and elsewhere in Australia, "fiber string bags" made of knotless fiber cordage netting and "dilly bags" made using twining, among other fiber constructions, most obviously serve utilitarian functions (Figures 1.8 and 1.9) (Davidson 1936; Isaacs n.d.). However, like other items of material culture, they also symbolize to Aboriginal groups complicated mythological beliefs related to the "Dream Time." Wally Caruana (1993:38–45, 74–86) reports: "The various types of string and pandanus-fibre bags, skirts, mats and nets form part of the symbolic imagery used to express the daily and the religious experience. . . . Objects made of woven fibres play prominent roles in ancestral events. Kunmatj, the sacred dilly bag, was carried by one of the major totemic beings, . . . Balangu, the Shark . . . Kunmatj, the dilly bag, appears as the custodian of the waterhole. . . ." Among many other groups, such as the Yekuana and Kayabí in South America, basketry and other fiber industries comparably symbolize a wide variety of mythological and other group beliefs (e.g., Guss 1989; Ribeiro 1987c; Rivière 1992). Thus, even dimensions of cognition and cultural meaning can be elucidated through the study of such artifacts.

Still elsewhere where traditional systems operate today, fiber industries serve other internal and external roles, from ethnic markers to an important means of market exchange and other economic activities. For the "Hill Tribes" of Southeast Asia, for example, clothing and related items continue to provide dramatic and immediately recognizable markers of the different ethnic groups, in spite of the ongoing acculturation to one another and the presence of a dominant national society, as in the case of Thailand; they also serve as a means of bringing in money from the outside (Figure 1.10) (Fraser-Lu 1988:122–124; Lewis and Lewis 1984). Indigenous fiber industries have become an important source of income necessary for participation in a market economy there and elsewhere where they are still produced, whether by aborigines in Australia or by native groups in North and South America (see Figures 1.4 and 1.5) (e.g., McBride 1990; McMullen 1992; Newton 1987).

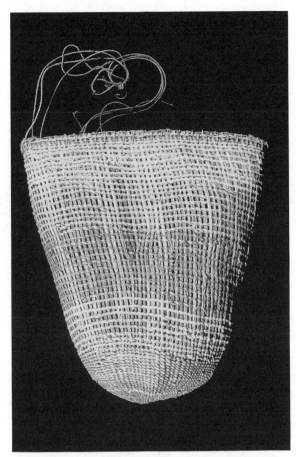

Figure 1.9. Recent Arnhem Land Aboriginal twined "dilly bag," with dyed elements, Northern Territory, Australia.

Figure 1.10. Recent Akha shoulder bag with geometric appliqué and embroidery, Chiang Rai province, Thailand.

Given acceptance of the basic tenets of the social function and cognitive approaches to the study of fiber industries, analyses should be structured to maximize identification of culturally sensitive attributes, as noted above. The first step ought to be more or less exhaustive and systematic description of the available sample. Comparison of the recorded attributes can follow as a form of hypothesis testing.

Some attributes can be particularly important in the assessment of social function, especially those that are commonly represented when specimens are preserved only as fragments or negative impressions. For example, it has been routinely demonstrated that cordage spin and twist, like spin and weft slant in twined fabrics, are reflective of their makers since they are made predominantly one

way or another (labeled S and Z, cf. Emery 1952; Osborne and Osborne 1954) by a particular population, often over a long period (e.g., Adovasio 1982; Andrews and Adovasio 1980; Fry and Adovasio 1970; Henning 1966; King 1974; Maslowski 1984, this volume; Petersen and Hamilton 1984; Taylor 1967; Wild 1988). Different forms of fiber raw materials sometimes can be correlated with different constructions (e.g., Bird and Hyslop 1985; Fenenga and Riddell 1948; Magers 1986; Maslowski 1985; Walton 1989), as evidenced by the analyses which consider a wide variety of attributes.

In a well-known example, Taylor (1967:132–134, 160–161) demonstrated the regional nature of the different basketry and cordage industries recovered from two areas of the Desert West, which he interpreted as two distinctive cultural configurations in these areas. Subsequent comparative analyses on a variety of more local scales have repeatedly demonstrated similar patterns in both eastern and western North America, again seemingly reflective of distinguishable populations in the archaeological record (e.g., Andrews et al. 1986:68–73; Croes 1989a, 1989b; Croes and Blinman 1980; Drooker 1992:207–232; Fry and Adovasio 1970; Goodman 1985; Lu 1987; Maslowski 1984, 1985, this volume; Morris and Burgh 1954; Petersen and Adovasio 1990; Petersen and Hamilton 1984; in particular, see Petersen this volume).

Copious data derived from the ethnographic record further substantiate the culturally sensitive nature of specific cordage and basketry attributes, among other forms of fiber artifacts. Only a small number of ethnographic examples can be cited here, but their careful review reflects the strong cultural patterning *and* potential functional complexity inherent in fiber industries (e.g., Buck 1964; Fowler and Matley 1979; Fraser-Lu 1988; Gigli 1974; Hames and Hames 1976; Lothrop 1929; Lowie 1924; Mason 1904; Newton 1987; O'Neale 1945, 1949; Osgood 1940; Pendergast 1987; Picton and Mack 1989; Ribeiro 1987a, 1987b; Rose 1983; Colin Turnbull 1965; Wheat 1967; Yde 1965).

One recent example may suffice. A detailed analysis of a large ethnographic sample of material culture from the Brazilian Yanomamo of Roraima (Couture-Brunette 1985, 1986) reflects that, among 45 twined "bowl" baskets, *all* have an S-weft slant. In addition, the 44 cotton and other fiber "aprons" in this sample include two or three different components: the "belt," or back portion, the "fringe," or front dangling portion, and the "cord," over which the fringe is twined and which connects the ends around the waist (see Figure 1.7).

Of these three components of Yanomamo "aprons," twined "belts" are found on 23 aprons in the studied sample; 19 (82.6%) have an S-weft slant and four (17.4%) have a Z-weft slant. Twined "fringe" occurs on 42 specimens; 35 (83.3%) have an S-weft slant, and seven (16.7%) have a Z-weft slant. "Cords" of variable configurations occur on all specimens; 40 (90.9%) have a final S-twist, and four (9.1%) have a final Z-twist. These and other specimens establish a clear preference for S-twist and S-weft slant across different categories of Yanomamo fiber industries, regardless of raw materials and construction techniques, confirming the above-mentioned typical preference for either S-twist and S-weft slant, or Z-twist and Z-weft slant configurations in a given population.

Criticism of this specific approach to the study of fiber industries has come from various quarters and is based, in part, upon healthy skepticism (e.g., O'Connell et al. 1982:228–229). Most notably, King (1992:4–5, personal communication 1993) has questioned whether reliance on single attribute modes such as cordage spin and twist direction really has "implications for ethnic affiliations." She says that since there are only two possible states, S or Z, "this has always seemed unlikely to me," but goes on to state that there "is no question, however, that in any given area there is a preference for one spin direction for any given fiber."

King (1992:5) supports this latter observation with data derived from archaeological specimens from Peru (e.g., Dransart 1992; Wallace 1979) and makes the valid point that when taken in conjunction with raw material differences, spin and/or twist can be regionally and/or temporally diagnostic, among other attributes. Her objections seem to stem from the ethnic implications derived by some analysts from merely one or two attributes in their data, not from the fact that such attributes can be spatially and/or temporally diagnostic.

King (1992, personal communication 1993) usefully points out that handedness, spinning techniques, and raw material types all may influence spin and twist attributes, among others. However, Adovasio has said repeatedly that even when handedness affects a given sample, it is the first logical explanation for the presence of a minority spin or twist, with the minority frequency likely correlating with the minority incidence of left-handed people. Other factors, such as cultural intermixing of craftspeople and/or trade in finished goods, also may be potentially reflected, but the clear domination of one spin and/or twist preference in many samples largely belies this point.

Differences in spinning techniques and raw materials are seemingly more pertinent, but, for the most part, these too are structured by a combination of cultural and/or environmental factors. While such differences may not be strictly correlated with ethnic groups in all cases, they are at least *potentially* controlled by a technological tradition and therefore may well also reflect social distinctions, given the obvious relationship between a technological tradition and culture. Although many of the chapters in this volume come down on the side of potentially seeing ethnicity in fiber industries, this issue obviously still needs critical study and debate.

One other matter of broad-scale anthropological significance bears specific mention in this consideration of fiber industries: the development of a general theory of style. Based on a discussion by Carr and Hinkle (1984), fiber industries can be used to test conceptions about the nature of style and its variable representation in dimensions based on individuals, internal and external social relations, and technological sophistication (cf. Adovasio and Gunn 1977; Chernela 1992; J. Schneider 1987; see also Carr and Maslowski 1995). Although not easily observable in all cases, the interface of these dimensions is inevitably represented in specific artifacts. When used with evolving conceptions of style hierarchies (Wiessner 1983, 1984), the study of these interfaces should ultimately enable better definition of the social contexts in which specific fiber industries functioned in the past and how they function today.

More specifically, fiber industries can be profitably studied as they reflect various forms of style, "iconological" and "isochrestic" style, for example, as two major contrastive forms have been called (e.g., Binford 1989; Sackett 1982, 1986; see also Wiessner 1983, 1984, 1990 for a different distinction between "emblemic" and "assertive" style). In this view, "iconological" style carries some sort of social message and is therefore "active." In contrast, "isochrestic" style is "passive" in that it represents a cultural choice which is "equivalent in use," that is, made without necessary intent. Nonetheless, "isochrestic" style may well be just as diagnostic of the maker as is "iconological" style from an external, etic perspective.

As emphasized above in the discussion of the social function of artifacts, fiber industries are often culturally sensitive, and thus they can be studied as reflections of one or both forms of style. Individual attributes, such as cordage twist, knot types, splices, etc., are likely reflective of "isochrestic" style, while overall combinations of attribute modes and some attributes in particular, such as decoration, are reflective of "iconological" style. Recognition and synthetic analysis of such forms of style in fiber industries will contribute to broader stylistic concerns in anthropology.

Of course, not every study of fiber industries needs to address ethnicity, style, or any of the other broad goals outlined above for both archaeological and ethnographic analyses. In fact, it is possible that some (or all) of these goals represent ambitious pursuits best achieved using carefully documented ethnographic information about fiber industries and their makers (e.g., Chernela 1992; MacKenzie 1992; Ribeiro 1987c; Rubinstein 1987; Weiner and Schneider 1989). In the end, the particular interests and experience of individual researchers will influence the nature of fiber artifact analyses as much as the available samples themselves.

FUTURE DIRECTIONS

As should be evident from this brief summary, the study of fiber industries from eastern North America is still in its formative stages. Following a previous discussion of ceramic material culture (Petersen 1985:14), the future challenge in the study of eastern North American fiber industries can be broken down largely into five tasks:

1. First and foremost, the definition of research questions to direct the analysis of fiber industries toward the solution of genuinely anthropological and humanistic problems;
2. Further development of standardized, systematic classification systems for the description of all forms of fiber industries, with the recognition that flexibility will be necessary;
3. Integration of specimen descriptions to begin to delimit assemblage composition within the limits of their preservation;

4. Correlation of data for archaeological fiber industries with stratigraphy and radiocarbon dates, and comparable correlation of ethnographic fiber industries with historical documentation of various sorts to develop local and regional sequences; in turn, these can be used to elucidate more broadly based chronologies for the full span of fiber artifact manufacture across eastern North America; and

5. Anthropological interpretation of archaeological and ethnographic fiber industries data based on intra-assemblage and inter-assemblage comparisons to address various issues of form, function, and meaning.

All five tasks will require considerable effort, but the first and last seem to be the most difficult challenges before us. However, all of these and other related issues should be addressed in the future. The utility of fiber industries in anthropological research can be strengthened through a combination of definition, description, and interpretation of specimens from archaeological and ethnographic contexts. In this way, the promise of material culture can be further developed as a significant component of contemporary anthropological research.

ACKNOWLEDGMENTS

The author again acknowledges the long-term support of James M. Adovasio and various others who have stimulated his interest in material culture. These others include Nathan Hamilton, Michael Heckenberger, William Johnson, Marjory Power, Brian Robinson, and Jack Wolford, among others. Thanks are also extended to Mary Elizabeth King (Black), Dwight Wallace, and Jack Wolford who provided useful comments on earlier drafts of this chapter. Finally, Nathan Hamilton, Michael Heckenberger, William Hillman, and Stephen Nelson helped provide illustrations and/or ethnographic artifacts, while Shirley Thompson patiently helped produce the final text. As is customary, all errors and omissions are the responsibility of the author.

NOTES

1. Although the Lower Pecos region is loosely included here in the East, it is, in fact, often related to the Desert (or Arid) West in terms of its culture-area classification, along with Trans-Pecos Texas. See, for example, the review by Fowler in this volume (also see Andrews and Adovasio this volume).

2. All ethnographic fiber perishables illustrated in this chapter are currently owned by the author.

REFERENCES CITED

Adovasio, J. M.
1970 The Origin, Development and Distribution of Western Archaic Textiles. *Tebiwa* 13(2):1–40.
1974 Prehistoric North American Basketry. In *Collected Papers on Aboriginal Basketry*, edited by Donald R. Tuohy and Doris L. Rendall, pp. 133–153. Nevada State Museum Anthropological Papers 16. Carson City.
1975–77 The Textile and Basketry Impressions from Jarmo. *Paleorient* 3:223–229.
1977 *Basketry Technology: A Guide to Identification and Analysis*. Aldine, Chicago.
1982 Basketry and Netting Impressions. In *The Prehistory of the Paintsville Reservoir, Johnson and Morgan Counties, Kentucky*, compiled by J. M.. Adovasio, pp. 826–845. Ethnology Monographs 6. Dept. of Anthropology, Univ. of Pittsburgh, Pittsburgh.
1984 Review of *Prehistoric Textiles of the Southwest* by Kate Peck Kent. *North American Archaeologist* 5(2):179–180.
1985 Style, Basketry, and Basketmakers: Another Look. Paper presented at the 50th annual meeting of the Society for American Archaeology, Denver.
1986 Artifacts and Ethnicity: Basketry as an Indicator of Territoriality and Population Movements in the Prehistoric Great Basin. In *Anthropology of the Desert West, Essays in Honor of Jesse D. Jennings*, edited by Carol J. Condie and Don D. Fowler, pp. 44–88. Univ. of Utah Anthropological Papers 110. Salt Lake City.
Adovasio, J. M., and R. L. Andrews
1976 Textile Remains and Basketry Impressions from Bab edh-Dhra and a Weaving Implement from Numeira. *Annual of the American School of Oriental Research* 43:57–60.
1985 *Basketry and Miscellaneous Perishable Artifacts from Walpi Pueblo, Arizona*. Ethnology Monographs 7. Dept. of Anthropology, Univ. of Pittsburgh, Pittsburgh.

Adovasio, J. M., and R. L. Andrews (with R. C. Carlisle)
1980 Basketry, Cordage and Bark Impressions from the
Northern Thorn Mound (46Mg78), Monongalia
County, West Virginia. *West Virginia Archeologist*
30:33–72.
Adovasio, J. M., and Joel D. Gunn
1977 Style, Basketry, and Basketmakers. In *The Individual
in Prehistory: Studies of Variability in Style in Prehistoric Technologies*, edited by James N. Hill and Joel
D. Gunn, pp. 137–153. Academic Press, New York.
1986 The Antelope House Basketry Industry. In *Archeological Investigations at Antelope House*, edited by
Don P. Morris, pp. 306–397. National Park Service,
U.S. Dept. of the Interior, Washington, D.C.
Adovasio, J. M., and Robert F. Maslowski
1980 Textiles and Cordage. In *Guitarrero Cave: Early Man
in the Andes*, by Thomas F. Lynch, pp. 253–290.
Academic Press, New York.
1988 Textile Impressions on Ceramic Vessels at Divostin.
In *Divostin and the Neolithic of Central Serbia*, edited
by Alan McPherron and Dragoslav Srejovic, pp.
345–357. Ethnology Monographs 10. Dept. of Anthropology, Univ. of Pittsburgh, Pittsburgh.
Alexander, Robert K.
1970 *Archaeological Excavations at Parida Cave.* Papers of
the Texas Archaeological Salvage Project 19. Univ.
of Texas, Austin.
Andrews, R. L., and J. M. Adovasio
1980 *Perishable Industries from Hinds Cave, Val Verde
County, Texas.* Ethnology Monographs 5. Dept. of
Anthropology, Univ. of Pittsburgh, Pittsburgh.
Andrews, R. L., J. M. Adovasio, and R. C. Carlisle
1986 *Perishable Industries from Dirty Shame Rockshelter,
Malheur County, Oregon.* Ethnology Monographs 9.
Dept. of Anthropology, Univ. of Pittsburgh, Pittsburgh.
Andrews, R. L., J. M. Adovasio, and D. G. Harding
1988 Textile and Related Perishable Remains from the
Windover Site (8BR246). Paper presented at the
53rd annual meeting of the Society for American
Archaeology, Phoenix.
Balfet, Helene
1957 Basketry: A Proposed Classification. Translated
by M. H. Baumhoff. *Annual Report of the Univer-
sity of California Archaeological Survey* 37(47):1–21.
Berkeley.
Barber, Elizabeth J. W.
1991 *Prehistoric Textiles: The Development of Cloth in the
Neolithic and Bronze Ages.* Princeton Univ. Press,
Princeton.

Bardwell, Kathryn
1986 The Case for an Aboriginal Origin of Northeast
Indian Woodsplint Basketry. *Man in the Northeast*
31:49–67.
Bar-Yosef, Ofer, and Tamar Schick
1989 Early Neolithic Organic Remains from Nahal Hemar
Cave. *National Geographic Research* 5(2):176–190.
Bell, Robert E., and David A. Baerreis
1951 A Survey of Oklahoma Archaeology. *Bulletin of
Texas Archaeological and Paleontological Society*
22:7–100.
Bell, Willis H., and Carl J. King
1944 Methods for the Identification of the Leaf Fibers of
Mescal *(Agave)*, Yucca *(Yucca)*, Beargrass *(Nolina)*,
and Sotol *(Dasylirion).* American Antiquity
10(2):150–160.
Bender Jorgensen, Lise
1992 *North European Textiles Until a.d. 1000.* Aarhus
Univ. Press, Aarhus.
Bernick, Kathryn
1987 The Potential of Basketry for Reconstructing Cultural Diversity on the Northwest Coast. In
Ethnicity and Culture, edited by Reginald Auger,
Margaret F. Glass, Scott MacEachern, and Peter H.
McCartney, pp. 251–257. Univ. of Calgary Archaeology Association, Calgary.
Binford, Lewis R.
1989 Styles of Style. *Journal of Anthropological Archaeol-
ogy* 8:51–67.
Bird, Junius B.
1960 The Long Sault Island Fabric. In *The Eastern Dis-
persal of the Adena*, by William A. Ritchie and Don
W. Dragoo, pp. 48–49. New York State Museum
and Science Service Bulletin 379. Albany.
Bird, Junius B., and John Hyslop
1985 *The Preceramic Excavations at the Huaca Prieta,
Chicama Valley, Peru.* Anthropological Papers of
the American Museum of Natural History 62(1).
New York.
Bower, Beth
1980 Aboriginal Textiles. In *Burr's Hill, A Seventeenth
Century Wampanoag Burial Ground in Warren, Rhode
Island*, edited by Susan Gibson, pp. 89–91, 140–144.
Haffenreffer Museum of Anthropology, Brown
Univ., Providence.
Brasser, Ted J.
1975 *A Basketful of Indian Culture Change.* Canadian Eth-
nology Service Paper 22. National Museum of
Man, Ottawa.

1987   By the Power of Their Dreams: Artistic Traditions of the Northern Plains. In *The Spirit Sings: Artistic Traditions of Canada's First Peoples*, pp. 93–131. Glenbow Museum and McClelland and Stewart, Toronto.

Browning, Kathryn
1974   Indian Textiles as Reconstructed from the Impressions Left on Long Island Pottery. *Archaeology of Eastern North America* 2(1):94–98.

Buck, Peter H.
1964   Twined Baskets. In *Arts and Crafts of Hawaii*, by Peter H. Buck, pp. 141–164. Bernice P. Bishop Museum Special Publication 45. Honolulu.

Burnham, Dorothy K.
1980   *Warp and Weft: A Textile Terminology*. Royal Ontario Museum, Toronto.

Burt, Jesse, and Robert B. Ferguson
1973   *Indians of the Southeast: Then and Now*. Abingdon Press, Nashville.

Carey, Henry A.
1941a   A Primitive Dagger Covering. In *Mt. Horeb Earthworks and the Drake Mound, Fayette County, Kentucky*, by W. S. Webb, pp. 185–191. Univ. of Kentucky Reports in Anthropology and Archaeology 5(2). Lexington.
1941b   Primitive Textiles from the Morgan Stone Mound. In *The Morgan Stone Mound, Site 15, Bath County, Kentucky*, by W. S. Webb, pp. 268–281. Univ. of Kentucky Reports in Archaeology and Anthropology 5(5). Lexington.

Carr, Christopher, and Kathleen Hinkle
1984   A Synthetic Theory of Artifact Design Applied to Ohio Hopewell Weavings. Paper presented at the 49th annual meeting of the Society for American Archaeology, Portland.

Carr, Christopher, and Robert F. Maslowski
1995   Cordage and Fabrics: Relating Form, Technology, and Social Processes. In *Style, Society, and Person: Archaeological and Ethnological Perspectives*, edited by Christopher Carr and Jill E. Neitzel, pp. 297–343. Plenum Press, New York.

Caruana, Wally
1993   *Aboriginal Art*. Thames and Hudson, New York.

Chapman, Carl H.
1980   *The Archaeology of Missouri, II*. Univ. of Missouri Press, Columbia.

Chapman, Jefferson
1985   *Tellico Archaeology: 12,000 Years of Native American History*. Report of Investigations 43. Dept. of Anthropology, Univ. of Tennessee, Knoxville.

Chapman, J., and J. M. Adovasio
1977   Textile and Basketry Impressions from Icehouse Bottom, Tennessee. *American Antiquity* 42(4):620–625.

Chernela, Janet M.
1992   Social Meaning and Material Transaction: The Wanano-Tukano of Brazil and Columbia. *Journal of Anthropological Archaeology* 11:111–124.

Church, Flora
1983   An Analysis of Textile Fragments from Three Ohio Hopewell Sites. *The Ohio Archaeologist* 33(1):10–15.
1984   Textiles as Markers of Ohio Hopewell Social Identities. *Midcontinental Journal of Archaeology* 9(1):1–25.

Coe, Joffre L.
1964   *The Formative Cultures of the Carolina Piedmont*. Transactions of the American Philosophical Society, New Series 54(5). Philadelphia.

Conway, Donna, and Mary Moser
1967   A Preliminary Analysis of the Cordage and Textile Industry of 36HU1. In *Archaeological Investigations of Sheep Rock Shelter, Huntingdon County, Pennsylvania*, vol. 1, edited by Joseph W. Michels and Ira F. Smith, pp. 257–301. Dept. of Sociology and Anthropology, Pennsylvania State Univ., Univ. Park.

Couture-Brunette, Lorraine
1985   Yanomama Material Culture in the Carnegie Museum of Natural History. Part I. Food Procurement and Household Articles. *Annals of Carnegie Museum* 54(15):487–532. Pittsburgh.
1986   Yanomama Material Culture in the Carnegie Museum of Natural History. Part II. Wearing Apparel and Festival Artifacts. *Annals of Carnegie Museum* 55(4):63–93. Pittsburgh.

Cowan, C. Wesley
1979   Excavations at Haystack Rock Shelters, Powell County, Kentucky. *Midcontinental Journal of Archaeology* 4(1):3–33.

Crawford, M. D. C.
1916   Peruvian Fabrics. *Anthropological Papers of the American Museum of Natural History* 12(4):107–187. New York.

Croes, Dale R.
1980   *Cordage from the Ozette Village Archaeological Site: A Technological, Functional, and Comparative Study*. Laboratory of Archaeology and History Project Reports 9. Washington State Univ., Pullman.
1989a   Prehistoric Ethnicity on the Northwest Coast of North America: An Evaluation of Style in Basketry and Lithics. *Journal of Anthropological Archaeology* 8:101–130.

1989b Lachane Basketry and Cordage: A Technological, Functional and Comparative Study. *Canadian Journal of Archaeology* 13:165–205.

1992 An Evolving Revolution in Wet Site Research on the Northwest Coast of North America. In *The Wetland Revolution in Prehistory*, edited by Byrony Coles, pp. 99–111. Wetland Archaeology Research Project Occasional Paper 6. Dept. of History and Archaeology, Univ. of Exeter, Exeter.

Croes, Dale R., and Eric Blinman (editors)
1980 *Hoko River: A 2500 Year Old Fishing Camp on the Northwest Coast of North America.* Reports of Investigations 58. Laboratory of Anthropology, Washington State Univ., Pullman.

Davidson, D. S.
1936 Australian Netting and Basketry Techniques. *Journal of the Polynesian Society* 35:257–299.

Dellinger, Samuel C.
1936 Baby Cradles of the Ozark Bluff Dwellers. *American Antiquity* 1(3):197–214.

DePratter, Chester B.
1979 Ceramics. In *The Anthropology of St. Catherine's Island 2. The Refuge-Deptford Mortuary Complex*, by David H. Thomas and Clark S. Larsen, pp. 109–132. Anthropological Papers of the American Museum of Natural History 56(1). New York.

D'Harcourt, Raoul
1962 *Textiles of Ancient Peru and Their Techniques.* Univ. of Washington Press, Seattle.

Doyle, Richard A., Nathan D. Hamilton, and James B. Petersen
1982 Early Woodland Ceramics and Associated Perishable Industries from Southwestern Maine. *Maine Archaeological Society Bulletin* 22(2):4–21.

Doyon-Bernard, S. J.
1990 From Twining to Triple Cloth: Experimentation and Innovation in Ancient Peruvian Weaving (ca. 5000–400 B.C.). *American Antiquity* 55(1):68–87.

Dragoo, Don W.
1963 *Mounds for the Dead.* Annals of Carnegie Museum 37. Pittsburgh.

Dransart, Penny
1992 Form and Function in the Basketry of the Central and South Central Andes: An Overview from Prehispanic Times to the Present. In *Basketmakers: Meaning and Form in Native American Baskets*, edited by Linda Mowat, Howard Morphy, and Penny Dransart, pp. 131–145. Univ. of Oxford Pitt Rivers Museum Monograph 5. Oxford.

Driver, Harold E.
1975 *Indians of North America,* 2nd Ed. Univ. of Chicago Press, Chicago.

Drooker, Penelope Ballard
1990 Textile Production and Use at Wickliffe Mounds (15Ba4), Kentucky. *Midcontinental Journal of Archaeology* 15(2):163–220.

1991 Mississippian Lace: A Complex Textile Impressed on Pottery from the Stone Site, Tennessee. *Southeastern Archaeology* 10(2):79–97.

1992 *Mississippian Village Textiles at Wickliffe.* Univ. of Alabama Press, Tuscaloosa.

Duggan, Betty J., and Brett H. Riggs
1991 *Studies in Cherokee Basketry.* Occasional Paper 9. The Frank McClung Museum, Univ. of Tennessee, Knoxville.

Dwyer, Jane P.
1979 The Chronology and Iconography of Paracas-Style Textiles. In *The Junius B. Bird Pre-Columbian Textile Conference*, edited by Ann P. Rowe, Elizabeth P. Benson, and Ann L. Schaffer, pp. 105–128. The Textile Museum, Washington, D.C.

Eckstorm, Fannie Hardy
1932 *The Handicrafts of the Modern Indians of Maine.* Lafayette National Park Museum Bulletin 3. Bar Harbor.

Emery, Irene
1952 Naming the Direction of the Twist of Yarn and Cordage. *El Palacio* 59(8):251–262.

1980 *The Primary Structure of Fabrics: An Illustrated Classification.* The Textile Museum, Washington, D.C.

Engel, Frederic
1963 *A Preceramic Settlement on the Central Coast of Peru, Asia, Unit 1.* Transactions of the American Philosophical Society, New Series 53(3). Philadelphia.

Epstein, Jeremiah F.
1963 Centipede and Damp Caves: Excavations in Val Verde County, Texas, 1958. *Bulletin of the Texas Archaeological Society* 33:1–129.

Evans, Clifford
1955 *A Ceramic Study of Virginia Archeology.* Smithsonian Institution Bureau of American Ethnology Bulletin 160. Washington, D.C.

Falk, Carole Portugal
1983 Cordage Impressed on Potomac Creek Pottery: Decoding the Corded Style Motifs and the Methods of Pattern Manufacture. *Maryland Archeology* 19(2):1–20.

Fang, Madeleine W., and Marilyn R. Binder

1990   *A Photographic Guide to the Ethnographic North American Indian Basket Collection, Peabody Museum of Archaeology and Ethnology.* Peabody Museum of Archaeology and Ethnology, Harvard Univ., Cambridge.

Fenenga, Franklin, and Francis A. Riddell

1949   Excavation of Tommy Tucker Cave, Lassen County, California. *American Antiquity* 14(3):203–214.

Flannery, Regina

1939   *An Analysis of Coastal Algonquian Culture.* Catholic Univ. of America Anthropological Series 7. Washington, D.C.

Fowke, Gerard, and Warren K. Moorehead

1894   Recent Mound Exploration in Ohio. In *Proceedings of the Academy of Natural Sciences of Philadelphia,* pp. 308–321. Philadelphia.

Fowler, Don D., and John F. Matley

1979   *Material Culture of the Numa, The John Wesley Powell Collection, 1867–1880.* Smithsonian Contributions to Anthropology 26. Smithsonian Institution, Washington, D.C.

Fowler, William S.

1966   Ceremonial and Domestic Products of Aboriginal New England. *Bulletin of the Massachusetts Archaeological Society* 27(3 & 4):33–66.

Fraser-Lu, Sylvia

1988   *Handwoven Textiles of South-East Asia.* Oxford Univ. Press, Singapore.

Fry, G. F., and J. M. Adovasio

1970   Population Differentiation in Hogup and Danger Caves, Two Archaic Sites in the Eastern Great Basin. *Nevada State Museum Anthropological Papers* 15:208–215. Carson City.

Funkhouser, W. D., and W. S. Webb

1929   *The So-called "Ash Caves" in Lee County, Kentucky.* Univ. of Kentucky Reports in Archaeology and Anthropology 1(2). Lexington.

1930   *Rock Shelters of Wolfe and Powell Counties, Kentucky.* Univ. of Kentucky Reports in Archaeology and Anthropology 1(4). Lexington.

Gardner, Joan S.

1980   *The Conservation of Fragile Specimens from the Spiro Mound, LeFlore County, Oklahoma.* Contributions from the Stovall Museum 5. Univ. of Oklahoma, Norman.

1988   Conservation of the Windover Fabrics and Wood. Paper presented at the 53rd annual meeting of the Society for American Archaeology, Phoenix.

Gigli, Jane Green

1974   Dat So La Lee, Queen of the Washo Basketmakers. In *Collected Papers on Aboriginal Basketry,* edited by Donald R. Tuohy and Doris L. Rendall, pp. 1–27. Nevada State Museum Anthropological Papers 16. Carson City.

Gilliland, Marion S.

1975   *The Material Culture of Key Marco, Florida.* Univ. Presses of Florida, Gainesville.

Gilmore, Melvin R.

1925   Arikara Basketry. *Indian Notes* 2(2):89–95. Museum of the American Indian, New York.

Goggin, John M.

1939   Louisiana Choctaw Basketry. *El Palacio* 46(6):121–123.

1949   Plaited Basketry in the New World. *Southwestern Journal of Anthropology* 5(2):165–168.

Goodman, Stacy

1985   Material Culture: Basketry and Fiber Artifacts. In *The Archaeology of Hidden Cave, Nevada,* edited by David H. Thomas, pp. 262–298. Anthropological Papers of the American Museum of Natural History 61(1). New York.

Gookin, Daniel

1792   *Historical Collections of the Indians in New England.* Belknap and Hall, Boston.

Green, Rayna

1992   Red Earth People and Southeastern Basketry. In *Basketmakers: Meaning and Form in Native American Baskets,* edited by Linda Mowat, Howard Morphy, and Penny Dransart, pp. 11–17. Univ. of Oxford Pitt Rivers Museum Monograph 5. Oxford.

Gregor, Thomas

1977   *Mehinaku: The Drama of Daily Life in a Brazilian Indian Village.* Univ. of Chicago Press, Chicago.

1985   *Anxious Pleasures: The Sexual Lives of an Amazonian People.* Univ. of Chicago Press, Chicago.

Griffin, James B.

1938   The Ceramic Remains from Norris Basin. In *An Archaeological Survey of the Norris Basin in Eastern Tennessee,* by William S. Webb, pp. 253–358. Smithsonian Institution Bureau of American Ethnology Bulletin 118. Washington, D.C.

1939   Report on the Ceramics of Wheeler Basin. In *An Archaeological Survey of Wheeler Basin on the Tennessee River in Northern Alabama,* by William S. Webb, pp. 127–165. Smithsonian Institution Bureau of American Ethnology Bulletin 122. Washington, D.C.

Guss, David M.

1989   *To Weave and Sing: Art, Symbol, and Narrative in the South American Rain Forest.* Univ. of California Press, Berkeley.

Haag, William G.
1942 A Description and Analysis of the Pickwick Pottery. In *An Archeological Survey of Pickwick Basin in the Adjacent Portions of the States of Alabama, Mississippi, and Tennessee,* by William S. Webb and David L. DeJarnette, pp. 509–526. Smithsonian Institution Bureau of American Ethnology Bulletin 129. Washington, D.C.

Haberlin, H. K., James A. Teit, and Helen H. Roberts
1928 Coiled Basketry in British Columbia and Surrounding Regions. In *Annual Report of the Bureau of American Ethnology, 1919–1924,* pp. 119–483. Smithsonian Institution, Washington, D.C.

Hadlock, Wendell S.
1947 The Significance of Certain Textiles found at Redbank, New Brunswick, in Relation to the History of the Culture Area. *Acadian Naturalist* 2(8):49–62.

Hald, Margrethe
1980 *Ancient Danish Textiles from Bogs and Burials: A Comparative Study of Costume and Iron Age Textiles.* Publications of the National Museum, Archaeological-Historical Series 21. Copenhagen.

Hames, Raymond B., and Ilene L. Hames
1976 Yekwana Basketry: Its Cultural Context. *Anthropologica* 44:3–58.

Hamilton, Henry W.
1952 The Spiro Mound. *The Missouri Archaeologist* 14:1–276.

Harper, J. Russell
1956 *Portland Point: Crossroads of New Brunswick History.* Historical Studies 9. New Brunswick Museum, Saint John.

Harrington, Mark R.
1924 The Ozark Bluff-Dwellers. *American Anthropologist* 26:1–21.

Henning, Amy E.
1966 Fabrics and Related Materials from Arnold Research Cave. *The Missouri Archaeologist* 28:41–53.

Hewitt, Nancy J.
1980 Fiber Artifacts. In *Cowboy Cave,* by Jesse D. Jennings, pp. 49–74. Univ. of Utah Anthropological Papers 104. Salt Lake City.

Holmes, William H.
1884 Prehistoric Textile Fabrics of the United States Derived from Impressions on Pottery. In *Annual Report of the Bureau of American Ethnology, 1881–1882,* pp. 393–425. Smithsonian Institution, Washington, D.C.
1888 A Study of the Textile Art in Its Relation to the Development of Form and Ornament. In *Annual Report of the Bureau of American Ethnology, 1884–1885,* pp. 189–252. Smithsonian Institution, Washington, D.C.
1896 Prehistoric Textile Art of the Eastern United States. In *Annual Report of the Bureau of American Ethnology, 1891–1892,* pp. 3–46. Smithsonian Institution, Washington.

Hurley, William M.
1974 *Silver Creek Woodland Sites, Southwestern Wisconsin.* Office of State Archaeologist Report 6. Univ. of Iowa, Iowa City.
1975 *An Analysis of Effigy Mound Complexes in Wisconsin.* Anthropological Papers 59. Museum of Anthropology, Univ. of Michigan, Ann Arbor.
1979 *Prehistoric Cordage: Identification of Impressions on Pottery.* Taraxacum, Washington, D.C.

Husted, Wilfred M.
1969 *Bighorn Canyon Archeology.* Smithsonian Institution River Basins Surveys Publications in Salvage Archeology 12. Lincoln.

Isaacs, Jennifer
n.d. *Aboriginal Baskets.* Aboriginal Arts and Crafts Pty. Ltd., Canberra.

Jakes, Kathryn A., Lucy R. Sibley, and Richard Yerkes
1994 A Comparative Collection for the Study of Fibres Used in Prehistoric Textiles from Eastern North America. *Journal of Archaeological Science* 21:641–650.

Jenkins, Ned J.
1981 *Gainesville Lake Area Ceramic Description and Chronology.* Report of Investigations 12. Office of Archaeological Research, Univ. of Alabama.

Jeppson, Britta D.
1964 A Study of Cordage and Rolled Copper Beads, Burial #6, Titicut Site. *Bulletin of the Massachusetts Archaeological Society* 25(2):37–38.

Johnson, William C.
1978 Ceramics. In 46SU3 Revisited, by Jan D. Applegarth, J. M. Adovasio, and Jack Donahue, pp. 41–65. *Pennsylvania Archaeologist* 48(1).
1982 Ceramics. In *The Prehistory of the Paintsville Reservoir, Johnson and Morgan Counties, Kentucky,* compiled by J. M. Adovasio, pp. 752–826. Ethnology Monographs 6. Dept. of Anthropology, Univ. of Pittsburgh, Pittsburgh.
1991 Cordage Twist Direction as a Tool in Delineating Territorial Boundaries and Demonstrating Population Continuity During the Late Prehistoric Periods in the Upper Ohio River Valley. Paper presented at the annual meeting of the Middle Atlantic Archaeological Association, Ocean City.

Jones, Volney H.
1935 Some Chippewa and Ottawa Uses of Sweet Grass. *Papers of the Michigan Academy of Science, Arts, and Letters* 21:21–31.

1936a The Vegetal Remains of Newt Kash Hollow Shelter. In *Rock Shelters in Menifee County, Kentucky,* by W. S. Webb and W. D. Funkhouser, pp. 147–165. Univ. of Kentucky Reports in Archaeology and Anthropology 3(4). Lexington.

1936b Notes on the Preparation and the Uses of Basswood Fiber by the Indians of the Great Lakes Region. *Papers of the Michigan Academy of Science, Arts, and Letters* 22:1–16.

1946 Notes on the Manufacture of Cedar-Bark Mats by the Chippewa Indians. *Papers of the Michigan Academy of Science, Arts, and Letters* 32:341–363.

1966 Two Textiles from the Valley Sweet Site. *The Michigan Archaeologist* 12(1):22–24.

Kehoe, Thomas F.
1973 *The Gull Lake Site: A Prehistoric Bison Drive Site in Southwestern Saskatchewan.* Publications in Anthropology and History 1. Milwaukee Public Museum, Milwaukee.

Kellar, James
1967 Material Remains. In *Angel Site: An Archaeological, Historical and Ethnological Study,* 2 volumes, by Glenn A. Black, pp. 431–487. Indiana Historical Society, Indianapolis.

Kent, Kate Peck
1983a *Prehistoric Textiles of the Southwest.* Univ. of New Mexico Press, Albuquerque.

1983b *Pueblo Indian Textiles: A Living Tradition.* School of American Research Press, Santa Fe.

Kenyon, W. A.
1982 *The Grimsby Site, A Historic Neutral Cemetery.* Royal Ontario Museum, Toronto.

Kidd, Kenneth E.
1953 The Excavation and Historical Identification of a Huron Ossuary. *American Antiquity* 18(4):359–379.

King, Mary E.
1968 Textile Fragments from the Riverside Site, Menominee, Michigan. *Verhandlungen des XXXVIII Internationalen Amerikanistenkongresses,* pp. 117–123.

1974 The Salts Cave Textiles: A Preliminary Account. In *Archeology of the Mammoth Cave Area,* edited by Patty Jo Watson, pp. 31–40. Academic Press, New York.

1975 Archaeological Textiles. In *Archaeological Textiles,* edited by Patricia L. Fiske, pp. 9–16. The Textile Museum, Washington, D.C.

1978 Analytical Methods and Prehistoric Textiles. *American Antiquity* 43(1):89–96.

1979 The Prehistoric Textile Industry of Mesoamerica. In *The Junius B. Bird Pre-Columbian Textile Conference,* edited by Ann P. Rowe, Elizabeth P. Benson, and Anne-Louise Schaffer, pp. 265–278. The Textile Museum, Washington, D.C.

1986 Preceramic Cordage and Basketry from Guilá Naquitz. In *Guilá Naquitz: Archaic Foraging and Early Agriculture in Oaxaca, Mexico,* edited by Kent V. Flannery, pp. 157–161. Academic Press, Orlando.

1992 The Perishable Preserved: Ancient Textiles from the Old World with Comparisons from the New World. *The Review of Archaeology* 13(1):2–11.

King, Mary E., and Joan S. Gardner
1981 The Analysis of Textiles from Spiro Mound, Oklahoma. In *The Research Potential of Anthropological Museum Collections,* edited by Ann-Marie E. Cantwell, James B. Griffin, and Nan Rothschild, pp. 123–139. Annals of New York Academy of Sciences 736. New York.

Kraft, Herbert C.
1976 The Rosenkrans Site, An Adena-Related Mortuary Complex in the Upper Delaware Valley, New Jersey. *Archaeology of Eastern North America* 4:9–49.

Kroeber, Alfred L.
1922 Basket Designs of the Mission Indians of California. *Anthropological Papers of the American Museum of Natural History* 20(2):151–183. New York.

Kuttruff, Jenna Tedrick
1980 Prehistoric Textiles Revealed by Potsherds. *Shuttle, Spindle and Dyepot* 11:40–41, 80.

1987 A Prehistoric Twined Bag from Big Bone Cave, Tennessee: Manufacture, Repair, and Use. *Ars Textrina* 8:125–153.

1988 *Textile Attributes and Production Complexity as Indicators of Caddoan Status Differentiation in the Arkansas Valley and Southern Ozark Regions.* Unpublished Ph.D. dissertation, Dept. of Textiles and Clothing, Ohio State Univ., Columbus.

1993 Mississippian Period Status Differentiation Through Textile Analysis: A Caddoan Example. *American Antiquity* 58(1):125–145.

Kuttruff, Jenna Tedrick, and Carl Kuttruff
1992 Textile Production and Use as Revealed in Fabric Impressed Pottery from Mound Bottom (40CH8), Tennessee. *Mississippi Archaeology* 27(2):1–27.

Lauersons, Judith
1984 *Teionkwahontasen: Basketmakers of Akwesasne.* Akwesasne Museum, Hogansburg.

Lehmer, Donald J.

1954 *Archeological Investigations in the Oahe Dam Area, South Dakota, 1950–1951.* Smithsonian Institution Bureau of American Ethnology Bulletin 158. Washington, D.C.

Lester, Joan

1987 "We Didn't Make Fancy Baskets Until We Were Discovered": Fancy-Basket Making in Maine. In *A Key into the Language of Woodsplint Baskets*, edited by Ann McMullen and Russell G. Handsman, pp. 38–59. American Indian Archaeological Institute, Washington, CT.

Levi-Strauss, Claude

1948 The Tribes of the Upper Xingu. In *The Tropical Forest Tribes*, edited by Julian H. Steward, pp. 321–348. Handbook of South American Indians, vol. 3. Smithsonian Institution Bureau of American Ethnology, Washington, D.C.

Lewis, Paul, and Elaine Lewis

1984 *Peoples of the Golden Triangle: Six Tribes in Thailand.* Thames and Hudson, London.

Lewis, Thomas M. N., and Madeline Kneberg

1946 *Hiwassee Island: An Archaeological Account of Four Indian Peoples.* Univ. of Tennessee Press, Knoxville.

1958 *Tribes That Slumber: Indians of the Tennessee Region.* Univ. of Tennessee Press, Knoxville.

Lismer, Marjorie

1941 *Seneca Splint Basketry.* Indian Handcrafts Pamphlet 4. Bureau of Indian Affairs, Washington, D.C.

Logan, Wilfred D.

1952 *Graham Cave: An Archaic Site in Montgomery County, Missouri.* Missouri Archaeological Society Memoir 2. Columbia.

1976 *Woodland Complexes in Northeastern Iowa.* Publications in Archeology 15. National Park Service, U.S. Dept. of the Interior, Washington, D.C.

Lothrop, S. K.

1929 The Henequen Industry of San Pablo, Guatemala. *Indian Notes* 6(2):120–129. Museum of the American Indian, New York.

Loud, Lewellyn L., and Mark R. Harrington

1929 *Lovelock Cave.* Univ. of California Publications in American Archaeology and Ethnology 25(1). Berkeley.

Lowie, Robert H.

1924 Notes on Shoshonean Ethnography. *Anthropological Papers of the American Museum of Natural History* 20(3):187–313. New York.

Lu, Yain Y.

1987 *Ecology, Subsistence and Boundary: Inference Based on a Cordage Dichotomy of Z-S Twist Ceramics of Central Maine.* Unpublished M.A. thesis, Dept. of Anthropology, Hunter College, New York.

MacKenzie, Maureen A.

1991 *Androgynous Objects: String Bags and Gender in Central New Guinea.* Harwood Academic Publishers, Chur, Switzerland.

MacNeish, Richard S., Antoinette Nelken-Terner, and Irmgard W. Johnson

1967 *Nonceramic Artifacts,* edited by Douglas S. Byers, pp. 3–258. The Prehistory of the Tehuacan Valley, vol. 2. Univ. of Texas Press, Austin.

Magers, Pamela C.

1986 Weaving and Miscellaneous Wooden and Vegetal Artifacts. In *Archeological Investigations at Antelope House,* edited by Don P. Morris, pp. 224–305. National Park Service, U.S. Dept. of the Interior, Washington, D.C.

Maslowski, Robert F.

1973 An Analysis of Cordmarked Watson Ware. *Pennsylvania Archaeologist* 43(2):1–12.

1984 The Significance of Cordage Attributes in the Analysis of Woodland Pottery. *Pennsylvania Archaeologist* 54(1–2):51–60.

1985 Cordage, Knots and Netting: Technological Approaches to Ethnicity and Cultural Stability. Paper presented at the 50th annual meeting of the Society for American Archaeology, Denver.

Mason, Otis T.

1885 Basket-Work of the North American Aborigines. In *Annual Report of the U.S. National Museum, 1884,* pp. 291–306. Washington, D.C.

1901 The Technique of Aboriginal American Basketry. *American Anthropologist* 3:109–128.

1904 Aboriginal American Basketry: Studies in a Textile Art Without Machinery. *Annual Report of the U.S. National Museum, 1902,* pp. 171–548. Washington, D.C.

McBride, Bunny

1990 *Our Lives in Our Hands: Micmac Indian Basketmakers.* Tillbury House, Gardiner.

McGregor, Roberta

1992 *Prehistoric Basketry of the Lower Pecos, Texas.* Prehistory Press Monographs in World Archaeology 6. Madison.

McMullen, Ann

1992 Talking Through Baskets: Meaning, Production and Identity in the Northeast Woodlands. In *Basketmakers: Meaning and Form in Native American Baskets*, edited by Linda Mowat, Howard Morphy, and Penny Dransart, pp. 19–36. Univ. of Oxford Pitt Rivers Museum Monograph 5. Oxford.

McMullen, Ann, and Russell G. Handsman (editors)

1987 *A Key into the Language of Woodsplint Baskets.* American Indian Archaeological Institute, Washington, CT.

McPherron, Alan L.

1967 *The Juntunen Site and the Late Woodland Prehistory of the Upper Great Lakes Area.* Anthropological Papers 30. Museum of Anthropology, Univ. of Michigan, Ann Arbor.

Miller, Carl F.

1960 The Use of *Chenopodium* Seeds as a Source of Food by the Early Peoples in Russell Cave, Alabama. *Southern Indian Studies* 12:31–32.

Mills, William C.

1907 Explorations of the Edwin Harness Mound. *Ohio Archaeological and Historical Quarterly* 16:113–193.

1909 Explorations of the Seip Mound. *Ohio Archaeological and Historical Quarterly* 18:269–321.

1922 *Exploration of the Mound City Group.* Certain Mounds and Village Sites in Ohio 3(4). Ohio State Archaeological and Historical Society, Columbus.

Miner, Horace

1936 The Importance of Textiles in the Archaeology of the Eastern United States. *American Antiquity* 1(3):181–192.

Moore, Carmella C., and A. Kimball Romney

1994 Material Culture, Geographic Propinquity, and Linguistic Affiliation on the North Coast of New Guinea: A Reanalysis of Welsch, Terrell, and Nadolski (1992). *American Anthropologist* 96(2):370–392.

Morris, Earl H., and Robert F. Burgh

1941 *Anasazi Basketry: Basket Maker II through Pueblo III: A Study Based on Specimens from the San Juan River Country.* Carnegie Institution of Washington Publication 533. Washington, D.C.

1954 *Basket Maker II Sites Near Durango, Colorado.* Carnegie Institution of Washington Publication 604. Washington, D.C.

Munger, Paul, and Robert McC. Adams

1941 Fabric Impressions of Pottery from the Elizabeth Herrell Site, Missouri. *American Antiquity* 7(2):166–171.

Neumann, Thomas W.

1978 Classification of Net Impressed Pottery from Central Minnesota. In *Some Studies of Minnesota Prehistoric Ceramics*, edited by Alan R. Woolworth and Mark A. Hall, pp. 56–65. Occasional Publications in Minnesota Anthropology 2. Minnesota Historical Society, St. Paul.

Newton, Dolores

1974 The Timbira Hammock as a Cultural Indicator of Social Boundaries. In *The Human Mirror, Material and Spatial Images of Man*, edited by Miles Richardson, pp. 231–251. Louisiana State Univ. Press, Baton Rouge.

1987 What to Do Before the Archaeologist Arrives: Doing Culture History in the Ethnographic Domain. In *Material Anthropology: Contemporary Approaches to Material Culture*, edited by Barrie Reynolds and Margaret A. Stott, pp. 129–153. Univ. Press of America, Lanham.

O'Connell, James F., Kevin T. Jones, and Stephen R. Simms

1982 Some Thoughts on Prehistoric Archaeology in the Great Basin. In *Man and Environment in the Great Basin*, edited by David B. Madsen and James F. O'Connell, pp. 227–240. Society for American Archaeology Papers 2.

O'Neale, Lila M.

1945 *Textiles of Highland Guatemala.* Carnegie Institution of Washington Publication 567. Washington, D.C.

1948 *Textiles of Pre-Columbian Chihuahua.* Carnegie Institution of Washington Publication 574. Washington, D.C.

1949 Basketry and Weaving. In *The Comparative Ethnology of South American Indians*, edited by Julian H. Steward, pp. 69–138. Handbook of South American Indians, vol. 5. Smithsonian Institution Bureau of American Ethnology, Washington, D.C.

Orchard, William C.

1920 *Sandals and Other Fabrics from Kentucky Caves.* Indian Notes and Monographs. Museum of the American Indian, New York.

Osborne, Douglas, and Carolyn Osborne

1954 Twines and Terminologies. *American Anthropologist* 56:1093–1101.

Osgood, Cornelius

1940 *Ingalik Material Culture.* Yale Univ. Publications in Anthropology 22. New Haven.

Over, W. H.

1936 The Archaeology of Ludlow Cave and Its Significance. *American Antiquity* 2(2):126–129.

Pelletier, Gaby
1982   *Abenaki Basketry.* Canadian Ethnology Service Paper 85. National Museum of Man, Ottawa.
Pelletier, Gaby (editor)
1977   *Micmac and Maliseet Decorative Traditions.* New Brunswick Museum, Saint John.
Pendergast, Mick
1987   *Te Aho Tapu: The Sacred Thread.* Univ. of Hawaii Press, Honolulu.
Petersen, James B.
1985   Ceramic Analysis in the Northeast: Resume and Prospect. In *Ceramic Analysis in the Northeast: Contributions to Methodology and Culture History,* edited by James B. Petersen, pp. 1–25. Occasional Publications in Northeastern Anthropology 9(2).
Petersen, J. B., and J. M. Adovasio
1990   Fiber Perishable Impressions. In *Prehistoric Ceramic Analysis,* by J. B. Petersen, pp. 155–188. Prehistory of the Bay Springs Rockshelters, Tombigbee River Multi-Resource District, Tishomingo County, Mississippi, vol. 3. Cultural Resource Management Program, Univ. of Pittsburgh, Pittsburgh.
Petersen, James B., and Nathan D. Hamilton
1984   Early Woodland Ceramic and Perishable Fiber Industries from the Northeast: A Summary and Interpretation. *Annals of Carnegie Museum* 53:413–445. Pittsburgh.
Petersen, James B., Nathan D. Hamilton, James M. Adovasio, and Alan L. McPherron
1984   Netting Technology and the Antiquity of Fish Exploitation in Eastern North America. *Midcontinental Journal of Archaeology* 9(2):199–225.
Petersen, James B., Tonya Largy, and Robert W. Carlson
1987   An Aboriginal Basketry Fragment from Lake Cochituate, Natick, Massachusetts. *Bulletin of the Massachusetts Archaeological Society* 48(1):2–8.
Petersen, Karen D.
1963   Chippewa Mat-Weaving Techniques. *Bureau of American Ethnology Bulletin* 186:211–285. Smithsonian Institution, Washington, D.C.
Phillips, Ruth B.
1987   Like a Star I Shine: Northern Woodlands Artistic Traditions. In *The Spirit Sings: Artistic Traditions of Canada's First Peoples,* pp. 51–92. Glenbow Museum and McClelland and Stewart, Toronto.
Picton, John, and John Mack
1989   *African Textiles.* Harper and Row, New York.
Quimby, George I.
1961   Cord Marking Versus Fabric Impressing of Woodland Pottery. *American Antiquity* 26(3):426–428.

Rachlin, Carol K.
1955   The Rubber Mold Technic for the Study of Textile-Impressed Pottery. *American Antiquity* 20(4):394–396.
1958   Historical Reconstruction from a Fossil Fabric, Angel Mounds Site, Newburgh, Indiana. *Indiana History Bulletin* 35(6):67–79.
1960   The Historic Position of the Proto-Cree Textiles in the Eastern Fabric Complex, An Ethnological-Archaeological Correlation. *National Museum of Canada Bulletin* 167:80–89. Ottawa.
Railey, Jimmy A. (editor)
1984   *The Pyles Site (15MS28), A Newtown Village in Mason County, Kentucky.* William S. Webb Archaeological Society Occasional Paper 1. Lexington.
Ribeiro, Berta G.
1987a   A Arte de Trancar: Dois Macroestílos, Dois Modos de Vida. In *Tecnologia Indígena,* edited by Berta G. Ribeiro, pp. 283–321. SUMA Etnológica Brasiliera, vol. 2, Darcy Ribeiro, general editor. Financiàdora de Estudes e Projetos, Petrópolis.
1987b   Artes Texteis Indígenas do Brasil. In *Tecnologia Indígena,* edited by Berta G. Ribeiro, pp. 351–395. SUMA Etnológica Brasiliera, vol. 2, Darcy Ribeiro, general editor. Financiàdora de Estudes e Projetos, Petrópolis.
1987c   Visual Categories and Ethnic Identity: The Symbolism of Kayabí Indian Basketry (Mato Grosso, Brazil). In *Material Anthropology: Contemporary Approaches to Material Culture,* edited by Barrie Reynolds and Margaret A. Stott, pp. 189–230. Univ. Press of America, Lanham.
Ritchie, William A.
1955   *Recent Discoveries Suggesting an Early Woodland Burial Cult in the Northeast.* New York State Museum and Science Service Circular 40. Albany.
1965   *The Archaeology of New York State.* Natural History Press, Garden City.
Ritchie, William A., and Richard S. MacNeish
1949   The Pre-Iroquoian Pottery of New York State. *American Antiquity* 15(2):97–124.
Ritzenthaler, Robert E., and Pat Ritzenthaler
1970   *The Woodland Indians of the Western Great Lakes.* Natural History Press, Garden City.
Rivière, Pierre
1992   Baskets and Basketmakers of the Amazon. In *Basketmakers: Meaning and Form in Native American Baskets,* edited by Linda Mowat, Howard Morphy, and Penny Dransart, pp. 147–159. Univ. of Oxford Pitt Rivers Museum Monograph 5. Oxford.

Rodman, Amy O.

1992 Textiles and Ethnicity: Tiwanaku in San Pedro de Atacama, North Chile. *Latin American Antiquity* 3(4):316–340.

Rose, Roger G.

1983 North American and Pacific Basketry: Some Perspectives. In *Pacific Basket Makers: A Living Tradition*, edited by Suzi Jones, pp. 37–56. Consortium for Pacific Arts and Cultures, Honolulu.

Rouse, Irving

1960 The Classification of Artifacts in Archaeology. *American Antiquity* 25(3):313–323.

Rowe, Ann Pollard

1981 *A Century of Change in Guatemalan Textiles.* Center for Inter-American Relations, New York.

Rozaire, Charles E.

1974 Analysis of Woven Materials from Seven Caves in the Lake Winnemucca Area, Pershing County, Nevada. In *Collected Papers on Aboriginal Basketry*, edited by Donald R. Tuohy and Doris L. Rendall, pp. 60–97. Nevada State Museum Anthropological Papers 16. Carson City.

Rubinstein, Donald H.

1987 The Social Fabric: Micronesian Textile Patterns as an Embodiment of Social Order. In *Mirror and Metaphor: Material and Social Constructions of Reality*, edited by Dan Ingersoll and Gordon Bronitsky, pp. 64–82. Univ. Press of America, Lanham.

Sackett, James R.

1982 Approaches to Style in Lithic Archaeology. *Journal of Anthropological Archaeology* 1:59–112.

1986 Isochrestism and Style: A Clarification. *Journal of Anthropological Archaeology* 5:266–277.

Schneider, Jane

1987 The Anthropology of Cloth. *Annual Review of Anthropology* 16:409–448.

Schneider, Mary J.

1984 An Investigation into the Origin of Arikara, Hidatsa, and Mandan Twilled Basketry. *Plains Anthropologist* 29(106):265–276.

Scholtz, Sandra Clements

1975 *Prehistoric Plies: A Structural and Comparative Analysis of Cordage, Netting, Basketry, and Fabric from Ozark Bluff Shelters.* Arkansas Archeological Survey Research Series 9. Univ. of Arkansas Museum, Fayetteville.

Sears, William H., and James B. Griffin

1950 Fabric-Marked Pottery in Eastern United States. In *Prehistoric Pottery of the Eastern United States.* Museum of Anthropology, Univ. of Michigan, Ann Arbor.

Seiler-Baldinger, Annemarie

1994 *Textiles, A Classification of Techniques.* Smithsonian Institution Press, Washington, D.C.

Shetrone, Henry C.

1931 *The Mound Builders.* D. Appleton and Company, New York.

Shippee, J. M.

1966 The Archaeology of Arnold Research Cave, Callaway County, Missouri. *The Missouri Archaeologist* 28:1–107.

Sibley, Lucy R., and Kathryn A. Jakes

1982 Textile Fabric Pseudomorphs, A Fossilized Form of Textile Evidence. *Clothing and Textiles Research Journal* 1:24–30.

1989 Etowah Textile Remains and Cultural Context: A Model for Inference. *Clothing and Textiles Research Journal* 7(2):37–45.

Skinner, Alanson

1921 *Material Culture of the Menomini.* Notes and Monographs 20. Museum of the American Indian, New York.

Smith, Harlan I.

1910 The Prehistoric Ethnology of a Kentucky Site. *Anthropological Papers of the American Museum of Natural History* 6(2):172–235. New York.

Speck, Frank G.

1911 Notes on the Material Culture of the Huron. *American Anthropologist* 13:208–228.

1914 *The Double-Curve Motive in Northeastern Algonkian Art.* Memoirs of the Canadian Geological Survey, Anthropological Series 1. Ottawa.

1920 Decorative Art and Basketry of the Cherokee. *Bulletin of the Public Museum of the City of Milwaukee* 2(2):53–86.

1940 *Penobscot Man: The Life History of a Forest Tribe in Maine.* Univ. of Pennsylvania Press, Philadelphia.

Stile, T. E.

1982 Perishable Artifacts from Meadowcroft Rockshelter, Washington County, Southwestern Pennsylvania. In *Meadowcroft: Collected Papers on the Archaeology of Meadowcroft Rockshelter and the Cross Creek Drainage*, edited by R. C. Carlisle and J. M. Adovasio, pp. 130–141. Dept. of Anthropology, Univ. of Pittsburgh, Pittsburgh.

Stott, Margaret, and Barrie Reynolds

1987 Material Anthropology: Contemporary Approaches to Material Culture. In *Material Anthropology: Contemporary Approaches to Material Culture*, edited by Barrie Reynolds and Margaret Stott, pp. 1–11. Univ. Press of America, Lanham.

Taylor, Walter W.

1966 Archaic Cultures Adjacent to the Northeastern Frontiers of Mesoamerica. In *Archaeological Frontiers and External Connections*, edited by Gordon F. Ekholm and Gordon R. Willey, pp. 59–94. Handbook of Middle American Indians, vol. 4. Univ. of Texas Press, Austin.

1967 *A Study of Archeology*. Southern Illinois Univ. Press, Carbondale.

1988 *Contributions to Coahuila Archaeology, with an Introduction to the Coahuila Project*. Southern Illinois Univ. at Carbondale Center for Archaeological Investigations Research Paper 52. Carbondale.

Trowbridge, H. M.

1938 Analysis of Spiro Mound Textiles. *American Antiquity* 4(1):51–52.

Trubowitz, Neal L.

1983 Caddoan Settlements in the Arkansas Ozarks: The Upper Lee Creek Valley. *Midcontinental Journal of Archaeology* 8(2):197–210.

Turnbaugh, Sarah Peabody, and William A. Turnbaugh

1986 *Indian Baskets*. Schiffer Publishing Ltd., West Chester.

1987 Weaving the Woods: Tradition and Response in Southern New England Splint Basketry. In *A Key into the Language of Woodsplint Baskets*, edited by Ann McMullen and Russell G. Handsman, pp. 76–93. American Indian Archaeological Institute, Washington, CT.

Turnbull, Christopher J.

1976 The Augustine Site: A Mound from the Maritimes. *Archaeology of Eastern North America* 4:50–62.

Turnbull, Colin M.

1965 The Mbuti Pygmies: An Ethnographic Survey. *Anthropological Papers of the American Museum of Natural History* 50(3):139–282. New York.

Wallace, Dwight T.

1979 The Process of Weaving Development on the Peruvian Coast. In *The Junius B. Bird Pre-Columbian Textile Conference*, edited by Ann P. Rowe, Elizabeth P. Benson, and Ann-Louise Schaffer, pp. 27–50. The Textile Museum, Washington, D.C.

Walthall, John A.

1980 *Prehistoric Indians of the Southeast: Archaeology of Alabama and the Middle South*. Univ. of Alabama Press, University, Alabama.

Walton, Penelope

1989 Textiles, Cordage and Raw Fibre from 16–22 Coppergate. In *The Small Finds*, edited by P. V. Addyman and V. E. Black, pp. 283–454. The Archaeology of York, vol. 17. Council for British Archaeology, London.

Watson, Patty Jo

1969 *Prehistory of Salts Cave, Kentucky*. Illinois State Museum Reports of Investigations 16. Springfield.

1974a Salts Cave (and Related) Material in East Coast Museum Collections. In *Archeology of the Mammoth Cave Area*, edited by Patty Jo Watson, pp. 167–180. Academic Press, New York.

1974b Mammoth Cave Archeology. In *Archeology of the Mammoth Cave Area*, edited by Patty Jo Watson, pp. 183–184. Academic Press, New York.

Webb, William S.

1938 *An Archaeological Survey of the Norris Basin in Eastern Tennessee*. Smithsonian Institution Bureau of American Ethnology Bulletin 118. Washington, D.C.

1939 *An Archaeological Survey of Wheeler Basin on the Tennessee River in Northern Alabama*. Smithsonian Institution Bureau of American Ethnology Bulletin 122. Washington, D.C.

1941 *Mt. Horeb Earthworks and the Drake Mound, Fayette County, Kentucky*. Univ. of Kentucky Reports in Archaeology 5(3). Lexington.

Webb, William S., and David L. DeJarnette

1942 *An Archeological Survey of Pickwick Basin in the Adjacent Portions of the States of Alabama, Mississippi, and Tennessee*. Smithsonian Institution Bureau of American Ethnology Bulletin 129. Washington, D.C.

Webb, W. S., and W. D. Funkhouser

1931 *The Tolu Site in Crittenden County, Kentucky*. Reports in Archaeology and Anthropology 1(5). Lexington.

1936 *Rock Shelters in Menifee County, Kentucky*. Univ. of Kentucky Reports in Archaeology and Anthropology 3(4). Lexington.

Webb, William S., and Charles E. Snow

1945 *The Adena People*. Univ. of Kentucky Reports in Anthropology and Archaeology 6. Lexington.

Weber, Ronald L.

1986 Ethnoarchaeological Analysis. In *Emmon's Notes on Field Museum's Collection of Northwest Coast Basketry*, edited by Ronald L. Weber, pp. 81–102. Fieldiana: Anthropology New Series 9. Field Museum of Natural History, Chicago.

Wedel, Waldo R.

1961 *Prehistoric Man on the Great Plains*. Univ. of Oklahoma Press, Norman.

Weiner, Annette B.

1976 *Women of Value, Men of Renown: New Perspectives in Trobriand Exchange*. Univ. of Texas Press, Austin.

1989 Why Cloth? Wealth, Gender, and Power in Oceania. In *Cloth and Human Experience*, edited by Annette B. Weiner, and Jane Schneider, pp. 37–72. Smithsonian Institution Press, Washington, D.C.

Weiner, Annette B., and Jane Schneider (editors)
1989 *Cloth and Human Experience.* Smithsonian Institution Press, Washington, D.C.

Weir, Glendon H.
1983 Analysis of Mammalian Hair and Plant Fibers in Cordage from a Texas Archaic Shelter. *Bulletin of the Texas Archaeological Society* 53:131–149.

Welsch, Robert L., John Terrell, and John A. Nadolski
1992 Language and Culture on the North Coast of New Guinea. *American Anthropologist* 94(3):568–600.

Weltfish, Gene
1930a Prehistoric North American Basketry Techniques and Modern Distributions. *American Anthropologist* 32(3):454–495.
1930b Coiled Gambling Baskets of the Pawnee and Other Plains Tribes. *Indian Notes* 7:277–295. Museum of the American Indian, New York.
1932 Problems in the Study of Ancient and Modern Basket Makers. *American Anthropologist* 34(2):108–117.

Wendrich, Willemina
1991 *Who Is Afraid of Basketry: A Guide to Recording Basketry and Cordage for Archaeologists and Ethnographers.* Centre for Non-Western Studies Publications 6. Leiden Univ., Leiden.

Wheat, Margaret M.
1967 *Survival Arts of the Primitive Paiutes.* Univ. of Nevada Press, Reno.

Whiteford, Andrew H.
1988 *Southwestern Indian Baskets: Their History and Their Makers.* School of American Research Press, Santa Fe.

Whitehead, Ruth H.
1980 *Elitekey, Micmac Material Culture from 1600 a.d. to the Present.* Nova Scotia Museum, Halifax.
1982 *Micmac Quillwork: Micmac Indian Techniques of Porcupine Quill Decoration, 1600–1950.* Nova Scotia Museum, Halifax.
1987 I Have Lived Here Since the World Began: Atlantic Coast Artistic Traditions. In *The Spirit Sings: Artistic Traditions of Canada's First Peoples,* pp. 17–49. Glenbow Museum and McClelland and Stewart, Toronto.
n.d. *Plant Fibre Textiles from the Hopps Site: BkCp-1.* Nova Scotia Museum Curatorial Report 59. Halifax.

Whitford, A. C.
1941 Textile Fibers Used in Eastern Aboriginal North America. *Anthropological Papers of the American Museum of Natural History* 38(1):5–22. New York.

Wiessner, Polly
1983 Style and Social Information in Kalahari San Projectile Points. *American Antiquity* 48(2):253–276.
1984 Reconsidering the Behavioral Basis for Style: A Case Study among the Kalahari San. *Journal of Anthropological Archaeology* 3:190–234.
1990 Is There a Unity to Style? In *The Uses of Style in Archaeology,* edited by Margaret Conkey and Christine Hastorf, pp. 105–112. Cambridge Univ. Press, Cambridge.

Wild, John P.
1988 *Textiles in Archaeology.* Shire Archaeology, Princes Risborough.

Wilder, Charles G.
1951 Kincaid Textiles. In *Kincaid: A Prehistoric Illinois Metropolis,* by Fay C. Cole and others, pp. 366–376. Univ. of Chicago Press, Chicago.

Willoughby, Charles C.
1905 Textile Fabrics of the New England Indians. *American Anthropologist* 7:85–93.
1924 *Indian Burial Place at Winthrop, Massachusetts.* Papers of the Peabody Museum of American Archaeology and Ethnology 11(1). Harvard Univ., Cambridge.
1932 History and Symbolism of the Muskhogeans. In *Exploration of the Etowah Site in Georgia,* by Warren K. Moorehead, pp. 8–67. Yale Univ. Press, New Haven.
1935 *Antiquities of the New England Indians.* Peabody Museum of American Archaeology and Ethnology. Harvard Univ., Cambridge.
1938 Textile Fabrics from the Burial Mounds of the Great Earthwork Builders of Ohio. *Ohio State Archaeological and Historical Quarterly* 47(4):273–287.
1952 Textile Fabrics from the Spiro Mound. *The Missouri Archaeologist* 14:107–118.

Wilson, Thomas
1889 Ancient Indian Matting from Petit Anse Island, Louisiana. *Annual Report of the U.S. National Museum, 1888,* pp. 673–676. Washington, D.C.

Winfree, R. Westwood
1972 A New Look at Cord-Marked Pottery. *Quarterly Bulletin of the Archaeological Society of Virginia* 26(4):179–189.

Wintemberg, W. J.
1946 The Sidey-Mackay Village Site. *American Antiquity* 11(3):154–182.

Wood, W. Raymond (editor)
1976 *Fay Tolton and the Initial Middle Missouri Variant.* Missouri Archaeological Society Research Series 13. Columbia.

Word, James H., and Charles L. Douglas
1970 *Excavations at Baker Cave, Val Verde County, Texas.* Bulletin of the Texas Memorial Museum 16. Univ. of Texas, Austin.

Wright, James V.

1987 Archaeological Evidence for the Use of Furbearers in North America. In *Wild Furbearer Management and Conservation in North America*, edited by Milan Novak, James A. Baker, Martyn E. Obbard, and Bruce Malloch, pp. 3–12. Ontario Ministry of Natural Resources, Ottawa.

Yde, Jens

1965 *Material Culture of the Waiwai.* Nationalmuseets Skrifter Ethnografisk Roekke 10. National Museum of Copenhagen, Copenhagen.

2

R. L. Andrews and J. M. Adovasio

The Origins of Fiber Perishables Production East of the Rockies

The genesis and subsequent evolution of aboriginal basketry and textile production east of the Rocky Mountains can be examined in terms of process and product. Though relatively uncommon by the "preservational standards" of the Arid West and Southwest, extant basketry and textile remains from archaeological contexts in the East are sufficient to reconstruct the broad outlines of so-called "perishable production" from the Paleoindian through the Late Archaic periods. Data from varied and widespread areas conclusively indicate that the manufacture of twining and/or plaiting underlies *all* subsequent development in perishable manufacture in eastern North America *as* in western North America. Furthermore, available evidence indicates that the quality and quantity of aboriginal basketry and textile production is at least as great east of the Rockies as it is in the prehistoric West. Data on these perishables present an unbroken, if imperfectly documented, developmental sequence throughout prehistory.

In the context of this chapter, the term "fiber perishables" subsumes a minimum of six basic compositional classes of vegetal artifacts—basketry, cordage, netting, knotted fibers, sandals, and miscellaneous fiber constructions. The constituents of these classes are treated here as the products of closely interrelated but technologically distinct prehistoric industries, the output of which are normally subject to rapid decomposition in unprotected depositional settings—hence, they are truly perishable.

Basketry herein encompasses several distinct kinds of items, including rigid and semi-rigid containers or baskets proper, matting, and bags. Matting includes items that are essentially two-dimensional or flat, while baskets are three-dimensional. Bags can be viewed as intermediate forms because they are two-dimensional when empty but three-dimensional when filled. As Driver (1961:159) points out, these artifacts can be treated as a unit because the overall technique of manufacture is the same in all instances. Specifically, all forms of basketry are manually woven without any frame or loom. Since all basketry is woven, it therefore is technically a class or variety of textile, although that term is sometimes restricted to cloth fabrics.

There are three major kinds or subclasses of basketry that are generally mutually exclusive: twining, coiling, and plaiting. The term twining denotes a subclass of basket weaves manufactured by the passing of moving (or "active") horizontal elements called wefts around stationary (or "passive") vertical elements called warps. Twining techniques can be employed to produce containers, mats, and bags, as well as fish traps, cradles, hats, clothing, and other "atypical" basketry forms.

The term coiling denotes a subclass of basket weaves manufactured by sewing stationary, horizontal elements (the foundation) with moving vertical elements (stitches). Coiling techniques are used almost exclusively in the production of containers and hats, but rarely for bags. Mats and other forms are seldom, if ever, produced by coiling.

The term plaiting denotes a subclass of basket weaves in which all elements pass over and under each other without any engagement. For this reason, plaited basketry is technically described as unsewn. Plaiting can be used to make containers, bags, mats, and a wide range of other, less-standard forms.

The term cordage denotes a class of elongate fiber constructions whose components are generally subsumed under the English terms string and rope. Netting, in this context, subsumes a class of openwork fabrics built up by the repeated interworking of a single continuous element with itself (see Emery 1966:30).

Two remaining classes, knotted fibers and miscellaneous fiber constructions, represent respectively the "end" products of a spectrum of functionally specific activities and a residual "catchall" category. Knotted fibers probably served a multiplicity of functions and are precisely what the term implies—single, paired, or bunched fibers with one or more knots. Miscellaneous fiber constructions are perishables that cannot be accommodated within any of the other five compositional classes.

This class contains such diverse artifacts as braids, latticework constructions, fiber rings, "fish sandwiches," etc.

Sandals are herein synonymous with open or closed, vegetal-fiber footwear normally referred to in English as shoes or slippers. Despite the exclusion of sandals and the various remaining classes of fiber perishables from additional treatment, we nonetheless stress that all such constructions are properly characterized as fiber constructions. And, although the present discussion focuses on basketry, cordage, and netting, we also wish to emphasize that these other fiber constructions certainly were as ancient and important—if not occasionally more important—than the categories discussed below.

The geographical "limits" set in this chapter encompass essentially all of North America east of the Rocky Mountain Front and its outliers. Specifically included are all the physiographic provinces from that convenient border to the Atlantic Ocean and specifically excluded is most of the state of Texas. Despite the fact that much of this latter perishables-rich area technically lies east of the Cordillera, basketry and related developments in that region are an integral part of the Arid West and hence may be omitted from consideration here.

The use of the Cordillera and its outliers as the western limits of the area considered in this presentation is not purely arbitrary. Indeed, this physiographic boundary marks the western margin of several prehistoric and ethnographic culture areas. It also marks what is, for all intents and purposes, the eastern limits of a series of interrelated fiber industries centered in the Great Basin and American Southwest (again, excluding Texas).

The area under study has a relative wealth of carbonized, metallic-salt-encrusted, and (more rarely) desiccated or water-logged specimens. Also represented are thousands of negative impressions of perishables, principally on ceramics or, less often, on partially-fired earth (e.g., see Maslowski 1973; Adovasio and Andrews [with Carlisle] 1980). However, *no* extensive, attribute-oriented, synthetic or comparative studies of prehistoric basketry, textile, netting, or cordage manufacture across eastern North America have ever been accomplished. Nevertheless, there are sufficient published data to sketch very briefly the broad outlines of the evolution of these crafts and to illustrate the general character of Woodland period fiber industries in the East.

Extensive studies of prehistoric basketry, textile, and cordage manufacture in western North America, including Mexico, conclusively indicate that the production of cordage (and presumably netting) was established in the western half of the continent by at least the tenth millennium B.C. The manufacture of basketry occurred only slightly thereafter. Moreover, these industries continued to be evidenced, often in a more elaborated state, through the period of Euroamerican contact (see Adovasio 1970a, 1970b, 1971, 1974, 1975a, 1975b, 1976, 1977, 1980a, 1980b, 1980c, 1986a, 1986b, n.d. a, n.d. b, n.d. c; Adovasio and Andrews 1980, 1983, 1985, 1987, n.d.; Adovasio et al. 1976; Adovasio et al. n.d.; Adovasio et al. 1982; Adovasio et al. 1978; Adovasio and Gunn 1975, 1977, 1986; Adovasio and Lynch 1973; Adovasio and Maslowski 1980; Andrews and Adovasio 1980, 1989; Andrews et al. 1986; Andrews et al. 1988; Cosgrove 1947; Cressman et al. 1942; Frison, Adovasio, and Carlisle 1986; Frison, Andrews, Adovasio, Carlisle, and Edgar 1986; Guernsey and Kidder 1921; Heizer and Krieger 1956; King 1974a, 1974b, 1979, 1986; Lindsay et al. 1968; Loud and Harrington 1929; MacNeish et al. 1967; Morris and Burgh 1941; Price 1957; Rozaire 1957, 1969, 1974; Tuohy 1970, 1974; Weltfish 1932).

Significantly, the earliest basketry subclass recovered from *any* portion of the greater American West with associated dates *prior* to the middle of the eighth millennium B.C. is twining, which at that point was already so sophisticated in execution as to suggest that its antecedents must lie in the remote past. The same observations can be made on the quality of the earliest western cordage and netting.

Given these facts, Adovasio has postulated that cordage, netting, and basketry manufacture, as well as the production of related fiber perishables may well have been part and parcel of the techno-logical milieu of the first migrants to the New World. In this regard, it is perhaps illuminating that Adovasio recently observed fine-gauge cordage suitable for sewing or netting production on an Upper Paleolithic living floor at the site of Khosoutshy in Moldavia, located between Ukraine and Romania. Additionally, during the 1991 excavations at the Mezhirich archaeological locality in Ukraine, Adovasio recovered cordage in flotation samples associated with mammoth-bone houses of fifteenth millennium B.C. ascription (Adovasio et al. 1992). An even more hoary antiquity for fiber working is now directly documented by the recovery of three specimens of Z-twisted "cordage" from a twentieth millennium B.P. context at Ohalo II, near the Sea of Galilee (Nadel et al. 1994) and the recent reanalysis of some fired-clay samples with negative impressions from Pavlov I in the Czech Republic (Adovasio et al. 1995). These latter impressions include clear examples of open simple twining, Z-twist weft, and open diagonal twining, S-twist weft, in the form of bags, mats, or nonloom woven cloth attributable to the twenty-seventh millennium B.P.

These discoveries not only document the use of fiber perishables in the Old World well before the end of the Pleistocene, but also provide some support for the postulation that these items were integral to the impedimenta of the first migrants to the New World. While confirmation of the presence or role of cordage, basketry, and netting in the tool kits of the first Paleoindians may never be forthcoming, data from western North America, Mesoamerica, and South America indicate that basketry and cordage production were established across the length and breadth of the New World by the eighth millennium B.C. at the latest (Adovasio and Lynch 1973; Adovasio and Maslowski 1980; King 1979).

Examination of the admittedly much "thinner" fiber perishable data base available from eastern North America (Table 2.1) would seem to confirm this fact. In the following pages, the extant fiber perishable record from archaeological contexts in North America east of the Rockies is examined by chronological period, from Paleoindian through terminal Late Archaic, and an overview is offered.

Table 2.1. Distribution of Select Fiber Perishable Types by Site and Temporal Period

Perishable Class	Construction Technique	Late Archaic 4000–1000 B.C.	Middle Archaic 6000–4000 B.C.	Early Archaic 8000–6000 B.C.	Paleoindian ?–8000 B.C.
Plaiting:	simple (1/1)	Meadowcroft Rockshelter, Salts Cave,[a] Ozark Bluff[a]	Meadowcroft Rockshelter, Windover		Meadowcroft Rockshelter
	twill (2/2)	Salts Cave,[a] Ozark Bluff[a]			Petit Anse Island (?)
	twill (3/3 or greater)	Ozark Bluff[a]			
Twining:	Close Simple, S-twist wefts	Salts Cave,[a] Ozark Bluff[a]	Windover[b]	Graham Cave	
	Close Simple, S- and Z-twist wefts	Salts Cave,[a] Ozark Bluff[a]			
	Open Simple, Z-twist wefts	Ozark Bluff,[a] Riverside[a]	Windover	Graham Cave (?), Icehouse Bottom	
	Open Simple, S-twist weft	Hart Falls, Riverside,[a] Ozark Bluff[a]		Graham Cave	
	Close Diagonal, S-Twist weft		Windover[b]		
	Open Diagonal, S-twist weft	Ozark Bluff[a] Riverside,[a]			
	Open Diagonal, Z-twist weft	Ozark Bluff[a]	Graham Cave (?)		
	Wrapped	Ozark Bluff[a]	Russell Cave		
	Type Unknown	Long Branch, Salts Cave[a]			
Coiling:	Close Coiling, 1 rod foundation	Ozark Bluff[a]			
	Close Coiling, bundle foundation	Ozark Bluff[a]			
	Close Coiling, 2 rod stocked foundation	Ozark Bluff[a]			
Cordage:	Two ply, S-Spun, Z-Twist (Z^S_s)	Ozark Bluff[a]	Windover		
	Two ply, Z-spun, S-Twist (S^Z_z)	Ozark Bluff,[a] Salts Cave,[a] Picton	Windover		
	Braided	Salts Cave,[a] Ozark Bluff[a]			
Netting:	Sheetbend knots	Ozark Bluff[a] (?)	Icehouse Bottom		
Misc. Construction:	Cordage	Ozark Bluff[a]	Squaw Rockshelter		

Note: Tentative identifications are marked (?). [a]Exact chronological placement unknown. [b]Includes both paired and trebled S-twist weft types.

PALEOINDIAN (?–8000 B.C.)

Perishable remains of any kind are extremely rare in Paleoindian contexts east of the Rocky Mountains (Map 2.1). The oldest reliably dated unequivocal specimen analyzed to date derives from middle Stratum IIa at Meadowcroft Rockshelter, Washington County, Pennsylvania. The item is a fragmentary wall (i.e., body fragment lacking selvage) constructed of simple plaiting with a 1/1 interval (Stile 1982:133) and single elements, which is bracketed by radiocarbon dates of 10,850 ±870 B.C. (12,800 ±870 B.P.) and 9350 ±700 B.C. (11,300 ±700 B.P.). The specimen lacks selvages, shifts, splices, and decoration. While the "finished" form of the plaiting fragment cannot be ascertained, it was manufactured (as with all of the Meadowcroft basketry) of a cut, birch-like (*Betula* sp.) bark (Stile 1982:133).

A far older but more tentatively classified perishable from Meadowcroft Rockshelter is of lowest Stratum IIa provenience and is directly dated to 17,650 ±2400 B.C. (19,600 ±2400 B.P.). The specimen again consists of a single element of cut, birch-like (*Betula* sp.) bark which is not dissimilar in overall configuration to the strips employed in all of the later Meadowcroft simple plaiting. If the specimen is a portion of a plaited construction, it is at once the oldest basket in eastern North America and the rest of the continent.

Interestingly, plaiting is also represented in an apparently ancient context some 1,500 mi (2,414 km) south of Meadowcroft Rockshelter at Petit Anse Island, Louisiana, on the Gulf of Mexico. Wilson (1889:674–675) reported that a single specimen of plaited matting was discovered near the surface of a salt dome, 2 ft (0.6 m) *below* the tusks and bones of a "fossil elephant" and ca. 14 ft (4.3 m) beneath the present soil horizon (Wilson 1889:674). The fragment is twill plaiting (2/2 interval) with several perhaps intentional 2/3/2 shifts (Wilson 1889:Figure CVII). The specimen probably represents a portion of either a large burden basket or mat and does not exhibit selvages or decoration. Splicing was apparently effected by securing the new element beneath the exhausted strip close to the plaiting juncture. The fragment was made with

strips of the outer bark of the southern cane (*Arundinaria macrosperma*) (Wilson 1889:674). Herein it should be stressed that while Wilson (1889:675) himself questioned the antiquity of the Petit Anse plaiting fragment, particularly given its occurrence in what must have been a faulted salt diapir, a late Pleistocene ascription would not be out of place given the demonstrated age of the Meadowcroft plaiting.

EARLY ARCHAIC (8000–6000 B.C.)

By the onset of essentially modern climatic conditions, which was concomitant with the initiation of the Early Archaic period (ca. 8000 B.C.), perishables were somewhat better represented in widely separated portions of eastern North America (see Map 2.1). A single specimen from Level 6 (Zone IV) at Graham Cave in Montgomery County, Missouri, ranges from 7750 ±500 B.C. (9700 ±500 B.P.) to 7340 ±300 B.C. (9290 ±300 B.P.) in age and may be assigned to the very beginning of this period (Klippel 1971:22; Logan 1952:74). This fired-clay impression, erroneously identified as "coiled" (Logan 1952:58), is actually the oldest evidence of twining in eastern North America. Examination of a clay positive made directly from the impression indicates that the specimen is composed of close simple twining with S-twist wefts. The paired wefts appear to be single elements of loosely Z-"spun" fibers, while the composition of the warps is not discernible. If the warps were rigid, the specimen probably represents a container of some sort, and if they were flexible, it may be a bag fragment.

The condition of the impression precludes the determination of splicing techniques or any other detail of construction save to note that the specimen is not structurally decorated. Similarly, the raw material employed in construction cannot be ascertained.

Later levels (zones) at Graham Cave produced additional basketry impressions, again on fired clay (Logan 1952:58). A minimum of two types of twining were recovered (Logan 1952:Plate XXI) from Level 5 (Zone IV/III), Level 4 (Zone III), and Level 2 (Zone II). Collectively, these specimens

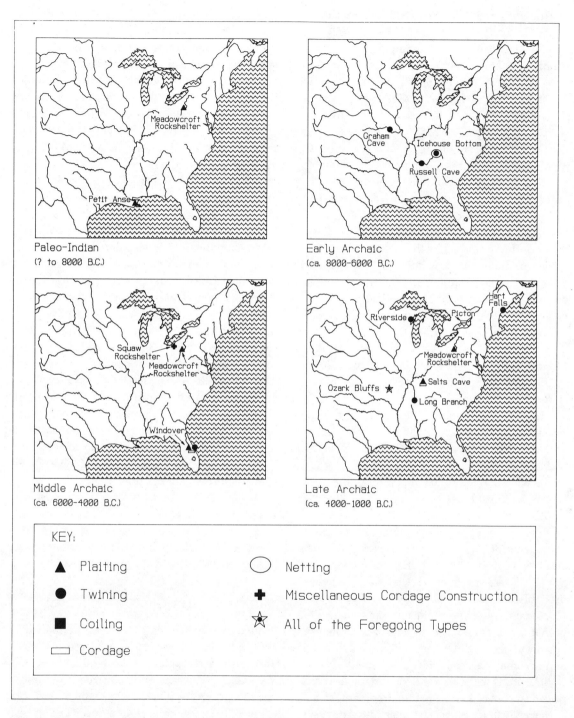

Map 2.1. Distribution of select fiber perishable–bearing sites in eastern North America by chronological period.

date between 6880 ±500 B.C. (8830 ±500 B.P.) and 5680 ±120 B.C. (7630 ±120 B.P.). One of these types (Logan 1952:Plate XXIc) is an impression of open simple S-twist twining over what appears to be two ply, Z-spun, S-twist (S_z^2) cordage warps, while the other (Logan 1952:Plate XXIb) is either a representative of the same type (except with Z-twist warps), or it is open diagonal twining, again with Z-twist warps. (It should be noted that diagonal twining as used in this discussion is essentially identical to alternate pair twining as discussed by Emery [1966:202]. Diagonal or alternate pair twining may have the weft rows either closely spaced or spaced at intervals sufficiently wide to expose the underlying warps.) As the "fibrous nature" of the warps and wefts may indicate, these two wall fragments probably represent portions of flexible containers, such as bags. The specimens lack selvages, splices, or decoration and are composed of indeterminate raw materials.

Southeast of Graham Cave, Icehouse Bottom in Monroe County, Tennessee (Chapman and Adovasio 1977:620), also yielded an assemblage of impressions of Early Archaic vintage. Among the 30 specimens from Icehouse Bottom, 27 originated in strata M–O, the Lower Kirk horizon, and span a period of 7500–7300 B.C. (9450–9250 B.P.) (Chapman and Adovasio 1977:623). The remaining three fragments were derived from strata L and J, the Upper Kirk horizon, and may be ascribed to a 7300–6900 B.C. (9250–8850 B.P.) time interval.

Twenty-nine specimens represent impressions of open simple twining with Z-twist wefts. Warps and wefts consist of two ply, S-spun, Z-twist cordage (Z_s^s). These specimens lack selvages and were probably originally flexible; thus, they probably represent impressions of the undecorated "walls" of matting or bags. Further, some of these items appear to be radially twined, although splice types and raw materials cannot be determined.

Stratum O of the Lower Kirk horizon also produced the oldest known netting fragment from eastern North America (Chapman and Adovasio 1977:622). It is a portion of a single-element fragment built up of a series of knotted loops of single ply, S-spun cordage forming an open diamond mesh. The knot employed in the looping process is a sheetbend or weaver's knot. The specimen is unmended, undecorated, and lacks selvages and splices. The raw material is again unknown.

While the Graham Cave and Icehouse Bottom perishables are *clearly* of Early Archaic ascription, somewhat less certain is the placement of fiber perishable specimens from Layer G at Russell Cave, located in northeastern Alabama (see Map 2.1). This "unit" is dated between 7000 B.C. (8950 B.P.) and 5000 B.C. (6950 B.P.) and has yielded four examples of what is alleged to be over-and-under lacing—that is, simple plaiting (Griffin 1974:62). While the single published photograph does not allow exact determination of actual construction techniques or any other details of manufacture, the specimen appears to be twined. Specifically, the illustrated item clearly seems to be functional wrapped twining, with one semi-rigid fixed weft and one flexible "running weft." Though rare in the extreme, this type is represented in the archaeological records of the Pacific Northwest and the Lower Pecos in Texas. The illustrated Russell Cave specimen apparently represents a (flexible?) wall fragment (without selvage) of a container of unspecified configuration and is unspliced, unmended, and undecorated. Lamentably, the problematic identification and interpretation of the Layer G artifacts is further compounded by the fact that these materials may be intrusive from later levels. Whatever the type or age of the Russell Cave assemblage, the data from Icehouse Bottom and Graham Cave clearly indicate that well-made fiber perishables were *definitely* in use in the East at this time.

MIDDLE ARCHAIC (6000–4000 B.C.)

Until very recently, Middle Archaic period sites with associated fiber perishables were nearly as rare as similarly endowed Paleoindian sites east of the Rockies. This lack of data has been partially rectified in spectacular fashion by the Florida State University excavations at the Windover Bog Cemetery (8BR2176), located in the St. Johns River drainage near Cape Canaveral, Florida (see Map 2.1) (Doran and Dickel 1988a, 1988b). The 1986 and

1987 excavations at that remarkable waterlogged locality yielded 87 specimens of technologically sophisticated textiles and other perishable materials from 37 burials of mid-sixth millennium B.C. (ca. 7500 B.P.) ascription. Since this assemblage currently includes the oldest textiles per se from both North and South America, an extended presentation of this intensively studied collection is warranted, particularly given the fact that none of this material has ever been published except in summary fashion. The following comments are abstracted from Andrews, Adovasio, and Harding (1988).

Eighty-seven perishable artifacts (excluding wood and bone), probably representing 67 once-complete items, were recovered during the 1986–87 excavations at Windover (see Doran and Dickel 1988b:Figure 5). The basketry includes four examples of twining. The textiles are represented by 49 specimens of twining and by a single example of plaiting. Of the cordage samples, 10 consist of "spun" and twisted fiber, and two of braided elements. One composite fiber construction is also included in the assemblage.

Twined specimens were allocated to four bona fide structural types and to three additional residual twining categories which accommodate specimens that cannot be completely classified as to type based on the number and sequence of warps engaged at each weft crossing and/or on the spacing of the weft rows. These items also were analyzed for selvage, method of starting, method of insertion of new warp and weft elements, method of preparation of warps and wefts, form, wear pattern, function, decorative pattern and mechanics, type and mechanics of mending, and raw material. Width of individual warp and warp unit, number of warps per centimeter, width of individual weft ply and weft unit, weft gap, and number of wefts per centimeter also were recorded for each twined specimen.

The single plaited textile specimen was allocated to a structural type based on interval of element engagement. This specimen was analyzed for selvage treatment, shifts, method of preparation of elements, form, wear pattern, function, type and mechanics of mending, and decorative pattern and mechanics. Width, orientation, and angle of plaited element crossing also were recorded.

The 10 pieces of "spun" and twisted cordage were assigned to a single structural type based upon the number of plies and the direction of "spin" and twist. Length, overall diameter, and individual ply diameter, angle of twist, and number of twists per centimeter were recorded for the cordage.

The two braided specimens were allocated to a single structural type based on the number of plaited elements. Length, overall diameter, and diameter of individual plies were noted for each item. Finally, the composite fiber construction was described on the basis of its manufacture components: cordage and cut fronds.

The four formal structural types and three residual untyped twining categories account for 98.1% of the Windover basketry/textile assemblage. The 73 samples represent a minimum of 53 originally complete twining forms, and it is upon these forms that the following observations are based. The four twining types represented at the Windover site are close twined. Two of the three untyped residual categories are close twined; the third is open twined. Following Emery's (1966:200–201) terminology, all of the Windover twining is weft twined, and the Type I and Type III specimens utilize paired weft rows. In the Type II and Type IV specimens, three wefts are employed in the twining process, a technique which Emery (1966:315) calls three strand weft twining.

All of the close twined specimens (i.e., those containing typable warp material) exhibit twisted and/or "spun" and twisted cordage warps. Herein it must be noted that the small diameter, wet state, and friability of the warps themselves sometimes hindered the exact determination of ply formulae. The identifiable variants include S-twist; Z-twist; two ply, Z-"spun," S-twist; and two ply, S-"spun," Z-twist cordage warps. It is possible, however, that the single ply versions were originally part of multiple ply constructions. In the discussion that follows, all warps are described only on the basis of their final twist.

Of all the close twined specimens with typable warps, S-twisted and Z-twisted warps each compose

47.6% of the total. Curiously enough, two samples (which represent the remaining 4.8% of the total) of the Type III—Close Diagonal Twining, Paired S-Twist Weft varieties—and Type IV—Close Diagonal Twining, Trebled S-Twist Weft varieties—each exhibit both S-twisted and Z-twisted warp material (in roughly equal proportions) within the same piece of cloth.

Type I: Close Simple Twining, Paired S-Twist Weft specimens (n = 4) make up 7.5% of the total twining sample. Unlike the three other twining types identified in the assemblage, Type I specimens contain only Z-twisted warps. Due to the low numerical frequency of this type in the assemblage, its correlation with warp type is not statistically significant.

Type II: Close Simple Twining, Trebled S-Twist Weft (n = 2); Type III: Close Diagonal Twining, Paired S-Twist Weft (n = 26); and Type IV: Close Diagonal Twining, Trebled S-Twist Weft specimens (n = 14) account for 3.8%, 49.1%, and 26.4% of the total twining assemblage, respectively. Specimens within these types contain either Z-twisted or S-twisted cordage warps. Further, the Z-twisted and S-twisted warp variations are represented almost equally within each type. Specifically, the S-twisted warp variants make up 50%, 57%, and 55% of Types II, III, and IV, respectively.

The single example of open twining represents a mere 1.9% of the total twining assemblage. As post-depositional deterioration has obscured its detail, this specimen cannot be ascribed to a formal type. Its warps consist of unspun bundles of grass.

All of the Windover close twining specimens contain S-twisted wefts. Further, the individual weft ply is inevitably composed of loosely Z-twisted plant material. The weft itself is composed of either two or three of these loosely twisted plies. Paired and trebled weft varieties compose some 67.3% and 30.8% of the close twined sample, respectively. The number of weft plies cannot be ascertained on one specimen (1.9% of the close twined sample).

In direct contrast to the close twining, the single open twined item exhibits Z-twisted wefts. The weft is paired and composed of untwisted plant material.

Unfortunately, none of the centers of the Type III: Close Diagonal Twining, Paired S-Twist Weft bags are intact; thus, the method by which twining was initiated cannot be determined. Based on specimen configuration, however, it is likely that radial twining on crossed warps was employed. This technique is often seen on Basketmaker II and III bags from the Southwest.

Five of the Windover twining samples exhibit intact portions of side selvages. All selvages are of the continuous weft variety and are found on examples of Type III: Close Diagonal Twining, Paired S-Twist Weft (three specimens) and Type IV: Close Diagonal Twining, Trebled S-Twist Weft (two specimens). In one of these Type IV: Close Diagonal Twining, Trebled S-Twist Weft selvages, the weft courses are reinforced with four rows (spaced ca. 8 mm apart) of simple looping. The sewn "thread" consists of two ply, Z-"spun," S-twist cordage, and the work direction is left to right.

Only one of the close twined specimens from Windover preserves an end selvage. This sample, a Type IV: Close Diagonal Twining, Trebled S-Twist Weft globular bag fragment, exhibits an elaboration of a 180° self end selvage. Each two ply, Z-spun, S-twist cordage warp "end" was given three counterclockwise twists as it was drawn over a two ply, S-spun, Z-twist cord which probably served to close the bag. The warp end is twisted in a counterclockwise direction twice about itself, and it is stabilized with a single binding course of close simple twining with paired wefts. The single example of open twining recovered from the Windover site does not retain side or end selvages.

Among the Windover perishables, the "laid in" splice is the most frequent technique for inserting new weft elements into close twining. In this method, additional weft material is simply inserted beneath the exhausted weft ply. Examples of this splice type are evident in Type I: Close Simple Twining, Paired S-Twist Weft (three specimens); Type II: Close Simple Twining, Trebled S-Twist Weft (three specimens); Type III: Close Diagonal Twining, Paired S-Twist Weft (15 specimens); Type IV: Close Diagonal Twining, Trebled S-Twist Weft (nine specimens); and the residual specimen of close twining with paired, S-twist wefts. Additionally, in three examples, "laid in" splices occur in combination with a technique in which new material is looped around a warp. In another Type III specimen, standard "laid in" splices are coupled using a method in which the additional weft material is folded and then "laid in." Finally, a third variation is illustrated by a Type IV example, where "laid in" splices are combined with a technique where new material is looped around the exhausted weft ply.

Warp splices employed by the Windover weavers in close twining include the simple insertion of new warp material into a pre-existing weft crossing (Type III: Close Diagonal Twining, S-Twist Weft; one specimen) and the "V" splice, in which additional warp material is folded into a "V" and inserted into pre-existing weft crossings. Windover examples of the "V" technique include single "V" (Type II: Close Simple Twining, S-Twist Weft; two specimens) and double "V" (Type III: Close Diagonal Twining, S-Twist Weft; two specimens) variations. The single open twining specimen recovered from the Windover locality does not exhibit splices.

One of the Windover close-twined specimens (Type III: Close Diagonal Twining, Paired S-Twist Weft) appears to have been mended in antiquity. A group of five cords, consisting of loose warps and wefts, are joined with a square knot. Another repair occurs ca. 3.5 cm from this mend and consists of knotted wefts, though the knot itself is unidentifiable. The open-twined specimen is unmended. A single example of Type III: Close Diagonal Twining, S-Twist Weft from the Windover locality is charred.

Unless the stitching adjacent to the close-twined 180° end selvage on the Type III: Close Diagonal Twining, S-Twist Weft specimen represents an attempt at structural decoration, none of the Windover perishables are decorated, at least not by any technique that has been preserved or that has been detected to date by the many and various physical methods of examination employed in their study.

Excluding the grass warps contained in the single open-twined specimen, 54.9% of the Windover twining specimens show wear patterns typical of pre-depositional attrition/abrasion. The vast majority (88.2%) of the items with wear are lightly worn (48.4% of the total twining). The frequency of wear by type is variable (Type II: Close Simple Twining, Trebled S-Twist Weft, 100%; Open Twining, Z-Twist Weft, 100%; Type IV: Close Diagonal Twining, Trebled S-Twist Weft, 44.4%; Type III: Close Diagonal Twining, Paired S-Twist Weft, 41.2%; Type I: Close Simple Twining, Paired S-Twist Weft, 25%). Some 11.8% of the twined samples that show wear (6.5% of the total twining) are moderately worn (Type I: Close Simple Twining, Paired S-Twist Weft, 25%; Type III: Close Diagonal Twining, Paired S-Twist Weft, 5.9%). The specimens without attrition wear account for 45.1% of the total (Type III: Close Diagonal Twining, Paired S-Twist Weft, 52.9%; Type I: Close Simple Twining, Paired S-Twist Weft, 50%; Type IV: Close Diagonal Twining, Trebled S-Twist Weft, 42%).

Three genera of raw materials were employed in the manufacture of the Windover twined perishables. All but two (8.5%) of the specimens are composed of the fibers of a member of the palm family (*Arecaceae*), either cabbage palmetto (*Sabal* spp.) or saw palmetto (*Serenoa repens*) (L. Newsom, personal communication 1986). These exceptions include a single specimen of Type IV: Close Diagonal Twining, Trebled S-Twist Weft, and the solitary example of open twining. In both instances, the weft material is either palm/palmetto or saw palm. However, the Type IV warps consist of highly deteriorated fibers that bear a marked resemblance to yucca (*Yucca* spp.). The warps of the open twined specimen are grass bundles of unknown taxa.

Attempts to further identify aboriginal plant sources utilized in the Windover perishables has included comparative histological studies (L. Newsom, personal communication 1986; D. K. Hess, personal communication 1987), phytolith identification (D. Piperno, personal communication 1987), pyrolytic mass spectrometry (J. Boon, personal communication 1988), analysis of associated pollen (K. Barnosky, personal communication 1988; F. King, personal communication 1988), and scanning electron microscopy (SEM) of a series of modern plant species. These studies thus far have proven incon-

Fiber Perishables East of the Rockies   39

clusive at the level of plant genus, but it is likely that scanning electron microscopy of the conserved/stabilized Windover fibers (following the research of Catling and Grayson 1982) will result in a more specific identification of raw material. Such scrutiny will also provide a gauge of the overall effectiveness of the conservation process.

Catling and Grayson (1982) suggest that each plant species exhibits a unique surface structure and tip configuration, and SEM performed on selected modern floral taxa from the Windover area that are known to have been used aboriginally in making perishables supports this claim. Comparison of modern specimens with nonstabilized prehistoric samples has been inconclusive to date due to the physical distortion of the archaeological specimens caused by desiccation. The examination of conserved/stabilized Windover fibers, once undertaken, may result in new and more substantive data on aboriginal choices of plant raw materials. Ongoing histological and pyrolytic mass spectrometry analysis of the Windover fibers and of unmodified prehistoric plant remains preserved at the Windover site also may contribute to the identification of plant species exploited so effectively by these prehistoric Floridians.

In all specimens except the open twined warp material, the plant epidermis apparently was removed from the leaf or frond before the fibers were extracted. The vast majority (79.6%) of the specimens retain no evidence of the original plant cortex (Residual Untyped Twining, 100%; Type IV: Close Diagonal Twining, Trebled S-Twist Weft, 92.3%; Type III: Close Diagonal Twining, Paired S-Twist Weft, 83%). In the remaining twined specimens (20.4%), the fibers contain widely distributed, minute epidermal patches (Type I: Close Simple Twining, Paired S-Twist Weft, 100%; Type II: Close Simple Twining, Trebled S-Twist Weft, 100%; Type III: Close Diagonal Twining, Paired S-Twist Weft, 16.7%).

The technique by which plant fibers were extracted from the leaf or frond has yet to be determined, but 64% of the twined fibers (excluding the open twined warp material) apparently were extracted by scraping the plant with some rigid tool (i.e., flaked stone tool, wooden scraper, shell, etc.)

and/or by mastication. Of these specimens, 66.6% are lightly altered (Type I: Close Simple Twining, Paired S-Twist Weft, 100%; Type II: Close Simple Twining, Trebled S-Twist Weft, 50%; Type III: Close Diagonal Twining, Paired S-Twist Weft, 40%; Type IV: Close Diagonal Twining, Trebled S-Twist Weft, 55.5%). The remaining altered specimens, which make up 33.4% of all altered specimens, exhibit a moderate degree of alteration (Type II: Close Simple Twining, Trebled S-Twist Weft, 50%; Type III: Close Diagonal Twining, Paired S-Twist Weft, 30%; Type IV: Close Diagonal Twining, Trebled S-Twist Weft, 22.2%). No evidence of mechanical alteration or mastication of the fibers is detected in 36% of the twining assemblage (Type III: Close Diagonal Twining, Paired S-Twist Weft, 30%; Type IV: Close Diagonal Twining, Trebled S-Twist Weft, 22.2%; Residual Untyped Twining, 100%).

All of the Windover twined perishables were directly associated with human skeletal remains. Preliminary aging and sexing by D. Dickel (personal communication 1988) indicate that 62.3% of the twining is from the burials of young adults or adults. Of these, 15 are male, 13 are female, and the sex of four skeletons is presently undetermined. Some 19.6% of the twining specimens in the sample are associated with preteens or teenagers. The gender of only one of this group, a female, is currently available. Of the remaining twined sample, 13.7% of the specimens were recovered with the remains of children, and 3.9% were found with infants or neonates.

As noted previously, six of the Windover twined specimens are encrusted with a veneer of yellowish red (5 YR 4/6) debris tentatively identified during the field excavation as red ocher (iron oxide). Nuclear magnetic resonance imaging conducted on this veneer was inconclusive (J. Brunberg, personal communication 1987), but diffuse reflectance infrared spectroscopy (L. Galya, personal communication 1988), light microscopy with stains (J. Perper, personal communication 1987), SEM coupled with energy dispersive X-ray scrutiny (G. Cooke, personal communication 1987), and initial amino acid analysis involving short-term hydrolysis independently suggest to the contrary that this substance is organic. Further, the architecture and histochemical properties of this residue are consistent with that of collagenous connective tissue, though there are no discernible differences in the samples that might reflect separate anatomical residues (J. Perper, personal communication 1988). It is hoped that immunological testing will determine whether this protein is of human or nonhuman (e.g., animal hide?) origin.

Five of the Windover twined fabric samples submitted for histological examination revealed pollen grains adhering to and caught between twisted sections of the plant material (D. K. Hess, personal communication 1987). This pollen is identified as a conifer, most probably pine (*Pinus* spp.) (K. Barnosky, personal communication 1988; F. King, personal communication 1988). A pine ascription is not unexpected given the paleodistribution of this plant, but the interdigitation of pine pollen and fabric fibers suggests that the raw material for at least five of the twined specimens was processed, and possibly woven, in the spring (K. Barnosky, personal communication 1988; F. King, personal communication 1988). Additional pollen studies are in progress.

Space precludes an expanded commentary here, but it should be noted that sharpened and unsharpened stakes, parallel bundles of unidentified grass stems (which may represent decomposed warp units of open-twined matting), cordage, bone fragments, fish scales, cheno-am seeds, and gastropod remains (*Heliosoma* spp.?) were observed during laboratory analysis in direct association with one or another type of twining. Particularly noteworthy is a Type IV: Close Diagonal Twining, Trebled S-Twist Weft blanket, cape, toga-like garment, or shroud that is encrusted with what may be the remains of an aboriginal "meal." This residue, which consists of minute fish bones and scales (taxa unknown) as well as cheno-am seeds, derives from the lower abdominal region of the associated burial.

Although the Windover perishables were recovered in a mortuary context, a relatively wide range of technomorphological forms is evident. All of the data presented above suggest that the majority (47 specimens: 88.7%) of the twined items are pieces of cloth from lightweight blankets, capes, toga-like garments, or shrouds. Two finer-gauged fabrics

may represent clothing of yet some other form, and another item adhering directly to a human cranium may be a portion of a cap, hood, or bag. This specimen exhibits "V" expansion splices that could occur in any of these forms. Two specimens certainly represent bag fragments, probably from globular bags. Interestingly, one is associated with a "cache" of bone needles that may have been contained within it (G. Doran, personal communication 1987; D. Dickel, personal communication 1987). The other bag was situated beneath or around the remains of a neonate juxtaposed between the lower limbs of a mature female (G. Doran, personal communication 1987; D. Dickel, personal communication 1987). The single open twined specimen is almost certainly a mat fragment.

A single plaited specimen recovered from the Windover locality accounts for 1.5% of the perishable assemblage. This finely woven item consists of Type V: Balanced Plainweave, Simple, 1/1 Interval Plaiting. Plaiting elements are single, cross at a ca. 90° angle, and are S-twisted. No shifts, selvages, or splices are evident. The specimen is uncharred, unmended, and undecorated. Wear from attrition is minimal. The cloth was positioned directly beneath a Type III: Close Diagonal Twining, Paired S-Twist Weft blanket, cape, toga-like garment, or shroud, and is associated with an interred 10- to 11-year-old individual of undetermined sex. This item was made with decorticated, highly masticated, or shredded palmetto/palm (*Sabal* spp.) or saw palm (*Serenoa repens*). The fine-gauge weave (i.e., 10 elements/cm) and its association and position with the burial suggest that this is an item of clothing which, although of unknown configuration, was perhaps worn next to the skin as a modern-day T-shirt or shift might be worn.

The 10 specimens of Type I: Two Ply, Z-"Spun," S-Twist cordage account for 83.3% of the Windover cordage. These specimens are highly fragmented, unknotted, and exhibit "laid in" splices. They are also unmended, uncharred, and undecorated. The Windover "spun" and twisted cordage is always found in direct association with (and usually superimposed upon) specimens of the blanket, cape, tunic-like garment, or shroud configuration. In conjunction with the stakes, it is possible that they served to immobilize the body after interment. The cordage is composed of decorticated, lightly to moderately masticated/macerated fiber. One of the items is constructed with one ply of what appears to be yucca (*Yucca* spp.) and another of palm/palmetto (*Sabal* spp.) or saw palm (*Serenoa repens*). The remaining cords are also palm/palmetto.

The two specimens of Type II: Three Strand Braid cordage recovered from the Windover site account for 16.7% of the cordage assemblage. The specimens consist of three tightly braided, S-twisted elements. There is no indication of knots, splices, mends, decoration, or charring. One of the items is directly associated with a wooden paddle that probably functioned as a bent-snare "spring," perhaps constituting a portion of some type of trap. The Type II: Three Strand Braid is either palm/palmetto (*Sabal* spp.) or saw palm (*Serenoa repens*).

As noted above, the single composite fiber construction from the Windover Bog site was classified according to the attributes of its manufacture. In this specimen, two aboriginally truncated fronds of what appears to be sabal palm (*Sabal* spp.) are crossed at a ca. 25° angle and are secured near their midsection with a knotted cord. Specifically, two ply, S-"spun" and Z-twisted cordage secures the fronds with a figure-eight knot (Shaw 1972). The cordage itself exhibits "laid in" splices. The item is uncharred and unworn. This construction was associated with an adult male burial. The cordage is decorticated, lightly masticated or macerated, palm/palmetto (*Sabal* spp.) or saw palm (*Serenoa repens*). This enigmatic item may, we speculate, represent a votive bundle of perishable construction material for use in the "next life."

The unexpected complexity of the Windover perishables is dimly mirrored by a fiber construction recovered from Test Unit II at Squaw Rockshelter, located in Cuyahoga County, Ohio (Andrews and Adovasio 1989). This item, which is ascribable to a level radiocarbon dated at ca. 3500 B.C. (5450 B.P.), represents a rather intricately interwoven, elaborately knotted complex of four Z-spun single elements to which a final S-twist is imparted; it is attributed to the late Middle Archaic

period by its excavator (Brose 1989). While the details of manipulation are too lengthy and complex to present here, a simple description follows. Initially, two unspun single ply elements were secured in and subsequently affixed to another pair of unspun elements with two respective overhand knots. Six of the eight emergent ends were imparted a slight Z-spin, intricately interlooped and overhand knotted with four of the plies, finally S-twisted together, and terminated with a final whipping knot. While the function of this complex construction is unknown, it is thoroughly charred and undecorated. It is possible that this specimen represents a mend or splice of a larger and quite elaborate cordage construction, or it may simply constitute a "doodle."

With the exception of one of the three simple plaited fragments from lower Stratum IIb at Meadowcroft Rockshelter, no other *directly* dated Middle Archaic period perishables are represented east of the Rockies. The Meadowcroft specimen, which differs in no way from its Paleoindian predecessor or its Late Archaic/Woodland period successors at the site (see below), exhibits a 1/1 plaiting interval without shifts. It is made of a birch-like (*Betula* sp.) bark and lacks selvages. This specimen, which dates from ca. 4720 ±140 B.C. (6670 ±140 B.P.) to 3350 ±130 B.C. (5300 ±130 B.P.), was directly associated with hackberry (*Celtis* sp.) seeds and may represent a portion of a circular or rectangular container.

Though it is certain that twining continued to be produced perhaps across the entire breadth of eastern North America and, further, that plaiting may well have been highly elaborated by this time, evidence for both these contentions is nil unless some of the well-preserved perishables from Arnold Research Cave in Missouri (Henning 1966) are indeed of Middle Archaic age, as noted by Chapman (1975:159).

LATE ARCHAIC (4000–1000 B.C.)

Not surprisingly, perishable-bearing sites of Late Archaic ascription/affinity are much more common than those of earlier periods (see Map 2.1). The fiber perishables themselves are far more numerous, generally better provenienced, and more typologically varied than in any of the preceding periods. J. Petersen (personal communication 1984) reports "ghost images" of twining from the Hart Falls (Overlock I) site on the St. George River in central Maine. The twining occurs on six ground slate hexagonal "bayonets" which are consigned to the later portion of the Late Archaic period Moorehead complex, dated from ca. 2000 to 1800 B.C. (3950 to 3750 B.P.). These specimens consist of open simple twining, S-twist wefts over loosely twisted (single?) warps. The wefts are apparently uniform in diameter and composed of unidentified fibrous material. The twined images most likely represent the remnant stains of a twined cloth or bag which enwrapped the cache of "bayonets" (J. Petersen, personal communication 1984; Whitehead n.d.:Appendix II).

Two of the simple plaited Meadowcroft Rockshelter basketry fragments from upper Stratum IIB and one specimen from Stratum III are ascribable to the Late Archaic period. Collectively, these specimens date from ca. 2000 to 900 B.C. (3950 to 2850 B.P.). One of them is directly dated at 1820 ±90 B.C. (3770 ±90 B.P.). All three specimens are composed of simple plaiting (1/1 interval) without apparent shifts. All three fragments are unmended and undecorated. The single and rarely doubled strips of birch-like (*Betula* sp.) bark are of apparently equal width (Stile 1982:133). The plaiting element size, coupled with the large size of a few specimens (Stile 1982:133) and their direct association with hackberry (*Celtis* sp.) seeds, raspberry (*Rubis* sp.) seeds, and nuts (Stile 1982:134), suggest that these specimens may represent fragments of large circular or rectangular containers (Stile 1982:133). Stile (1982:133) also reports that the largest specimen is collapsed onto itself. Further, one of the specimens contains a selvage described by Stile (1982:133) as follows: "In this example, which may be the edge of a circular container of unknown size, the end or rim selvage is of the 180° self type folded over a rod which circumscribes the exterior of the rim. The elements have been folded over the rod (which is a whole, undecorticated twig of presently unknown species), and then sewed to the body of the basket with cordage of an unknown number of plies, initial spin or final twist."

From the Long Branch site on the Tennessee River, Alabama, a fragment of twining was discovered in association with the midsection of a human burial (Webb and DeJarnette 1942:189). The burial is assigned to the Lauderdale focus (DeJarnette 1952), which spans an interval of 4000–1000 B.C. (5950–2950 B.P.; Walthall 1980:69). Unfortunately, the small size of the photograph illustrating this specimen (Webb and DeJarnette 1942:Plate 217) renders it untypable and precludes the determination of all other technological attributes.

Of almost equally precise chronological placement are the generally more numerous and often more spectacular perishable remains from the Salts Cave area of Kentucky, the Ozark Bluff shelters of Arkansas, the Picton site in Ontario, Canada, and the Riverside site in Michigan.

King (1974c:31–40) details a collection of exceptionally well-preserved perishables from Salts Cave including both twined and plaited objects, as well as "spun," twisted, and braided cordage. Though space precludes an extensive discussion of this remarkable collection, it minimally includes close twined sandals (called slippers) with S-twist only or both S-twist and Z-twist, two ply wefts; open twined sandals with an unknown weft stitch slant; and simple and twill plaited basketry and/or sandal fragments. Cordage in this assemblage includes two ply, Z-spun, S-twist (S_Z^2); three strand braided; and perhaps still other varieties. At least some of these artifacts are probably Late Archaic in age, although available dates from the site range from 1190 ±150 B.C. (3140 ±150 B.P.) to A.D. 30 ±160 (1920 ±160 B.P.; Watson 1974). Similarly, at least *some* of the truly myriad plaiting types, as well as a portion of the twining from the Ozark Bluff shelters (Scholtz 1975), are also probably Late Archaic in age, though the few extant radiocarbon dates are *considerably* later (see below).

The Ozark Bluff shelters lie at the juncture of the eastern border of the Great Plains and the western border of the Southeast. This crossroads position is reflected in the perishable assemblage, which has definite affinities both to prehistoric centers in

Texas and historic groups on the Plains and in the Southeast. The basketry of the Ozark Bluff shelters, meticulously analyzed and described by Scholtz (1975), includes plaited, twined, and coiled materials. While many simple and complicated types of twining are represented (see Table 2.1), the most diagnostic specimens in that basketry assemblage are coiled and plaited items.

The Ozark Bluff coiling includes three major foundation types: one rod, two rod stacked, and bundle. The one rod and two rod stacked specimens are extremely coarse and appear to be either local innovations or extremely inept copies of similar types from Texas. Interestingly, the "local" one rod and two rod coiling is quite similar in execution and vessel form to the gambling trays of historic Plains Indians groups and could possibly provide the prototype for these later items.

The bundle foundation specimens from the Ozark Bluff shelters are quite well made and are virtual duplicates of certain bundle foundation varieties from Lower Pecos, Trans-Pecos, and central Texas. This similarity extends to the splices, spacing of the stitches, and rim finish. While these items are not numerous at the Ozark Bluff shelters, they do point to connections with developments in Texas. Whatever its individual or collective affinities, the Ozark Bluff coiling is the *only* preceramic coiling located outside Texas and east of the Rockies.

The Ozark Bluff plaiting, while sharing certain features with Lower Pecos and Trans-Pecos Texas plaiting, more clearly resembles later historic materials from the Southeast. In historic times, plaiting was the norm in the Southeast, and the beginnings of this tradition can be found in contexts like the Ozark Bluff shelters.

Little more can be said about the Ozark Bluff basketry, particularly in the near total absence of radiocarbon dates from the sites. While Adovasio (1970a:21) originally viewed the Ozark Bluff basketry as relatively late (A.D. 400–700; 1550–1250 B.P.), it could prove to be much earlier. In fact, the incredible complexity of the twining types bespeaks a very long antecedent development. It should be noted that whatever their age, the fiber perishables from the Ozark Bluff shelters are indicative of the complexity of prehistoric basketry making in the Southeast, particularly, and in the East, generally.

In a sense, the other "end" of the Late Archaic preservational and technological spectrum is represented by archaeological localities like the Picton site on the Trent Waterway in southeastern Ontario, Canada (Ritchie 1949). At this locality, the *only* recovered perishables were lengths of two ply, Z-spun, S-twist (S_z^z) cordage preserved by fortuitous contact with copper salts (Ritchie 1949:38) in two burials. The site is ascribed to the Glacial Kame complex, dated at ca. 2000–1000 B.C. (ca. 3950–2950 B.P.).

Also preserved by contact with copper salts, but far more spectacular than the Picton perishable artifacts is the assemblage of twined items from the Riverside site in Michigan (King 1968). Feature 29 at that site, a cremation pit surrounded by vertical, burned oak logs, yielded ca. 3 ft^2 (0.28 m^2) of textiles associated with charred human bones, ovate bifaces, and copper beads (King 1968:117–118). Although Feature 29 itself is undated, Feature 6 at the site is dated at 1081 ± 300 B.C. (3031 ± 300 B.P.; Crane and Griffin 1958:1120). Five other miscellaneous charcoal samples from the site, however, range from 510 B.C. (2460 B.P.) to A.D. 1 (1949 B.P.; Hruska 1967:255).

King (1968:120) distinguishes three twining variants in the Riverside assemblage which constitute no more than two complete textiles. A single fragment of open simple twining with S-twist wefts over single warps adhered to a biface (King 1968:120). The warps are apparently unshredded and untwisted, while the finer wefts occasionally exhibit a slight S-twist. Wear patterns noted on the bifaces (Hruska 1967, cited in King 1968:120), as well as their respective positions (Hruska 1967:29), suggest that this twined fragment represents a portion of a carrying cloth or bag (King 1968:120).

The remaining specimens from the Riverside site consist of open simple S-twist twining over paired warps (King 1968:120). The warp pairs are normally untwisted and function as single elements, though occasionally some pairs are twisted. Wefts consist of two ply, Z-spun, S-twist (S_Z^Z) cordage. Adjacent warp pairs are subsequently wrapped with a figure-eight stitch composed of a split leaf. This treatment conceals one face of the twining. The opposite surface is obscured by a "pile" measuring ca. 2 cm (0.79 in) long and composed of bundles of shredded fiber which are secured by the weft row. In some of the open-twined specimens, bands of openwork are generated by crossing adjacent warps in a false cross-warp or diagonally twined fashion. These warps are apparently engaged by the same kinds of wefts evidenced in the closely twined specimens, though this not directly verifiable. According to King (1968:121), another fragment of this textile exhibits an additional row of open simple Z-twist twining which may actually be a portion of another fabric.

As with the Ozark Bluff perishables, whatever their exact age or configuration, the Riverside materials provide eloquent testimony to the skill and technological sophistication of preceramic weavers in the broad study area as defined here. Moreover, they constitute an excellent transition to the Woodland industries discussed elsewhere in this volume.

In conclusion, the data summarized on the preceding pages and in Table 2.1 suggest that:

1. The available radiocarbon assessments indicate that the manufacture of so-called fiber perishables is as old in eastern North America as it is west of the Rocky Mountains. Given the possibility of both a coastal entryway as well as an interior route via the so-called Ice-Free Corridor, perishables producing populations may well have been in place penecontemporaneously in the unglaciated portions of the entire North American continent. Indeed, the antiquity of fiber perishables in both the eastern and western portions of the continent underscores their probable inclusion in the tool kits of the first migrants to the New World.
2. Direct evidence suggests that both plaiting and twining were produced by the beginning of the eighth millennium B.C. *at the very latest*, as was cordage and knotted netting.
3. The oldest eastern North America fiber perishables include a variety of forms, notably, flexible bags or mats, containers of unspecified configuration, and nets. However, the exact forms and attendant functions of these articles are often difficult to reconstruct. Moreover, the favored raw materials used in their construction and certain details of their manufacture remain elusive.
4. By Middle Archaic times, sophisticated twined textiles were evidenced in the Southeast and perhaps elsewhere in eastern North America as well. It is noteworthy that the earliest southeastern textiles occur in mortuary contexts.
5. Twining was highly elaborated by Late Archaic times, especially in the Northeast, while plaiting was the norm in most of the Southeast. Coiling was always very rare and apparently restricted to the Ozark Bluff area of Arkansas, where it probably represents an introduction from Texas. Unfortunately, detailed developmental sequences cannot be generated in any area east of the Rockies.
6. By the onset of the Woodland period, the technological foundations of fiber perishable production had been firmly established over the *entire* eastern half of the continent, as evidenced by the manufacture of typologically diverse and technologically sophisticated forms in *no way inferior* to their better-preserved counterparts in the Arid West. Continuing a pattern which is apparently quite ancient, some of these forms were recovered in mortuary contexts.

As a final note, we should mention that the very early appearance and incredible longevity of plaiting in eastern North America may well be due to a surfeit of suitable dicotyledonous plants producing bast fibers or canes and a concomitant lack of monocots (e.g., yucca, sotol, agave, etc.) for such constructions. Though the preceding summary is admittedly skeletal, it is assumed (or at least hoped) that further work east of the Rockies will add some flesh to the bare bones exhumed herein.

ACKNOWLEDGMENTS

Like this entire volume, this chapter is dedicated to the memory of the late R. L. Andrews, the finest perishables analyst I have ever known. This manuscript was typed and edited by David Pedler, editor-in-chief, Mercyhurst Archaeological Institute, Mercyhurst College, Erie, Pennsylvania. Computer-aided drafting was also performed by David Pedler.

REFERENCES CITED

Adovasio, J. M.
1970a The Origin, Development and Distribution of Western Archaic Textiles. *Tebiwa* 13(2):1–40.
1970b Textiles. In *Hogup Cave*, by C. Melvin Aikens, pp. 133–153. Univ. of Utah Anthropological Papers 93. Salt Lake City.
1971 Some Comments on the Relationship of Great Basin Textiles to Textiles from the Southwest. *University of Oregon Anthropological Papers* 1:103–108. Eugene.
1974 Prehistoric North American Basketry. In *Collected Papers on Aboriginal Basketry*, edited by Donald R. Tuohy and Doris L. Rendall, pp. 133–153. Nevada State Museum Anthropological Papers 16. Carson City.
1975a Prehistoric Great Basin Textiles. In *Archaeological Textiles, Irene Emery Roundtable on Museum Textiles*, edited by Patricia L. Fiske, pp. 141–148. The Textile Museum, Washington, D.C.
1975b Fremont Basketry. *Tebiwa* 17(2):67–76.
1976 Basketry from Swallow Shelter (42Bo268). In *Swallow Shelter and Associated Sites*, by Gardiner F. Dalley, pp. 167–169. Univ. of Utah Anthropological Papers 96. Salt Lake City.
1977 *Basketry Technology: A Guide to Identification and Analysis*. Aldine, Chicago.
1980a Prehistoric Basketry of Western North America and Mexico. In *Early Native Americans: Prehistoric Demography, Economy and Technology*, edited by David L. Browman, pp. 341–362. Mouton, The Hague.
1980b The Evolution of Basketry Manufacture in Northeastern Mexico, Lower and Trans-Pecos Texas. In *Papers on the Prehistory of Northeastern Mexico and Adjacent Texas*, edited by Jeremiah F. Epstein, Thomas R. Hester, and Carol Graves, pp. 93–102. The Univ. of Texas at San Antonio Center for Archaeological Research Special Report 9. San Antonio.
1980c Fremont: An Artifactual Perspective. In *Fremont Perspectives*, edited by David B. Madsen, pp. 35–40. Utah State Historical Society, Antiquities Section Selected Papers 16. Salt Lake City.
1986a Artifacts and Ethnicity: Basketry as an Indicator of Territoriality and Population Movements in the Prehistoric Great Basin. In *Anthropology of the Desert West, Essays in Honor of Jesse D. Jennings*, edited by Carol J. Condie and Don D. Fowler, pp. 43–88. Univ. of Utah Anthropological Papers 110. Salt Lake City.
1986b Prehistoric Basketry. In *Great Basin*, edited by Warren L. d'Azevedo, pp. 194–205. Handbook of North American Indians, vol. 11, William G. Sturtevant, general editor. Smithsonian Institution, Washington, D.C.
n.d. a Coahuila Coiled Basketry. In *Contributions to Coahuila Prehistory*, by Walter W. Taylor et al.; edited by J. M. Adovasio. Ethnology Monographs. Dept. of Anthropology, Univ. of Pittsburgh, Pittsburgh (in preparation).
n.d. b Basketry. In *Technology and Visual Arts*. Handbook of North American Indians, vol. 16, William G. Sturtevant, general editor. Smithsonian Institution, Washington, D.C. (in press).
n.d. c Basketry from Moorehead Cave. In *Moorehead Cave*, by Robert F. Maslowski. Ethnology Monographs. Dept. of Anthropology, Univ. of Pittsburgh, Pittsburgh (in press).

Adovasio, J. M., and R. L. Andrews
1980 Basketry and Miscellaneous Perishable Artifacts from Walpi. In *Textiles, Basketry and Shell Remains from Walpi*, by K. P. Kent, J. M. Adovasio, R. Andrews, J. D. Nations, and J. L. Adams, pp. 1–93. Walpi Archaeological Project-Phase II, vol. 6. Museum of Northern Arizona, Flagstaff. Submitted to the Heritage, Conservation and Recreation Service, Interagency Archeological Services, San Francisco.
1983 Material Culture of Gatecliff Shelter: Basketry, Cordage and Miscellaneous Fiber Constructions. In *The Archaeology of Monitor Valley 2. Gatecliff Shelter*, by David H. Thomas, pp. 279–289. Anthropological Papers of the American Museum of Natural History 59(1). New York.
1985 *Basketry and Miscellaneous Perishable Artifacts from Walpi Pueblo, Arizona*. Ethnology Monographs 7. Dept. of Anthropology, Univ. of Pittsburgh, Pittsburgh.
1987 Basketry and Miscellaneous Perishable Artifacts from Walpi: A Summary. *American Archaeology* 6(3):199–213.
n.d. Basketry from Baker Cave. In *Baker Cave*, by Thomas R. Hester (in press).

Adovasio, J. M., and R. L. Andrews (with R. C. Carlisle)
1980 Basketry, Cordage and Bark Impressions from the Northern Thorn Mound (46Mg78), Monongalia County, West Virginia. *West Virginia Archeologist* 30:33–72.

Adovasio, J. M., R. L. Andrews, and R. C. Carlisle
1976 The Evolution of Basketry Manufacture in the Northern Great Basin. *Tebiwa* 18(2):1–8.

Adovasio, J. M., R. L. Andrews, R. C. Carlisle, and R. D. Drennan
n.d. Fur Cordage from Avayalik Island, Extreme Northern Labrador. In *Avayalik Island*, by Richard H. Jordan and William W. Fitzhugh. Smithsonian Contributions to Anthropology. Smithsonian Institution, Washington, D.C. (in press).

Adovasio, J. M., R. L. Andrews, and C. S. Fowler
1982   Some Observations on the Putative Fremont "Presence" in Southern Idaho. *Plains Anthropologist* 27:19–27.

Adovasio, J. M., R. C. Carlisle, and R. L. Andrews
1978   An Evolution of Anasazi Basketry: A View from Antelope House. *New World Archaeology* 2(5):1–5.

Adovasio, J. M., and Joel D. Gunn
1975   Basketry and Basketmakers at Antelope House. *The Kiva* 4(1):71–80.
1977   Style, Basketry and Basketmakers. In *The Individual in Prehistory: Studies of Variability in Style in Prehistoric Technologies*, edited by James N. Hill and Joel D. Gunn, pp. 137–53. Academic Press, New York.
1986   The Antelope House Basketry Industry. In *Archeological Investigations at Antelope House*, edited by Don P. Morris, pp. 306–397. National Park Service, U.S. Dept. of the Interior, Washington, D.C.

Adovasio, J. M., and T. F. Lynch
1973   Preceramic Textiles from Guitarrero Cave, Peru. *American Antiquity* 38(1):84–90.

Adovasio, J. M., and Robert F. Maslowski
1980   Textiles and Cordage. In *Guitarrero Cave: Early Man in the Andes*, by Thomas F. Lynch, pp. 253–290. Academic Press, New York.

Adovasio, J. M., O. Soffer, D. Dirkmaat, C. Pedler, D. Pedler, D. Thomas, and R. Buyce
1992   Flotation Samples from Mezhirich, Ukrainian Republic: A Micro-View of Macro-Issues. Paper presented at the 57th annual meeting of the Society for American Archaeology, Pittsburgh.

Adovasio, J. M., O. Soffer, and B. Klima
1995   Paleolithic Fiber Technology: Data from Pavlov I, ca. 27,000 B.P. Paper presented at the 60th annual meeting of the Society for American Archaeology, Minneapolis.

Andrews, R. L., and J. M. Adovasio
1980   *Perishable Industries from Hinds Cave, Val Verde County, Texas*. Ethnology Monographs 5. Dept. of Anthropology, Univ. of Pittsburgh, Pittsburgh.
1989   Knotted Cordage from Squaw Rockshelter, Aurora Run, Cuyahoga County, Ohio. *Kirtlandia* 44:59–62. The Cleveland Museum of Natural History, Cleveland.

Andrews, R. L., J. M. Adovasio, and R. C. Carlisle
1986   *Perishable Industries from Dirty Shame Rockshelter, Malheur County, Oregon*. Ethnology Monographs 9. Dept. of Anthropology, Univ. of Pittsburgh, Pittsburgh.

Andrews, R. L., J. M. Adovasio, and D. G. Harding
1988   Textile and Related Perishable Remains from the Windover Site (8BR246). Paper presented at the 53rd annual meeting of the Society for American Archaeology, Phoenix.

Andrews, R. L., J. M. Adovasio, and T. G. Whitley
1988   Coiled Basketry and Cordage from Lakeside Cave (42BO385), Utah. Paper presented at the 21st annual Great Basin Anthropological Conference, Park City.

Brose, David S.
1989   The Squaw Rockshelter (33CU34): A Stratified Archaic Deposit in Cuyahoga County. *Kirtlandia* 44:17–53. The Cleveland Museum of Natural History, Cleveland.

Catling, D., and J. E. Grayson
1982   *Identification of Vegetable Fibers*. Chapman and Hall, New York.

Chapman, Carl H.
1975   *The Archaeology of Missouri, I*. Univ. of Missouri Press, Columbia.

Chapman, J., and J. M. Adovasio
1977   Textile and Basketry Impressions from Icehouse Bottom, Tennessee. *American Antiquity* 42(4):620–625.

Cosgrove, C. B.
1947   *Caves of the Upper Gila and Hueco Areas in New Mexico and Texas*. Papers of the Peabody Museum of Archaeology and Ethnology 24(2). Cambridge.

Crane, H. R., and James B. Griffin
1958   University of Michigan Radiocarbon Dates, III. *Science* 128(3332):1117–1123.

Cressman, Luther S., F. C. Baker, H. P. Hansen, P. Conger, and R. F. Heizer
1942   *Archaeological Researches in the Northern Great Basin*. Carnegie Institution of Washington Publications 538. Washington, D.C.

DeJarnette, David L.
1952   Alabama Archeology: A Summary. In *Archeology of the Eastern United States*, edited by James B. Griffin, pp. 272–284. Univ. of Chicago Press, Chicago.

Doran, Glen H., and David N. Dickel
1988a Radiometric Chronology of the Archaic Windover Archaeological Site (8Br246). *The Florida Anthropologist* 41(3):365–380.
1988b Multidisciplinary Investigations at the Windover Site. In *Wet Site Archaeology*, edited by Barbara A. Purdy, pp. 263–289. Telford Press, Caldwell.

Driver, Harold E.
1961   *Indians of North America*. Univ. of Chicago Press, Chicago.

Emery, Irene
1966   *The Primary Structure of Fabrics: An Illustrated Classification*. The Textile Museum, Washington, D.C.

Frison, George C., J. M. Adovasio, and R. C. Carlisle
1986   Coiled Basketry from Northern Wyoming. *Plains Anthropologist* 31:163–167.

Frison, George C., R. L. Andrews, J. M. Adovasio, R. C. Carlisle, and Robert Edgar
1986 A Late Paleoindian Animal Trapping Net from Northern Wyoming. *American Antiquity* 51(2):352–361.

Griffin, John W.
1974 *Investigations in Russell Cave*. National Park Service Publications in Archeology 13. U.S. Dept. of the Interior, Washington, D.C.

Guernsey, Samuel J., and Alfred V. Kidder
1921 *Basketmaker Caves of Northeastern Arizona*. Papers of the Peabody Museum 8(2). Harvard Univ., Cambridge.

Heizer, Robert F., and Alex D. Krieger
1956 *The Archaeology of Humboldt Cave, Churchill County, Nevada*. Univ. of California Publications in American Archaeology and Ethnology 47(1). Berkeley.

Henning, Amy E.
1966 Fabrics and Related Materials from Arnold Research Cave. *The Missouri Archaeologist* 28:41–53.

Hruska, Robert
1967 The Riverside Site: A Late Archaic Manifestation in Michigan. *The Wisconsin Archaeologist* 48(3):145–260.

King, Mary E.
1968 Textile Fragments from the Riverside Site, Menominee, Michigan. *Verhandlungen des XXXVIII Internationalen Amerikanistenkongresses*, pp. 117–123.
1974a Medio Period Perishable Artifacts: Textiles and Basketry. In *Casas Grandes: A Fallen Trading Center of the Gran Chichimeca*, by Charles C. DiPeso, John B. Rinaldo, and Gloria J. Fenner, pp. 76–113. Northland Press, Flagstaff.
1974b Espanoles Period Perishable Artifacts. In *Casas Grandes: A Fallen Trading Center of the Gran Chichimeca*, by Charles C. DiPeso, John B. Rinaldo, and Gloria J. Fenner, pp. 114–125. Northland Press, Flagstaff.
1974c The Salts Cave Textiles: A Preliminary Account. In *Archeology of the Mammoth Cave Area*, edited by Patty Jo Watson, pp. 31–40. Academic Press, New York.
1979 The Prehistoric Textile Industry of Mesoamerica. In *The Junius B. Bird Pre-Columbian Textile Conference*, edited by Ann P. Rowe, Elizabeth P. Benson, and Anne-Louise Schaffer, pp. 265–278. The Textile Museum, Washington, D.C.
1986 Preceramic Cordage and Basketry from Guilá Naquitz. In *Guilá Naquitz: Archaic Foraging and Early Agriculture in Oaxaca, Mexico*, edited by Kent V. Flannery, pp. 157–161. Academic Press, Orlando.

Klippel, Walter E.
1971 *Graham Cave Revisited: A Re-evaluation of Its Cultural Position During the Archaic Period*. Missouri Archaeological Society Memoir 9. Columbia.

Lindsay, A. J., J. R. Ambler, M. A. Stein, and P. M. Hobler
1968 *Survey and Excavations North and East of Navajo Mountain, Utah, 1959–1962*. Museum of Northern Arizona Bulletin 45. Flagstaff.

Logan, Wilfred D.
1952 *Graham Cave: An Archaic Site in Montgomery County, Missouri*. Missouri Archaeological Society Memoir 2. Columbia.

Loud, Llewellyn L., and Mark R. Harrington
1929 *Lovelock Cave*. Univ. of California Publications in American Archaeology and Ethnology 25(1). Berkeley.

MacNeish, R. S., Antoinette Nelken-Terner, and Irmgard W. Johnson
1967 *Nonceramic Artifacts*, edited by Douglas S. Byers, pp. 3–258. The Prehistory of the Tehuacan Valley, vol. 2. Univ. of Texas Press, Austin.

Maslowski, Robert F.
1973 An Analysis of Cordmarked Watson Ware. *Pennsylvania Archaeologist* 43(2):1–12.

Morris, Earl H., and Robert F. Burgh
1941 *Anasazi Basketry: Basket Maker II through Pueblo III: A Study Based on Specimens from the San Juan River Country*. Carnegie Institution of Washington Publication 533. Washington, D.C.

Nadel, D., A. Danin, E. Werker, T. Schick, M.E. Kislev, and K. Stewart
1994 19,000-Year-Old Twisted Fibers from Ohalo II. *Current Anthropology* 35(4):451–457.

Price, Sara S.
1957 Textiles. In *Danger Cave*, by Jesse D. Jennings, pp. 235–264. Univ. of Utah Anthropological Papers 27. Salt Lake City.

Ritchie, William A.
1949 *An Archaeological Survey of the Trent Waterway in Ontario, Canada, and its Significance for New York State Prehistory*. Researches and Transactions of the New York State Archaeological Association 12(1).

Rozaire, Charles E.
1957 *Twined Weaving and Western North American Prehistory*. Unpublished Ph.D. dissertation, Dept. of Anthropology, Univ. of California, Los Angeles.
1969 The Chronology of Woven Materials from Three Caves at Falcon Hill, Washoe County, Nevada. *Nevada State Museum Anthropological Papers* 14:181–186. Carson City.
1974 Analysis of Woven Materials from Seven Caves in the Lake Winnemucca Area, Pershing County, Nevada. In *Collected Papers on Aboriginal Basketry*, edited by Donald R. Tuohy and Doris L. Rendall, pp. 60–97. Nevada State Museum Anthropological Papers 16. Carson City.

Scholtz, Sandra Clements

1975 *Prehistoric Plies: A Structural and Comparative Analysis of Cordage, Netting, Basketry, and Fabric from Ozark Bluff Shelters.* Arkansas Archeological Survey Research Series 9. Univ. of Arkansas Museum, Fayetteville.

Shaw, George R.

1972 *Knots.* Collier Books, New York.

Stile, T. E.

1982 Perishable Artifacts from Meadowcroft Rockshelter, Washington County, Southwestern Pennsylvania. In *Meadowcroft: Collected Papers on the Archaeology of Meadowcroft Rockshelter and the Cross Creek Drainage,* edited by R. C. Carlisle and J. M. Adovasio, pp. 130–141. Dept. of Anthropology, Univ. of Pittsburgh, Pittsburgh.

Tuohy, Donald R.

1970 The Aboriginal Containers of Baja California, Mexico: A Search for Origins. *Tebiwa* 13(2):41–51.

1974 A Cache of Fine Coiled, Feathered and Decorated Baskets from Western Nevada. In *Collected Papers on Aboriginal Basketry,* edited by Donald R. Tuohy and Doris L. Rendall, pp. 28–46. Nevada State Museum Anthropological Papers 16. Carson City.

Walthall, John A.

1980 *Prehistoric Indians of the Southeast: Archaeology of Alabama and the Middle South.* Univ. of Alabama Press, University, Alabama.

Watson, Patty Jo (editor)

1974 *Archeology of the Mammoth Cave Area.* Academic Press, New York.

Webb, William S., and David L. DeJarnette

1942 *An Archeological Survey of Pickwick Basin in the Adjacent Portions of the States of Alabama, Mississippi, and Tennessee.* Smithsonian Institution Bureau of American Ethnology Bulletin 129. Washington, D.C.

Weltfish, Gene

1932 Problems in the Study of Ancient and Modern Basket Makers. *American Anthropologist* 34(2):108–117.

Whitehead, Ruth H.

n.d. *Plant Fibre Textiles from the Hopps Site: BkCp-1.* Nova Scotia Museum Curatorial Report 59. Halifax.

Wilson, Thomas

1889 Ancient Indian Matting from Petit Anse Island, Louisiana. *Annual Report of the U.S. National Museum, 1888,* pp. 673–676. Washington, D.C.

3

Michael J. Heckenberger

James B. Petersen

Frances B. King

Louise A. Basa

Fiber Industries from the Boucher Site:
An Early Woodland Cemetery
in Northwestern Vermont

Aboriginal fiber industries are seldom recovered from archaeological sites in northeastern North America, or the Northeast. In the far Northeast, fewer than a dozen sites have produced reliably dated prehistoric fiber artifacts, or "perishables," and fewer still have been thoroughly described. Textiles and cordage from the Boucher site, located near Lake Champlain in northwestern Vermont, constitute the largest securely dated sample of prehistoric fiber artifacts yet known in the far Northeast, including at least 99 textile and 56 cordage specimens.

The Boucher site is an aboriginal cemetery attributable to the Early Woodland period, ca. 1000–100 B.C. It is located in the town of Highgate, Franklin County, Vermont, in the Champlain Lowlands physiographic region (Map 3.1) (Jacobs 1950). More specifically, the site is situated on a glacial outwash delta formation adjacent to the modern floodplain of the Missisquoi River and roughly 8 km to the east of Lake Champlain. This cemetery

was accidentally discovered and partially disturbed in April 1973 during excavation of a private house cellar and a brief episode of amateur collecting. Archaeological salvage operations were immediately undertaken by the University of Vermont (UVM) under the direction of Louise Basa. An area of approximately 340 m^2 was ultimately excavated in 1973 (Map 3.2), which constituted near total recovery of the site. Many of the endangered burials were taken out *en masse* for subsequent excavation in the UVM anthropology laboratory, the last of which was completed in 1988.

The cemetery contained 43 unequivocal inhumation (unburned) burials and 17 cremation burials. An additional three burials contained both cremated and unburned individuals for a total of 63 burials which preserved human skeletal remains. Of the 43 inhumations, two were double inhumations and three of the cremations contained two cremated individuals. At least one additional unburned individual was recovered prior to the

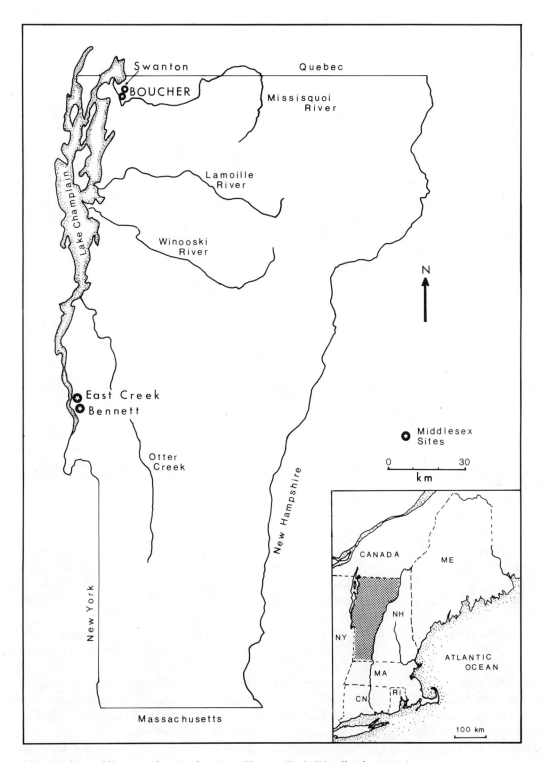

Map 3.1. State of Vermont showing location of known Early Woodland cemeteries.

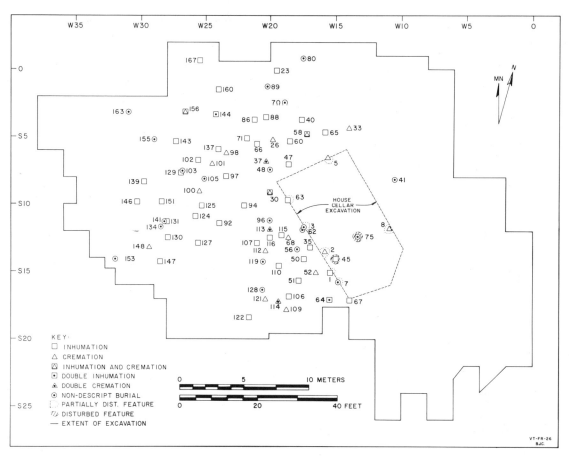

Map 3.2. Plan view of the Boucher site. Note the house cellar excavation which led to original disturbance and discovery of the site.

UVM investigations. In sum, a minimum of 72 individuals are known from the skeletal remains. Inhumations at the Boucher site included individuals of both sexes and all age groups (i.e., infant, child, adolescent, subadult, adult, and old adult) and consisted of primary (predominantly flexed), two-stage and secondary interments (Heckenberger et al. 1990a, 1990b; Krigbaum 1986). Apparently, there was no systematic placement of the burials across the site, although conditions of preservation, disturbance, and recovery may have obscured any such pattern.

Recent radiocarbon assays of various Boucher samples yielded 16 dates considered reliable by the authors; these dates range from an early date of 2835 ± 35 years B.P.: 885 B.C. (PITT-0761) to a late date

of 2065 ± 25 B.P.: 115 B.C. (PITT-0030) (Heckenberger et al. 1990b). Cross-dated lithic and ceramic artifacts from the site are consistent with these radiometric measurements. The combined data indicate a clear attribution of the Boucher site to most, if not all, of the full span of the Early Woodland period, ca. 1000–100 B.C.

Many lithic artifacts from the site closely resemble artifacts attributed to the Adena "culture" of the Midwest, and, in fact, midwestern lithic raw materials are well represented at Boucher, along with others from northeastern Canada and Maine. Additional artifacts from the site, including copper and shell, indicate ties with still other distant portions of eastern North America. Several dozen sites across the far Northeast and nearby areas can be comparably related to Adena manifestations in the Midwest, but most are small, incompletely known, and/or partially reported (e.g., Kraft 1976; Loring 1985; Mounier 1981; Ritchie 1965; Ritchie and Dragoo 1960; Ritchie and Funk 1973; Thomas 1970; Turnbull 1976).

Based on Adena-related burial sites in New York state and elsewhere, Ritchie and Dragoo (1960) defined the Middlesex phase, or "complex," a designation which has been used to describe this mortuary pattern in the far Northeast since then. During the temporal span of the Middlesex complex, exotic raw materials and finished goods were exchanged over a broad area through extensive interregional trade networks. Various technological attributes and burial practices represented at Boucher are characteristic of Middlesex complex sites. The material attributes include blocked-end tubular pipes, lobate-stemmed Adena projectile points, boatstones, pendants and gorgets, ovate "cache" bifaces, interior/exterior fabric-paddled Vinette I ceramics, and, notably, the extensive use of both copper and shell beads.

Among the exotic goods interred with Middlesex complex burials at various sites, strands of copper beads and copper tools placed in some graves have enabled the preservation of otherwise highly perishable organic remains. This unusual degree of preservation is largely attributable to the biocidic action of the oxidizing copper, as known elsewhere (e.g., Janaway 1985:30; King 1978:89; Wright 1987:5). A minimum of 155 fragmentary fiber artifacts were so preserved at the Boucher site. Besides partially preserved skeletal remains and the fragmentary fiber artifacts, numerous other artifacts made from wood, hide, and bone, as well as unmodified organics, were preserved in many of the Boucher burials.

The preservation of actual fiber artifacts at the Boucher site is particularly significant given the paucity of archaeological specimens of comparable antiquity and complexity in eastern North America. The extant fiber artifacts from Boucher constitute one of the largest samples of Early Woodland period antiquity from the broad Northeast. Although more completely preserved than many samples, the Boucher fiber artifacts document broad-scale relationships with perishables

from contemporaneous sites in eastern North America. The striking similarities among these samples provide further evidence of the extensive social interaction that was characteristic of the Early Woodland period in general.

In total, 99 fragments of textiles were preserved at the Boucher site (Table 3.1). Almost all of these are assignable to five structural types: open simple twining, S-twist weft slant; open simple and diagonal twining, S-twist weft slant; close simple twining, Z-twist weft slant; close wrapped twining, Z-twist weft slant; and braiding or oblique interlacing (Adovasio 1977; Emery 1980). A total of 56 fragments of cordage were also preserved. These are divisible into four varieties consisting of single, two, three, and four ply constructions. All cordage was spun down to the left, or Z-spun, and then twisted to the right, or S-twisted (Adovasio 1982:827; Hurley 1979:6).

Of the 155 extant fiber artifacts from the Boucher site, all retain sufficient structural integrity to warrant analysis. All specimens are completely dehydrated, usually quite friable, and therefore difficult to handle due to their curation in dry and often hot conditions since recovery. Given that the use of chemicals might preclude or limit future analysis, no preservatives or consolidants were employed during the analysis, but all specimens were cleaned using low-pressure directed air. All specimens were analyzed using a stereoscopic microscope and measurements were taken using Helios dial calipers accurate to 0.05 mm and a pocket comparator. The analysis of all specimens was recorded using standardized forms.

THE BOUCHER SITE
CORDAGE ASSEMBLAGE

Strands of copper and shell beads were often draped around the head and neck, and sometimes around the wrists and lower arms, of the individuals buried at the Boucher site. These beads, unmodified raw copper, and a single copper tool promoted favorable conditions for preservation. The strands of beads were strung using a variety of materials, including spun and unspun hide thongs and vegetal fiber strands. Fragments of the hide thong and

Table 3.1. Structural Types in the Boucher Site Textile Assemblage by Feature Designation (Part 1)

Textile Structural Type		41 2520±70 (Beta-37059)	45 *1240±150 (Pitt-0021)	47 1845±95 (Pitt-0022)	58	65	94 2665±20 (Pitt-0025)	107 2620±95 (Pitt-0760)	110 2335±50 (Pitt-0026)	Subtotal of Fabrics
TWINING										
Type I	Open Simple Twining									
Subtype I	paired S-wefts, cordage elements	—	—	P	P	P	—	P	—	4
Subtype II	paired S-wefts, and wrapped element engaging successive warps	B	—	—	—	—	S	—	—	2
Subtype III	2 rows paired S-wefts, 2 rows trebled S-wefts, cordage elements	—	—	—	—	—	—	—	—	0
Subtype IV	paired S-wefts, unspun elements	—	—	—	—	P	—	P	—	2
Type II	Open and Simple Diagonal Twining, S-wefts, cordage elements	—	—	—	—	—	—	S	—	1
Type III	Close Simple Twining, Z-wefts, cordage wefts and unspun warps	—	—	—	—	—	—	—	P	1
Type IV	Close Wrapped Twining, Z-wefts, cordage passive wefts and warps, animal hair active wefts	—	—	—	—	—	—	—	P	1
BRAIDING										
Type V										
Subtype I	3 element braid, unspun elements	—	P	—	—	—	—	—	—	1
Subtype II	3 element braid, cordage elements	—	—	—	—	—	—	—	P	1
TOTAL BY FEATURE		1	1	1	1	2	1	3	3	13

KEY: S = Shroud   B = Bag   P = Present—unknown function   * = Radiocarbon date is considered unreliable   ** = Probable variant (selvage?) of Subtype II fabric.

Table 3.1. Structural Types in the Boucher Site Textile Assemblage by Feature Designation (Part 2)

Textile Structural Type	124 2620±45 (Pitt-0027)	129 2185±70 (Pitt-0028)	130 2300±50 (Pitt-0762)	131 2075±70 (Pitt-0029B)	139 2265±40 (Pitt-0763)	151	156 2415±35 (Pitt-0032)	167 2550±195 (Pitt-0034)	Subtotal of Fabrics	Total Number of Fabrics
TWINING										
Type I Open Simple Twining										
Subtype I paired S-wefts, cordage elements	P	P	—	B	—	—	P	P	5	9
Subtype II paired S-wefts, and wrapped element engaging successive warps	—	P	P	—	—	S	—	—	3	5
Subtype III 2 rows paired S-wefts, 2 rows trebled S-wefts, cordage elements	—	—	—	—	—	P	—	P**	P**	P**
Subtype IV paired S-wefts, unspun elements	—	—	—	—	—	—	—	—	0	2
Type II Open and Simple Diagonal Twining, S-wefts, cordage elements	—	—	—	—	—	—	—	—	0	1
Type III Close Simple Twining, Z-wefts, cordage wefts and unspun warps	—	—	—	—	—	—	—	—	0	1
Type IV Close Wrapped Twining, Z-wefts, cordage passive wefts and warps, animal hair active wefts	S	—	—	—	—	—	—	—	1	2
BRAIDING										
Type V										
Subtype I 3 element braid, unspun elements	—	—	—	—	P	—	—	—	1	2
Subtype II 3 element braid, cordage elements	—	—	—	—	—	—	—	—	0	1
TOTAL BY FEATURE	2	2	1	1	1	1	1	1	10	23 forms

KEY   S = Shroud   B = Bag   P = Present—unknown function   * = Radiocarbon date is considered unreliable   ** = Probable variant (selvage?) of Subtype II fabric.

twisted vegetal fiber strands, the latter denoted as cordage, were commonly preserved within the copper and shell beads. Only the vegetal fiber cordage is reported here, however. Of the total of 56 cordage fragments from the Boucher site, all but a few were closely associated with copper beads.

Following Adovasio and Andrews (with Carlisle) (1980:54), cordage is considered to be "a class of elongate fiber constructions, the components of which are generally subsumed under the common terms 'string' and 'rope.'" Cordage has been assigned to structural types based on the number of plies, direction of initial spin, whether down to the left (Z) or down to the right (S), and the direction of final twist, similarly either Z or S, following standard criteria described elsewhere (e.g., Adovasio 1977; Emery 1980:10–13; Hurley 1979:6).

Select attributes of the cordage were measured and recorded. Measurements of cordage diameter, twists per cm, and helix angle were made using standard procedures specified by Emery (1980:11). Additionally, each fragment was examined for the presence of splices and/or knots. Finally, a preliminary assessment of the fibrous raw materials used in the construction of the cordage was made and any coloring or staining of the specimens was recorded.

Four structural types of cordage were identified from the site. These include: single ply, Z-spun; two ply, Z-spun, S-twist; three ply, Z-spun, S-twist; and four ply, Z-spun, S-twist. In all cases, multiple ply cordage is always Z-spun and S-twisted.

All cordage was constructed using fine, retted vegetal fibers. While the absolute identity of all fibers used in the cordage remains incompletely known, preliminary analysis of selected samples of cordage and textile specimens by Frances King includes examples of common milkweed (*Asclepias* sp.), and/or Indian hemp (*Apocynum* sp.), basswood *(Tilia americana)*, and slippery elm *(Ulmus rubra)* (Table 3.2). Thus, both fine fibers, such as milkweed and/or Indian Hemp, and coarser fibers, like basswood and elm, are present in the overall sample. Curiously, the cordage specimens which were obviously made as discrete structures, rather than for use in textiles, are all fine fibers, while cordage used in textiles is largely composed of the coarser fibers, predominantly basswood. In any case, these identifications are not unexpected given several previous studies of vegetal fiber raw materials used elsewhere in the region (e.g., Browning 1974; Jones 1936; Whitford 1941).

The great majority of the extant cordage is two ply, Z-spun, S-twist (Figure 3.1A). This type includes 50 specimens, or 89.2% of the total cordage sample. Likewise, all Boucher textiles which were manufactured using cordage employ this structural type. Overall, the two ply, Z-spun, S-twist cordage is quite consistent in both overall diameter and tightness of the twist. The range in overall cordage diameter is 0.30 mm to 2.10 mm, the helix angle range is 15° to 45°, and the range in number of segments per centimeter is 3 to 10. However, the overall mean values for these attributes reflect a high degree of uniformity in this type of cordage. The mean diameter of this type is 1.04 mm, with over 74% falling between 0.70 mm and 1.20 mm. On the basis of a mean helix angle of 35° and a mean of 5.6 segments per cm, all of this cordage is tightly twisted, with no exceptions (cf. Emery 1980:12).

The second most common structural type of cordage represented in the Boucher sample is single ply, Z-spun. Single ply cordage may represent unraveled plies of multi-ply cordage; however, the single ply specimens do not exhibit the twists or kinks typical of unraveled plies. In any case, this structural type includes only four specimens from a single feature (7.1% of the total cordage sample). The range in diameter for single ply, Z-spun cordage is only 0.40–0.50 mm.

Table 3.2. Botanical Materials Represented in the Boucher Site Cordage and Textiles by Feature Designation

Botanical Material	Cordage	Textile
Milkweed (*Asclepias* sp.)/ Indian hemp (*Apocynum* sp.)	40, 77, 125, 131, 160	129
Bast (*Tilia americana*)	—	65, 94, 107(1), 107(2), 110, 131, 151
Bast (*Ulmus rubra*)	—	124
Grass stem	—	107(3), 139

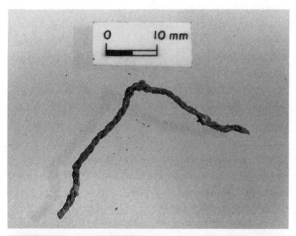

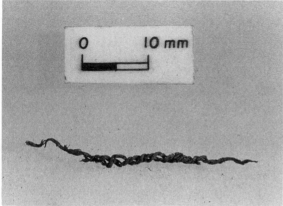

Figure 3.1. Cordage specimens from the Boucher site: A) two ply, Z-spun, S-twist from feature 131; B) three ply, Z-spun, S-twist from feature 65.

The final two structural types of cordage include three ply, Z-spun, S-twist, and four ply, Z-spun, S-twist. Both are represented by single specimens, or 1.7% of the cordage sample each. The three ply fragment consists of a two ply, Z-spun, S-twist strand and an additional added ply that is smaller than the other two plies (see Figure 3.1B). The diameter of this cord is 0.70 mm, with a helix angle of 35°. The four ply specimen is 1.20 mm in diameter, with a helix angle of 40°. This latter fragment may represent a two ply strand doubled back on itself, but no clear evidence of this is preserved.

The final stage of cordage analysis involved the tentative identification of coloring or staining where present. Much of the cordage retains a reddish hue (Munsell 7.5 R 4/12), but this coloration is most likely inadvertent staining due to the large amount of red ocher included in many burials. Some coloration may represent aboriginal dye or pigment, but this remains to be proven. In contrast, two fragments of cordage, one from feature 45 and one retrieved from a private collection, seemingly preserve probable intentional coloring produced by a pigment or dye. These specimens have a uniform bluish/indigo color (Munsell 10 B 4/10) over their entire length. They have not been subjected to a rigorous analysis, however, and this color may be attributable to unique conditions of copper staining.

THE BOUCHER TEXTILE ASSEMBLAGE

Structural analysis of the Boucher textiles involved three levels of examination. First, analysis of the structure of the fabric was conducted, and each specimen was then assigned to one of five structural types, or a sixth "unidentifiable" or "residual" category. Secondly, the individual structural elements (i.e., warps and wefts) were examined. Finally, supplementary elements not integral to the structure of the fabric were described. In addition, preliminary evaluation of the fiber raw materials used to construct all elements, both structural and ancillary, was undertaken. As with the cordage specimens, this final level of analysis was largely based on comparison with contemporary analogues, as well as the identified fibers from other prehistoric and ethnographic fiber assemblages.

Before description of the textile types, a brief explanation of relevant terminology is necessary. The terms "textile" and "fabric" are used here interchangeably to describe a diverse range of woven artifacts, minimally including bags, garmenture, and straps. In general, these objects meet the criteria suggested by Adovasio for basketry, that is, items manually woven without a loom or frame. It is possible, however, that a simple frame was employed in the manufacture of at least some of the fabrics. All textile structures are described following Adovasio (1977), except where noted. The measurements presented below for each structural type are an average of the means obtained for each measurement from each sample (Table 3.3).

Table 3.3. Select Metric Attributes for the Boucher Site Twined Textiles

Twining Structural Type	Diameter of Warps		Number of Warps per/cm		Diameter of Wefts		Weft Row Separation		Number of Weft Rows per/cm		Diameter of Trebled Weft	
	Range	Mean	Range	Mean	Range	Mean	Range	Mean	Range	Mean	Range	Mean
Type I												
Subtype I	0.3–1.25	0.63 (n = 8)	3.5–6.0	5.0 (n = 6)	0.2–1.0	0.44 (n = 8)	2.5–10.0	5.5 (n = 8)	1.0–3.5	2.0 (n = 8)	—	—
Subtype II	0.55–1.30	0.82 (n = 11)	5.0–8.0	5.7 (n = 9)	0.45–1.0	0.67 (n = 9)	3.2–7.5	4.85 (n = 11)	1.0–3.0	2.1 (n = 9)	—	—
Subtype III	—	0.9 (n = 1)	NA	NA	—	0.5 (n = 1)	—	3.5 (n = 1)	—	2.5 (n = 1)	—	1.2 (n = 1)
Subtype IV	3.3–3.5	3.4 (n = 2)	1.0–2.0	1.5 (n = 2)	1.0–1.5	1.25 (n = 2)	12.7–24.5	18.6 (n = 2)	0.5–1.0	0.75 (n = 2)	—	—
Type II	1.5–3.2	2.4 (n = 4)	—	3.0 (n = 1)	1.1–1.4	1.25 (n = 2)	7.9–8.3	8.1 (n = 2)	NA	NA	—	—
Type III	0.9–1.4	1.03 (n = 3)	5.0–6.0	5.5 (n = 2)	0.7–0.8	0.76 (n = 5)	—	0.4 (n = 1)	6.0–8.0	7.33 (n = 3)	—	—
Type IV	0.4–1.15	0.74 (n = 4)	6.0–8.0	6.5 (n = 4)	*0.4–1.1	0.78 (n = 8)	2.8–3.9	0.36 (n = 2)	6.0–10.0	7.56 (n = 8)	—	—

*Diameter of active (moving) weft.
All measurements in millimeters (where applicable).

A total of 99 textile fragments were identified. The large majority of these specimens are assignable to four structural types of twining: 1) open simple twining, S-weft slant; 2) open simple and diagonal twining, S-weft slant; 3) close simple twining, Z-weft slant; and 4) close wrapped twining, Z-weft slant; and one structural type of plaiting.[1] At least 84% of the textile sample, or a total of 83 specimens, were twined (Figure 3.2).

Twining refers to weaves which are usually produced by "passing moving (active) horizontal elements, called wefts, around passive (stationary) vertical elements, or warps" (Adovasio 1977:15). The single form of plaiting represented in the Boucher assemblage is usually referred to as braiding (e.g., Miner 1936:185).

Determination of the fabric structure was based on the number and sequence of warps engaged at each weft crossing, the spacing of weft rows, and the stitch slant of the weft rows. All specimens were also inspected for selvages, starts, splices, knots, or other forms of mending. Consideration was also given to form, function, decoration, and raw material, when appropriate. Attribution of more than one specimen to a single fabric was based on structural similarities and provenience within individual burials. In total, 20 individual twined fabrics were identified, one of which was identified on the basis of a color slide. This specimen from feature 58 was removed from the collection in 1976 and is presumed lost.

The most common structural type of twining was open simple twining with an S-weft slant.

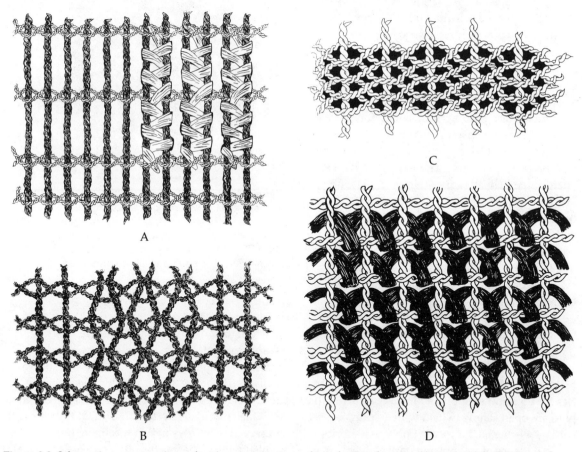

Figure 3.2. Schematic reconstructions of various twining types from the Boucher site: A) open simple twining with wrapping element (Type I, Subtype II); B) open simple and diagonal twining (Type II); C) close simple twining (Type III); D) close wrapped twining (Type IV).

Also known as two strand weft twining (Emery 1980:197), 60 unequivocal specimens of this type from 24 samples were identified. These constitute 16 (70%) of the 23 individual textiles identified in the overall sample including the missing specimen from feature 58. This structural type of textile, designated here as Type I, is a common weave which involves engagement of single successive warps by two paired (or doubled) wefts per row. The weft rows are spaced so that they do not conceal the warp elements. Open simple twining was identified from 13 burials: features 41, 47, 58, 65, 94, 107, 124, 129, 130, 131, 151, 156, and 167.

Four subtypes of Type I open simple twining are described on the basis of warp and weft preparation, or the presence of nonstructural elements. Invariably, all open twined fabrics exhibit an S-weft slant. The specimens included in Subtype I were constructed with S-twist cordage warp and weft elements. The Subtype II specimens were also constructed using S-twist cordage elements; however, an auxiliary element was wrapped around paired warps. The single fragment of Subtype III was also constructed using cordage elements. Subtype IV was constructed using unspun warp and weft elements.

Twenty-nine textile specimens are attributable to Subtype I and comprise nine (56%) of the 16 open simple twined fabrics (Figure 3.3A). Subtype I textiles were identified in 12 samples from 9 features including 47, 58, 65, 107, 124, 129, 131, 156, and 167. The missing specimen from feature 58 is attributed to this subtype as well since all of its elements appear to be Z-spun, S-twist cordage and no evidence of additional elements can be discerned from the available photograph of it.

A total of 28 specimens of Subtype II constitute five (31%) of the total of open simple twined forms (Figures 3.4–3.6). Fourteen samples from five features contained Subtype II textiles. These include features 41, 94, 129, 130, and 151.[2] Subtype II fabrics are identical to Subtype I in basic structure (i.e., both are open simple twined with Z-spun, S-twist cordage elements). However, Subtype II fabrics show evidence of a supplementary element wrapped around successive warps in a figure-eight manner (see Figures 3.2A and 3.6). The wrapping

Figure 3.3. Complex series of textiles from feature 107 at the Boucher site: A) two open simple twined fabrics—outermost textile is Type I, Subtype I, and inner textile is Type I, Subtype IV; B) open simple and diagonal twined (Type II), probably a burial shroud. Note A and B show the reverse sides of the same specimen preserved en masse.

element passes over successive weft rows. The wrapped elements range between 0.80 mm and 1.30 mm (mean = 1.08 mm), and there are five wraps per cm for all measurable specimens.

Only a single textile fragment is assignable to Subtype III (Figure 3.7A), and this specimen is almost certainly a fragment from the Subtype II fabric which originated in feature 151. Of the four preserved weft rows in this specimen, two involve trebled wefts, whereas the other two are the usual doubled weft rows. This weft row variation is related to some sort of decoration, or more likely it is

Figure 3.4. Textile specimen from feature 94 at the Boucher site: A) open simple twined probable garment (Type I, Subtype II); B) Close-up view of open simple twined specimen. Note faunal remains encased in a hide bag are visible protruding from the upper portion of the specimen in A.

Figure 3.5. Textile specimen from feature 151 at the Boucher site: A) open simple twined (Type I, Subtype II) probable burial shroud; B) close-up of open simple twined fabric.

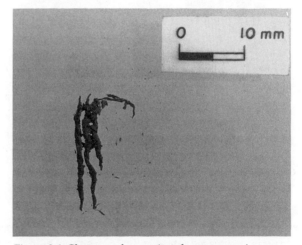

Figure 3.6. Close-up of wrapping element engaging a pair of warps in the open simple twined fabric from feature 130 at the Boucher site.

a portion of the selvage. The measurements for this fragment accord well with the Subtype II specimens from feature 151 in any case.

Specimens classified as Subtype IV of Type I were constructed with unspun warp and weft elements (see Figures 3.3 and 3.7B). Two features, 65 and 107, each yielded one fragment of this subtype and comprise two (13%) of the 16 open simple twined forms.

The textile form here designated as Type II is an unusual variant of open simple twining in which six successive warps are engaged by the wefts differently than the remainder of the warps (see Figures 3.2B and 3.3B). These six warps are paired and engaged

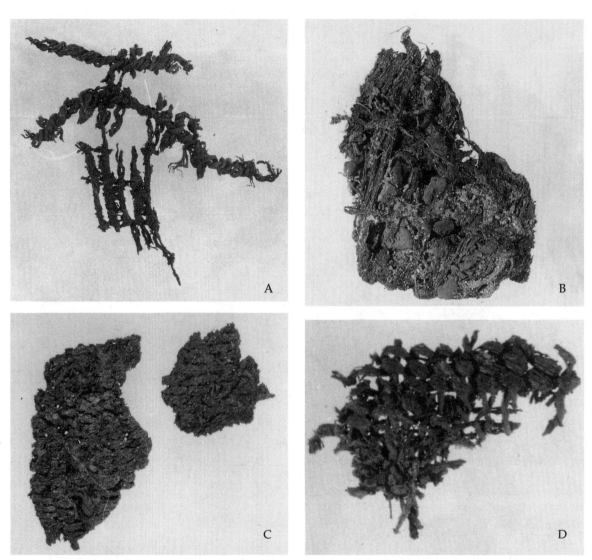

Figure 3.7. Twined fabrics from the Boucher site: A) Close-up view of open simple twined possible selvage (Type I, Subtype III) from feature 151; B) close-up view of open simple twined (Type I, Subtype IV) specimen from feature 65; C) close-up view of close simple twined (Type III) specimen from feature 110; D) close-up view of close wrapped twined (Type IV) specimen from feature 124.

alternately at each weft crossing, a technique de-scribed as diagonal twining (Adovasio 1977:16) or as alternate-pair weft twining (Emery 1980:202). All elements are cordage, Z-spun, S-twist, and in fact, the cordage used to construct this fabric is the coars-est known among the Boucher fiber perishables. This structural type is identical to the open simple twin-ing, S-weft slant forms from the site, with the excep-tion of its usage of at least six diagonal twined

warps. Defined herein as open simple and diagonal twining, this type is represented by two fragments from feature 107, constituting a single fabric. The S-weft slant is uniform over the entire specimen.

Specimens of close simple twining, Z-weft slant are designated as Type III (see Figures 3.2C and 3.7C). The 10 specimens of this type are from six samples, all recovered from feature 110, and are most likely fragments of the same fabric. An additional 12 textile fragments from feature 110 could not be conclusively assigned to this fabric and since two other textiles (a close wrapped twined fabric and a braid, both described below) were associated, these specimens cannot be included in Type III or any other type. Some of these unassigned or "residual" specimens, notably four fragments which may be small selvage remnants, are almost certainly part of the close simple twined textile, however. In any case, this structural type constitutes only one (5%) of the 20 individual forms of twining. This feature 110 fabric is the only simple twined form in the assemblage which has a Z-weft slant. In all cases, its warps are S-twist cordage and the wefts are unspun single elements. This twining type is also designated as compact two strand weft twining (Emery 1980:197).

Eleven specimens of close wrapped twining, designated as Type IV, were identified in nine samples from two features, 110 and 124, and are likely from two fabrics (10% of the 20 twined fabrics) (see Figures 3.2D and 3.7D). Also known as "bird cage" twining (Emery 1980:210), this technique involves the use of one active weft element and one passive weft element in each weft row. The rigid weft is bound to one side by the flexible moving element or weft (Adovasio 1977:19). Since in wrapped twining, one element of the weft pair does not pass over and under the warps, only one side of the fabric demonstrates an oblique weft slant (defined on the reverse side) which in this case is a Z-weft slant, like the close simple twining of Type III. The warps and rigid wefts are cordage (S-twist) in all instances, and the moving wefts are all unspun flat animal hair fibers. In the case of the fabric from feature 124, two varieties (species?) of hair were used differentially across the textile to create a geometric decorative design.

The single structural type of plaiting present in the Boucher textile assemblage is braiding (Figure 3.8). These four specimens have been assigned to a single major category designated here as Type V. Also referred to as oblique interlacing, this technique consists of three or more active elements which start at a common point, trend in a common direction, and are bent to reintroduce them into the weave

(Emery 1980:62). The Boucher assemblage includes three forms of three element braiding. One form from feature 45 and another form from feature 139 are designated as Subtype I. They were constructed of single unspun elements. The other form including three specimens from feature 110, designated as Subtype II, employed paired strands of S-twist cordage.

The Subtype I braided construction from feature 45 is 10.0 mm wide and the width of each element ranges from 2.70 to 4.50 mm (n = 2). The feature 139 Subtype I braided specimen measures between 8.1 mm and 8.5 mm in width, with a mean width of 8.33 mm (n = 4). The width of the individual elements ranges between 3.4 mm and 3.7 mm; the mean is 3.55 mm (n = 4). The sample from feature 110, Subtype II, consists of three fragments which range in width from 6.20 to 7.10 mm, with a mean width of 6.73 mm. The width of each doubled cordage element ranges from 2.40 to 2.90 mm, with a mean of 2.66 mm. The mean diameter of the cordage is 1.20 mm.

Figure 3.8. Braided (Type V, Subtype I) specimen from feature 45 at the Boucher site.

Internal Correlations

The fiber industries from the Boucher site constitute one of the largest thoroughly studied samples of such artifacts from the far Northeast and much of eastern North America. While the extant specimens undoubtedly do not reflect the full range of fiber artifacts used by the population who buried their dead at Boucher, they do provide an intriguing sample. The most basic inference is that the available sample is regrettably deficient since it appears that fiber artifacts were only preserved when in direct contact with, or in close proximity to, large amounts of copper. In those burials which preserved evidence of the relationship between fiber artifacts and individual skeletons, textile and cordage fragments were only associated with the upper portion of each skeleton, as would be expected since copper was almost always a form of upper body adornment. Other perishables such as sandals and the lower portions of fabrics which may have encapsulated the body apparently had little chance of preservation and are therefore missing in the sample.

The uniform structural characteristics of the textiles and the complicated nature of their construction indicates that the Boucher population possessed a well-developed fiber technology. Rare structural varieties, such as wrapped twining and open simple twining with wrapped warps, are products of a highly sophisticated nonloom technology, and they were undoubtedly manufactured by exceptional craftspeople. The regularity of warp and weft elements, weft row spacing, and general structural patterns further attest to the high level of competency of these weavers.

The Boucher cordage specimens are quite fine overall; that is, they are composed of relatively thin, delicate elements, whether used in individual constructions or as components of textiles. The cordage exhibits a minimum diameter of 0.35 mm and a mean diameter just slightly greater than 1.00 mm for all specimens. The consistency of the cordage is also notable in regard to its fineness and the tightness of twist.

Since differential preservation has presumably biased the number and types of available fiber artifacts, few absolutely reliable inferences can be suggested on the basis of the relative frequencies of fiber artifacts within the preserved sample. The extant fiber artifacts do allow some meaningful observations, however; most notable is the overwhelming preference for Z-spun, S-twist cordage. Cordage twist and other fiber attributes are rooted in the motor habits of a given population and they are resistant to change (e.g., Maslowski 1984:51). Moreover, it has been repeatedly emphasized that cordage twist can be a useful indicator of cultural boundaries (e.g., Adovasio 1977:4–5; Hurley 1979:141–145; Petersen and Hamilton 1984:430–438). In any case, the preference of Early Woodland populations for S-twist cordage and S-weft twined basketry is manifest at a variety of sites throughout eastern North America (e.g., Adovasio 1982:835–845; Adovasio and Andrews [with Carlisle] 1980:60–72; Heckenberger and Petersen 1988:110–116; Petersen and Hamilton 1984:430).

Additional characteristics of the Boucher fiber artifacts are likewise worthy of note. These include the predominance of open simple twining with an S-weft slant among the preserved textiles, constituting 16, or 80%, of the total 20 individual twined forms. Open simple twining apparently was the most popular type included with the human burials; in fact, it may represent the most common form of twining manufactured by the Boucher population, at least for use as garments. It is interesting to note that the open twined fabrics from Boucher, both open simple and open simple and diagonal twining, exhibit an S-weft slant, while the close twined fabrics from Boucher, both close simple and close wrapped twining, have a Z-weft slant. As with cordage twist, twining weft slant can be an important indicator of cultural boundaries, and it seems to be so at Boucher.

Certainly more rare than data on structural types, a number of textiles from Boucher can be confidently ascribed to specific forms and probable functions. Open simple twined specimens from features 41 and 131 are bags. The bag from feature

Figure 3.9. Open simple twined (Type I, Subtype II) bag with hide lining containing copper nuggets from feature 41 at the Boucher site.

41 encased a cache of copper fragments, some of which appear to be unmodified raw material (Figure 3.9). The bag is approximately 5 cm x 6 cm in size and is lined with hide. As discussed further below, the feature 41 textile bag was apparently decorated by differentially introducing nonstructural fibers into the weave (see description for textile Type I, Subtype II). The feature 131 textile was defined as a bag on the basis of extant textile fragments attached to and negative impressions left on a large (10 cm x 12 cm) consolidated clump of powdered red ocher. The fabric or impressions of it were present on all exterior surfaces of the red ocher. This bag and its contents were interred over the chest area of a mid-adult probable female flexed burial in feature 131.

Other bags made from dressed hide were present in Boucher features 45 and 94. The hide bag from feature 94 contained a mass of ritually interred faunal remains and several artifacts (see Heckenberger et al. 1990b:Figures 22 and 23). Intact portions of dressed and possibly sewn hide, which tightly conform to the concentration of animal bones, substantiate that the hide originally enveloped the entire mass. The bag may have measured approximately 15 cm x 20 cm or greater when full.

Animal bones present within the feature 94 bag minimally include pine marten *(Martes americana)*, American mink *(Mustela vison)*, red fox *(Vulpes vulpes)*, timber rattler *(Crotalus horridus)*, black rat snake *(Elaphe obsoleta)*, raccoon *(Procyon lotor)*, and unidentified cervid and bird (small duck?). This hide bag was interred near the shoulder of an old adult male who was wrapped in a textile shroud, or clothed in a garment of some sort. The small hide bag from feature 45 contained the remains of a black rat snake *(Elaphe obsoleta)* (see Heckenberger et al. 1990b:Figure 22). These latter two bags are interpreted as ritual pouches, or "medicine bags," and it is quite possible that all four bags had specific magico-religious functions.

Personal garments are also present among the Boucher textiles and, like the bags, are little known in the archaeological record. Several features contained fabrics which represent some form of secular or ritual apparel based on their relative size and intimacy with the human remains, as well as their overall quality. The wrapped twining specimens from feature 124, the open simple and diagonal twined specimen from feature 107, and open simple twined fabrics from features 94 and 151 all exhibit structural and contextual attributes which indicate a function as upper-body clothing.

In the case of the wrapped twined specimen from feature 124, the delicacy of the fabric and its association with the individual strongly suggest a garment. The moving weft of the fabric was constructed with strands of animal hair, and the weave of the specimen is extremely delicate. The fabric is directly adhering to the scapula (shoulder) of the individual and was also present at the base of the skull. This fabric was also preserved around and amongst the hand bones. In fact, the feature 124 fabric was folded several times in the area of the hand, testifying to its supple quality. A similar fabric was preserved in feature 110; however, it was too fragmentary to ascribe a possible function.

The textile from feature 107, an open simple and diagonal twined fabric, was also intimately associated with the body. The feature 107 fabric had been wrapped around the individual, apparently as a shroud or cowl. This twined form was the innermost of at least three separate fabric forms included in the feature 107 burial and seems to have had a special relationship to the human body, probably as an outer garment or shroud (see Figure 3.3B). The individual in feature 107 was directly clothed in a tailored hide garment which was also enveloped by the fabric. In feature 151, impressions of a large open simple twined fabric indicate that it once enveloped the upper body (see Figure 3.5A), as is apparent on hide adhering to both scapulas. This is suggestive of a similar arrangement to that encountered in feature 107, that is, an individual wearing a hide garment (shirt?) wrapped in an outer textile garment or shroud. In both cases, strands of copper beads, wrapped around the head and neck of the individual, were present outside of the hide garment and inside the textile in relation to the body. Parenthetically, features 107 and 151 both contained juvenile humans.

The feature 94 textile was likewise intimately associated with the head and shoulder area of the individual, an old adult male. This large fragment of open simple twining (Type I, Subtype II) (see Figure 3.4A) was apparently wrapped around the upper body, along with a strand of copper beads. The hide "medicine bag" described above was present outside of the textile near or on the shoulder of the individual.

The majority of Boucher textiles, 20 of the 23 forms, were constructed using solely or predominantly Z-spun, S-twist cordage elements. These structural elements are consistent with the range in diameter and tightness of twist of the individual cordage fragments. Again, no Z-twist cordage was present in the available textile assemblage. Of special note, the active elements of the close wrapped twining from feature 124 are unspun strands of animal hair, as are the wrapping elements of the open simple twining (Type I, Subtype II) from features 41, 94, 129, 130, and 151. In fact, the close wrapped twining from feature 124 was manufactured with two varieties (most likely two species) of hair, a brown colored hair (also used in the Type I, Subtype II textiles) and a black-colored hair. The brown hair differs in no significant way from other

Middlesex complex perishables, which include some usage of moose hair (*Alces alces*) at sites such as Augustine Mound (C. Turnbull, personal communication 1987).

One final aspect of the sample, the apparent use of decoration on several forms, merits attention since it is truly unique. No other unequivocal fabric decoration has been reported from Early Woodland period sites in the far Northeast. The wrapped twined garment or shroud from feature 124 preserves unequivocal evidence of decoration (Figure 3.10). A chevron decoration was created by weaving successive rows of black hair against a brown hair background, as described above. One twining fragment from feature 124 preserves two sets of black lines, approximately 0.5–1.0 cm wide, each of which meet to form two pointed V's, pointing in opposite directions. This decoration is similar to early Contact period decorated fabrics from New England in terms of the use of linear geometric designs, in contrast to the more stylized floral designs favored by native populations after prolonged contact with Europeans (Richardson 1977:113–119).

Additionally, the wrapping elements used in the open simple twined fabrics from features 41, 94, 129, 130, and 151 may have been meant to serve as decorative elements. The wrapping in all these

Figure 3.10. Decorated close wrapped twined probable shroud fragment from feature 124 at the Boucher site. Note chevron decoration visible in upper left corner of specimen.

cases served no necessary structural purpose. For example, in the case of the feature 41 bag and the possible shroud from feature 151, the wrapping elements were clearly used discontinuously over the specimens. The wrapping apparently was employed to create geometric designs on these fabrics.

External Correlations

Although twined basketry was clearly established in eastern North America by the eighth millennium B.C. (Andrews and Adovasio this volume), fiber artifacts predating the Woodland period before ca. 1000 B.C. are extremely scarce. At present, few extant fiber perishables or impressions thereof are attributable to the Early and Middle Archaic periods, ca. 8000–4000 B.C., and few can be assigned to the Late Archaic period, ca. 4000–1000 B.C., with any certainty. Twined basketry fragments from the Riverside site in Michigan (King 1968), the Ozark Bluff shelters in Arkansas (Scholtz 1975), and Salts Cave in Kentucky (King 1974; Watson 1969) are all tentatively assigned to the Late Archaic period. However, the available radiocarbon dates seem to indicate a possible attribution to the Early Woodland period for the Riverside site specimens and perhaps most of those from Salts Cave (Hruska 1967:255; Watson 1969:50–51).

Negative images of open twining with S-twist wefts over single warps, perhaps representing a bag form, are known from the Hart Falls (Overlock I) site in Maine (Petersen et al. 1984; Whitehead n.d.:Appendix B). These stained images, the earliest evidence of basketry in New England and the Canadian Maritimes, occur on ground slate "bayonets" attributable to the later portion of the Moorehead complex (phase), ca. 2000–1800 B.C. (cf. Bourque 1976). This twining is similar to both earlier and later twined forms known in the broad region including those from the Boucher site, and it seemingly indicates long-term technological continuity.

The vast majority of known fiber perishables from the Northeast are attributable to the Woodland period. In part, this is due to the development of ceramics at about the onset of the Early Woodland period, whereby the characteristic use of fiber artifacts in surface finishing and/or decorating ceramics preserved them as negative impressions on pottery surfaces. Although a large number of sites have yielded such ceramics, few samples of the fiber perishables have yet to be analyzed. Nonetheless, it seems certain that diverse forms of cordage, netting, and textiles were present in the far Northeast by the onset of the Early Woodland period (Petersen and Hamilton 1984; Petersen et al. 1984:419).

Throughout the broad region, a variety of actual fiber artifacts attributable to the first millennium B.C. have been described, mostly from mortuary contexts (e.g., Adovasio 1982:826–845; Adovasio and Andrews [with Carlisle] 1980:33–72; Dragoo 1963:129, 224; King 1968:117–123; Ritchie and Dragoo 1960:16, 20; Shetrone 1931:81–84; Webb 1941:185–190; Webb and Snow 1945). In the far Northeast, these most notably include specimens from the Morrow site in New York, which produced a specimen of close simple twining (Z-wefts) and netting associated with dates of 630 B.C. ±250 and 562 B.C. ±100 (Ritchie 1965:186–187), and the Rosenkrans site in New Jersey which yielded two open twined specimens (S-wefts) with associated radiocarbon dates of 610 B.C. ±120 and 450 B.C. ±60 (Kraft 1976:12). The Mason cemetery in central Maine preserved open simple twining (S-wefts) with unspun warps and wefts. Two radiocarbon dates of 460 B.C. ±60 and 10 B.C. ±70 have been obtained for this Early Woodland component at the Mason cemetery (Klein 1983:633; Moorehead 1922:42). Other Early Woodland cemeteries in Vermont (Loring 1985:110), New York (Ritchie 1955:103, 109; Ritchie and Dragoo 1960) and New Jersey (Mounier 1981:60) also preserved fragments of actual fiber artifacts.

Augustine Mound in New Brunswick preserved the largest comparable assemblage of Early Woodland fiber artifacts from the far Northeast. Textiles recovered from several burials at Augustine Mound are among the most spectacular specimens in the broad region. Excellent examples of open simple twining (S-wefts; unspun and cordage elements), simple and twill plaiting (unspun and cordage elements), and braiding were encountered in several burials. Six radiocarbon dates, ranging between 1000 B.C. ±75 and 380 B.C. ±110, have been obtained for Augustine Mound (Turnbull 1976:55; C. Turnbull, personal communication 1987).

Twining continued throughout the Woodland period and at least into the early Contact period. A fragment of actual twined basketry from Lake Cochituate, Massachusetts, possibly attributable to the Middle or Late Woodland period, has been reported (Petersen et al. 1987). Negative impressions and extant specimens of twining attributable to the Middle and Late Woodland periods are known from across the far Northeast and nearby areas (e.g., Heckenberger and Petersen 1988; Michels and Smith 1967; Petersen this volume; Petersen and Power 1983; Petersen and Sanger 1991). Likewise, a variety of aboriginal specimens of twining, as well as plaiting and braiding, are known from Contact period archaeological contexts in the broad region (e.g., Bower 1980; G. Brown [Gustafson], personal communication 1986; Whitehead n.d.; Willoughby 1905).

Possibly the most outstanding aspect of the Boucher fiber artifact assemblage is its consistency with other samples from Early Woodland period sites across the broad region, particularly those relating to classic Adena and the Middlesex complex. Several general traits considered characteristic of Adena fiber industries are present at the Boucher site. These traits, first suggested by Webb and Snow (1945:27), include the presence of both simple (or "plain") and diagonal twining, lattice or wrapped twining, and the use of three ply cordage. A dramatic preponderance of S-twist cordage and S-weft slant basketry is also characteristic among Early Woodland Adena/Middlesex fiber artifacts (Petersen and Hamilton 1984:430). Of further interest, the Boucher textiles include several varieties which are presently known only in other Early Woodland samples and then only rarely. In the case of Boucher, these rare varieties include the open simple twined forms with wrapped warps, the active wrapped or "bird cage" twined form, and the open simple and diagonal twined form.

The open simple twined forms at Boucher that have warps wrapped with nonactive elements are virtually identical to rare fabrics known from several other sites in eastern North America. A nearly identical nonactive wrapping technique on twining is reported from a mortuary context at the Riverside site (King 1968:121). Based on personal observation, a nearly identical technique is also present in the textile assemblage from Augustine Mound. In the case of the Augustine Mound fabrics, the wrapping elements have been positively identified as moose hair (Alces alces), as noted above. The wrapping elements in the Boucher fabrics differ in no significant way from the moose hair at Augustine Mound and are assuredly animal hair as well. Based on cross-dated artifacts and the available radiocarbon dates, Augustine Mound is firmly dated to the Early Woodland period. Although no conclusive date is available for the Riverside fabric, five radiocarbon dates from the site and cross-dated lithic artifacts suggest that it too is roughly contemporaneous with the Boucher site and Augustine Mound.

The active wrapped or "bird cage" close twined fabrics from the Boucher site are some of the few examples of this technology known to the authors from the broad region. The single unequivocal analogue for the Boucher active wrapped fabrics is from Mt. Horeb Mound in Kentucky, where open wrapped twining was described by Carey (in Webb 1941:185–190) as "lattice" or "bird-cage" twining. Mt. Horeb Mound has been attributed to the Early Woodland period on the basis of cross-dated artifacts. Close wrapped twining of some sort is also associated with the first millennium B.C. on the basis of ceramic impressions from Tick Island in Florida (Harding 1988). An even older wrapped twining analogue (of some sort) may be attributable to the Early Archaic period at Russell Cave in Alabama (Andrews and Adovasio this volume). However, the close wrapped twined fabrics from the Boucher site are considerably more delicate than any of the above mentioned analogues, and they clearly represent exceptionally refined weaves which incorporated animal hair and vegetal fibers.

The simple and diagonal twined fabric from the Boucher site is also a very rare textile form in the far Northeast and elsewhere throughout North America. The only analogous specimen reported anywhere in the broad region is the fabric from the Riverside site mentioned above. The Riverside example apparently differs from the Boucher site fabric in that the structure changes from simple to diagonal twining across weft rows, rather than across warps (King 1968:121), but in both cases the diagonal twining is confined between simple twined portions of the fabric. However, King (1968:121) notes: "[O]ne fragment suggests that in some cases the openwork bands may not have extended the entire width of the fabric but were combined with wrapped pile areas—possibly producing a pattern. Unfortunately, with such small fragments it is impossible to be sure."

In the final analysis, the Boucher specimens attest to the fact that Early Woodland fiber industries must have had ancient antecedents in the more remote past. In the far Northeast, these industries were highly developed by the onset of the Early Woodland period and undoubtedly played a significant role in Early Woodland material culture. This treatment has been confined to the actual fiber artifacts from mortuary contexts at the Boucher site. However, the presence of fabric-impressed ceramics at the site indicates that fiber industries were not confined to ritual activities. Virtually all of the various textile forms identified in the Boucher assemblage likely functioned or had correlates in the secular life of these people as well.

The paucity of extant fiber artifacts predating the Contact period in the far Northeast makes it difficult to precisely define characteristics which were unique to a discrete population, or a group of culturally-related populations. However, the notable similarities among the known Early Woodland fiber industries, in conjunction with the consistency of other artifact and raw material traits across the broad region, attest to the interdependence of these populations and/or their common origins. The interregional exchange of diverse goods documents links between Early Woodland groups which undoubtedly involved well-established avenues for the exchange of ideas and per-haps individuals as well. The material correlates across the region thus reflect not only transported goods but also document a common cultural milieu.

Of further interest, fine-grained analysis also reveals that localized variations in material culture can be documented within the context of regional interdependence. Preservation biases certainly complicate the record, but the identification of localized artifact distributions promises to be relevant for reconstruction of cultural interaction across the region during the Early Woodland period. Further isolation of local developments, along with better definition of those with far-flung regional correlates, should be pursued through future research.

ACKNOWLEDGMENTS

The authors owe thanks to a large number of individuals and institutions who have graciously granted access to their collections and research data over an extended period. Most notably, Christopher J. Turnbull, New Brunswick provincial archaeologist, kindly allowed Heckenberger and Petersen to examine materials from Augustine Mound. Likewise, these two authors would like to thank Robert E. Funk at the New York State Museum and J. V. Wright at the Canadian National Museum of Civilization who permitted perusal of the voluminous collections in these museums. UMF faculty development funds awarded to Petersen supported these research trips. A special note of thanks is due William A. Haviland of the University of Vermont who kindly provided continued access to the Boucher site collections prior to their repatriation to the Western Abenaki in Vermont. The late Robert Stuckenrath provided most of the radiocarbon dates for the Boucher site; a grant from the Cecil Howard Charitable Trust supported the AMS dates. At UMF, Kara Ohlund and Shirley Thompson typed the manuscript on disk and Belinda Cox drafted the site map. Finally, Stephen Nelson and Stanley Lantz are thanked for their help and expertise in photography of the Boucher fiber artifacts. All errors and omissions are the sole responsibility of the authors.

NOTES

1. Twelve specimens from feature 110 at Boucher were not assignable to a specific structure type due to their fragmentary condition and the presence of three fabrics within the feature. Four of the 12 fragments are apparently related to the close simple twined fabric from feature 110 and may be, in fact, simple selvage fragments. Three other fragments may be related to the braid from feature 110. The other five specimens are so fragmentary that their original structural type cannot even be guessed. All of these 12 unassigned specimens are composed of S-twist cordage elements.

2. Two feature 130 fabric specimens (130-6 and 130-66) can be classified as open simple twining, but do not preserve adequate structures to be fully described. It is assumed that these two fragments are related to the Type I, Subtype II fabric from feature 130, and they are therefore included with other specimens from it.

REFERENCES CITED

Adovasio, J. M.
1977   *Basketry Technology: A Guide to Identification and Analysis.* Aldine, Chicago.
1982   Basketry and Netting Impressions. In *The Prehistory of the Paintsville Reservoir, Johnson and Morgan Counties, Kentucky,* compiled by J. M. Adovasio, pp. 826–845. Ethnology Monographs 6. Dept. of Anthropology, Univ. of Pittsburgh, Pittsburgh.

Adovasio, J. M., and R. L. Andrews (with R. C. Carlisle)
1980   Basketry, Cordage and Bark Impressions from the Northern Thorn Mound (46Mg78), Monongalia County, West Virginia. *West Virginia Archeologist* 30:33–72.

Bourque, Bruce J.
1976   The Turner Farm Site: A Preliminary Report. *Man in the Northeast* 11:21–30.

Bower, Beth
1980   Aboriginal Textiles. In *Burrs Hill, A Seventeenth Century Wampanoag Burial Ground in Warren, Rhode Island,* edited by Susan Gibson, pp. 89–91, 140–144. Haffenreffer Museum of Anthropology, Brown Univ., Providence.

Browning, Kathryn
1974   Indian Textiles as Reconstructed from the Impressions Left on Long Island Pottery. *Archaeology of Eastern North America* 2(1):94–98.

Dragoo, Don W.
1963   *Mounds for the Dead.* Annals of Carnegie Museum 37. Pittsburgh.

Emery, Irene
1980   *The Primary Structure of Fabrics: An Illustrated Classification.* The Textile Museum, Washington, D.C.

Harding, Deborah G.
1988   Some Early Florida Basketry Types from Mat Impressed Pottery. Unpublished ms. on file, Division of Anthropology, Carnegie Museum of Natural History, Pittsburgh.

Heckenberger, Michael J., and James B. Petersen
1988   Aboriginal Perishable Fiber Industries. In *Archaeological Investigations at the Pearl Street Park Sites in Essex, Chittenden County, Vermont,* by James B. Petersen, Michael J. Heckenberger, and Peter A. Thomas, pp. 110–116. Univ. of Vermont Dept. of Anthropology Report 95. Burlington.

Heckenberger, Michael J., James B. Petersen, and Louise A. Basa
1990a   Early Woodland Period Ritual Use of Personal Adornment at the Boucher Site. *Annals of Carnegie Museum* 59(3):173–217. Pittsburgh.

Heckenberger, Michael J., James B. Petersen, Louise A. Basa, Ellen R. Cowie, Arthur E. Spiess, and Robert E. Stuckenrath
1990b   Early Woodland Period Mortuary Ceremonialism in the Far Northeast: A View from the Boucher Cemetery. *Archaeology of Eastern North America* 18:109–144.

Hruska, Robert
1967   The Riverside Site: A Late Archaic Manifestation in Michigan. *The Wisconsin Archaeologist* 48(3):145–260.

Hurley, William M.
1979   *Prehistoric Cordage: Identification of Impressions on Pottery.* Taraxacum, Washington, D.C.

Jacobs, Eldridge
1950   *The Physical Features of Vermont.* Vermont State Development Commission, Montpelier.

Janaway, R. C.
1985   Dust to Dust: The Preservation of Textile Materials in Metal Artifact Corrosion Products with Reference to Inhumation Graves. *Science and Archaeology* 27:29–34.

Jones, Volney H.
1936   Notes on the Preparation and the Uses of Basswood Fiber by the Indians of the Great Lakes Region. *Papers of the Michigan Academy of Sciences, Arts, and Letters* 22:1–16.

King, Mary E.

1968 Textile Fragments from the Riverside Site, Menominee, Michigan. *Verhandlungen des XXXVIII Internationalen Amerikanistenkongresses*, pp. 117–123.

1974 The Salts Cave Textiles: A Preliminary Account. In *Archeology of the Mammoth Cave Area*, edited by Patty Jo Watson, pp. 31–40. Academic Press, New York.

1978 Analytical Methods and Prehistoric Textiles. *American Antiquity* 43(1):89–96.

Klein, J. I.

1983 Current Research. *American Antiquity* 48(4):626–633.

Kraft, Herbert C.

1976 The Rosenkrans Site, An Adena-related Mortuary Complex in the Upper Delaware Valley, New Jersey. *Archaeology of Eastern North America* 4:9–49.

Krigbaum, John

1986 *An Osteological Analysis of VT-FR-26, An Early Woodland Cemetery.* Unpublished senior thesis, Dept. of Anthropology, Univ. of Vermont, Burlington.

Loring, Stephen

1985 Boundary Maintenance, Mortuary Ceremonialism and Resource Control in the Early Woodland: Three Cemetery Sites in Vermont. *Archaeology of Eastern North America* 13:93–127.

Maslowski, Robert F.

1984 The Significance of Cordage Attributes in the Analysis of Woodland Pottery. *Pennsylvania Archaeologist* 54(1–2):51–60.

Michels, Joseph W., and Ira F. Smith (editors)

1967 *Archaeological Investigations of Sheep Rock Shelter, Huntingdon County, Pennsylvania.* Dept. of Sociology and Anthropology, Pennsylvania State Univ., Univ. Park.

Miner, Horace

1936 The Importance of Textiles in the Archaeology of the Eastern United States. *American Antiquity* 1(3):181–192.

Moorehead, Warren K.

1922 *A Report on the Archaeology of Maine.* Dept. of Anthropology, Phillips Academy, Andover.

Mounier, R. Alan

1981 Three Possible Middlesex Sites in Southern New Jersey. *Archaeology of Eastern North America* 9:52–63.

Petersen, James B., and Nathan D. Hamilton

1984 Early Woodland Ceramic and Perishable Fiber Industries from the Northeast: A Summary and Interpretation. *Annals of Carnegie Museum* 53:413–445. Pittsburgh.

Petersen, James B., Nathan D. Hamilton, James M. Adovasio, and Alan L. McPherron

1984 Netting Technology and the Antiquity of Fish Exploitation in Eastern North America. *Midcontinental Journal of Archaeology* 9(2):199–225.

Petersen, James B., Tonya Largy, and Robert W. Carlson

1987 An Aboriginal Basketry Fragment from Lake Cochituate, Natick, Massachusetts. *Bulletin of the Massachusetts Archaeological Society* 48(1):2–8.

Petersen, James B., and Marjory W. Power

1983 *The Winooski Site and the Middle Woodland Period in the Northeast.* Dept. of Anthropology, Univ. of Vermont. Submitted to Interagency Archeological Services, Mid-Atlantic Region, National Park Service, Philadelphia.

Petersen, James B., and David Sanger

1991 An Aboriginal Ceramic Sequence for Maine and the Maritimes. In *Prehistoric Archaeology in the Maritimes: Past and Present Research,* edited by Michael Deal and Susan Blair, pp. 121–178. Council of Maritime Premiers, Fredericton.

Richardson, James B.

1977 The Impact of European Contact on Northeastern Iroquois and Algonkian Art Styles. In *Current Perspectives on Northeastern Archaeology: Essays in Honor of William A. Ritchie,* edited by Robert E. Funk and Charles F. Hayes, pp. 113–119. Researches and Transactions of the New York State Archaeological Association 17(1). Rochester.

Ritchie, William A.

1955 *Recent Discoveries Suggesting an Early Woodland Burial Cult in the Northeast.* New York State Museum and Science Service Circular 40. Albany.

1965 *The Archaeology of New York State.* Natural History Press, Garden City.

Ritchie, William A., and Don W. Dragoo

1960 *The Eastern Dispersal of the Adena.* New York State Museum and Science Service Bulletin 379. Albany.

Ritchie, William A., and Robert E. Funk

1973 *Aboriginal Settlement Patterns in the Northeast.* New York State Museum and Science Service Memoir 20. Albany.

Scholtz, Sandra Clements

1975 *Prehistoric Plies: A Structural and Comparative Analysis of Cordage, Netting, Basketry, and Fabric from Ozark Bluff Shelters.* Arkansas Archeological Survey Research Series 9. Univ. of Arkansas Museum, Fayetteville.

Shetrone, Henry C.

1931 *The Mound Builders.* D. Appleton and Company, New York.

Snow, Dean R.
1980   *The Archaeology of New England*. Academic Press, New York.

Thomas, Ronald A.
1970   Adena Influence in the Middle Atlantic Coast. In *Adena: The Seeking of an Identity*, edited by B. K. Swartz, pp. 56–87. Ball State Univ. Press, Muncie.

Turnbull, Christopher J.
1976   The Augustine Site: A Mound from the Maritimes. *Archaeology of Eastern North America* 4:50–62.

Watson, Patty Jo
1969   *Prehistory of Salts Cave, Kentucky*. Illinois State Museum Reports of Investigations 16. Springfield.

Webb, William S.
1941   *Mt. Horeb Earthworks and the Drake Mound, Fayette County, Kentucky*. Univ. of Kentucky Reports in Archaeology 5(3). Lexington.

Webb, William S., and Charles E. Snow
1945   *The Adena People*. Univ. of Kentucky Reports in Anthropology and Archaeology 6. Lexington.

Whitehead, Ruth H.
n.d.   *Plant Fibre Textiles from the Hopps Site: BkCp-1*. Nova Scotia Museum Curatorial Report 59. Halifax.

Whitford, A. C.
1941   Textile Fibers Used in Eastern Aboriginal North America. *Anthropological Papers of the American Museum of Natural History* 38(1):5–22. New York.

Willoughby, Charles C.
1905   Textile Fabrics of the New England Indians. *American Anthropologist* 7:85–93.

Wright, James V.
1987   Archaeological Evidence for the Use of Furbearers in North America. In *Wild Furbearer Management and Conservation in North America*, edited by Milan Novak, James A. Baker, Martyn E. Obbard, and Bruce Malloch, pp. 3–12. Ontario Ministry of Natural Resources, Ottawa.

4

Lucy R. Sibley

Kathryn A. Jakes

Lewis H. Larson

Inferring Behavior and Function from an Etowah Fabric Incorporating Feathers

Human behavior and fabric function can be inferred from fabrication, compositional, and provenience data for a fabric fragment incorporating feathers, hair, and unidentified fibers from the Etowah site in Georgia. These materials were combined in a wrapping yarn around a bast core in this Mississippian period fabric. Three sets of behavior are potentially associated with it, including fabric production, usage, and ultimate placement in a burial context. As discussed further below, the evidence supports identification of the fabric fragment as the remains of a valued ceremonial garment, likely worn on special occasions to demonstrate political and/or religious status.

The fabric, embedded in clay, was recovered from Mound C at the Etowah site, in conjunction with other burial goods such as copper and shell. The copper at least partially accounts for preservation of the fabric, which exhibits a partially mineralized, distinctive structure. It includes apparent feathers, hair, and other fine fibrous materials in one of its yarn systems. These were twisted together and encircle bast core yarns

(Sibley and Jakes 1986). Some areas of the wrapping material are green, which indicates the occurrence of at least partial "pseudomorphs" replicating the original structure of the fiber; pseudomorphs are formed in the replacement of organic structures by mineral compounds. Gray, brown, and black areas are also discernible in the wrapping, but these are more likely the results of degradative processes rather than original colors present in the fabric.

Whatever the original coloration may have been, enough of this Etowah fabric survives to document a series of decisions concerning the production of complex yarn structures from a mixture of fibrous materials. Although these fibers can be difficult to manipulate, aboriginal craftspeople certainly were able to blend disparate elements into coherent and integrated fabrics, as identified in past studies of Middle Woodland period Hopewell and other Mississippian period textiles in eastern North America (e.g., King and Gardner 1981; Sibley et al. 1989; Whitford 1941). This fabric fragment from Etowah helps to better define the complicated behaviors inherent in the archaeological textile record of the region.

Etowah is one of the more imposing sites attributed to the Mississippian period, ca. A.D. 800–1600, in southeastern North America, or the Southeast. Located on the north bank of the Etowah River about 3.3 km (2 mi) south of Cartersville, Georgia, the site proper includes the remains of a town that covered an area of about 21 hectares. Its major features include three large, truncated, pyramidal mounds arranged around two plazas. The largest of the mounds, Mound A, is approximately 10,000 m² in size and rises almost 20 m above the surrounding floodplain. The other two large mounds, B and C, are each approximately 2116 m² and about 5–6 m high (Larson 1972).

Excavation of Mound C has permitted interpretation of the nature and function of the earthwork. It was first built as an earthen platform on which was constructed a mortuary temple. In turn, the temple apparently contained the bodies of the members of high status or chiefly lineage of the aboriginal town. Mound C was subsequently enlarged, and the temple on its summit was rebuilt four more times. Each construction phase was accompanied by the erection of a palisade of posts around the base of the mound which screened it from the plaza. At the time of each new construction phase, the bodies held in the mortuary temple were buried in graves made into the earthen floor of the temple, as well as in graves that encircled the base of the existing mound (Larson 1971). In all, over 350 burials were placed into or around the mound while it was used for mortuary purposes.

This Mississippian site is closely identified with the Southeastern Ceremonial complex, or Southern Cult (Waring and Holder 1945), and its fabrics and other artifacts are significant in broad regional contexts. Very little is known about Mississippian fabrics in general (King and Gardner 1981) and Etowah fabrics in particular. Thus, examination of the fragment from Mound C provides an important opportunity to add to available knowledge of aboriginal fabrics and their role in the prehistory of complex societies in eastern North America.

Previous analyses of Etowah fabrics have been conducted using fragments recovered: 1) during the 1920s by an "expedition" led by Warren K. Moorehead (Moorehead 1932; Byers 1962a, 1962b); and 2) during the 1950s by Lewis H. Larson (Larson 1959; Sibley and Jakes 1986, 1989; Sibley et al. 1989). Byers (1962b) noted that the lack of provenience information for the fabrics excavated during the 1920s hindered research. In contrast, those recovered during the 1950s do have associated provenience data. The research reported here infers human behavior and fabric function from evidence obtained using recent fabrication, compositional, and provenience analyses for a fragmentary fabric recovered from Etowah by Larson (catalogue no. 1145 from burial 103 in Mound C).

A fundamental relationship exists between human behavior and the function of a fabric (or any other artifact) since the latter is a product of the former. Although all artifacts are shaped by human behavior, some, such as fabrics and other fiber industries, provide a greater number of clues about behavior since they were produced through complicated processes of manufacture and for multiple uses. If a fabric is a "product of a configuration of interrelated choices," as Wallace (1975:101) proposes, then this Etowah fabric with wrapping yarns provides an opportunity to construct a cognitive map of the interrelated behavioral choices associated with its manufacture, usage, and discard. Fabric manufacture is directly related to cultural decisions to meet one or more functional needs.

Whether completely conscious or not, numerous decisions must be made to maneuver hairlike fibrous materials into various fabric structures. The resultant shape itself is evidence of function and, ultimately, of associated human behavior, given the numerous ways in which fibrous materials can be manipulated (Sibley and Jakes 1989). At the same time, a single fabric may well have functioned in various ways. For example, a fabric manufactured to function as a mantle or some other garment also may have served as a blanket, among other uses, and ultimately may have been placed in a burial as a covering.

Decisions associated with manufacture, usage, and discard of fabrics are all potentially identifiable through examination of fibers, yarns, and fabric structural evidence, as well as any available contextual provenience data. A "map" of interrelated decisions and behavior can be derived from the combined classes of evidence. Not all the details of the "map" will be discernible necessarily for any given fabric (or other fiber artifact), but enough may be visible to allow identification of the major landmarks of its cultural context.

DESCRIPTION OF THE ETOWAH FABRIC

The fabric fragment described here actually consists of two related specimens which exhibit the same characteristics and were recovered adjacent to each other. Emphasis is placed on the larger of the two fragments, fragment 1, which is approximately 10 cm x 15 cm in size. Although much of the fragment is clay encrusted, no attempt was made to remove the clay since it now supports the fabric structure. The clay matrix hindered the fabrication analysis, but, fortunately, certain portions of the fabric are relatively well exposed, and a series of parallel yarn-like structures are visible in these areas (Figure 4.1).

Fabric System Evidence for the Etowah Fabric

Microscopic examination revealed the presence of complex yarn structures, each consisting of a core with a fibrous wrapping material surrounding it, as well as a possible third element, the function of which is not certain. The complex yarns can be designated as "system A" for purposes of clarity in terms of the structural analysis (Sibley and Jakes 1986).

A second less obvious series of strands appears perpendicular to the system A yarns and some 5

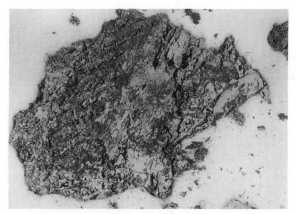

Figure 4.1. Fabric fragment 1 (cat. no. 1145) from burial 103 in Mound C at the Etowah site.

cm above them (see Figure 4.1). These strands are designated as "system B" yarns. No interworking of the two systems was observed, and no selvage was discovered. The system B yarns are fine and lack the multiple components present in those of system A. Clay covers nearly all the system B yarns and so it is impossible to make further statements about the second set of elements.

Microscopic evaluation of the reverse side of fragment 1 confirmed the fact that the two systems are not interworked. It also revealed the presence of a split-cane matting structure between the two wrapped yarn fabric layers. So, the clay matrix contains both fabric and matting specimens. A structure composed of at least two sets of elements, systems A and B, is postulated from the evidence. The lack of any identifiable interworking of the two systems precludes identification of the precise type of fabric structure, however.

Yarn Evidence for the Etowah Fabric

Classification of the system A complex yarns depends upon identification of their constituent parts. Scholtz (1975) interpreted a feather-wrapped cord as being "replied" because plied yarns are twisted around each other, but the system A yarns of fragment 1 do not precisely match that description. First, the core yarns consist of at least a pair of two ply, S-twist (\) yarns (Figure 4.2). In some areas, the number of yarns used in the core increases. These core yarns maintain their own structural integrity and do not spiral around each other; they are held together by the wrapping yarns.

The second constituent of the system A yarns is the wrapping portion, which incorporated feather-like entities, or feather barbules, apparently twisted around the minimally paired core yarns. The wrapping material itself is not plied, but it is twisted around the core. An alignment of fibers including featherlike materials, suggestive of intentional manipulation, is visible in certain sections of the wrapping (Figure 4.3). Since the wrapping fibers are loosely twisted, no regular twist direction is obvious, as is normally present in twisted or spun yarns. Likewise, there is no indication of any other yarn twisted around the fibrous wrapping. The core and wrapping

Figure 4.2. Etowah fabric fragment 1, system A core, with wrapping (9.4 x magnification).

are interworked simply by the twisting action of the wrapping element, in other words. The wrapping may be considered the "active" component of the structure and the core is the "passive" component.

Technically, the system A yarns are not replied, since not all elements are plied; yet, "replied cord" or "wrapped yarn elements" are more accurate terms than "yarn," since the latter describes either a twisted single yarn, or one produced by twisting two already twisted strands together (Joseph 1981). These units might be also called "complex yarns," or yarns with unlike elements (core, effect, and binder) twisted together, given the interrelation of different components, as present in the system A units. None of these terms is completely satisfactory, however, and so several are used herein to designate the system A units.

For the most part, the wrapping material simply encircles the core and does not show evidence of

any spinning or twisting. In one section, however, a black/brown fibrous mass is caught between the two core yarns (see Figure 4.3). In another area, the gray-green wrapping is broken and reveals a series of fine S-twisted yarns which are perpendicular to the core and parallel to the wrapping combinations (Figure 4.4). These yarns may have secured the wrapping to the core as a binder or may have been a foundation for the wrapping. It is likely that the wrapping material originally covered both core and foundation/binder so well that neither was visible.

Fiber Evidence for the Etowah Fabric

In addition to photomicrographic study, small samples of yarn components were taken for compositional analysis by scanning electron microscopy (SEM) and energy dispersive analysis of X-rays (EDS). Work in progress includes X-ray diffraction and infrared analyses to determine the extent of mineralization and to characterize the chemical composition of the material.

The physical structure of the core yarns of system A is typical of bast material, i.e., bundles of vegetal fibers of irregular size and shape used as one strand. These structures are still apparent (Figure 4.5), although occluded by soil particles; EDS data confirm the presence of the soil elements Al, Si, K, Ca, and Fe, with additional quantities of phosphorus due to the presence of plant material and copper (Table 4.1). The latter stems from association of the fabric with copper in the burial and incipient mineralization of the fibers, as noted above.

Figure 4.3. Etowah fabric fragment 1, system A wrapping (19.1 x magnification).

Figure 4.4. Etowah fabric fragment 1, system A wrapping/ binder (18.9 x magnification).

Table 4.1. Elemental Analysis of Yarn Components in Etowah Fabric Fragment 1 (Cat. No. 1145) from Burial 103 in Etowah Mound C

Sample	Elements												
	Na	Mg	Al	Si	P	S	Cl	K	Ca	Ti	Cr	Fe	Cu
Soil	—	trace	x	x	trace	—	—	x	x	x	x	x	trace
Core Yarn	—	—	x	x	x	x	—	x	x	—	—	x	x
Wrapping Yarn:													
Analysis 1	x	—	x	x	x	x	—	—	x	—	—	x	x
Analysis 2	—	—	x	x	x	x	—	x	x	x	—	x	x
Analysis 3	—	—	x	x	—	x	x	—	—	—	—	—	—
Analysis 4	—	—	x	x	—	x	—	—	x	—	—	x	trace
Analysis 5	—	—	—	x	—	x	—	—	—	—	—	x	x
Yarn, Reverse side	—	—	x	x	x	x	—	—	x	—	—	—	x

x = presence of elements.

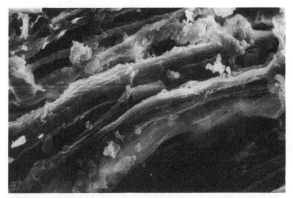

Figure 4.5. Scanning electron micrograph of core yarn of bast fibers (1485 x magnification).

The wrapping material encircling the bast core varies in combination of fibrous elements, as well as color. In some areas, the wrapping is fine and black, while nearby the wrapping is of different texture and color. Both types of material are wrapped around the same core yarns and appear contiguous. A sample of the fine black material consists of pronged nodular fiber structures which are similar to the barbules of feathers in the order *Falconiformes* (Day 1966) (Figures 4.6–4.7). This order includes the golden eagle (*Aquila chrysaetus*) and the sparrow hawk (*Accipter nisus*), among other species. The pronged structures of the barbules appear regularly throughout the samples studied, but are less common than other constituents in the wrapping elements. Previous examination of the wrapping material demonstrated the presence of a feather barbule of an unidentifiable genus (Sibley and Jakes 1986); its node structure differs from the *Falconiformes* structure and so it appears that several types of feathers were employed. The lack of a rachis suggests that the feather material is composed of down, not the entire feather.[1]

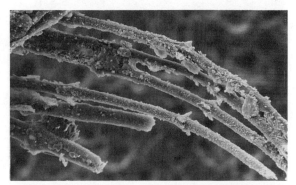

Figure 4.6. Scanning electron micrograph of feathers in wrapping material (1031 x magnification).

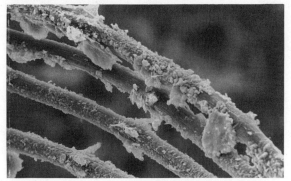

Figure 4.7. Scanning electron micrograph of feathers in wrapping material (2062 x magnification).

It is difficult to identify the other wrapping constituents without further study, but in some there is an indication of a scalar structure typical of hair (Figure 4.8). In another sample of the same wrapping yarn, predominantly gray and green fibers with a twisted shape (Figure 4.9) and unpeeling layers (Figure 4.10) can be seen. Certainly, these fibers are different than the other fibers described above, but more work remains to be done to identify them. Since little is known concerning the change in physical structure of fibers as they degrade in archaeological contexts, it is hazardous to specify a fiber type without more data. Swelling, fibrillation of fiber, and loss of distinctive morphological characteristics, all of which occur in archaeological textiles, generally hinder accurate identification of fibers (e.g., Jakes and Sibley 1983; King 1978).

Figure 4.10. Scanning electron micrograph of unpeeling fiber layers in wrapping material (2062 x magnification).

The physical structure of the yarn fibers on the reverse of the Etowah fabric is very different from those described above. Flat, ribbonlike fibers are obvious (Figure 4.11), but at present neither their specific identity nor general classification can be suggested. The relation of the flat fibers to those of the fabric incorporating feathers is not known. It may be another fiber used in the wrapping, perhaps a foundation or binder yarn.

Large quantities of sulfur were indicated by the EDS analysis of the wrapping yarn and this evidence supports the presence of protein in the down/feathers and hair. Varying relative amounts of sulfur and phosphorus in the analyzed samples reflect different fiber compositions; variation in the amount of soil elements reflects differing soil contaminants (see Table

Figure 4.8. Scanning electron micrograph of possible hair fibers in wrapping material (2062 x magnification).

Figure 4.9. Scanning electron micrograph of unknown fibers in wrapping material (4125 x magnification).

Figure 4.11. Scanning electron micrograph of yarn from fabric fragment 1 reverse side (1923 x magnification).

4.1). Similarly, varying quantities of copper indicate differential mineralization of these fibers. Further study of the process of pseudomorph development may prove useful in the identification of these fibers.

Burial Context for the Etowah Fabric

The Etowah site has long excited the interest of professional prehistorians and the public alike. It was first brought to the attention of nineteenth-century antiquarians and savants by the Reverend Elias Cornelius, a missionary traveling among the Cherokee. In 1818, Cornelius published an account of his visit to Etowah with his Cherokee hosts. He described the great earthworks that are its most noteworthy features and speculated about their origin and use (Cornelius 1818:322–324).

In the last decades of the nineteenth century, Cyrus Thomas of the Bureau of American Ethnology (BAE), Smithsonian Institution, undertook a broad-scale archaeological program of prehistoric mound exploration across the eastern United States. As a result, John Rogan, working for Thomas, began the first scientific investigation of the Etowah site during the 1880s. Directed by Warren K. Moorehead (1932), the R. S. Peabody Foundation of Phillips Academy later carried out three seasons of excavation at Etowah from 1927 through 1929. Both Rogan and Moorehead concentrated their efforts on Mound C. In 1952, the state of Georgia purchased the site, and in 1954 the Georgia Historical Commission began six seasons of archaeological work under the direction of Lewis Larson. That work continued investigation of Mound C and ultimately resulted in the complete excavation of the earthwork.

The Etowah fabric described here was recovered from burial 103, one of the burials encircling the base of Mound C, by Larson during the 1957 season. It was one of a series of burials associated with what was apparently the first rebuilding of the mound. Based on its location, burial 103 had been placed inside the post palisade that encircled the earliest of the mound construction phases; it is therefore interpreted as one of the first group of burials to have been interred in Mound C. These burials are tentatively assigned to the Etowah II period, probably dating from ca. A.D. 1300–1400.

At the time of interment, burial 103 was placed at the base of the back of the mound, i.e., the western side near the southwestern corner. It was put into a rectangular grave pit lined with stone slabs (Map 4.1). The long axis of the grave was north-south, and it contained a single individual lying on its left side, with the legs partially flexed and the arms tightly flexed against the chest. The head was to the south.

As was the case with much of the Mound C skeletal material, the preservation of the burial 103 bone was very poor. Nevertheless, an examination of bone from burial 103 by Robert Blakely, a physical anthropologist, tentatively identified the single individual as a male 25 to 28 years of age (Blakely n.d.). Blakely also noted that the burial 103 skeleton had "extensive copper staining and copper residue . . . [on the] ribs, metacarpals, and phalanges l[eft] radius, l[eft] ulna, l[eft] and r[ight] clavicles, [and] manubrium" (Blakely n.d.).

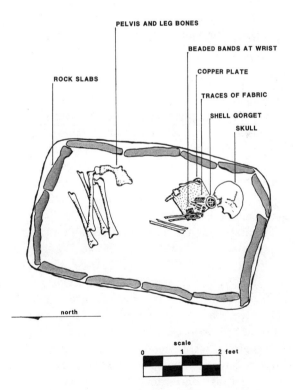

Map 4.1. Plan view of burial 103 in Mound C at the Etowah site.

The individual in burial 103 was accompanied by a number of artifacts. Bands of tubular beads were present on the wrists; each bead is approximately 8 mm long and 4 mm in diameter. The beads had been strung together to form bands 13 to 14 beads wide (i.e., about 65 mm wide) on each wrist. The hands and wrists of the individual lay atop a rectangular copper plate which lay over his upper chest. The plate, made of thin sheet copper, is too badly corroded to determine if it bore an embossed decoration; it measures approximately 14 cm on each side. An engraved and excised shell gorget was found on top of the copper plate. About 5 cm in diameter, the gorget was presumably worn at the throat suspended from a cord around the neck. The design on the gorget is a simple cross formed by two interlocked ovals that resemble two opposed chain links, framed by a plain circular border about 5 mm wide. The fabric described herein lay on the copper plate which enabled its partial preservation.

RECONSTRUCTION OF ASSOCIATED BEHAVIOR AND FUNCTION FOR THE ETOWAH FABRIC

Inferring human behavior and function for the Etowah fabric fragment begins with the realization that there are three general sets of potential behavior involved. Each set is related to a stage in the movement of a fabric through its cultural system, and each stage can be considered a "physiographic region" on the overall "cognitive map" of interrelated choices pertinent to that fabric.

The first "region" consists of decisions and actions related to fabrication of the fabric. The second "region" entails behavior related to use of the fabric in its cultural or systemic context (Schiffer 1972), or its function, in other words. The final "region" encompasses behavior related to placement of the fabric in a burial, or its discard, in an archaeological context. The second and third sets of behavior can be combined if the fabric was prepared solely as a burial good, i.e., if its function was strictly related to accompanying the dead. These sets of related behavior and their concomi-

tant functions may need to be expanded if a recycling mechanism is part of the cultural system, following Schiffer (1972).

One additional matter bears mention. While raw materials may be directly obtained from one or more nearby environmental settings, it is also possible to indirectly acquire them through trade with other populations who draw on other environments. Moreover, fabrics are easily transportable and thus may move through an exchange system at any stage in their production, i.e., as raw materials, as processed yarn, or as finished fabrics (Petersen and Hamilton 1984).

Region One of the "Cognitive Map"

The manufacture of the Etowah fabric involved harvesting and processing bast fibers, as well as feathers and animal hair. Although interrelated, the behavior associated with manipulating feathers and hair would be somewhat different than preparing bast fibers.

The choice of a bast type would be dictated by its potential pliability and relative fineness, and the technological processes necessary to produce bast fibers would first involve the removal of the outer woody layer of the plant. This is known as retting in the production of flax (Joseph 1981). Since bast fibers occur in fiber bundles in the stem of a plant, it is relatively easy to work them into a continuous structure in contrast to short, single fibers, which are more difficult to work (Sibley 1986).

The remaining manufacture processes would depend upon the type of yarn desired: the finer the yarn, the greater the amount of processing time required to achieve the size demanded. Twisting the separate fiber bundles into a plied yarn would increase the length and strength of the strand. By using groups of two ply core yarns, the Etowah people produced a strand or cord capable of sustaining the down-hair wrapping.

On the other hand, decisions about the use of down-hair elements would have to consider how well the prospective material covered the core of bast, as well as the weight and perhaps the potential warmth of the finished product. Colors and traditional patterns may have affected the selection of types of feathers, hair, and other fibers as well. Since it was impossible to classify the gray-green wrapping fiber as either plant or animal material, it is difficult to comment further about the behavior associated with its production. It does appear to have been incorporated into the wrapping yarn of down and hair, although probably it was not blended with them. The unidentified fiber may have had a color/pattern function in the fabric. Its relation to the binder yarn of bast is puzzling, but analysis is hampered by the condition of the fragment.

The support or binder yarn identified in one small portion of the fabric fragment also affected the choice of down-hair and other fiber wrapping constituents. The support or binder yarn appears as an S-twist structure perpendicular to the core. If it too is bast, additional choices had to be made about its processing and size in relation to the core, feathers, and hair.

The selection of appropriate raw materials has cultural implications beyond those of technology. King and Gardner (1981) reported the use of turkey down (Meleagris gallopavo) clearly spun into yarns in some fabrics from Craig Mound at the Spiro site in Oklahoma; other feather-wrapped yarns also occurred at Spiro (M. E. King, personal communication 1993). King and Gardner (1981) related the use of turkey down to the importance accorded the turkey as a symbol in the Southern Cult. So, separate sets of human behavior related to the fabric may be interrelated as well, i.e., symbolic and/or function-use decisions may well have affected fabric production decisions.

Preparation of the down-hair yarn undoubtedly presented a distinctive set of challenges to the craftspeople who produced the original fabric. Since feathers and down lack the typical length-to-width ratio of vegetal fibers, they require a means of either joining them into a long continuous strand or incorporating them individually into a strand. For the first alternative, spinning is the logical answer, but King and Gardner (1981) found that turkey down is difficult to spin by itself and requires from 10% to 50% mammal hair to achieve a strand suitable for use in a fabric. In the case of the Etowah specimen, down from possibly two genera

of birds and animal hair were apparently spun or twisted to form the wrapping yarn.

Another way to prepare a feather yarn was through the use of a binder yarn to attach feathers to the core by anchoring the "proximal ends to the cords with fine twine" (Willoughby 1952:112). Although Willoughby's work incorporated analyses of Spiro feather cords and ethnohistorical references to Maidu feather cloaks, he did not refer to the spinning of feathers. Rather, he indicated that separate, single feathers were bound to the cord so that both binder and core were hidden.

Scholtz (1975) focused on the structure of feather-wrapped yarns, how the feathers were attached to the core, and differences in the size of the core. She identified two means to secure feathers to the core. One method uses a regular binding to attach the feathers and the other involves the trapping of quills between two or more core yarns. The latter method was apparently used at Etowah, but not for anchoring individual feather quills; instead, the entire feather-hair yarn was caught between two core yarns (see Figure 4.3).

The imprecise congruence among these three analyses of feather constructions may result from differences in the original choice of raw materials, feathers versus down, as well as obviously different manufacture techniques related to yarn construction and yarn wrapping. Even feathers from small birds would have greater coherence than would down, and hence the use of hair to stabilize the structure was likely important in yarn constructions involving down.

Just as the down strands would have to be anchored to the core, so too would the system A yarns of the fabric structure need to be stabilized by a second system. Given the circumstances of burial and the elaborate nature of the down-hair yarns in system A, it is doubtful that system B is simply cordage or any of the one-system structures noted by Emery (1966). Instead, evidence preserved in fabric fragment 1 suggests a structure with interworking of two sets of elements, one perpendicular to the other. The type and extent of the interworking would have affected the fabric's function, as well as any behavior associated with its use. Interworking of two sets of elements necessitates other actions on the part of the fabric makers, and the specific structure affects the particular behavior involved.

Fabric structures identified in textiles from Craig Mound at Spiro (King and Gardner 1981; Scholtz 1975; Willoughby 1952; Whitford 1941) are weft twining, spaced weft twining, twill tapestry twining, and even a woven fabrication. The identification of a spaced octagonal twined fabric among the Etowah structures (Sibley and Jakes 1986) suggests the likelihood that some form of twining was used for the Etowah wrapped yarn fabric.

Willoughby (1952) indicated that the feather yarns in the Spiro fabrics are warp cords of a weft twined fabric. He noted that although the feather yarns appeared separate, close examination revealed the remains of weft yarns at half-inch (12.7 mm) intervals concealed by the feathers. Again, he turned to the ethnographic Maidu to support his identification of the feather yarns as warp elements in a mantle. If Willoughby is correct, then the Spiro fabric structure should be labeled a spaced weft twine, according to Emery's (1966) classification. The Etowah fragment does not display the remains of regular weft-yarn interworking along the system A yarns, however.

Aboriginal fabrics in eastern North America apparently were often constructed for a specific function and with a specific person in mind. In contrast, historic European (and other) textiles are produced generally by the yard, with no specific person or purpose in mind (Wilson 1980). The latter are used as fabric raw material, later shaped by cutting and sewing into various types of garments or furnishings, as needed, while Mississippian fabrics became mantles, kilts, or sleeping blankets, among other forms, immediately during the process of manufacture.

The relative value of the Etowah fabric may be inferred from its structure and the choice of materials used in its manufacture. The effort required to prepare down-hair wrapped fabrics must have been considerable since preparation of the down-hair yarns was undoubtedly time consuming and required considerable dexterity. It is reasonable to assume that the more time consuming the production process, the higher the status associated with the fabric in general. A corollary might be applicable to the Etowah fabric: the scarcer the raw materials or the greater the value accorded them, the higher the status of the fabric's user.

Region Two of the "Cognitive Map"

The intended function of the burial 103 fabric would have at least partially determined the choices relevant to its production. All of this decision making may have taken place before preparation of the first yarn. At whatever point production decisions were made, they inevitably led to a second set of behaviors related to the fabric, that is, its intended usage within a living cultural (or systemic) context. Use of the fabric implies its function, and the result is a circular relationship between human behavior and fabric function. Behaviors related to production of the fabric generated a structure incorporating feathers and hair to be used in some cultural context, but its use depended upon its primary function as body covering, shelter, or another object.

In the search for possible primary functions of the Etowah fabric, one is limited by the structure and fragmentary nature of the fabric itself. Whether the fabric consisted of tassel-like cords swinging from a weft-anchor system or a spaced weft twined fabric structure, it lacked the sturdiness essential for shoes, belts, or headdresses. Cordage, basketry, or matting would not be feasible because of the nature of the material. The flexibility implied by the available fabric evidence is more consistent with a mantle or perhaps a kilt. Use as a blanket would not be precluded either.

Both kilts and mantles were typical garments worn by other Mississippian populations. The wearers of the Spiro garments, for example, used a variety of body garments, including mantles, kilts (skirts), breechcloths, belts, and sashes, as well as head and footwear (King and Gardner 1981). Of these, it is not certain how many were made from feather fabrics. Willoughby (1952) noted that feather cords were used only in mantles, although not all mantles were constructed using feathers.

Certainly, the Etowah mantle, illustrated by Willoughby in Moorehead's original report (1932), did not incorporate feathers. Byers (1962b) described in detail a fabric recovered from the same burial (grave 19) as the mantle fragment originally illustrated by Willoughby, but he did not specify its function. Earlier still, Holmes (1896) linked feather yarns to garments in his review of ethnohistoric works describing fabrics. He quoted du Pratz, among others, to support his argument that feather yarns were used in mantles. From another source, Holmes reported the use of fabrics incorporating feather yarns as blankets.

Given the limited preservation and the ambiguity of the context in burial 103 at Etowah, it is impossible to provide more than speculation about the ways in which the down-hair-bast fabric might have been used. Certainly, garments or burial coverings are only two possible and obvious uses that might account for the presence of the fabric in the burial. However, one major problem with an interpretation of the fabric as a garment is its location; it apparently covered the chest or upper body of the interment. Representations of a human with a garment covering the upper body are very rare in Mississippian period art. Further, in the few examples that can be cited, it is difficult to say with certainty that these representations are depictions of a garment, rather than of body paint or tattooing.

Unarguable Mississippian period representations of garments do exist, and these make credible the interpretation of the burial 103 fabric as a possible garment. For example, Phillips and Brown (1978:Plate 20) illustrate fragments of a Spiro engraved shell cup that depicts male human figures wearing tunics that cover one shoulder and a portion of the chest. One of a group of six human figures engraved on the Rocky Creek limestone slab (Parker 1949:Figure 2) is shown wearing a cloak-like garment that covers the shoulders, one arm, all but the lower part of the other arm, and the entire torso.

Equivocal representations of garments over the upper body include two almost identical shell gorgets from Mound C at Etowah, one of which came from the 1884 BAE excavations (Thomas 1894:Figure 190), and the other (unpublished) from burial 19 excavated in 1954 by Larson. The dual human figures have the upper body and arms covered with parallel lines that may represent a garment, but they may instead depict body paint or tattooing. The Pine Harbor figurine of modeled and fired clay (Larson 1955:Figures 1 and 3) represents a headless, presumably human figure. Details of a falcon costume are shown by incised lines. Over the chest and extending to the belted waist are a series of vertical incised lines that give the appearance of a pleated "dress" shirt. It remains uncertain whether these were intended to represent a garment (also see MacCurdy 1915).

Human behavior associated with feather garments would probably involve ceremonial activities, i.e., a set of actions designed to remind the wearer and his or her society of political and/or religious affiliation and rank (Sibley et al. 1992). The elite nature of the fabric evidence and the burial context warrant such an inference here. Mound C apparently supported a mortuary temple which, in turn, served as the focus of an elaborate complex of funerary rituals associated with a high status social group at Etowah (Larson 1971). This social group almost certainly dominated the political structure of Etowah (and perhaps a larger area) and in all likelihood constituted a kin unit where the hereditary political offices were held.

The burials of this group were made through the floors of the temples that occupied the five distinct stages of mound construction, as well as around the base of each of the mound stages. Many of the burials contained grave goods that have been interpreted as the paraphernalia and costume associated with the political and/or religious office of the interred individuals. These goods are usually related to the Southeastern Ceremonial Complex, or Southern Cult, although present interpretation allows that they do not constitute a ceremonial complex and certainly were not utilized within a single cult across the entire Southeast.

Many of the burial goods are either exotic themselves or were crafted locally from materials that are exotic to the specific locales where they have been recovered. Marine shells, mineral materials, marine turtle shell, shark teeth, and ceramics are a partial inventory of materials brought to Etowah from relatively distant parts of the Southeast and even beyond. The presence of these materials at Etowah and the presence of materials thought to have originated at Etowah in other parts of the Southeast (Phillips and Brown 1978:185) support an argument for an extensive system of exchange relationships throughout the Southeast during the Mississippian period.

Although the sparrow hawk and the golden eagle, for example, were indigenous to the region, feathers from both local and nonlocal birds might have been available in such an exchange system. The decision to use down from either of these two species would have been related more to the cultural value or significance accorded them than strictly to their availability.

Despite the fact that down-hair-bast combinations would provide a lightweight, soft fabric, the value of the Etowah feather mantle or kilt likely resided in its ceremonial function, rather than in its protective capabilities. In all likelihood, its use as a ceremonial garment would have been restricted to ritual occasions, rather than to daily use by high-status individuals. A second consideration has to do with the wearer. Blakely's tentative identification of the skeletal remains as a male, 25–28 years old, means that the body covering was probably worn by an adult male.

If the garment was worn during rituals to remind the wearer and viewers of some political and/or religious role and status, then its use would have been closely tied to the types of rituals and the part the wearer played in them. Furthermore, kinship affiliation (and hereditary office) might have been demonstrated by the type of feathers chosen for the mantle or kilt and/or by the patterning of the wrapping yarn. The combination of fibrous materials from different species and genera in the wrapping yarn may well indicate important patterning decisions on the part of the fabricator. Such patterning may have had profound significance for the wearer, his kin group, and other members of their society.

Region Three of the "Cognitive Map"

The third set of actions associated with the Etowah feather fabric has to do with the removal of the fabric from its systemic context. In the case of this Etowah fabric fragment, it was placed in a select burial context, rather than a midden or trash heap. The high value of the fabric is supported by recovery of associated grave goods typically related to high status, i.e., shell and copper gorgets and beads. Its proximity to the copper facilitated its fragmentary survival and caused its partial mineralization in an archaeological context (see Map 4.1).

As noted above, split-cane matting was discovered between two layers of the fabric, and this is of some interest too. Although the presence of matting is not surprising, its position is. Matting was typically included in the Mound C graves, either as flat mats or baskets. The fabric with feathers and hair wrapping may have been positioned between the body and a mat, i.e., the fabric may have functioned as a burial covering, or shroud. During the decomposition of the body and of most of the fabric and matting, migration may have occurred. Perhaps a layer of fabric shifted outside the matting, while the copper products from the corrosion of the copper plate maintained the fabric structure. In this scenario, if the fabric acted as a burial covering, then it is more likely to have been a larger construction more like a mantle than a kilt.

An alternative course of action concerning the burial may have involved the placement of what was a fabric garment near or over the body, rather than a burial covering per se. In this case, both kilt or mantle would remain possibilities for the fabric's primary function. However, matting between the two layers of fabric may indicate that the garment was folded at one time, or even that a set of two down-hair-bast garments is involved. One layer might have been a kilt and another might have been a mantle, for example.

The relative position of the fabric remnant with respect to the copper plate, shell gorget, and skeletal remains seemingly supports its use to wrap the body. The plate and gorget were placed on top of the fabric, while wide bands of beads were placed on the wrist. Possibly attired in ritual garments, this individual was placed on his left side. Subsequent to burial, the plate and gorget slipped from the chest to the matting floor of the burial pit, and the lower arms and manubrium slumped on to the fabric, copper plate and gorget which lay beneath. In this case, one layer of the down-hair-bast fabric fragment might be the remains of the back of a mantle and the other, the front. Again, possible migration within the archaeological context limits reliance on any one explanation.

It seems clear that high status goods were consigned to Mound C graves. Placement of valuable goods in the burials may have deprived the members of the group of valued raw materials and products. This decision must have stemmed from a religious ideology because the down-hair-bast mantle or kilt was lost from its systemic context once it was placed into the burial. If this fabric was made solely for burial, then it was not likely used prior to its interment. Obviously, the clay matrix hinders any identification of the micro- and macro-morphological evidence of wear for the Etowah down-hair-bast fabric and thus, this possibility cannot be ruled out.

In summary, results of the fabrication, compositional, and provenience analyses indicate that clay-encrusted fragment 1 from Etowah consists of two layers of fabric with matting sandwiched between them. Although no definite interworking of yarn systems was identified, the evidence apparently indicates a fabric structure with two systems. System A of the fabric has replied cords or complex yarns incorporating a mixture of down, hair and fiber in yarns surrounding two ply, bast core yarns. The compositional analyses indicate that copper is widespread in these yarns as a result of at least partial mineralization of the fabric. Sulfur is present in the down and hair. This finding is not surprising since this element is a basic component of proteinaceous materials. Two other types of fiber could not be identified. One is part of the wrapping yarn and the other is found on the reverse of fabric fragment 1. System B yarns are finer than those of system A, but clay obscures most of the details concerning these yarns.

The down-hair-bast fabric was recovered from burial 103, located in the southwestern corner of Mound C at Etowah; it is assignable to Etowah II period, ca. A.D. 1300–1400. Mound C burials are noted for their rich assortment of high-status burial goods. Analysis of the human remains from burial 103 has tentatively identified an adult male, 25–28 years old. The fabric fragment was associated with copper and shell gorgets in the upper torso-shoulder area of this burial.

A "cognitive map" of interrelated decisions and behaviors relevant to this fabric began with selection and manufacture of at least three animal (feathers and hair) and plant (bast) materials. Decisions at this stage were somewhat affected by expectations about the eventual use of the fabric. Subsequent details of the "cognitive map" involved further decisions related to the more specific function of the fabric within its systemic context. The fabrication and provenience data suggest that this fabric fragment represents the surviving portion of a highly valued mantle or kilt. It may have been a ceremonial garment, possibly worn on special occasions to demonstrate political and/or religious status. Undoubtedly, decisions concerning the use of down/feathers were affected by the ritual nature of the fabric in any case. Furthermore, kinship affiliation, if not leadership, may have been denoted by the specific motifs in the fabric's structure.

Placement of the fabric within a burial context is the final physiographic region of the "cognitive map." The position of the fabric fragment near the individual's shoulders may mean that it is a mantle or burial shroud remnant. On the other hand, it is conceivable that it was a ritual garment which was folded and placed on the body, or just under the body in the same area. The garment also may have been a product of merging the second and third sets of behavior, combining functions related to cultural (systemic) and burial (archaeological) contexts, but this remains uncertain. Nonetheless, the combined fabrication, compositional, and burial provenience data enable us to make inferences about human behavior and possible functions related to this fabric and others in the archaeological record. Even when fragmentary and incomplete, such evidence is of inestimable value for the examination of how technology can be used to establish relative social status and to adapt to natural and social environments.

ACKNOWLEDGMENTS

The authors are indebted to the state of Georgia for permission to study the fabric from the Etowah site described in this chapter.

NOTE

1. The term "feather" is used here in a general sense to refer to feathers and down that cover birds. The more specific term "down" is used here to indicate material composed of downy barbules with no rachises present.

REFERENCES CITED

Blakely, Robert L.
n.d. Etowah Skeletal Analysis, Mound C Burials, Numbers 1 to 140. Unpublished ms. on file, Archaeological Laboratory, West Georgia College, Carrollton.

Byers, Douglas S.
1962a The Restoration and Preservation of Some Objects from Etowah. *American Antiquity* 28 (2):206–216.
1962b Two Textile Fragments and Some Copper Objects from Etowah, Georgia. *Actas y Memorias* 1. XXXV Congreso Internacional de Americanistas, Mexico City.

Cornelius, Elias
1818 A List of Plants Found in the Neighbourhood of Connasarga River (Cherokee Country), where Springplace is Situated; made by Mrs. Gambold, at the request of the Rev. Elias Cornelius. *The American Journal of Science* I(VI):245–328. New Haven.

Day, M. G.
1966 Identification of Hair and Feather Remains in the Gut and Faeces of Stoats and Weasels. *Zoology* 148:201–217.

Emery, Irene
1966 *The Primary Structure of Fabrics: An Illustrated Classification.* The Textile Museum, Washington, D.C.

Holmes, William H.
1896 Prehistoric Textile Art of the Eastern United States. In *Annual Report of the Bureau of American Ethnology, 1891–1892,* pp. 3–46. Smithsonian Institution, Washington, D.C.

Jakes, Kathryn A., and Lucy R. Sibley
1983 Survival of Cellulosic Fabrics in Archaeological Contexts. *Science and Archaeology* 25:31–38.

Joseph, Marjory L.
1981 *Introductory Textile Science.* Holt, Rinehart and Winston, New York.

King, Mary E.
1978 Analytical Methods and Prehistoric Textiles. *American Antiquity* 43(1):89–96.

King, Mary E., and Joan S. Gardner
1981 The Analysis of Textiles from Spiro Mound, Oklahoma. In *The Research Potential of Anthropological Museum Collections,* edited by Ann-Marie E. Cantwell, James B. Griffin, and Nan Rothschild, pp. 123–139. Annals of New York Academy of Sciences 736. New York.

Larson, Lewis H., Jr.
1955 Unusual Figurine from the Georgia Coast. *The Florida Anthropologist* 8(3):75–81.
1959 A Mississippian Headdress from Etowah, Georgia. *American Antiquity* 25:109–112.
1971 Archaeological Implications of Social Stratification at the Etowah Site, Georgia. In *Approaches to the Social Dimensions of Mortuary Practices,* edited by James A. Brown, pp. 58–67. Memoirs of the Society for American Archaeology 25.
1972 Functional Considerations of Warfare in the Southeast During the Mississippian Period. *American Antiquity* 37(3):383–392.

MacCurdy, George G.
1915 Shell Gorgets from Missouri. *American Anthropologist* 15:395–414.

Moorehead, Warren K.
1932 *Etowah Papers.* Yale Univ. Press, New Haven.

Parker, Malcolm
1949 A Study of the Rocky Creek Pictoglyph. *Tennessee Archaeologist* 5(2):13–17.

Petersen, James B., and Nathan D. Hamilton
1984 Early Woodland Ceramic and Perishable Fiber Industries from the Northeast: A Summary and Interpretation. *Annals of Carnegie Museum* 43:413–445. Pittsburgh.

Phillips, Philip, and James A. Brown
1978 *Pre-Columbian Shell Engraving from the Craig Mound at Spiro, Oklahoma, Part I.* Peabody Museum of Archaeology and Ethnology, Harvard Univ., Cambridge.

Schiffer, Michael B.

1972 Archaeological Context and Systemic Context. *American Antiquity* 37:156–165.

Scholtz, Sandra Clements

1975 *Prehistoric Plies: A Structural and Comparative Analysis of Cordage, Netting, Basketry, and Fabric from Ozark Bluff Shelters.* Arkansas Archeological Survey Research Series 9. Univ. of Arkansas Museum, Fayetteville.

Sibley, Lucy R.

1986 The Use of Textile Fabric Pseudomorphic Evidence in the Reconstruction of Ancient Technologies. In *Proceedings of the 24th International Archaeometry Symposium*, edited by J. S. Olin, and M. J. Blackman, pp. 153–163. Smithsonian Institution Press, Washington, D.C.

Sibley, Lucy R., and Kathryn A. Jakes

1986 Characterization of Selected Prehistoric Fabrics of Southeastern North America. In *Historic Textile and Paper Materials Construction and Characterization*, pp. 253–275. Advances in Chemistry Series 212. American Chemical Society.

1989 Etowah Textile Remains and Cultural Context: A Model for Inference. *Clothing and Textiles Research Journal* 7(2):37–45.

Sibley, Lucy R., Kathryn A. Jakes, and Cheunsoon Song

1989 Fibers and Yarn Processing by Prehistoric People of North America: Examples from Etowah. *Ars Textrina* 11:191–209.

Sibley, Lucy R., Kathryn A. Jakes, and Mary E. Swinker

1992 Etowah Feather Remains from Burial 57: Identification and Context. *Clothing and Textiles Research Journal* 10:21–28.

Thomas, Cyrus

1894 Report on the Mound Explorations of the Bureau of Ethnology. *Annual Report of the Bureau of Ethnology, 1890–91*, pp. 1–742. Smithsonian Institution, Washington, D.C.

Wallace, Dwight T.

1975 The Analysis of Weaving Periods: Examples from the Early Periods in Peru. In *Archaeological Textiles, Proceedings of the Irene Emery Roundtable on Museum Textiles*, edited by Patricia L. Fiske, pp. 101–116. The Textile Museum, Washington, D.C.

Waring, Anthony J., and Preston Holder

1945 A Prehistoric Ceremonial Complex in the Southeastern United States. In *The Waring Papers*, edited by Stephen Williams, pp. 9–29. Papers of the Peabody Museum 58. Harvard Univ., Cambridge.

Whitford, A. C.

1941 Textile Fibers Used in Eastern Aboriginal North America. *American Museum of Natural History Anthropological Papers* 38(1):5–22. New York.

Willoughby, Charles C.

1952 Textile Fabrics from the Spiro Mound. *The Missouri Archaeologist* 14:107–118.

Wilson, Kax

1980 *A History of Textiles*. Westview Press, Boulder.

5

Robert F. Maslowski

Cordage Twist and Ethnicity

Cordage and fabric structure analysis should be an integral part of reports on archaeological sites which produce perishable textiles or cord-marked pottery. In the western United States and elsewhere, cordage and textiles have been used to determine prehistoric and ethnographic cultural boundaries. In the Ohio River Valley, cordage twist patterns have been analyzed using samples from numerous archaeological sites since 1973. These include Middle Woodland, Late Woodland, Late Prehistoric, and Protohistoric period sites, covering a time span about 1500 years long, ca. A.D. 200–1680. The Ohio Valley twist patterns are typically recorded using latex or plasticene casts made from negative impressions on pottery since actual fiber artifacts are seldom present (Maslowski 1973, 1984a). Results of these analyses have been used to interpret cultural relationships between sites and groups of sites, as discussed here in some detail.

These cordage twist studies began as an attempt to identify new pottery attributes for the development of more sensitive ceramic chronologies in the upper Ohio Valley (Maslowski 1973). The middle and upper Ohio Valley region is characterized by an abundance of seemingly mundane prehistoric pottery types that are basically plain or cord-marked, with relatively small percentages of fabric-impressed, net-impressed, and grooved-paddle surface treatments also present. Different forms of pottery decoration are relatively rare and consist of various incised designs, punctations, and minor rim modifications. As a result, past chronologies and cultural distinctions largely have been based on variations in pottery temper types, or ratios of plain to cord-marked pottery using simple frequency counts.

After analyzing a pottery sample from the Watson site in the upper Ohio Valley (Maslowski 1973) and various extant cordage and textile assemblages from Texas and Peru (Adovasio and Maslowski 1980; Maslowski 1978a), it became evident that cordage twist and twining weft slant were very stable, highly standardized attributes among various cultural groups. For example, in the Coahuiltecan area of Trans-Pecos Texas,[1] two ply, S-spun, Z-twist was the dominant twist pattern for unretted hard fibers for 8000 years (Maslowski 1978a). Left, or Z-twist, cordage is also characteristic of the six Coahuila sites studied by Walter W. Taylor (1948:160, 1988). However, at Danger Cave in Utah, two ply S-twist and Z-twist cordage co-existed in approximately even percentages for over 10,000 years (Jennings 1957:230), while Lovelock Cave in Nevada produced a sample of 99% right, or S-twist, cordage (Loud and Harrington 1929; Taylor 1948:160).

Similar patterns of twist distribution have become evident in the Ohio Valley over the past 20 years, leading to the conclusion that cordage twist patterns are very useful in delineating cultural groups and reconstructing culture historical models and settlement systems (Maslowski 1984a). Over time, these ideas have been generally accepted by the few regional investigators who are familiar with the analysis of fiber perishables. Unfortunately, many generalists and some pottery specialists have been reluctant to accept the significance of S-twist or Z-twist cordage preferences in the analysis and interpretation of the archaeological and ethnographic entities. In one respect the critics are justified, given that so little has been written about the theoretical and methodological background to cordage analysis. As should be obvious, however, the potential of this research is significant in local and broad regional contexts.

THEORETICAL APPROACH

Basically, there are two approaches to the analysis of cordage. Hurley and Wagner (1972), Hurley (1979), and, more recently, Falk (1983) have considered cordage more or less as a decorative attribute of pottery. They have dealt primarily with complex decorated ceramics on which cordage or composite constructions including cordage were applied as a primary form of decoration. In this view, cordage and other fiber perishables are another form of pottery decoration, rather than a separate form of material culture worthy of independent study.

An alternative approach taken here is that cordage twist patterns are the result of highly standard-ized, culture-specific motor habits. Such motor habits are learned at an early age and are transmitted from generation to generation within family groups or work groups. Hence, cordage twist patterns often have greater temporal continuity than decoration or environmentally influenced attributes of material culture (Maslowski 1985; see also Carr and Maslowski 1995).

Various technological attributes such as initial spin and final twist in cordage have no adaptive value; that is, the different directions of spin and twist have no value beyond the utility of alternating them so that they interlock to produce a stable structure. Although there are exceptions to this strategy of alternating the directions of spin and twist, they are relatively rare in multiple ply constructions due to the basic mechanical principle at work here. Taylor (1948) and Roth (1924:112) before him pointed out that "it seems to be a mechanical principle of string-making that the direction must be reversed in each successive twisting." As later pointed out by Wallace (1979:32), the use of multiple plies "can produce a more consistent strength by minimizing irregularities of the individual strands and, when spin and ply [twist] direction are opposite, by stabilizing the twist so that any tendency to untwist is countered or cancelled out." So, the use of multiple plies will strengthen a structure, especially when the configurations are alternated between initial spin and final twist. However, there is no advantage afforded by use of either a Z or S initial spin or final twist, as long as they are alternated between spinning and twisting.

Simply stated, two ply, S-spun, Z-twist cordage is equally as easy to make and as sturdy as two ply, Z-spun, S-twist cordage, at least for most raw materials. Likewise, there is no functional difference between twining with Z-twist plied wefts and twining with S-twist plied wefts. Thus, the choice between these alternatives is a culturally specific one in both cases.

Other material culture attributes, such as decoration, are also specific to particular cultures. However, selection of particular decorative attributes depends on stylistic preferences, which can change relatively quickly over time. In contrast, cultural preferences involved in the transmission of established motor habits, such as those used in cordage making, are apparently much more resistant to change (Maslowski 1985). Children make Z-twist cordage (or vice-versa) because parents or other members of the community show them how to roll fiber down the leg to get the initial S-spin and combine two plies by rolling them up the leg to get the final Z-twist. While some cordage makers and spinners are quite conscious of duplicating culturally preferred cordage styles (e.g., Roth 1924; Underhill 1944), others may not even be aware of the cultural choice involved in initial spin and final twist patterns, unlike decorative attributes and contrary to Taylor's (1948:161) interpretation of his information from archaeological sites in Coahuila.

Variations in spin and twist patterns do obviously exist. No large collections of cord-marked pottery from Ohio Valley sites exhibit exclusively S-twist or Z-twist cordage. Some variation in twist patterns can be expected due to handedness or other idiosyncratic behavior. Different spin and twist patterns within a sample eventually may be attributed to different segments within the population. For example, perhaps both males and females made cordage. If so, it is possible that they had different cordage-making preferences, resulting in varying percentages of S-twist and Z-twist cordage within some samples.

A direct relationship exists between certain twist patterns and fiber and cordage manufacturing technologies (Maslowski 1978b). In much of the Southwest, Mexico, and Trans-Pecos Texas, two ply, S-spun, Z-twist cordage was the dominant type for 8000 years. When cotton was introduced, it likely came with a new manufacturing technique, the spindle, and the predominant cordage twist pattern changed to two ply, Z-spun, S-twist, perhaps in part because cotton spins more easily in the Z direction, as some analysts have maintained (M. E. King, personal communication 1993). However, archaeological and ethnographic data suggest that both S and Z initial spin and S and Z final twist cotton cordage have been produced in different settings, using various techniques such as the spindle, among others (e.g., Bird 1979; Couture-

Brunette 1985, 1986; Fraser-Lu 1988; Wallace 1979). These data suggest that even if there is a natural tendency for cotton to spin more easily in the Z direction it may not fully explain the switch in initial spin and final twist preferences when cotton was introduced in the Southwest and nearby regions.

It is structurally advantageous and therefore quite typical to use a final twist which is opposite the initial spin in multiple ply elements, for example, but it is *not* absolutely necessary (e.g., Couture-Brunette 1985:Table 1; Hurley 1979). Consequently, when analyzing collections of extant cordage, it has proven most useful to compare distributions in terms of *initial* spin rather than *final* twist, especially when compound cordage is included in the collections. When possible, *both* initial spin and final twist should be reported, along with other pertinent details.

In a comparison of compound cordage from Lovelock Cave, Nevada, and six caves in northern Coahuila, Taylor (1948:160) concluded that Coahuila people reversed the initial spin direction so that the final twist was the same for both two ply and compound cordage. At Lovelock Cave, the two plied cordage was simply replied into a compound cord, resulting in an opposite final twist. Taylor (1948:161) further observed:

[T]he Coahuila people, when they desired a strong compound cord, visualized the whole process and reversed their normal procedure at the start so that the final product would conform to their idea of how finished cordage should be twisted. The Lovelock people, on the other hand, appear to have been unconcerned with the final form and merely continued their usual procedure one step further and by the machinations of technique, came out with the compound cords having a spiral different from the majority of their cordage.

It should be noted that Taylor's samples of compound cordage were rather small, including eight specimens from Lovelock Cave and four specimens from one Coahuila cave. An alternate explanation based on the analysis of the cordage from Moorehead Cave (Maslowski 1978b) suggests that the compound cordage in Trans-Pecos Texas was generally made with retted yucca rather than with decorticated agave. A different manufacturing technique

was introduced with the use of retted yucca, resulting in a different spin and twist pattern. Utilitarian
hard fiber cordage in Trans-Pecos Texas was made
with decorticated agave or yucca by manually twisting and splicing bundles of fiber consisting of complete vascular structures (Maslowski 1978b:2). The
retted yucca cordage was most likely made by the
traditional method of rolling bundles of fiber on the
leg. Furthermore, most of the compound cordage at
Moorehead Cave and most of the other Coahuiltecan
sites was used in the manufacture of aprons which
did not require a "strong compound cord." In most
assemblages compound cords make up a relatively
small percentage of the total cordage, however, and do
not affect the interpretations of the generally established twist and spin patterns for local populations.

OHIO VALLEY CORDAGE DATA

During the Late Prehistoric and Protohistoric periods, ca. A.D. 1100–1680, two distinct distributions of
cordage twist patterns were represented in the
Ohio Valley. Monongahela sites in the Monongahela
drainage and Fort Ancient sites along the upper
and middle Ohio River to the mouth of the Scioto
River had a strong preference for two ply, Z-twist
cordage (Map 5.1, Tables 5.1 and 5.2). Fort Ancient
sites in the New River, Kanawha River, and Big
Sandy drainages also had a strong preference for
two ply, Z-twist cordage (see Map 5.1, Tables 5.2
and 5.3). However, sites of this same time period in
the Scioto drainage and the Glaciated Allegheny
Plateau of Ohio and Pennsylvania had a different

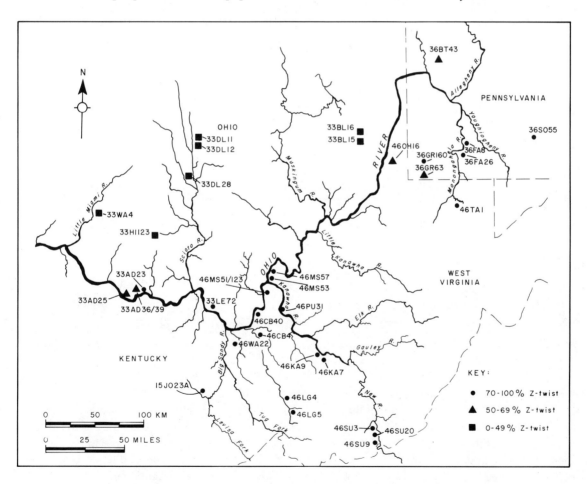

Map 5.1. Distribution of Late Prehistoric and Protohistoric cordage twist patterns in the Ohio Valley.

Table 5.1. Cordage Twist Frequencies for Late Prehistoric and Protohistoric Monongahela Sites

Site	Component and Temper	Approx. Date A.D.	No. Z-Twist	% Z-Twist	No. S-Twist	% S-Twist	References
Gnagey 36SO55	Monongahela, limestone	1000–1100	196	98.0	4	2.0	George 1983:29*
Throckmorton 36GR160	Monongahela, shell	1500–1600	68	97.0	2	3.0	NPW Consultants 1983:149*
Henderson Rocks 46TA1	Page, limestone	1200	41	95.0	2	5.0	Baker 1981
Redstone Old Ft. 36FA8	Monongahela, shell	1300–1500	97	87.4	14	12.6	Maslowski 1984a*; Michael 1983
Campbell 36FA26	Monongahela, shell	1400–1500	37	83.7	7	16.3	Johnson 1981
Duvall 46OH16	Monongahela, shell	1200	34	68.0	16	32.0	Dunnell 1964*, 1980
Gensler 36GR63	Monongahela, shell	1300	18	55.0	15	45.0	NPW Consultants 1983:50*
Bonnie Brook 36BT43	Monongahela, shell	1400	27	52.0	25	48.0	Herbstritt 1981
Hunt 33BL16	Monongahela, shell	1500	14	35.0	26	65.0	Prufer and McKenzie 1975
Tower 33BL15	Monongahela, shell	1200–1300	16	28.1	41	79.9	Brown 1978; Maslowski 1984a*

*Reference from which cordage data were taken; other references are published site descriptions, while an unspecified reference indicates that data were taken from the author's files.

Table 5.2. Cordage Twist Frequencies for Late Prehistoric and Protohistoric Bluestone, Clover, and Feurt Phase Fort Ancient Sites

Site	Component and Temper	Approx. Date A.D.	No. Z-Twist	% Z-Twist	No. S-Twist	% S-Twist	References
French Farm 46SU20	Bluestone, shell	1400	24	96.0	1	4.0	Solecki 1949
Barker's Bottom 46SU3	Bluestone, shell	1200–1400	57	80.3	14	19.7	Solecki 1949
Island Creek 46SU9	Bluestone, shell	1200	14	74.0	5	26.0	Solecki 1949
Marmet Village 46KA9	Clover, shell	1600	43	100.0	0	0.0	Maslowski 1984b*
Logan 46LG4	Clover, shell	1600	76	98.7	1	1.3	Maslowski 1984b*
Buffalo 46PU31	Clover, shell	1600	91	97.8	2	2.2	Maslowski 1984b*
Rolfe Lee #2 46MS123	Clover, shell	1640	92	92.0	8	8.0	Maslowski 1984b*
Rolfe Lee #1 46MS51	Clover, shell	1640	50	87.7	7	12.3	Maslowski 1984b*
Clover 46CB40	Clover, shell	1600	179	84.8	32	15.2	Maslowski 1984b*
Lewis Farm 46MS57	Feurt, shell	1300	4	100.0	0	0.0	Kuhn and Spurlock 1982
Roseberry Farm 46MS53	Feurt, shell	1300–1400	74	90.2	8	9.8	Graybill 1981
Marmet Bluffs 46KA7	Feurt, shell	1300–1400	11	78.5	3	21.5	

*Reference from which cordage data were taken; other references are published site descriptions, while an unspecified reference indicates that data were taken from the author's files.

preference; that is, two ply, S-twist cordage was typical (see Map 5.1, Table 5.3). Given that the size and structure of the cordage seems generally comparable across all of these samples, this difference suggests that these populations may have been distinctive for hundreds or possibly thousands of years. It should be further pointed out that while the cordage raw materials are incompletely understood, since they are only represented in positive casts, these too seem generally comparable across the samples, at least in terms of the size, character, and processing of constituent fibers.

Table 5.3. Cordage Twist Frequencies for Late Prehistoric Baum, Anderson, Cole, and Generalized Fort Ancient Sites

Site	Component and Temper	Approx. Date A.D.	No. Z-Twist	% Z-Twist	No. S-Twist	% S-Twist	References
Cole 33DL11	Cole, grit	1200–1300	0	0.0	10	100.0	Barkes n.d.*
Decco 33DL28	Cole, grit	1100–1200	0	0.0	5	100.0	Barkes n.d.*
Paint Cr. #7 33HI123	Baum, grit	1300	13	15.7	70	84.3	Prufer and McKenzie 1975; Maslowski 1984a*
Anderson Village 33WA4	Anderson, shell/limestone	1200	22	42.0	30	58.0	Marwitt et al. 1984:52*
Mann Site 46LG5	Woodside, shell	1450	111	89.5	13	10.5	Maslowski 1984b*
Ufferman 33DL12	Cole, grit	1200–1300	16	48.5	17	51.5	Barkes n.d.*
Killen-Grimes 33AD36/39	Ft. Ancient, shell/grit	1200?	17	51.5	16	48.5	Marwitt et al. 1984:52*
Island Creek 33AD25	Ft. Ancient, shell/limestone	1300	106	61.0	67	39.0	Marwitt et al. 1984:52*
Wamsley 33AD23	Ft. Ancient, shell/limestone	1300	38	76.0	12	24.0	Marwitt et al. 1984:52*
Gue Farm 46CB4	Ft. Ancient, shell	1500	93	89.4	11	10.6	Maslowski 1984a*
Goldcamp 33LE72	Ft. Ancient, shell	1400	13	92.8	1	7.2	Bender 1971; Maslowski 1984a*
Dameron 15JO23A	Ft. Ancient, shell	1300–1400	10	100.0	0	0.0	Adovasio 1982:764*
46WA22	Ft. Ancient, shell	1300–1400	24	100.0	0	0.0	

* Reference from which cordage data were taken; other references are published site descriptions, while an unspecified reference indicates that data were taken from the author's files.

Some Monongahela sites, such as Bonnie Brook (36BT43) and Duvall (46OH16) closer to the border of the Glaciated Allegheny Plateau, apparently had more evenly distributed percentages of S-twist and Z-twist cordage. This situation may be reflective of the mixing of distinct ethnic populations since there is no evidence to suggest changes in cordage-making technology across the region for reasons other than cultural ones. Likewise, there is no evidence for the maintenance of two or more distinct manufacturing techniques for utilitarian cordage within those populations in terms of different structural complexity or raw material types.

Below the mouth of the Scioto River, there was again more variability in the distribution of S-twist and Z-twist cordage. The four Fort Ancient sites in the present sample range from 42% Z-twist at Anderson Village (33WA4) to 76% Z-twist at Wamsley (33AD23). This may reflect a mixing of populations, or it may reflect the established ratios of S-twist and Z-twist cordage within these particular cultural groups for some other reason. Simi-

lar distributions are exhibited at the Sand Ridge site (33HA17), which is attributable to the Late Woodland Newtown complex.

During the earlier Middle and Late Woodland periods, there was much more variability in the cordage twist patterns in the upper Ohio Valley, Kanawha Valley, and central West Virginia (Map 5.2, Tables 5.4 and 5.5). The Late Woodland period Watson site exhibits predominant Z-twist cordage, while to the south the Middle Woodland period Fairchance site exhibits predominant S-twist cordage. In the Parkersburg area, the Late Woodland Big Run site (46WD53) exhibits 96.3% Z-twist cordage, while Muskingum Island (46WD61) exhibits 100% S-twist cordage. Similar situations are found in the distributions of cordage twist in the Kanawha Valley and central West Virginia (see Map 5.2, Tables 5.4 and 5.5). The distribution of these cordage twist preferences suggests that there were probably several distinct ethnic groups interspersed throughout the region with no clearly definable territorial boundaries, at least at this level of analysis.

Table 5.4. Cordage Twist Frequencies for Middle/Late Woodland Complexes: Levisa Cordmarked, Buck Garden, Watson, Fairchance, and Newtown

Site	Component and Temper	Approx. Date A.D.	No. Z-Twist	% Z-Twist	No. S-Twist	% S-Twist	References
15J042	Levisa, sandstone	500	0	0.0	10	100.0	Adovasio 1982:764*
Blanton 15JO32	Levisa, sandstone	500	9	11.5	69	88.5	Adovasio 1982:764*
Dameron 15JO23A	Levisa, sandstone	500	14	15.2	78	84.8	Adovasio 1982:764*
Fairchance 46MR13	Fairchance, limestone	500	8	18.6	35	81.4	Hemmings 1984*
Childers 46MS121	Childers, limestone/grit	400–600	37	28.2	94	71.8	Maslowski and Dawson 1980*
Morrison Shelter 46NI18	Buck Garden, limestone/grit	600–900	11	31.4	24	68.6	Maslowski 1984a*
Glade Branch 15JO50	Levisa, sandstone	500	6	35.3	11	64.7	Adovasio 1982:764*
Sand Ridge 33HA17	Newtown, grit & limestone	800–900	76	61.8	47	38.2	
Meadowcroft 36WH297	Watson, limestone	900–1000	13	61.9	8	38.1	Johnson 1977*
Buck Garden 46NI49	Buck Garden, grit	600–900	79	84.0	15	16.0	McMichael 1965
Watson 46HK34	Watson, limestone	400–1000	163	86.0	26	14.0	Maslowski 1973*

*Reference from which cordage data were taken; other references are published site descriptions, while an unspecified reference indicates that data were taken from the author's files.

Table 5.5. Cordage Twist Frequencies for Unidentified Woodland Components in the Ohio and Kanawha Valleys

Site	Component and Temper	Approx. Date A.D.	No. Z-Twist	% Z-Twist	No. S-Twist	% S-Twist	References
Alloy 46FA189	Woodland, siltstone/grit	400–1100	0	0.0	47	100.0	
Muskingum Is. 46WD61	Woodland, limestone/grit	400–1100	0	0.0	21	100.0	
Reed WW 46KA166	Woodland, sandstone/siltstone	400–1100	4	18.1	18	81.9	
Cash Farm 46PU79	Woodland, siltstone/sandstone	400–1100	58	72.5	22	27.5	
Weed Shelter 46CB56	Woodland, limestone/siltstone	400–1100	16	80.0	4	20.0	Kuhn et al. 1978*
Tompkins Farm 46KA6	Woodland, grit	800	7	87.5	1	12.5	
Big Run 46WD53	Woodland, limestone/grit	400–1100	26	96.3	1	3.7	
Jarvis Farm 46KA105	Woodland, siltstone/grit	800	21	100.0	0	0.0	

*Denotes cordage data from published reference has been supplemented with additional data from author's files, while an unspecified reference indicates that data were taken from the author's files.

In eastern Kentucky, the Paintsville Reservoir sites, such as Blanton (15JO32), Dameron (15JO23A), and Glade Branch (15JO50), all have high percentages of S-twist cordage. The samples are small, but 83.4% of the 216 sandstone tempered sherds from 14 sites exhibit S-twist cordage (Adovasio 1982:764). This suggests a highly standardized cordage industry for a distinct ethnic group. Clearly defined territorial boundaries seem to be correlated with this group, as currently understood.

CORDAGE TWIST PREFERENCES AND ARCHAEOLOGICAL PHASES

The analysis of cordage twist patterns can be extremely useful in defining archaeological complexes and phases because twist patterns are more culture specific than many lithic and pottery attributes. For example, the Monongahela complex of the upper Ohio Valley obviously had a strong

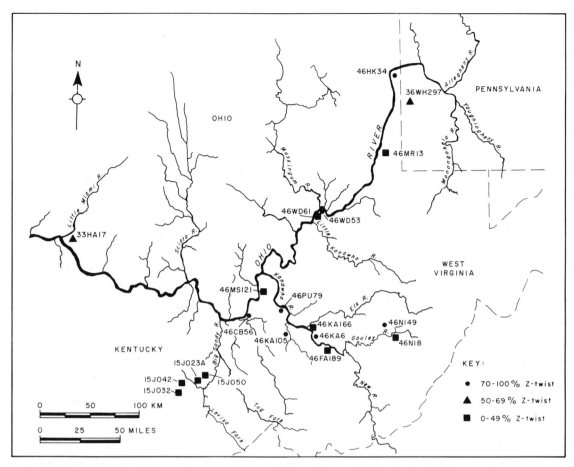

Map 5.2. Distribution of Middle and Late Woodland cordage twist patterns in the Ohio Valley.

preference for Z-twist cordage and appears to have historically evolved from the Watson complex, which also showed a strong preference for Z-twist cordage (Maslowski 1984a). This preference continued into the Protohistoric period, based on Herbstritt's analysis of seven Foley Farm phase sites which exhibit dominant Z-twist cordage in each case. These occurrences range from 71% to 97% (Maslowski 1985). Of note, the four sites of the Foley Farm phase with the largest samples exhibit 96%–97% Z-twist cordage.

Some archaeologists have argued that the McFate complex of northwestern Pennsylvania should be included in the Monongahela complex on the basis of shell tempering and a few decorative attributes, while others feel that McFate was a distinct complex. Johnson (personal communication) has checked the cordage twist patterns for McFate and they are predominantly S-twist, which relates McFate to the archaeological complexes of the Glaciated Allegheny Plateau. Also, "Ohio Monongahela" sites, such as Tower (33BL15) and Hunt (33BL16), have opposite (S-twist) cordage patterns, even though they share other, less diagnostic attributes such as shell tempering and a similar upland settlement pattern with Monongahela complex sites in Pennsylvania and West Virginia. Investigators should take a closer look at these sites, along with Bonnie Brook (36BT43), Gensler (36GR63), and Duvall (46OH16), to determine their appropriate placement within the Monongahela cultural complex.

In the Fort Ancient area, the Feurt, Bluestone, and Clover phases and the Woodside phase of eastern Kentucky and southern West Virginia all had a strong preference for Z-twist cordage, while the Baum and Anderson phases had high percentages of S-twist cordage. Preliminary analysis of cordage from the Anderson site (33WA4) and Paint Creek #7 site (33HI23) documents a high correlation between guilloche (a decoration consisting of interlaced bands and openings), grit temper, and S-twist cordage. Guilloche decoration has been reported for sites of the Feurt, Bluestone, and Clover phases but in such small quantities that it cannot be used to relate them culturally to the Scioto Valley and lower Ohio Valley Fort Ancient. The Cole complex north of Columbus also had a very high percentage of S-twist cordage, suggesting strong cultural ties with the Fort Ancient complexes to the south and earlier Late Woodland complexes in the Scioto drainage.

Potentially, cordage twist analysis can be used quickly and accurately for preliminary attribution of sites to specific cultural phases, even with small collections. This is especially useful when adequate numbers of rim and/or decorated sherds are not available. A vessel level of analysis, however, is preferred whenever possible to prevent sample bias.

By the same token, cordage twist analysis can be used to verify previous attributions of sites to particular cultural phases. No one has yet to offer a completely logical explanation for how sites with opposite cordage twist patterns can be closely related, that is, assigned to the same cultural phase and temporal period. Many researchers feel that archaeological phases are arbitrary constructs that do not *necessarily* correspond to actual prehistoric cultural groups, but, in fact, they may be correlated. Obviously, archaeological phases and other spatial and temporal constructs should be developed (or redefined) on the basis of combinations of culture-specific attributes, including cordage twist data, which best correspond to the original cultural groups.

CORDAGE TWIST AND ETHNICITY

About twenty years ago, Newton (1974) provided one of the few ethnographic studies relating cordage twist and twining patterns to ethnic boundaries. In a more recent study, Croes (1989) measured the degree of similarity across basketry and cordage assemblages from wet sites on the Northwest Coast and found continuities in cultural styles for 3000 years. He concluded that distinct Wakashan and Salishan basketry and cordage styles can be traced back for at least this long on the Northwest Coast.

While cordage twist analysis is useful in the identification of cultural or ethnic groups, it should be used in conjunction with other diagnostic artifacts whenever possible. Cordage analysis can play a highly important role in archaeological interpretation, especially when it is used to correlate different technologies at a single site, as is potentially the case in many portions of eastern North America where fiber perishables are preserved directly on ceramics. A cord-marked potsherd certainly demonstrates a 100% correlation between cordage and ceramic attributes within a particular group, given the impression of the fiber artifact directly into the pottery. If pottery exhibits cordage marking and/or net or fabric impressions, there may be a 100% correlation between two or even three distinct but contemporaneous technologies (i.e., ceramics, cordage, and weaving) for the group. Coupled with evidence for other technologies and cultural practices, such analyses can contribute to the better definition of ethnic groups in the archaeological record.

The co-occurrence of the same cordage technology certainly does not prove a direct cultural relationship between two or more groups or sites, however. Z-twist cordage is characteristic of Late Prehistoric sites from western Pennsylvania, West Virginia, and eastern Kentucky. These sites represent distinct cultural groups which may have been related at some point in the distant past, but not necessarily the recent past during the Late Prehistoric period. Broad ethnographic studies reveal that styles and technologies can crosscut ethnic boundaries on variable levels (e.g., Hodder 1982; Stanislawski 1978). However, in many cases, styles and technologies do *not* crosscut ethnic boundaries, and thus they correspond with such boundaries in the archaeological and ethnographic records (e.g., Adovasio 1982; Wiessner 1983).

Unfortunately, even though cordage data exist for nearly 100 archaeological sites in the Ohio Valley, none of the samples can be directly related to specific linguistic or tribal groups, due, in large part, to the paucity of ethnographic information for the region. The idea that basic cordage technologies may correlate in some way with macrolinguistic groups has been informally discussed before. However, historic aboriginal collections have yet to be analyzed for the Ohio Valley given their apparent rarity.

The Protohistoric Clover phase has been tentatively associated with the Yuchi or eastern Siouan-speaking groups in the middle and upper Ohio Valley (Maslowski 1984b). If this association can be ultimately supported with evidence from historic sites, it would establish a highly standardized cordage assemblage (84.8%–100% Z-twist) with an identified cultural and linguistic group. Unfortunately, historic aboriginal sites in this area are again rare and lack good documentation for cultural and linguistic associations. Such associations will have to come from the Southeast, Northeast, or elsewhere where historically documented aboriginal villages have been or can be excavated.

ACKNOWLEDGMENTS

I wish to thank Jodi L. Woody for drafting the preliminary maps, programming the cordage data for the tables, and proofing the manuscript; at UMF, Belinda J. Cox prepared the final versions of the maps. James Petersen and Nathan Hamilton offered several useful suggestions on the revised version of this chapter, as did Mary E. King and Dwight Wallace. Jeffery Graybill of the Blennerhassett Historic Commission, Alan Tonetti and Jeffery Brown of the Ohio State Historic Preservation Office, Edward Hussey of the West Virginia Archeological Society, and James T. Herbstritt of the Society for Pennsylvania Archaeology provided collections which were analyzed as part of the research reported here.

NOTE

1. As used here, Trans-Pecos Texas includes both the Lower Pecos and Trans-Pecos areas, where Coahuiltecan-speaking populations were present at the time of contact; these areas are differentiated by some researchers.

REFERENCES CITED

Adovasio, J. M. (compiler)
1982   *The Prehistory of the Paintsville Reservoir, Johnson and Morgan Counties, Kentucky.* Ethnology Monographs 4. Dept. of Anthropology, Univ. of Pittsburgh, Pittsburgh.

Adovasio, J. M., and Robert F. Maslowski
1980   Textiles and Cordage. In *Guitarrero Cave: Early Man in the Andes,* by Thomas F. Lynch, pp. 253–290. Academic Press, New York.

Baker, S. W.
1981   The Henderson Rocks Site (46TA1): A Preliminary Look at Cultural Perseverance in the Rugged Uplands Region of Northern West Virginia. *West Virginia Archeologist* 32:1–27.

Barkes, Buela M.
n.d.   An Analysis of Late Woodland Ceramics from the Decco (33DL28), Ufferman (33DL12), and W. S. Cole (33DL11) Sites: The Cole Complex Reconsidered. Unpublished ms. in the possession of the author.

Bender, Harold D.
1971   The Goldcamp Site: A Multi-Component Site in Lawrence County, Ohio. *The Ohio Archaeologist* 21(3):19–20.

Bird, Junius B.
1979   Fiber and Spinning Procedures in the Andean Area. In *The Junius B. Bird Pre-Columbian Textile Conference,* edited by Ann P. Rowe, Elizabeth P. Benson, and Ann-Louise Schaffer, pp. 13–17. The Textile Museum, Washington, D.C.

Brown, Jeffery D.
1978   Vertebrate Fauna from the Tower Site (33BL15). *The Ohio Archaeologist* 28(3):36–39.

Carr, Christopher, and Robert F. Maslowski
1995   Cordage and Fabrics: Relating Form, Technology, and Social Processes. In *Style, Society, and Person: Archaeological and Ethnological Perspectives,* edited by Christopher Carr and Jill E. Neitzel, pp. 297–343. Plenum Press, New York.

Couture-Brunette, Lorraine

1985 Yanomama Material Culture in the Carnegie Museum of Natural History. Part I. Food Procurement and Household Articles. *Annals of Carnegie Museum* 54(15):487–532. Pittsburgh.

1986 Yanomama Material Culture in the Carnegie Museum of Natural History. Part II. Wearing Apparel and Festival Artifacts. *Annals of Carnegie Museum* 55(4):63–93. Pittsburgh.

Croes, Dale R.

1989 Prehistoric Ethnicity on the Northwest Coast of North America: An Evaluation of Style in Basketry and Lithics. *Journal of Anthropological Archaeology* 8:101–130.

Dunnell, Robert C.

1964 The Duvall Site: A Monongahela Settlement in Central Ohio County, West Virginia. Unpublished ms. on file, West Virginia Geological Survey, Morgantown.

1980 Duvall: A Monongahela Settlement in Northern West Virginia. *West Virginia Archeologist* 29:1–37.

Falk, Carol Portugal

1983 Cordage Impressed on Potomac Creek Pottery: Decoding the Corded Style Motifs and the Methods of Pattern Manufacture. *Maryland Archeology* 19(2):1–20.

Fraser-Lu, Sylvia

1988 *Handwoven Textiles of South-East Asia.* Oxford Univ. Press, Singapore.

George, Richard L.

1983 The Gnagney Site and the Monongahela Occupation of the Somerset Plateau. *Pennsylvania Archaeologist* 53(4):1–97.

Graybill, Jeffery R.

1981 *The Eastern Periphery of Fort Ancient (a.d. 1050–1650): A Diachronic Approach to Settlement Variability.* Unpublished Ph.D. dissertation, Dept. of Anthropology, Univ. of Washington, Seattle.

Hemmings, E. Thomas

1984 Fairchance Mound and Village: An Early Middle Woodland Settlement in the Upper Ohio Valley. *West Virginia Archeologist* 36(1):3–68.

Herbstritt, James T.

1981 Bonnie Brook: A Multicomponent Aboriginal Locus in West-Central Pennsylvania. *Pennsylvania Archaeologist* 51(3):1–59.

Hodder, Ian

1982 *Symbols in Action: Ethnoarchaeological Studies of Material Culture.* Cambridge Univ. Press, Cambridge.

Hurley, William M.

1979 *Prehistoric Cordage: Identification of Impressions on Pottery.* Taraxacum, Washington, D.C.

Hurley, William M., and Norman E. Wagner

1972 *Ceramic Analysis: A Class and Attribute List for the Northeast.* Anthropological Series No. 13. Dept. of Anthropology, Univ. of Toronto, Toronto.

Jennings, Jesse D.

1957 *Danger Cave.* Univ. of Utah Anthropological Papers 27. Salt Lake City.

Johnson, William C.

1977 Ceramics. In Meadowcroft Rockshelter: Retrospect 1976, by J. M. Adovasio, J. D. Gunn, J. Donahue, and R. Stuckenrath, pp. 59–64. *Pennsylvania Archaeologist* 47(2–3).

1981 The Campbell Farm Site (36FA26) and Monongahela: A Preliminary Examination and Assessment. Paper presented at the 4th Monongahela Symposium, California State College, California, Pennsylvania.

Kuhn, Thomas C., Dewey Sanderson, and Robert F. Maslowski

1978 Excavations at Weed Shelter, 46CB56: A Preliminary Report. *West Virginia Archeologist* 27:16–27.

Kuhn, Thomas C., and Beverly Spurlock

1982 Lewis Old Town (46MS57): A Late Prehistoric Village Site in Mason County, West Virginia. *West Virginia Archeologist* 33:37–45.

Loud, Lewellyn L., and Mark R. Harrington

1929 *Lovelock Cave.* Univ. of California Publications in American Archaeology and Ethnology 25(1). Berkeley.

Marwitt, John P., Brenda Davis, Stephen Batug, V. Albaneso, Thomas Yokum, and Richard Stallings

1984 *Test Excavations at the Island Creek Village Site (33AD25).* Submitted to the U.S. Army Corps of Engineers, Huntington District, Huntington.

Maslowski, Robert F.

1973 An Analysis of Cordmarked Watson Ware. *Pennsylvania Archaeologist* 43(2):1–12.

1978a *The Archeology of Moorehead Cave: Val Verde County, Texas.* Unpublished Ph.D. dissertation, Dept. of Anthropology, Univ. of Pittsburgh, Pittsburgh.

1978b Moorehead Cave Cordage Analysis: Its Culture and Technological Implications. Paper presented at the 43rd annual meeting of the Society for American Archaeology, Tucson.

1984a The Significance of Cordage Attributes in the Analysis of Woodland Pottery. *Pennsylvania Archaeologist* 54(1–2):51–60.

1984b Protohistoric Villages in Southern West Virginia. In *Upland Archeology in the East, Symposium 2*, edited by Michael B. Barber, pp. 148–165. James Madison Univ., Harrisonburg.

1985 Cordage, Knots and Netting: Technological Approaches to Ethnicity and Cultural Stability. Paper presented at the 50th annual meeting of the Society for American Archaeology, Denver.

Maslowski, Robert F., and David L. Dawson

1980 Childers (46-MS-121): A Terminal Late Woodland Village. *West Virginia Archeologist* 30:4–32.

McMichael, Edward V.

1965 *Archeological Survey of Nicholas County, West Virginia*. Archeological Series 1. West Virginia Geological and Economic Survey, Morgantown.

Michael, Ronald L.

1983 Redstone Old Fort (36FA8): A Hilltop Monongahela Site. *Pennsylvania Archaeologist* 53(1–2):1–10.

Newton, Delores

1974 The Timbira Hammock as a Cultural Indicator of Social Boundaries. In *The Human Mirror, Material and Spatial Images of Man*, edited by Miles Richardson, pp. 231–251. Louisiana State Univ. Press, Baton Rouge.

NPW Consultants, Inc.

1983 *Excavation of Two Monongahela Sites: Late Woodland Gensler (33GR63) and Proto-historic Throckmorton (33GR160)*. Submitted to Consolidated Coal Company, Pittsburgh.

Prufer, Olaf H., and Douglas H. McKenzie (editors)

1975 *Studies in Ohio Archeology*. Kent State Univ. Press, Kent.

Roth, Walter E.

1924 An Introductory Study of the Arts, Crafts, and Customs of the Guiana Indians. *Annual Report of the Bureau of American Ethnology 1916–1917*, pp. 25–745. Smithsonian Institution, Washington, D.C.

Solecki, Ralph S.

1949 An Archeological Survey of Two Rivers in West Virginia: The Bluestone Reservation. *West Virginia History* 10(4):319–432.

Stanislawski, Michael B.

1978 If Pots Were Mortal. In *Explorations in Ethnoarchaeology*, edited by Richard A. Gould, pp. 201–227. Univ. of New Mexico Press, Albuquerque.

Taylor, Walter W.

1948 *A Study of Archeology*. American Anthropological Association Memoir No. 69.

1988 *Contributions to Coahuila Archaeology, with an Introduction to the Coahuila Project*. Southern Illinois Univ. at Carbondale Center for Archaeological Investigation Research Paper 52. Carbondale.

Underhill, Ruth

1944 *Pueblo Crafts*. U.S. Dept. of Interior, Branch of Education, Washington, D.C.

Wallace, Dwight T.

1979 The Process of Weaving Development on the Peruvian Coast. In *The Junius B. Bird Pre-Columbian Textile Conference*, edited by Ann P. Rowe, Elizabeth P. Benson, and Ann-Louise Schaffer, pp. 27–50. The Textile Museum, Washington, D.C.

Wiessner, Polly

1983 Style and Social Information in Kalahari San Projectile Points. *American Antiquity* 48(2):253–276.

6

James B. Petersen

Fiber Industries from Northern New England: Ethnicity and Technological Traditions during the Woodland Period

Aboriginal fiber industries of any antiquity have been rarely recognized in archaeological contexts across eastern North America and even more rarely reported in full. This circumstance has been due to various factors: unusual preservation of actual fiber artifacts; the extremely fragmentary condition of those which have been recovered; and correspondingly limited experience in the stabilization, analysis, and reporting of such artifacts among regional researchers (Adovasio and Andrews [with Carlisle] 1980:64; King 1975). As a result, synthetic analyses of archaeological fiber industries, or "perishables," have yet to be conducted over this broad region, with some notable exceptions (e.g., Drooker 1990; Hurley 1975; Maslowski 1984).

An attribute-oriented study of archaeological fiber industries has been undertaken to rectify this situation in a portion of northeastern North America, the far Northeast. It is one component of a long-term examination of aboriginal technology and social interaction in this region (e.g., Petersen

1980, n.d.; Petersen and Hamilton 1984; Petersen and Power 1985; Petersen and Sanger 1991).

A wide range of aboriginal ceramics with fiber artifact impressions preserved on them and actual fiber artifacts from northern New England have been studied, minimally spanning the entire Woodland (Ceramic) period and Contact period, ca. 1000 B.C.–A.D. 1750, and back into the Archaic period as well. This work is based, in part, on a series of individual site-oriented analyses in Maine, Vermont, and (to a much lesser degree) New Hampshire, and more recent broad-scale studies (e.g., Petersen and Sanger 1991). Ultimately, various issues should be addressed through the cross-correlation of attributes of technology and style for ceramics and fiber industries across an area of some 136,000 km^2 and over a period of at least 3700 years (e.g., Plog 1983; Wiessner 1983). The present discussion is confined to an available sample of fiber industries from northern New England, some 558 specimens dated between ca. 2000 B.C. and A.D. 1750.[1]

Extant aboriginal fiber perishables have been previously recovered only from a small number of archaeological sites in the broad Northeast. These specimens nonetheless provide a glimpse of the traditional diversity of regional fiber industries, with most samples attributable to the Protohistoric or Contact period after A.D. 1500–1550 (e.g., Bower 1980; Harper 1956; Whitehead n.d.; Willoughby 1924, 1935:244–247). Rare examples of extant fiber artifacts of greater antiquity are also known and have been variably reported (e.g., Heckenberger et al. 1990, this volume; King 1968; Michels and Smith 1967; Ritchie 1965; Ritchie and Dragoo 1960; Stile 1982; Watson 1974; Willoughby 1938). In all cases, unusual conditions of preservation are typically due to some combination of carbonization, contact with metallic salts, water saturation, or aridity.

More importantly for the present case, a large, if yet little studied, inventory of fiber industries can be derived from impressions on plastic materials, particularly ceramics. Negative impressions of fiber artifacts are present as the result of surface finish and/or decoration on many aboriginal ceramic forms all across eastern North America. This avenue of fiber artifact reconstruction is often difficult, in part, because of the small size and imprecise nature of the impressions. It is neither novel or new, but instead has had a tenure over the past century or so (e.g., Holmes 1884; Smith 1910; Miner 1936; Kellar 1967; Hurley 1975; Chapman and Adovasio 1977; Adovasio and Andrews [with Carlisle] 1980). Not surprisingly, the record of fiber industries across eastern North America generally begins with the introduction of ceramics, which occurred by about 1000 B.C. in most areas.

METHODS

Sample Selection and Context

The present sample of fiber industries is no exception to the aforementioned situation. Out of a total of 558 specimens, less than ten are actual fiber artifacts derived from one site (the Boucher cemetery,[2] or VT-FR-26), with the balance being reconstructions taken from negative impressions preserved on aboriginal ceramics of different ages and, in one case, slate tools attributable to the Late Archaic period.

The largest portion (n = 466) of the sample has been derived from 64 sites in Maine (see Bonnichsen et al. n.d.; Borstel 1982; Bourque 1976; Bourque and Cox 1981; Cox 1983; Doyle et al. 1982; Hamilton and Yesner 1985; Petersen and Sanger 1991; Sanger et al. 1977; Sanger et al. 1980; Spiess et al. 1983). The Maine sample has been split into two subsamples, coastal and interior, for reasons given below. These subsamples have been somewhat arbitrarily distinguished on the basis of their environmental settings; that is, sites situated on salt water environments have been labeled as *coastal* sites and all others on fresh water have been labeled as *interior* sites. The largest portion of the sample is attributable to the first and the last four periods of a seven-part aboriginal ceramic sequence, spanning ca. 1000 B.C.–A.D. 1750 (Petersen n.d.; Petersen and Sanger 1991) (Table 6.1).

This chronological sequence has been developed on the basis of radiocarbon assays, stratigraphic associations, and cross-dates from northern New England and the broader Northeast. Parenthetically, it should be noted that this seven-part se-

Table 6.1. Northern New England Chronological Periods for Fiber Industries

Designation(s)	Date Range
Late Archaic period (Moorehead complex)	2500 B.C.–1800 B.C.
Ceramic period 1 (Early Woodland)	1000 B.C.–100 B.C.
Ceramic period 4 (late-terminal Middle Woodland)	A.D. 600–A.D. 1000
Ceramic period 5 (early Late Woodland)	A.D. 1000–A.D. 1300
Ceramic period 6 (late Late Woodland)	A.D. 1300–A.D. 1550
Ceramic period 7 (Contact)	A.D. 1550–A.D. 1750

Adapted from Petersen and Sanger 1991.

quence can be equated with the Woodland (Ceramic) period and so-called Contact period, as used more generally in the Northeast. In addition, singular evidence exists in Maine of at least one fiber artifact reconstruction from the late portion of the Late Archaic period Moorehead complex (phase), ca. 2000–1800 B.C., which is the *oldest* known such specimen from New England and much of the far Northeast (see Andrews and Adovasio this volume; Petersen et al. 1984; Whitehead n.d.:Appendix II).

The balance of the currently available sample, some 92 specimens, derives from five sites in the Lake Champlain and Connecticut River drainages of Vermont and New Hampshire. These datable specimens likewise span the entire range of local aboriginal ceramic manufacture, ca. 1000 B.C.–A.D. 1750 (Petersen and Power 1983, 1985; Petersen et al. 1985; Thomas 1973, 1979; Thomas and Robinson 1981).

Overall, this sample of fiber industries (n = 558) has been derived from 69 archaeological sites across much of northern New England. It should be emphasized that most of the available sample undoubtedly represents those fiber artifacts which were variably chosen by aboriginal potters for use in the surface finish and/or decoration of ceramics. This sample is almost certainly incomplete in comparison with the entire range of fiber industries within the original technological inventory across this area (see Heckenberger et al. this volume). It should be stressed that the absence of fiber industries for Ceramic periods 2 and 3 is due to their apparent local absence (or near absence) as implements for the surface finish and/or decoration of ceramics between ca. 100 B.C. and A.D. 600, the early and middle portions of the Middle Woodland (Ceramic) period. Farther west and to the south, fiber industries were used for ceramic surface finish and decoration during this period and, thus, are more commonly represented (e.g., Ritchie 1965; Ritchie and Funk 1973).

System of Classification

The term fiber industries, or "perishables," is used here to denote basketry, other fabrics, cordage, netting, and composite combinations of these materials (e.g., cord-wrapped "sticks," cord-

wrapped "cords," etc.), as well as their positive casts as obtained from impressions on ceramics. Following Adovasio and Andrews (with Carlisle) (1980:34), cordage is considered "a class of elongate fiber constructions, the components of which are generally subsumed under the common terms 'string' and 'rope'." Cordage undoubtedly served a variety of important functions in aboriginal societies including use as a tool for the decoration of ceramics (Hurley 1979). Netting is considered "a class of openwork fabrics built up by the repeated interworking of a single continuous element with itself" (Andrews and Adovasio [with Carlisle] 1980:27; see Emery 1980).

Composite manipulations of cordage include: 1) cord-wrapped "cords," or cordage wrapped around a thin, obviously flexible foundation; 2) cord-wrapped "sticks," or cordage wrapped around a thin, linear, largely rigid implement; and 3) cord-wrapped "paddles," or cordage wrapped around a broad, flat, rigid implement. In the latter case, cord-wrapped paddles have been distinguished from fabrics, etc., on the basis of a series of parallel, discrete, noninterwoven elements, even though little evidence of "paddles" *per se* can be discerned. Similarly, although the use of "stick" or "cord" foundations could be clearly identified in only a few cases, these terms have been adopted as a semantic convention to differentiate between the usage of a rigid versus nonrigid foundation around which cordage was wrapped. These complex manipulations of cordage were apparently manufactured primarily—and perhaps solely—as tools for the decoration and/or surface finish of ceramics (Hurley 1979:84–108).

Basketry is a diverse class of perishables woven without a frame or loom and commonly includes three major manufacture techniques: coiling, plaiting, and twining. Of these techniques, only twining and plaiting are represented here. Twining is "manufactured by passing moving (active) horizontal elements called wefts around stationary (passive) vertical elements or warps," and it is employed in the production of containers, mats, bags, fish traps, cradles, hats, clothing, and other less typical items (Adovasio 1977; Adovasio and Andrews [with

Carlisle] 1980:33). Plaiting, on the other hand, is a technique "in which all elements pass over and under each other without any engagement. . . . Plaiting can be used to make containers, bags, and mats as well as a wide range of other less standard forms" (Andrews and Adovasio 1980:27; see Adovasio 1977).

RESULTS

Fiber Artifact Structural Types

The structural types identified in this sample (Tables 6.2–6.4) include two predominant forms of cordage: two ply, S-spun, Z-twist and two ply, Z-spun, S-twist (Figures 6.1 and 6.2). Infrequent representation of braided cordage and a residual category of indeterminate cordage are also pertinent.

Six forms of composite or compound cordage constructions have been noted (Figures 6.3 and 6.4). These include the use of Z-twist and S-twist cordage in conjunction with variable foundations as noted above: "sticks," "cords," and "paddles." Knotted netting was also discerned as a small constituent of the overall sample, with largely unknown type(s) of knots.

Six forms of open and close twining were noted, with the greatest variety discernible in the open forms (Figures 6.4–6.7). In addition, one form of coarse plaiting and one apparent form of interlinked "fabric" were noted; the latter form is technically another form of plaiting (Figure 6.8). Several small residual categories, separable on the basis of cordage twist or other attributes, were also defined.

Table 6.2. Fiber Artifact Structural Types from Coastal Sites in Maine

Structural Form(s) and Twist or Weft Slant	Ceramic Periods				
	CP1	CP4	CP4/5	CP5	CP6/7
Cord-wrapped stick, Z-twist cordage	—	33	37	67	—
Cord-wrapped stick, S-twist cordage	—	25	20	9	—
Cord-wrapped stick, ?-twist cordage	—	—	1	1	—
Cord-wrapped cord, Z-twist cordage	—	—	5	3	—
Cord-wrapped cord, S-twist cordage	—	—	2	—	—
Close simple (?) twining, Z-wefts	5	1	—	13	1
Close simple (?) twining, S-wefts	—	—	—	—	—
Open simple twining, Z-wefts	3	—	—	22	1
Open simple twining, S-wefts	3	—	—	—	—
Open diagonal twining, S-wefts	—	—	—	1	—
Open cross warp twining, Z-wefts	—	—	—	1	—
Cord-wrapped paddle, Z-twist cordage	—	—	3	7	—
Interlinked fabric, Z-twist cordage	1	—	—	6	—
Interlinked fabric, S-twist cordage	1	—	—	—	—
Knotted netting, Z-twist cordage	—	—	1	—	—
Unknown form, Z-twist cordage	6	—	3	5	2
Unknown form, S-twist cordage	4	—	—	—	—
Twill plaited (?)	—	1	—	—	—
TOTAL Z	15	34	49	124	4
PERCENT OF TOTAL (Z)	65%	58%	69%	93%	100%
TOTAL S	8	25	22	10	—
PERCENT OF TOTAL (S)	35%	42%	31%	7%	—

Table 6.3. Fiber Artifact Structural Types from Interior Sites in Maine

Sructural Form(s) and Twist or Weft Slant	Late Archaic	Ceramic Periods				
		CP1	CP4	CP4/5	CP5	CP6/7
Cord-wrapped stick, Z-twist cordage	—	—	10	5	14	3
Cord-wrapped stick, S-twist cordage	—	—	27	5	4	—
Cord-wrapped stick, ?-twist cordage	—	—	—	—	2	—
Cord-wrapped cord, Z-twist cordage	—	—	—	1	—	—
Cord-wrapped cord, S-twist cordage	—	—	—	1	—	—
Close simple (?) twining, Z-wefts	—	2	1	3	6	6
Close simple (?) twining, S-wefts	—	14	—	—	—	3
Close simple (?) twining, S- and Z-wefts	—	—	1	—	—	—
Open simple twining, Z-wefts	—	5	—	2	10	4
Open simple twining, S-wefts	1+	10	—	2	—	—
Open simple twining, S- and Z-wefts	—	—	1	—	—	—
Open simple twining, braided wefts	—	—	—	1	—	1
Cord-wrapped paddle, Z-twist cordage	—	—	—	—	1	2
Cord-wrapped paddle, S-twist cordage	—	1	—	—	—	—
Interlinked fabric, Z-twist	—	—	—	—	1	2
Interlinked fabric, S-twist	—	—	—	1	—	—
Knotted netting, Z-twist cordage	—	—	—	—	1	—
Unknown form, Z-twist cordage	—	—	—	1	4	3
Unknown form, S-twist cordage	—	5	1	1	1	—
Unknown form, braided cordage	—	—	—	1	—	—
TOTAL Z	—	7	11	12	37	20
PERCENT OF TOTAL (Z)	—	19%	28%	55%	88%	87%
TOTAL S	1	30	28	10	5	3
PERCENT OF TOTAL (S)	100%	81%	72%	45%	12%	13%

Table 6.4. Fiber Artifact Structural Types from Sites in Vermont and New Hampshire

Structural Form(s) and Twist or Weft Slant	Ceramic Periods			
	CP1	CP4	CP5	CP6/7
Cordage, Z-twist	1	1	1	—
Cordage, S-twist	4	2	1	—
Cord-wrapped stick, Z-twist cordage	—	3	14	—
Cord-wrapped stick, S-twist cordage	—	16	—	—
Cord-wrapped stick, ?-twist cordage	—	—	10	—
Cord-wrapped cord, S-twist cordage	—	3	—	—
Close simple (?) twining, Z-wefts	—	1	6	3
Close simple (?) twining, S-wefts	—	1	1	6
Open simple twining, Z-wefts	—	1	4	1
Open simple twining, S-wefts	—	—	—	1
Cord-wrapped paddle, Z-twist cordage	—	—	2	—
Cord-wrapped paddle, S-twist cordage	—	4	1	—
Knotted netting, S-twist cordage	—	—	—	—
TOTAL Z	1	6	27	4
PERCENT OF TOTAL (Z)	20%	19%	90%	36%
TOTAL S	4	26	3	7
PERCENT OF TOTAL (S)	80%	81%	10%	64%

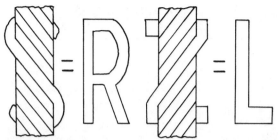

Figure 6.1. Direction of spin, twist, or weft slant and symbols employed in their description. (After Hurley 1979.)

Figure 6.2. Cordage specimen from feature 131 at the Boucher site (VT-FR-26), Franklin County, Vermont, radiocarbon dated to 2075 ± 70 B.P., or 125 B.C. (PITT-0029B). Specimen is a two ply, Z-spun, S-twist construction; total length is about 45.0 mm and diameter is about 1.35 mm.

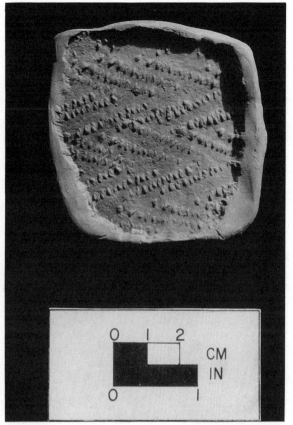

Figure 6.3. Positive cast from the Toll Bridge site (VT-WN-46) in the Springfield area, Windsor County, Vermont. It is an exterior cast showing S-twist cord-wrapped stick decoration attributable to Ceramic period 4 or Ceramic period 5, ca. A.D. 600–1300.

Figure 6.4. Positive casts from site ME 155-8 in the Munsungan Lake area, Piscataquis County, Maine. All are attributable to Ceramic period 4 or Ceramic period 5, ca. A.D. 600–1300. Upper left: exterior cast from vessel 2 rim sherd showing Z-twist cord-wrapped stick decoration; upper right: exterior cast from vessel 3 rim sherd showing S-twist
cord-wrapped stick decoration; lower left and lower right: exterior casts from vessel 3 neck sherds showing S-twist
cord-wrapped stick decoration and probable open simple twining, S-weft slant.

Figure 6.5. Twined fabric from feature 94 at the Boucher site (VT-FR-26), Franklin County, Vermont, radiocarbon dated at 2665 ± 20 B.P., or 715 B.C. (PITT-0025). Specimen is an open simple twined, S-weft slant construction (Type I, Subtype II), which likely represents a garment. Total length of specimen is about 210.0 mm (not shown). Native copper bead in lower section (fourth bead from left) is about 6.80 mm in length.

Figure 6.6. Ceramic body sherd and positive casts from the Rhoda site (ME 90-2A) in the Milo area, Piscataquis County, Maine. Upper: interior surface of ceramic body sherd (Vinette-I-like) attributable to Ceramic period 1, ca. 1000–100 B.C.; lower left: interior cast showing probable open simple twining, Z-weft slant; lower right: exterior cast showing smoothed probable open simple twining, Z-weft slant. The latter cast is indistinct because of exterior smoothing which followed the fabric paddling.

Figure 6.7. Ceramic rim sherds and positive casts from several sites in the Munsungan Lake area, Piscataquis County, Maine. Upper left: vessel 1 rim sherd from site ME 154-13 attributable to Ceramic period 4 or Ceramic period 5, ca. A.D. 600–1300; lower left: ME 154-13 vessel 1 positive exterior cast showing open simple twining, S- and Z-weft slants; upper right: vessel 4 rim sherd from site ME 155-8 attributable to Ceramic period 4 or Ceramic period 5, ca. A.D. 600–1300; lower right: ME 155-8 vessel 4 positive exterior cast showing open simple twining, S- and Z-weft slants.

Figure 6.8. Ceramic body sherd and positive cast from the Hirundo site (ME 73-9), Penobscot County, Maine. Left: vessel 30 body sherd attributable to Ceramic period 6 or Ceramic period 7, ca. A.D. 1300–1750; right: vessel 30 plasticene exterior cast showing interlinked fabric, Z-twist elements (crossed right over left).

A wide variety of other attributes have been recorded for these various structural types, but are not reported here. These include such things as metrics and more precise details of composition and construction (for details see Hamilton 1985; Hedden n.d.; Petersen n.d.; Petersen and Power 1983).

Temporal and Spatial Distribution of Perishables

A preliminary statistical analysis of spatial and temporal continuities was conducted with a series of Chi-square tests. The Chi-square tests included a Yates's continuity correction. In both cases using the distribution of Z (twist/weft slant) and S (twist/weft slant) as the independent variable, these simple tests were utilized to examine both synchronic and diachronic distributions of fiber industries between coastal and interior environments. Each relationship was assessed first using solely the portion of the sample from Maine and then repeated to include the Vermont and New Hampshire samples in the interior category.

These tests reveal several highly significant discontinuities (Table 6.5), with rejection of the null hypothesis (Ho:P = 0.50) that cordage twist or weft slant is randomly distributed in space and time within the given sample. In particular, significant discontinuities are apparent between coastal and interior portions of the sample in Ceramic periods 1–4, ca. 1000 B.C.–A.D. 1000, for both the Maine portion of the sample and the combined sample. This discontinuity remained constant between Ceramic periods 1 and 4, as revealed by an independent Chi-square test (Map 6.1).

Table 6.5. Intra-Sample Spatial and Temporal Distributions

	Chi-Square Value	Rejection Sig. at .05 df = 1	Rejection Sig. at .01 df = 1
SPATIAL RELATIONSHIPS*			
(Z-and S-twist/weft slant)			
Coast-Interior CP 1 (ME)	11.2	*	*
Coast-Interior CP 1 (ME & VT)	13.7	*	*
Coast-Interior CP 4 (ME)	6.6	*	*
Coast-Interior CP 4 (ME & VT)	13.2	*	*
Coast-Interior CP 4/5 (ME)	1.0	—	—
Coast-Interior CP 5 (ME)	0.5	—	—
Coast-Interior CP 5 (ME & VT)	0.6	—	—
Coast-Interior CP 6/7 (ME)	N.A.	—	—
Coast-Interior CP 6/7 (ME & NH)	N.A.	—	—
TEMPORAL RELATIONSHIPS**			
(Z- and S-twist/weft slant)			
CP 1–4 (ME)	0.8	—	—
CP 1–4 (ME & VT)	0.4	—	—
CP 4–4/5 (ME)	7.1	*	*
CP 4/5–CP 5 (ME)	25.3	*	*
CP 4–CP 5 (ME)	65.5	*	*
CP 4–CP 5 (ME & VT)	105.2	*	*
CP 5–CP 6/7 (ME)	N.A.	—	—
CP 5–CP 6/7 (ME & NH)	8.7	*	*

*Ho:P = 0.50.   **CP = Ceramic Period.

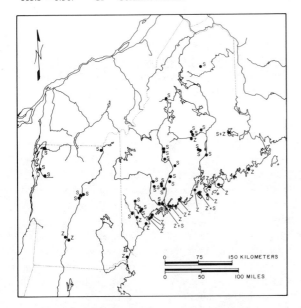

Map 6.1. Distribution of dominant cordage twists and weft slants at archaeological sites in northern New England during Ceramic period 1-Ceramic period 4, ca. 1000 B.C.–A.D. 1000.

The coastal-interior distinction disappeared in Ceramic period 5, however, as evidenced by the failure to reject the null hypothesis of differential distribution of Z and S preferences and highly significant rejection of continuity between Ceramic periods 4 and 5 (Map 6.2). Curiously, something of an apparent resumption of the difference is evident in the combined sample for northern New England in Ceramic periods 6/7, although the small size of Ceramic period 6/7 samples leaves this result tentative.

In sum, significant continuities and discontinuities in the cultural preferences for cordage twist and weft slant across some (or all) of northern New England have been demonstrated. What remains is the more difficult matter of interpretation.

Style, Interaction, and "Ethnicity" in Woodland Fiber Perishables

One of the commonly accepted tenets of archaeology is that attributes of technology and style can be used to assess behavioral continuities across space

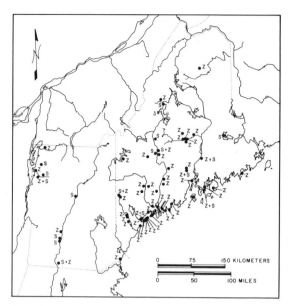

Map 6.2. Distribution of dominant cordage twists and weft slants at archaeological sites in northern New England during Ceramic period 5 to Ceramic period 7, ca. A.D. 1000–1750.

and time, and thereby social interaction and perhaps "ethnicity" can be addressed in the archaeological record (e.g., Adovasio 1986; Clarke 1970, 1979; Croes 1989a; Flannery 1976; Taylor 1967; Wiessner 1983). Despite various criticisms of different aspects of this endeavor (e.g., Binford and Sabloff 1982; Hodder 1979, 1982; Stanislawski 1978), these material clues do, in fact, provide an avenue for exploration of behavioral chains or linkages through the archaeological record, given the development of appropriate levels of analysis.

In this study, the most common available stylistic attributes have been employed, that is, cordage twist and twining weft slant. These attributes are significant because of their ubiquity in most fiber artifact assemblages, as well as their relatively low, or basic, position in the hierarchy of social information content (Plog 1983; Wobst 1977). Following Wiessner (1983:258), cordage twist and twining weft slant can be best ascribed to the category of *assertive style*, as distinguished from *emblemic style*, a distinction which will be returned to below. Still following Wiessner, it should be emphasized that assertive style has no distinct referent. Consequently,

it may be widespread and thus provide a measure of social interaction. Furthermore, assertive style can operate on either a conscious *or* unconscious level (in contrast to emblemic style) and *may* therefore operate independently of and at a different rate of change than identity-marking emblemic style. This is significant in the present case because of the obvious presence of higher order (in the hierarchy of social information content) emblemic style represented by widespread ceramic horizon styles, which do not immediately provide evidence of local group affiliation in the far Northeast.

Little overt emphasis on cordage twist or weft slant as stylistic elements can be expected, but nonetheless these attributes carry information supporting, rather than necessarily symbolizing, individual identity as they are reflective of individual patterns within group-learning networks (Plog 1983; Stanislawski 1978). In the present case, the central problems are: 1) definition of the particular level of group-learning networks; and 2) further explication of the dynamics of such networks on the basis of the recognized spatial and temporal distributions.

Before being considered heretical here, it should be stressed that twist direction in cordage and weft (or stitch) slant in twined fabrics are very highly sensitive, *normally* population-specific attributes in fiber industries, as long noted by various analysts (e.g., Adovasio 1977, 1979, 1986; Andrews and Adovasio 1980; Bird 1979:16; Croes 1989a, 1989b:175, 190; Drooker 1990:176; Fry and Adovasio 1970; Jorgensen 1992:13; Maslowski 1984, 1985; Wallace 1979:45; Weltfish 1932). This position can be summarized as follows:

"Population" in this sense explicitly equates with an ethnic group in the sense that Pima or Paiute, Karok or Kwakiutl, Cheyenne or Shawnee are ethnic groups. While several linguistically related or unrelated groups may share the same stitch slant (as well as other aspects of production), rarely if ever does any one group regularly employ both of them *even* if some individuals *may* opt to use a non-customary pattern. Put another way, although a minor amount of idiosyncratic variation in twining weft manipulation preference may exist within a given population of weavers, rarely, if ever will any group systematically exploit *both* possible stitch slants. Twining stitch slant (like work direction in the production of coiled baskets as well as initial spin or final twist in cordage manufacture) is not dependent on handedness. The preponderance of one or another twist direction or its apparent coexistence in some numbers cannot be explained on the basis of idiosyncratic terms alone. Indeed, there are virtually no ethnographic parallels for the coexistence of both twining twist directions in the same residence unit unless two different populations of weavers have been amalgamated, peacefully or otherwise. (Adovasio and Carlisle 1982:848)

Numerous archaeological and ethnographic examples substantiate the diagnostic nature of the attributes mentioned by Adovasio and Carlisle (e.g., Adovasio 1986; Andrews and Adovasio 1980; Bender Jorgensen 1992; Bower 1980; Croes 1980, 1989a, 1989b; Epstein 1963; Fowler and Matley 1979; Johnson this volume; Maslowski this volume; O'Neale 1945; Osgood 1940; Wallace 1979). A preferred twist or weft slant in fiber industries typically ranges between 60% and 80% and often exceeds 90% in large samples. The important point here is that once a population adopts a particular cordage twist or twined weft slant, they rarely, if ever, change it. As long reported by various anthropologists (e.g., Taylor 1967), basic motor habits can be conditioned by one's culture during enculturation. Once an individual's physical reflexes are conditioned by cultural convention, it is likely to be uncomfortably difficult to deliberately "unlearn" habits that "come easily." In this way, human cultures develop and maintain both conceptual *and* physical manifestations of cultural traditions.

Recent criticisms of this approach aside (e.g., King 1992; O'Connell et al. 1982), as discussed at greater length elsewhere (Petersen this volume), it seems evident on the basis of cordage and weft slant attributes that distinctive and different learning networks for fiber artifact production can be distinguished in Maine and are likely to be distinguishable across northern New England by at *least* the onset of the Early Woodland period (Ceramic period 1) at ca. 1000 B.C. These different networks were apparently aligned along a coastal/interior environmental distinction, a matter which may well be more than coincidental and is likely to be correlated with different patterns of adaptation and/or social

networks. This distinction apparently persisted through the late or terminal Middle Woodland period (Ceramic period 4), or until about A.D. 1000.

Given that the distribution of twist or weft preferences is not uniform in any one time period, it can be inferred that the proportion of about 80:20 is indicative of right handedness versus left handedness. The striking differences observed in the present case are all the more remarkable in light of the likelihood of *some* intergroup (coastal-interior, etc.) exchange of fiber industries, ceramics, and other goods, as known elsewhere in the archaeological record (e.g., Adovasio 1977; Clarke 1979; McPherron 1967a; Penney 1981; Spielman 1983). Such material exchange is even better known in the ethnographic record (e.g., Ernst 1978; Teit 1905, 1930; Wiessner 1982; Wood 1980; Wright 1967).

Other ceramic data, including attributes of temper, vessel morphology, design elements, etc., allow suggestion of increased interaction between local populations by the terminal Middle Woodland period (late Ceramic period 4), ca. A.D. 800 and thereafter. These data, in fact, independently suggest actual exchange of ceramic vessels by this time. In the subsequent early Late Woodland period (Ceramic period 5), the "coastal" pattern of Z-twist and Z-weft slant fiber industries completely "swamped" the presence of S-twist and S-weft slant specimens all across interior environments in Maine and western Vermont, quite likely for different reasons. For instance, Maine ceramic data establish that *greater* than 60% of all early Late Woodland (Ceramic period 5) vessels were predominantly tempered with shell, which in at least some cases seems to be attributable to several saltwater molluscan species. Identification of ceramic vessels so tempered at sites farther than 160–200 km from the coast in interior upland Maine suggests increased exchange of ceramic vessels and/or greater group mobility by ca. A.D. 1000 (Petersen and Sanger 1991). In Vermont, it is possible that the advent of "foreign" influences and/or visitors (i.e., Iroquoian groups) contributed to a shift in cordage twist and twining weft preferences (Petersen 1990).

Identification of contemporaneous and similar shell-tempered ceramics, albeit in small amounts, is even possible in Late Woodland material from the Lake Champlain and the Connecticut River drainages of Vermont and New Hampshire. Moreover, continuation of long-term technological traditions *and* the apparent intrusion and coexistence of a distinctive technological tradition correlated with proto-Iroquoian developments to the west and north can be discerned (see Petersen 1990; Ritchie 1965; Ritchie and Funk 1973; Wright 1966). Although an Iroquoian preference for Z-twist and Z-weft slant fiber industries is tentatively suggested here, this matter bears detailed examination through future research using Iroquoian samples from New York, Ontario, and Quebec. Data from the late Late Woodland and/or Contact period (Ceramic periods 6 and 7), the last era of fully traditional fiber artifact and ceramic manufacture in the region, seems to corroborate the early Late Woodland (Ceramic period 5) pattern(s), but unfortunately the available samples are too small for this precise definition.

The implications of the coastal-interior distinction as represented by cordage twist and twining weft preference are potentially complex, but it seems safe to suggest that distinctive *technological* populations, reflecting different learning networks, were present in coastal and interior environments over much of the span of the entire Woodland (Ceramic) period, with a late prehistoric change at ca. A.D. 1000. Models of population replacement (Adovasio 1979:729), or changing patterns of marriage partner exchange (McPherron 1967b) might be posited, however, and thus the matter clearly remains unresolved. Nonetheless, the available data permit questioning of previous ethnohistoric models of seasonal movement between coastal and interior environments in Maine and the Maritimes (e.g., Snow 1978; Speck 1940), paralleling arguments presented by Sanger (1982) on the basis of subsistence data.

The social implications of these observations are potentially diverse: How do technological populations correlate with social groups? What factors best account for technological differentiation in the first place? Finally, what does the identification of such populations mean in terms of regional culture history and previous behavioral reconstructions? It is suggested here that differentiation of technological populations can be *minimally* interpreted as being indicative of different social groups, whether local or regional macrobands or, in the case of the northern New England data, that previously unrecognized differences in ethnic populations will be ultimately detailed (e.g., Adovasio 1986; Andrews and Adovasio 1980; Wiessner 1983). It seems likely that the presence of these distinctive technological populations in northern New England will be *only* correlated with major distinctions (macroband or some other sociopolitical entity?) in any case. While the observed distinctions possibly may be related to some aspect of subsistence seasonality, symbolic/structural differentiation, and/or raw material availability, none of these factors drawn from the ethnographic record seems compelling in the explanation of these distinctions, especially given their relatively unobtrusive nature. Cordage twist and twining weft slant do *not* seem to represent emblemic style, but instead seem to reflect assertive style, or that which is unheralded and possibly unconsciously representative of particular cultural traditions in the present case.

In summary, ongoing research has demonstrated the presence of fiber industries in the technological inventories of northern New England aboriginal populations by at *least* ca. 2000 B.C., with the likelihood of much older antecedents locally and across eastern North America. The relatively diverse nature of these fiber industries is only clearly documented with the onset of the Early Woodland period (Ceramic period 1), by ca. 1000 B.C. and thereafter through the range of known native technologies, when conditions of preservation, largely through negative impressions on pottery, have provided a broader sample to work with.

Of greater potential significance, however, this chapter represents another example of the utility of fiber industries in documenting the existence of learning networks or technological populations in the archaeological record. Data from Maine (and elsewhere in northern New England) suggest a long-term differentiation of coastal and interior technological populations on the basis of fiber industries, spanning several thousand years at minimum and undergoing one or more notable changes during late prehistory. While the precise correspondence of these learning networks with social categories of more traditional anthropological usage cannot be addressed yet, it does seem evident that these technological populations do correlate with ethnic divisions on some level, most likely macrobands or something similar in Maine (and language groups in Vermont?). The dynamics underlying these observations certainly bear further examination in the future.

ACKNOWLEDGMENTS

This chapter represents a much revised version of a paper originally coauthored by Nathan Hamilton, with the assistance of Laureen LaBar-Kidd and Mark Hedden. In its present form it includes the combined efforts of a variety of individuals who kindly provided support in one form or another over a prolonged period of analysis. Collective thanks are owed to James Adovasio, Louise Basa, Joan Gardner, William Haviland, William Johnson, Robert Maslowski, Brian Robinson, Peter Thomas, Ken Varney, and the Vermont Archaeological Society for providing access to study collections and/or critical reference materials.

Thanks are also extended to Rob Bonnichsen, Bruce Bourque, Michael Brigham, Steven Cox, Richard Doyle, Nathan Hamilton, Mark Hedden, Walter Macdougall, David Sanger, Kathrin Williams, David Yesner, among others, and particularly Arthur Spiess of the Maine Historic Preservation Commission and the Maine Archaeological Society, all of whom made possible and encouraged an extended period of research in Maine. Elaine Hamilton long ago typed an early draft of this chapter, and Kara Ohlund and Shirley Thompson typed revised versions. Steve Bicknell and Tom Buchanan helped with the production of photographs, and Belinda Cox drafted the maps. Bill Haviland, Alice Kehoe, Mary Elizabeth King, Dwight Wallace, and Jack Wolford offered pointed criticisms of earlier drafts of this chapter. I hope their written and verbal comments have been adequately addressed. Finally, I would like to acknowledge the support of James B. Richardson III, chief curator, Section of Anthropology, Carnegie Museum of Natural History, and a Rea postdoctoral fellowship, which made it possible for me to produce and present this contribution in the first place.

NOTES

1. The fiber artifact sample discussed in this chapter includes those specimens studied as of the mid-1980s with little, if any, mention of those studied more recently. It should be noted that the observations discussed here have been much amplified by more recent studies of samples from the Lake Champlain and Connecticut River drainages of Vermont and New Hampshire, as well as coastal and interior settings in Maine (e.g., Heckenberger and others this volume; Petersen and Sanger 1991).
2. See Heckenberger and others this volume for more exhaustive discussion of the fiber perishables from the Boucher cemetery (VT-FR-26).

REFERENCES CITED

Adovasio, J. M.
1977 *Basketry Technology: A Guide to Identification and Analysis*. Aldine, Chicago.
1979 Comment on the Fremont and Sevier: Defining Prehistoric Prehistoric Agriculturists North of the Anasazi. *American Antiquity* 44(4):723–731.
1986 Artifacts and Ethnicity: Basketry as an Indicator of Territoriality and Population Movements in the Prehistoric Great Basin. In *Anthropology of the Desert West, Essays in Honor of Jesse D. Jennings*, edited by Carol H. Condie and Don D. Fowler, pp. 43–88. Univ. of Utah Anthropological Papers 110. Salt Lake City.
Adovasio, J. M., and R. L. Andrews (with R. C. Carlisle)
1980 Basketry, Cordage and Bark Impressions from the Northern Thorn Mound (46Mg78), Monongalia County, West Virginia. *West Virginia Archeologist* 30:33–72.
Adovasio, J. M., and R. C. Carlisle
1982 External Affinities of the Paintsville Reservoir Perishable Industry. In *The Prehistory of the Paintsville Reservoir, Johnson and Morgan Counties, Kentucky*, compiled by J. M. Adovasio, pp. 844–849. Ethnology Monographs 6. Dept. of Anthropology, Univ. of Pittsburgh, Pittsburgh.

Andrews, R. L., and J. M. Adovasio
1980 *Perishable Industries from Hinds Cave, Val Verde County, Texas.* Ethnology Monographs 5. Dept. of Anthropology, Univ. of Pittsburgh, Pittsburgh.

Bender Jorgensen, Lise
1992 *North European Textiles Until a.d. 1000.* Aarhus Univ. Press, Aarhus.

Binford, Lewis R., and Jeremy A. Sabloff
1982 Paradigms, Systematics and Archaeology. *Journal of Anthropological Research* 28(2):137–153.

Bird, Junius B.
1979 Spinning Procedures in the Andean Area. In *The Junius B. Bird Pre-Columbian Textile Conference,* edited by Ann P. Rowe, Elizabeth P. Benson, and Ann-Louise Schaffer, pp. 13–17. The Textile Museum, Washington, D.C.

Bonnichsen, R., V. Konrad, V. Clay, T. Gibson, and D. Schnurrenberger
n.d. *Archaeological Research at Munsungan Lake: 1980 Preliminary Technical Report of Activities.* Institute for Quaternary Studies, Univ. of Maine, Orono.

Borstel, Christopher L.
1982 *Archaeological Investigations at the Young Site, Alton, Maine.* Occasional Publications in Maine Archaeology 2. Maine Historic Preservation Commission, Augusta.

Bourque, Bruce J.
1976 The Turner Farm Site: A Preliminary Report. *Man in the Northeast* 11:21–30.

Bourque, Bruce J., and Steven L. Cox
1981 Maine State Museum Investigation of the Goddard Site. *Man in the Northeast* 22:3–27.

Bower, Beth
1980 Aboriginal Textiles. In *Burr's Hill, a Seventeenth Century Wampanoag Burial Ground in Warren, Rhode Island,* edited by Susan Gibson, pp. 89–91, 140–144. Haffenreffer Museum of Anthropology, Brown Univ., Providence.

Chapman, J., and J. M. Adovasio
1977 Textile and Basketry Impressions from Icehouse Bottom, Tennessee. *American Antiquity* 42(4):620–625.

Clarke, David L.
1970 *Beaker Pottery of Great Britain and Ireland,* 2 volumes. Cambridge Univ. Press, Cambridge.
1979 The Beaker Network—Social and Economic Models. In *Analytical Archaeologist: Collected Papers of David L. Clarke,* edited by his colleagues, pp. 333–362. Academic Press, New York.

Cox, Steven L.
1983 The Blue Hill Survey. *Maine Archaeological Society Bulletin* 23(2):21–30.

Croes, Dale R.
1980 Cordage. In *Hoko River: A 2500 Year Old Fishing Camp on the Northwest Coast of North America,* edited by Dale R. Croes and Eric Blinman, pp. 236–256. Reports of Investigations 58. Laboratory of Anthropology, Washington State Univ., Pullman.
1989a Prehistoric Ethnicity on the Northwest Coast of North America: An Evaluation of Style in Basketry and Lithics. *Journal of Anthropological Archaeology* 8:101–130.
1989b Lachane Basketry and Cordage: A Technological, Functional and Comparative Study. *Canadian Journal of Archaeology* 13:165–205.

Doyle, Richard A., Nathan D. Hamilton, and James B. Petersen
1982 Early Woodland Ceramics and Associated Perishable Industries from Southwestern Maine. *Maine Archaeological Society Bulletin* 22(2):4–21.

Drooker, Penelope Ballard
1990 Textile Production and Use at Wickliffe Mounds (15BA4), Kentucky. *Midcontinental Journal of Archaeology* 15(2):163–220.

Emery, Irene
1980 *The Primary Structures of Fabrics: An Illustrated Classification.* The Textile Museum, Washington, D.C.

Epstein, Jeremiah F.
1963 Centipede and Damp Caves: Excavations in Val Verde County, Texas, 1958. *Bulletin of the Texas Archaeological Society* 33:1–129.

Ernst, T. M.
1978 Aspects of Meaning of Exchanges and Exchange Items Among the Onabasulu of the Great Papuan Plateau. *Mankind* 11:187–197.

Flannery, Kent V.
1976 Introduction to Analysis of Stylistic Variation Within and Between Communities. In *The Early Mesoamerican Village,* edited by Kent V. Flannery, pp. 251–254. Academic Press, New York.

Fowler, Don D., and John F. Matley
1979 *Material Culture of the Numa, The John Wesley Powell Collection, 1867–1880.* Smithsonian Contributions to Anthropology 26. Smithsonian Institution, Washington, D.C.

Fry, G. F., and J. M. Adovasio
1970 Population Differentiation in Hogup and Danger Caves, Two Archaic Sites in the Eastern Great Basin. *Nevada State Museum Anthropological Papers* 15:208–215. Carson City.

Hamilton, Nathan D.
1985 *Maritime Adaptations in Western Maine: The Great Diamond Island Site.* Unpublished Ph.D. dissertation, Dept. of Anthropology, Univ. of Pittsburgh, Pittsburgh.

Hamilton, Nathan D., and David Yesner
1985   Early, Middle and Late Woodland Ceramic Assemblages from the Great Diamond Island Site, Casco Bay, Maine. In *Ceramic Analysis in the Northeast: Contributions to Methodology and Culture History*, edited by James B. Petersen, pp. 39–72. Occasional Publications in Northeastern Anthropology 9(2).

Harper, J. Russell
1956   *Portland Point, Crossroads of New Brunswick History*. Historical Studies 9. New Brunswick Museum, St. John.

Heckenberger, Michael J., James B. Petersen, and Louise A. Basa
1990   Early Woodland Period Ritual Use of Personal Adornment at the Boucher Site. *Annals of Carnegie Museum* 59(3):173–217.

Hedden, Mark H.
n.d.   Pottery from the Goddard Site. Unpublished ms. in the possession of the author.

Hodder, Ian
1979   Economic and Social Stress and Material Culture Patterning. *American Antiquity* 44(3):446–454.
1982   *Symbols in Action: Ethnoarchaeological Studies of Material Culture*. Cambridge Univ. Press, Cambridge.

Holmes, William H.
1884   Prehistoric Textile Fabrics of the United States Derived from Impressions on Pottery. *Annual Report of the Bureau of American Ethnology, 1881–1882*, pp. 393–425. Smithsonian Institution, Washington, D.C.

Hurley, William M.
1975   *An Analysis of Effigy Mound Complexes in Wisconsin*. Anthropological Papers 59. Museum of Anthropology, Univ. of Michigan, Ann Arbor.
1979   *Prehistoric Cordage: Identification of Impressions on Pottery*. Taraxacum, Washington, D.C.

Kellar, James
1967   Material Remains. In *Angel Site, An Archaeological, Historical and Ethnological Study*, 2 volumes, by Glenn A. Black, pp. 431–487. Indiana Historical Society, Indianapolis.

King, Mary E.
1968   Textile Fragments from the Riverside Site, Menominee, Michigan. *Verhandlungen des XXXVIII Internationalen Amerikanistenkongresses*, pp. 117–123.
1975   Archaeological Textiles. In *Archaeological Textiles, Irene Emery Roundtable on Museum Textiles*, edited by Patricia L. Fiske, pp. 9–16. The Textile Museum, Washington, D.C.
1992   The Perishable Preserved: Ancient Textiles from the Old World with Comparisons from the New World. *The Review of Archaeology* 13(1):2–11.

Maslowski, Robert F.
1984   The Significance of Cordage Attributes in the Analysis of Woodland Pottery. *Pennsylvania Archaeologist* 54(1–2):51–60.
1985   Cordage, Knots, and Netting: Technological Approaches to Ethnicity and Cultural Stability. Paper presented at the 50th annual meeting of the Society for American Archaeology, Denver.

McPherron, Alan L.
1967a *The Juntunen Site and the Late Woodland Prehistory of the Upper Great Lakes Area*. Anthropological Papers 30. Museum of Anthropology, Univ. of Michigan, Ann Arbor.
1967b On the Sociology of Ceramics: Pottery Style Clustering, Marital Residence, and Cultural Adaptations on an Algonkian–Iroquoian Border. In *Iroquois Culture, History and Prehistory: Proceedings of the 1965 Conference on Iroquois Research*, edited by Elizabeth Tooker, pp. 101–107. New York State Museum and Science Service, Albany.

Michels, Joseph W., and Ira F. Smith (editors)
1967   *Archaeological Investigations of Sheep Rock Shelter, Huntingdon County, Pennsylvania*. Dept. of Sociology and Anthropology, Pennsylvania State Univ., Univ. Park.

Miner, Horace
1936   The Importance of Textiles in the Archaeology of the Eastern United States. *American Antiquity* 1(3):181–192.

O'Connell, James F., Kevin T. Jones, and Stephen R. Simms
1982   Some Thoughts on Prehistoric Archaeology in the Great Basin. In *Man and Environment in the Great Basin*, edited by David B. Madsen and James F. O'Connell, pp. 227–240. Society for American Archaeology Papers 2.

O'Neale, Lila M.
1945   *Textiles of Highland Guatemala*. Carnegie Institution of Washington Publication 567. Washington, D.C.

Osgood, Cornelius
1940   *Ingalik Material Culture*. Yale Univ. Publications in Anthropology 22. New Haven.

Penney, Gerald
1981   A Point Peninsula Rim Sherd from L'Anse a Flamme, Newfoundland. *Canadian Journal of Archaeology* 5:171–173.

Petersen, James B.
1980   *The Middle Woodland Ceramics of the Winooski Site, a.d. 1–1000*. Vermont Archaeological Society New Series Monograph 1.
1990   Evidence of the Saint Lawrence Iroquoians in Northern New England: Population Movement, Trade, or Stylistic Borrowing? *Man in the Northeast* 40:31–39.

n.d.   Aboriginal Ceramic and Fiber Industries from
        Maine: An Investigation of Technology and Social
        Interaction during the Ceramic Period. Occasional
        Publications in Maine Archaeology (in preparation).

Petersen, James B., and Nathan D. Hamilton
1984   Early Woodland Ceramic and Perishable Fiber In-
        dustries from the Northeast: A Summary and In-
        terpretation. *Annals of Carnegie Museum*
        53:413–445. Pittsburgh.

Petersen, James B., Nathan D. Hamilton, James M.
        Adovasio, and Alan L. McPherron
1984   Netting Technology and the Antiquity of Fish Ex-
        ploitation in Eastern North America.
        Midcontinental Journal of Archaeology 9(2):199–225.

Petersen, James B., and Marjory W. Power
1983   *The Winooski Site and the Middle Woodland Period in
        the Northeast.* Dept. of Anthropology, Univ. of Ver-
        mont. Submitted to Interagency Archeological Ser-
        vices, Mid-Atlantic Region, National Park Service,
        Philadelphia.
1985   Three Middle Woodland Ceramic Assemblages from
        the Winooski Site. In *Ceramic Analysis in the Northeast:
        Contributions to Methodology and Culture History,* ed-
        ited by James B. Petersen, pp. 109–159. Occasional
        Publications in Northeastern Anthropology 9(2).

Petersen, James B., and David Sanger
1991   An Aboriginal Ceramic Sequence for Maine and
        the Maritimes. In *Prehistoric Archaeology in the
        Maritimes: Past and Present Research,* edited by
        Michael Deal and Susan Blair, pp. 121–178. Council
        of Maritime Premiers, Fredericton.

Petersen, James B., Jack A. Wolford, Nathan D. Hamilton,
        Laureen A. LaBar, and Michael J. Heckenberger
1985   Archaeological Investigations in the Shelburne
        Pond Locality, Chittenden County, Vermont. *An-
        nals of Carnegie Museum* 54(3):23–76.

Plog, Stephen
1983   Analysis of Style in Artifacts. *Annual Review of An-
        thropology* 12:125–142.

Ritchie, William A.
1965   *The Archaeology of New York State.* Natural History
        Press, Garden City.

Ritchie, William A., and Don W. Dragoo
1960   *The Eastern Dispersal of the Adena.* New York State
        Museum and Science Service Bulletin 379. Albany.

Ritchie, William A., and Robert E. Funk
1973   *Aboriginal Settlement Patterns in the Northeast.* New
        York State Museum and Science Service Memoir
        20. Albany.

Sanger, David
1982   Changing Views of Aboriginal Seasonality and
        Settlement in the Gulf of Maine. *Canadian Journal of
        Anthropology* 2(2):195–203.

Sanger, David, Ronald B. Davis, Robert G. McKay, and
        Harold W. Borns
1977   The Hirundo Archaeological Project—An Interdis-
        ciplinary Approach to Central Maine Prehistory. In
        *Amerinds and Their Paleoenvironments in Northeast-
        ern North America,* edited by Walter S. Newman
        and Bert Salwen, pp. 457–471. Annals of New York
        Academy of Sciences 288. New York.

Sanger, David, Barbara Johnson, James McCormick, and
        Marcella H. Sorg
1980   *Archaeological Salvage and Test Excavations, Fernald
        Point, Acadia National Park, Maine.* Dept. of Anthro-
        pology, Univ. of Maine, Orono. Submitted to the
        National Park Service, Denver.

Smith, Harlan I.
1910   The Prehistoric Ethnology of a Kentucky Site. *An-
        thropological Papers of the American Museum of Natu-
        ral History* 6(2):172–235. New York.

Snow, Dean R.
1978   Eastern Abenaki. In *Northeast,* edited by Bruce G.
        Trigger, pp. 137–147. Handbook of North Ameri-
        can Indians, vol. 15, William G. Sturtevant, general
        editor. Smithsonian Institution, Washington, D.C.

Speck, Frank G.
1940   *Penobscot Man: The Life History of a Forest Tribe in
        Maine.* Univ. of Pennsylvania Press, Philadelphia.

Spielmann, Katherine A.
1983   Late Prehistoric Exchange between the Southwest
        and Southern Plains. *Plains Anthropologist*
        28(102):257–272.

Spiess, Arthur E., James B. Petersen, and Mark Hedden
1983   The Evergreens: 5000 Years in Interior Northwest
        Maine. *Maine Archaeological Society Bulletin* 23(1):9–26.

Stanislawski, Michael B.
1978   If Pots were Mortal. In *Explorations in Ethnoarchae-
        ology,* edited by Richard A. Gould, pp. 201–227.
        Univ. of New Mexico Press, Albuquerque.

Stile, T. E.
1982   Perishable Artifacts from Meadowcroft
        Rockshelter, Washington County, Southwestern
        Pennsylvania. In *Meadowcroft: Collected Papers on
        the Archaeology of Meadowcroft Rockshelter and the
        Cross Creek Drainage,* edited by R. C. Carlisle and
        J. M. Adovasio, pp. 130–141. Dept. of Anthropol-
        ogy, Univ. of Pittsburgh, Pittsburgh.

Taylor, Walter W.

1967 *A Study of Archeology.* Southern Illinois Univ. Press, Carbondale.

Teit, J. A.

1905 The Lillooet Indians. *Memoirs of the American Museum of Natural History* 4(5):193–300. New York.

1930 The Salishan Tribes of the Western Plateaus. *Annual Report of the Bureau of American Ethnology* 45:23–396. Smithsonian Institution, Washington, D.C.

Thomas, Peter A.

1973 Squakheag Ethnohistory: A Preliminary Study of Culture Conflict on the Seventeenth Century Frontier. *Man in the Northeast* 5:27–36.

1979 *In the Maelstrom of Change, the Indian Trade and Cultural Process in the Middle Connecticut River Valley: 1635–1665.* Unpublished Ph.D. dissertation, Dept. of Anthropology, Univ. of Massachusetts, Amherst.

Thomas, Peter A., and Brian S. Robinson

1981 *Joseph C. McNeil Generating Station Borrow Area.* Univ. of Vermont Dept. of Anthropology Report 31. Burlington.

Wallace, Dwight T.

1979 The Process of Weaving Development on the Peruvian Coast. In *The Junius B. Bird Pre-Columbian Textile Conference,* edited by Ann P. Rowe, Elizabeth P. Benson, and Ann-Louise Schaffer, pp. 27–50. The Textile Museum, Washington, D.C.

Watson, Patty Jo (editor)

1974 *Archeology of the Mammoth Cave Area.* Academic Press, New York.

Weltfish, Gene

1932 Problems in the Study of Ancient and Modern Basket Makers. *American Anthropologist* 34(2):108–117.

Whitehead, Ruth H.

n.d. *Plant Fibre Textiles from the Hopps Site: BkCp-1.* Nova Scotia Museum Curatorial Report 59. Halifax.

Wiessner, Polly

1982 Risk, Reciprocity and Social Influences on !Kung San Economics. In *Politics and History in Band Societies,* edited by Eleanor Leacock and Richard Lee, pp. 61–84. Cambridge Univ. Press, Cambridge.

1983 Style and Social Information in Kalahari San Projectile Points. *American Antiquity* 48(2):253–276.

Willoughby, Charles C.

1924 *Indian Burial Place at Winthrop, Massachusetts.* Papers of the Peabody Museum of American Archaeology and Ethnology 11(1). Harvard Univ., Cambridge.

1935 *Antiquities of the New England Indians.* Peabody Museum of American Archaeology and Ethnology, Harvard Univ., Cambridge.

1938 Textile Fabrics from the Burial Mounds of the Great Earthwork Builders of Ohio. *Ohio Archaeological and Historical Quarterly* 47(4):273–287.

Wobst, H. Martin

1977 Stylistic Behavior and Information Exchange. In *Papers for the Director: Research Essays in Honor of James B. Griffin,* edited by Charles E. Cleland, pp. 317–342. Anthropological Papers 61. Museum of Anthropology, Univ. of Michigan, Ann Arbor.

Wood, W. Raymond

1980 Plains Trade in Prehistoric and Protohistoric Intertribal Relations. In *Anthropology on the Great Plains,* edited by W. Raymond Wood and Margot Liberty, pp. 98–109. Univ. of Nebraska Press, Lincoln.

Wright, Gary A.

1967 Some Aspects of Early and Mid-Seventeenth Century Exchange Networks in the Western Great Lakes. *The Michigan Archaeologist* 13(4):181–197.

Wright, James V.

1966 *The Ontario Iroquois Tradition.* National Museum of Canada Bulletin 210. Ottawa.

7

Nathan D. Hamilton

James B. Petersen

Alan L. McPherron

Fiber Industries in the Upper Great Lakes: A Late Woodland Case Study from the Juntunen Site

Products of certain fiber industries, including cordage, netting, and basketry, were used in the surface finish and decoration of prehistoric aboriginal ceramics in the Upper Great Lakes region and elsewhere in eastern North America. This chapter examines a sample of aboriginal fiber industries, or "perishables," as preserved on ceramics, along with several extant fiber artifacts, from three periods of occupation at the prehistoric Juntunen site, situated in the Straits of Mackinac between Lake Michigan and Lake Huron (McPherron 1967a). These three periods include the Mackinac, Bois Blanc, and Juntunen phases, ca. A.D. 800–1400, all of which are attributable to the Late Woodland period of regional prehistory (Mason 1981).

Located on the western end of Bois Blanc Island in the Straits of Mackinac, the Juntunen site was extensively excavated in 1960–61 by the Museum of Anthropology, University of Michigan, under the direction of Alan McPherron. Detailed analyses and interpretation of data from the site have been presented previously (e.g., Cleland 1966; McPherron 1967a, 1967b; Yarnell 1964), and they have been used as an important reference point in broad regional research over the past several decades (e.g., Brose 1978; Clark et al. 1992; Dawson 1977; Fitting 1970, 1976; Mason 1981; Noble 1983). McPherron originally investigated various aspects of anthropological archaeology in terms of subsistence technology, mortuary practices, and settlement for late prehistoric populations in this region. In particular, McPherron documented extensive social interaction in the Upper Great Lakes region during late prehistory on the basis of material culture remains, primarily ceramics.

Ceramics made up the largest category of material culture recovered from the Juntunen site: there were 101,477 sherds from 1688 vessels. In the present study, a sample of 222 fragmentary ceramic vessels was selected from the total sample of vessels on the basis of their relative completeness. This sample represents the largest and best preserved of the vessels and was employed here as a source of data on Juntunen fiber industries since only two actual fiber specimens were recovered during the excavations. Fiber industries have been reconstructed on the basis of positive plasticene and silicon casts made from negative impressions left on the vessels in the processes of applying decoration and/or some forms of surface finish (Figure 7.1). The several extant fiber artifacts have been included as well.

ANALYTICAL PROCEDURES

Analysis of the fiber artifact impressions preserved on ceramics from the Juntunen site was undertaken at the University of Pittsburgh during the 1980s. The Juntunen ceramics were then on loan from the Museum of Anthropology, University of Michigan.

The sample of 222 ceramic vessels (some represented by partially reconstructed vessels) was selected on the basis of relative size and completeness

Figure 7.1. Mackinac Banded vessel from the Juntunen site. Cord-wrapped cord and open twined decoration present, along with open twining-wrapped paddle surface treatment (see Figure 7.4 for detailed discussion of open twined decoration on neck). (McPherron 1967a:Plate XIVa; Mason 1981:Plate 8.11.)

of the fiber artifact impressions present on rim sherds. Vessels which illustrated sequential decorative patterns on their rim and the neck portions, often including separate surface finish attributes, were also selected (see Figure 7.1).

All rim sherds were initially compared against one another to establish vessel lots, an important practice employed in the original ceramic analysis conducted by McPherron (1967a). It is noteworthy that 1316 of the 1688 vessels isolated in the original study are represented by only a single sherd each. In any case, this form of sorting has proven utility as an important means of vessel reconstruction, especially in the comparison of attribute frequencies and establishment of spatial correlations (e.g., Hamilton and Yesner 1985; Petersen 1985; Wright 1980). Vessel lot analysis will provide a reliable means of elucidating variability in a given ceramic sample, as evident in past research in the Great Lakes region (e.g., Finlayson 1977; Pendergast 1973; Ramsden 1977; Stothers 1977; Wright 1967; Wright and Anderson 1963).

Once rims were sorted into vessel lots, each vessel was specifically examined using a standardized analysis of 52 attributes, including but not limited to techniques of manufacture, forms, applications, and patterns of decoration, and morphological characteristics (Appendix 1). Only attributes of vessel decoration and exterior surface finish are considered here, however, in accord with the objectives of this study.

Specific attributes given consideration in this analysis include interior, lip, and exterior decoration and surface finish, or, in other words, all areas where fiber artifact impressions were encountered (Appendix 2). Variations among the fiber perishables were addressed, including size, complexity, and combination of element attributes, as well as decorative motifs, the sequence and extent of the decoration, and specific tools used in decoration and/or surface finish. Other tool forms, such as punctate stamps and incising tools, and various other ceramic attributes have been studied using this same sample, but they are not discussed here.

Attributes of the fiber industries were isolated using the standardized categories of Adovasio (1977)

for the analysis of basketry and Hurley (1979) for the analysis of cordage. Other references were consulted as well (e.g., Andrews and Adovasio [with Carlisle] 1980; Emery 1980; Hurley 1974, 1975; Scholtz 1975), dealing with application of these techniques to a variety of North American fiber industries.

All ceramic specimens were carefully cleaned with fine hair brushes, and positive casts were taken with soft plasticene impressed on the surfaces of the ceramic sherds. Select positive casts were also made with a silicon casting technique. All measurements were taken with Helios needle-nosed dial calipers (accurate to 0.05 mm).

The silicon casts were prepared with Dow Corning 3110 RTV silicon rubber catalyzed with Dow Corning RTV catalyst. The silicon was applied to the entire surface of the larger ceramic specimens to secure an accurate representation of the various fiber industries applied as surface finish and/or decoration. Care was taken to apply the silicon and/or plasticene evenly so that the best possible casts of the fiber artifacts could be obtained.

Positive casts from the 222 analyzed vessel lots represent at least six structural types of cordage, one structural type of netting, four structural types of twined basketry, and nine structural types of complex combinations of perishables, with cord-wrapped stick, cord-wrapped cord and cord-wrapped paddle types. The cordage specimens have been assigned to structural types based on the number of plies, direction of initial spin S or Z, and the direction of final cordage twist and twining weft slant, following standardized criteria briefly summarized below.

Ply is used to describe "a strand or 'bunch' of fibrous materials that is almost always twisted and/or spun. These strands can be used alone to form single ply cordage, or in groups to form *multiple* ply cordage. Multiple ply cordage is produced by twisting two or more 'single' plys [or plies] together." (Adovasio and Andrews [with Carlisle] 1980:38). A ply is "simple" when it is homogenous, or composed of a single strand or bunch of fibers with the same twist/spin. A ply is "compound" when it is composed of multiple strands or bunches of fibers that are initially spun and then twisted together, typically in the opposite direction (see Adovasio and Andrews [with Carlisle] 1980).

Spin is used to note the initial configuration of individual strands or bunches of simple or compound cordage, whereas *twist* is the final direction in which the strands or bunches are twisted (or "plied") together to form a piece of cordage. The direction of spin or twist can be only S or Z, that is twisted to the right or left, respectively (Hurley 1979:6).

Besides the attributes of construction, each specimen was examined for the presence of splices, twists per cm, and angle of twist. Segment and twist measurements were taken using procedures specified by Hurley (1979:Figures 1 and 2).

A like set of criteria was used in the analysis of the other fiber industries, including netting, twined basketry, or fabrics, and complex combinations of cordage. In addition, the netting was classified on the basis of the form of looping present since netting is a term applied to openwork fabrics produced from the repeated interworking of a single flexible element with itself (Andrews and Adovasio 1980:30–31; Emery 1980).

Twining is a form of basketry or fabric "manufactured by passing moving (active) horizontal elements called wefts around stationary (passive) vertical elements or warps" (Adovasio and Andrews [with Carlisle] 1980:33). Determination of warp and weft elements was made using the above mentioned criteria and attention was also given, where possible, to the presence of selvages, splices, knots, mends, and other less frequently encountered attributes. Twining weft slant (or "twist"), either S or Z, was also recorded, denoting the direction of the twining, along with the constituent twist and spin where pertinent.

The complex combinations of perishables were similarly analyzed, with particular attention given to the form of the active elements, usually cordage, and the foundations. Foundations were classified as "cords" where directly observable or when obviously flexible in nature, whereas "sticks" were recognized by direct observation or where the foundation appeared relatively inflexible or rigid. "Paddle" foundations were inferred when cordage elements were aligned parallel to one another but

did not exhibit any connecting elements. In addition, direction of wrap, angle of wrap, and wrap spacing were noted for each specimen, as appropriate (e.g., Petersen and Power 1983).

SUMMARY OF RESULTS

Cordage: Six structural types of cordage have been delimited in the available sample (Table 7.1, Figure 7.2). These include: Type I: Two ply, S-spun, Z-twist; Type II: Two ply, Z-spun, S-twist; Type III: Three ply, Z-spun, S-twist; Type IV: Compound two ply, S-spun, Z-twist; Type V: Compound two ply, Z-spun, S-twist; Type VI: Compound three ply, Z-spun, S-twist.

Comments: The greatest number of specimens were Type IV: Compound two ply, S-spun, Z-twist cordage. It seems likely that most, if not all, of the compound two ply specimens were formed by doubling a piece of cordage back on itself, as evident in a number of looped ends. For example, Type V: Compound two ply, Z-spun, S-twist cordage was produced by doubling a cord of Type I: Two ply, S-spun, Z-twist back on itself and then twisting the doubled up strands together (see Figure 7.2D). Of the simple two ply forms, Type I: Two ply, S-spun, Z-twist and Type II: Two ply, Z-spun, S-twist were equally represented in the total sample (see Figures 7.2A and 7.2B).

In many cases, evidence of individual fibers could be observed in the positive casts, all of very fine size. However, raw materials typically cannot be identified by gross morphological features alone, as preserved in the positive casts. Most cordage specimens ranged between 1.0 and 3.0 mm in diameter. The application of cordage as decoration was confined to approximately the upper one-third of each vessel where it was employed.

Twined Basketry: Four structural types of twining (Table 7.2, Figures 7.3–7.5) and two residual categories have been discerned; the two residual categories include specimens with unclear wefts. The four structural types include: Type I: Close simple twining, Z-weft slant; Type II: Close simple twining, S-weft slant; Type III: Open simple twining, Z-weft slant; and Type IV: Open simple twining, S-weft slant.

Table 7.1. Structural Types of Cordage as Correlated with Juntunen Ceramic Types

Ceramic Type	No. of Vessels	Cordage					
		two ply, S-twist	two ply, Z-twist	three ply, Z-twist	compound two ply, S-twist	compound two ply, Z-twist	compound three ply, S-twist
MACKINAC							
Undecorated	35	—	4	—	2	9	—
Punctate	43	4	7	—	—	4	—
Cord-Impressed	56	6	6	5	5	19	1
Banded	49	8	6	5	2	18	—
Mackinac Subtotal	183	18	23	10	9	50	1
BLACKDUCK							
Banded	9	—	—	—	—	1	—
BOIS BLANC							
Braced Rim	6	—	—	—	1	1	—
Beaded Rim	9	2	—	—	—	1	—
Castellated Corded	13	2	2	—	1	4	—
Bois Blanc Subtotal	28	4	2	—	2	6	—
JUNTUNEN							
Drag and Jab	2	1	—	—	—	—	—
TOTAL	222	23	25	10	11	57	1

Comments: The predominant forms of twining were Type I: Close simple twining, Z-weft slant, and Type II: Close simple twining, S-weft slant. The paired weft elements were most often constructed with two ply, S-spun, Z-twist (Type I) and two ply, Z-spun, S-twist (Type II) cordage, respectively, over unobservable warps. Because of the generally fine nature of the cordage and apparent flexibility inherent in the construction, the twined basketry specimens which employed cordage are alternatively classifiable as fabrics, as are nearly all the other twined specimens.

Other specimens were clearly not produced with cordage but instead with single, more sizable spun fiber elements. In the open forms of twining, both cordage and single rigid warp foundations were evident (see Figure 7.4). Type III: Open simple twining, Z-weft slant basketry (or fabric) seems to have been manufactured for some utilitarian purpose and was only applied incidentally during the process of ceramic surface finish, after being wrapped around an unknown foundation or paddle of some sort.

The several extant fiber specimens recovered from the Juntunen site are examples of open simple twining, which may be attributable to a single original artifact or perhaps two artifacts. In any case, they originated in a single human burial and seemingly represent one (or more) twined bag(s) associated with a "personal kit" (see McPherron 1967a:210–211, Plate XLVI:n–o). The extant twining fragments are clearly related to Type IV: Open simple twining, S-weft slant, with the wefts crossing doubled warps (see Figure 7.3).

Netting: One structural type of netting was evident in the available sample, representing a variety of knotted looping apparently tied with fishnet knots (see Table 7.2, Figure 7.6). A relatively fine-sized mesh was evident in both cases, suggesting manufacture for seining (Petersen et al. 1984). The netting specimens were apparently stretched over some unknown foundation, presumably to aid in application. Netting was applied both as a form of decoration and as a means of surface finish.

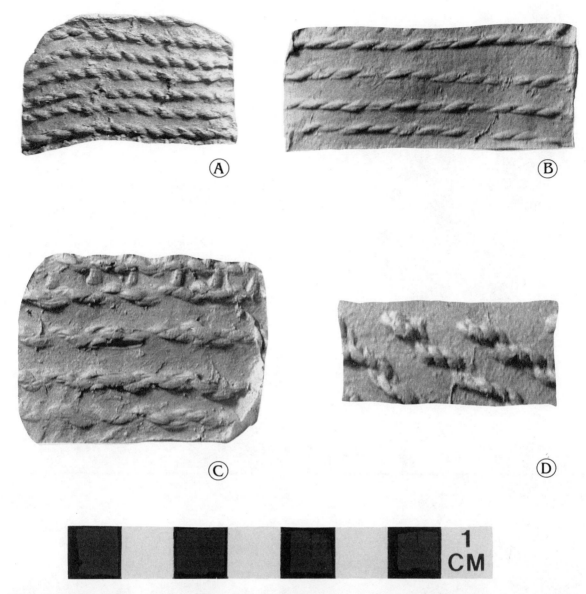

Figure 7.2. Positive cordage casts from the Juntunen site: A) two ply, S-spun, Z-twist cordage; B) two ply, Z-spun, S-twist cordage; C) three ply, S-spun, Z-twist cordage; D) compound two ply, Z-spun, S-twist cordage.

Figure 7.3. *Left*. Open simple twined extant fabric fragment, S-weft slant, from the Juntunen site. Note vertical orientation of the warps and diagonal orientation of the wefts.

Figure 7.4. *Below*. Positive open simple twining, Z-weft slant cast from the Juntunen site. The weft (left oblique orientation in photograph) is made with two ply, S-spun, Z-twist cordage, and the warp (right oblique orientation in photograph) is made with three ply, S-spun, Z-twist cordage, wrapped from left to right with two ply, Z-spun, S-twist cordage. Several overhand knotted splices are apparent and the selvage is of a crossed 90°–180° type with wrapped reinforcement. The mean of the mesh is 0.65 cm. Note orientation of cast as taken from a ceramic vessel (see Figure 7.1).

Figure 7.5. Positive close simple and open simple twining casts from the Juntunen site: A) close simple twining, S-weft slant; B) open simple twining, S-weft slant; C) open simple twining, Z-weft slant. Note orientation of casts as taken from ceramics.

Table 7.2. Structural Types of Twining and Netting as Correlated with Juntunen Ceramic Types

| Ceramic Type | No. of Vessels | Close Simple Twining | | | Open Simple Twining | | | Knotted Netting |
		S-twist weft	Z-twist weft	unknown weft	S-twist weft	Z-twist weft	unknown weft	two ply, S-twist
MACKINAC								
Undecorated	35	9	15	2	2	4	—	—
Punctate	43	11	10	3	3	2	1	—
Cord-Impressed	56	6	3	1	1	1	1	1
Banded	49	4	4	1	—	3	—	1
Mackinac Subtotal	183	30	32	7	6	10	2	2
BLACKDUCK								
Banded	9	—	—	—	—	—	—	—
BOIS BLANC								
Braced Rim	6	3	—	—	—	—	—	—
Beaded Rim	9	1	—	—	—	—	—	—
Castellated Corded	13	3	2	—	—	—	—	—
Bois Blanc Subtotal	28	7	2	—	—	—	—	—
JUNTUNEN								
Drag and Jab	2	—	1	—	—	—	—	—
TOTAL	222	37	35	7	6	10	2	2

Cord-Wrapped Cord: Five structural types of cord-wrapped cord complex constructions were defined, including two residual categories which were necessary since the foundations are unknown in some cases (Figure 7.7C). The two basic types of two ply cordage, Types I and II, were apparently wrapped around varying flexible foundations which, in some cases, were obviously strands of simple cordage; in other cases, compound cordage was used as a flexible foundation. Like the cord-wrapped stick specimens, the cord-wrapped cords (Table 7.3) were all apparently manufactured as decorative stamping tools. In a few cases, Type I: Two ply, S-spun, Z-twist cordage was apparently wrapped around a single element of a flexible nature, which has been distinguished here as a separate structural type.

Cord-Wrapped Stick: Two structural types of cord-wrapped stick complex constructions were defined (Figure 7.7A and 7.7B). The two basic forms of two ply cordage, dominated by Type II: Two ply, Z-spun, S-twist, as described above, were wrapped around foundations of varying sizes, usually small, but up to 10 mm in diameter (see Table 7.3). They were then applied as a form of decoration to the ceramic vessels. The types of cord-wrapped stick decorative tools were established in correspondence with the type of cordage wrapped around the rigid foundation, in some cases quite clearly a stick, as observed projecting beyond the cordage wrapping toward the ends of the positive casts. Overhand knots were occasionally evident where cordage was tied to the foundation.

Cord-Wrapped Paddle: Two structural types of cord-wrapped paddle complex constructions were defined, but only eight individual impressions were noted in the sample (see Table 7.3). Usage of cord-wrapped paddles was apparently uncommon as a form of surface finish, at least as represented among the rim sherds. The two structural types were differentiated on the basis of the two types of cordage, Types I and II, employed in wrapping the paddle foundations.

Internal Correlations

This analysis has delimited diverse and well-developed fiber industries, largely as preserved in

Figure 7.6. Knotted netting from the Juntunen site: A) ceramic rim sherd exhibiting negative netting impression; B) positive cast of netting with S-twist cordage and possible fishnet knots. Note orientation of cast as taken from the rim sherd.

negative impressions on ceramics from the Juntunen site. Most of these fiber perishables are attributable to the 183 selected Mackinac phase vessels, ca. A.D. 800–1000, but also include a lesser number of specimens (n = 28 vessels) for the later Bois Blanc phase, ca. A.D. 1000–1200, and only a few specimens (n = 2 vessels) for the Juntunen phase, ca. A.D. 1200–1400. The several extant specimens of open simple twining are clearly related to the Juntunen phase as well, on the basis of their recovery from a radiocar-

bon-dated ossuary (McPherron 1967a). In addition, nine vessels are clearly related to the northern Blackduck "culture" or complex, generally dated from ca. A.D. 800–1500. The decreasing numbers of fiber perishables used for decoration in the later phases at Juntunen should not be interpreted as anything other than a gradual shift toward different forms of ceramic decoration tools, not as a decreased production of cordage or basketry. Notably, the use of twined basketry for ceramic surface finish persisted throughout the sequence.

The key elements in the Juntunen fiber industries are the different structural types of cordage which were applied singularly or in conjunction with more complex constructions, such as rigid "stick" or flexible "cord" foundations, as forms of ceramic decoration. Much less frequent usage of netting and open simple twining as decorative stamps were also recorded in the sample. Other forms of twining, notably close simple twining, predominated among the fiber industries used for external surface finish.

The cordage is generally fine to medium sized (1.0 to 3.0 mm in diameter), and most often two ply or compound two ply cordage. Cordage was applied as decoration solely on the upper exterior, lip, and upper interior surfaces of the pots, in various combinations in terms of both structural category and location. While the cordage types serve as generally unifying features for the entire set of fiber industries from the Juntunen site, a trend toward reduction in the size of the cordage over time may be evident. The limited size of the samples from the later phases precludes confirmation of this trend, however. Similarly, the cordage on Mackinac phase ceramics seems generally more variable and clearly thicker on average than the contemporaneous, if less well represented, cordage on the Blackduck ceramics present in the sample.

The functions of the fiber industries within the economic system(s) of the Juntunen population(s) remain largely conjectural. Cordage was undoubtedly employed for a variety of utilitarian purposes apart from those documented on the ceramics, including manufacture of netting and basketry or fabrics, among other constructions. The more complex combinations of cord elements with rigid and non-

Table 7.3. Structural Types of Cord-Wrapped Cord, Cord-Wrapped Stick, and Cord-Wrapped Paddle Constructions as Correlated with Juntunen Ceramic Types

Ceramic Type	No. of Vessels	Cord-Wrapped Stick		Cord-Wrapped Paddle			Cord-Wrapped Cord					
							two ply S-twist on:			two ply Z-twist on:		
		two ply, S-twist	two ply, Z-twist	two ply, S-twist	two ply, Z-twist	two ply S-twist	compound two ply, S-twist	compound two ply Z-twist	N.A.	two ply, Z-twist	two ply, S-twist	N.A.
MACKINAC												
Undecorated	35	7	3	—	—	—	—	1	1	2	—	1
Punctate	43	11	8	3	4	4	—	—	1	1	—	—
Cord-Impressed	56	8	2	—	—	6	1	—	4	1	1	—
Banded	49	6	4	—	—	3	—	1	8	1	—	—
Mackinac Subtotal	183	32	17	3	4	13	1	2	14	4	1	1
BLACKDUCK												
Banded	9	3	5	—	—	—	—	—	—	—	—	1
BOIS BLANC												
Braced Rim	6	1	2	—	—	1	—	—	1	—	—	—
Beaded Rim	9	5	—	—	—	—	—	—	1	—	—	—
Castellated Corded	13	3	2	—	1	—	—	—	1	—	—	1
Bois Blanc Subtotal	28	9	4	—	1	1	—	—	3	—	—	1
JUNTUNEN												
Drag and Jab	2	2	—	—	—	—	—	—	—	—	—	—
TOTAL	222	46	26	3	5	14	1	2	17	4	1	3

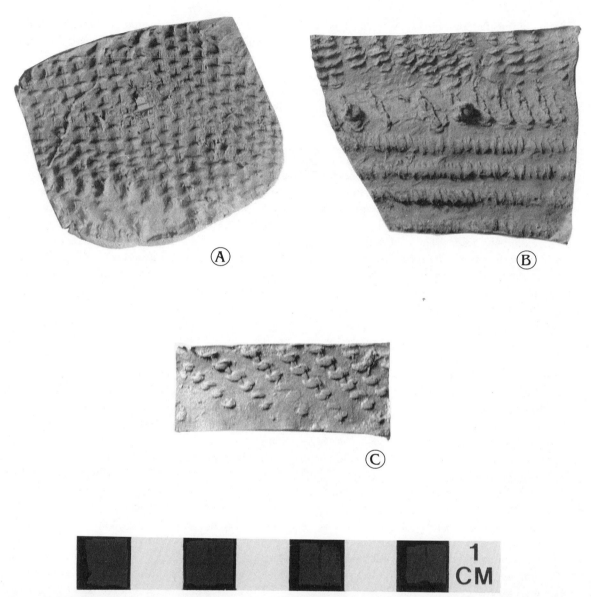

Figure 7.7. Positive cord-wrapped cord and cord-wrapped stick complex construction casts from the Juntunen site: A) cord-wrapped stick, two ply, S-spun, Z-twist cordage; B) cord-wrapped stick, two ply, Z-spun, S-twist cordage; C) cord-wrapped cord, two ply, S-spun, Z-twist cordage around two ply, S-spun, Z-twist cordage.

rigid elements, however, were likely manufactured specifically for use as tools for decoration of the ceramics. The reconstructed array of the composite constructions, again for use as tools for decoration, reflects a high degree of competency among the craftsmen and an unusual latitude in their manipulations of cordage and foundation types (e.g., Figure 7.4).

The netting and some of the open-twined specimens may well have been manufactured for use as fish nets, which were also stretched and applied to ceramics during the processes of surface finish and/or decoration. Other open-twined and close-twined specimens may have been manufactured as fabrics or basketry. The fineness of the elements and the obvious flexibility in many cases suggests that they were fabrics, as clearly reflected by the few extant specimens which may represent one or more bags (see Figure 7.3). Still other close-twined specimens were seemingly less flexible, with rigid warps and elements of larger size. These may have functioned primarily as semi-flexible basketry containers or mats.

In all cases, the raw materials employed in manufacture remain unknown. Various vegetal fibers were undoubtedly employed, processed by a combination of retting and spinning into a variety of elements, again as clearly exemplified in the several extant specimens. The well-developed and diversified nature of these processes is readily apparent in the available sample. The overall complexity of the fiber industries suggests a long antecedent development prior to their earliest representation at the Juntunen site.

Notably, the frequencies of cordage twists and twining weft slants exhibited in the available sample of Juntunen cordage, netting, complex cordage constructions, and twining are somewhat enigmatic since elsewhere most assemblages of fiber artifacts from a particular site and limited temporal span reflect a clear preference for either S-twist or Z-twist/weft slant constructions (see Johnson this volume; Maslowski this volume; and Petersen [chapter 1] this volume for extended discussion). Although such a preference can be, in fact, elucidated for the Juntunen fiber industries, this only pertains to the cordage, netting, and complex cordage construction, while the twining shows a contrary admixture.

The frequencies of the simple two ply cordage specimens are balanced, with final S-twist (n = 23) and final Z-twist (n = 25) nearly even among the analyzed specimens. However, the compound two ply specimens show a strong preference for a final Z-twist (n = 57) relative to a final S-twist (n = 11). In each case, these represent doubled two ply cordage, however, with the compound two ply, Z-twist specimens consisting of doubled two ply, S-twist specimens, for example. Thus, consideration of merely the *final* cordage twist regardless of ply structure reveals that S-twist (n = 35) is dominated by Z-twist

(n = 92). In reality, recognition of the basic two ply structure inherent in the sample indicates that the cordage is actually composed of predominant S-twist based structures (n = 80) relative to Z-twist based structures (n = 47). A fundamental preference for a basic S-twist structure is therefore recognizable.

Examination of the complex cordage constructions shows the same basic preference for two ply, S-twist cordage. Of the outer wrapped cordage among the cord-wrapped cord specimens, two ply, S-twist structures (n = 33) clearly predominate over Z-twist structures (n = 8). Among the cord-wrapped cord foundations, the basic structures show the same preference for two ply, S-twist (n = 16) over Z-twist (n = 5) structures, where this attribute could be determined. Likewise, among the cord-wrapped stick specimens, S-twist structures (n = 46) dominate Z-twist structures (n = 26). The cord-wrapped paddle specimens show a different preference, with S-twist structures (n = 3) slightly dominated by Z-twist structures (n = 5). However, the small number of specimens in this latter category renders this distinction inconclusive.

In contrast to the preference for basic S-twist configurations among the cordage and composite constructions, the twining structures show a precisely even mixture of final S-weft slants (n = 45) and Z-weft slants (n = 45), while the two examples of knotted netting were both constructed of two ply, S-twist cordage. The even mixture of the twining weft slants is not easily explainable on the basis of structure alone. Most twining samples typically demonstrate a preference for either an S-weft slant or a Z-weft slant, not a mixture as evident here.

Thus, the available data for cordage twists and twining weft slants at the Juntunen site do not precisely conform to expectations about such attributes. While the cordage shows a clear preference for S-twist structures when the basic two ply constructions are examined, the twining weft slants show no preference on the basis of available data. Thus, it is possible that several distinctive populations were responsible for the manufacture of the Juntunen fiber industries and, by extension, for the ceramics on which they are preserved.

External Correlations

The Juntunen site ceramics exhibit a variety of external relationships both within and beyond the Upper Great Lakes region. Unfortunately, relatively little research has been devoted to fiber industries in the Upper Great Lakes and broader northeastern North America in general, making correlations on this basis tenuous. Thus, emphasis must be given to comparison of the ceramics rather than strictly to the associated fiber industries for delineation of their external correlations.

As first reported by McPherron (1967a), the external relationships of the Mackinac phase ceramics, or Mackinac ware (Map 7.1), include similarities with Heins Creek ware of the Door Peninsula of Wisconsin (Mason 1966), Madison ware of the Effigy Mound tradition of central Wisconsin (Hurley 1975), ceramics of the Early Lakes phase of northwestern Wisconsin (Brose 1978; Salzer 1974), and Blackduck ceramics of adjoining portions of the Upper Great Lakes (Anfinson 1979; Evans 1961; Lugenbeal 1978; MacNeish 1958). A number of sherds, morphologically identical with Blackduck ware ceramics but having some physical characteristics of the other associated wares, were recovered from the Juntunen site, suggesting some sort of social interaction between Mackinac and Blackduck populations or, less likely, distinct occupations of the site by these different populations. Mackinac ware has been most closely associated with these various western wares (e.g., Brose 1978; Fitting 1970:185; McPherron 1967a:269–275).

This broad variability, well represented in ceramics (and associated fiber industries) from the Juntunen site, has long been recognized in ceramic samples all across the Upper Great Lakes (e.g., Brose 1978; Dawson 1977, 1979; Mason 1981; Wright 1966a, 1969, 1972). Wright (1966a:88) has specifically suggested: "The association of two or more ceramic complexes in a single occupation level appears to be a general characteristic of Late Woodland sites along . . . Lake Superior and is expressive, perhaps, of the mobility of the sparse nomadic population that occupied the area."

Other less closely related but contemporaneous wares with the Mackinac phase materials include ceramics of the Allegan, Spring Creek, and Wayne traditions in the Lake Erie and Lake Michigan drainage basins (Brashler 1981; Fitting 1965; Prahl, Brose, and Stothers 1976; Stothers and Pratt 1981), and the late Point Peninsula and subsequent Owasco tradition in southern Ontario and New York (Ritchie 1965; Ritchie and Funk 1973). In point of fact, many northeastern ceramics exhibit general similarities during the period A.D. 500 to A.D. 1400, and later. Certain vessel forms and the common use of fiber perishables for surface finish and decoration of ceramics are characteristic within the context of regionally diversifying cultural systems during this period (e.g., Fitting 1978:52; Mason 1981:298–299; McPherron 1967a:276; Petersen and Power 1983:407–455).

Well-studied fiber industries of any time period are *extremely* rare in the Northeast in general and in the broad Great Lakes region in particular. Fiber artifacts attributable to the Late Archaic or Early Woodland and Middle Woodland periods are known in the Great Lakes (e.g., Bisbing and Martin 1993; Hurley 1975; King 1968). Samples attributable to the Effigy Mound tradition in Wisconsin, ca. A.D. 200–1100, are particularly relevant to the Upper Great Lakes materials from the Juntunen site. A wide variety of fiber perishables have been reconstructed by Hurley (1974, 1975, 1979) from Madison ware ceramics, including types similar to those from the Juntunen site.

Elsewhere in the broad Northeast, a small number of actual fiber specimens have been recovered, mostly from late prehistoric and early historic contexts (Heckenberger and others this volume; Kenyon 1982; Michels and Smith 1967; Ritchie 1965). Still other fiber industries have been reconstructed from clay and ceramic negative impressions which span the last 2500–3000 years of prehistory (e.g., Adovasio 1982; Adovasio and Andrews [with Carlisle] 1980; Petersen and Power 1983:183–196). Fiber industries also have been reconstructed using samples derived from the margin of the Great Plains to the west (e.g., Nicholson 1990; Rachlin 1960; Reid and Rajnovich 1980). None of these latter fiber

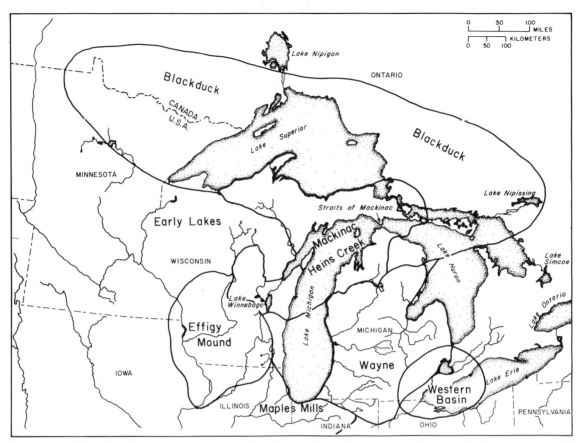

Map 7.1. Early Late Woodland cultural manifestations in the Upper Great Lakes region. (After Brose 1978:Figure 2a.)

assemblages *apparently* matches the complexity of the Juntunen and Effigy Mound samples, however, at least in terms of combinations of cordage and twining elements used for decoration and surface finish of ceramics. Moreover, the Juntunen and Effigy Mound samples are apparently distinctive relative to each other, as well as other regional samples on the basis of available information.

The relationships of the later Bois Blanc and Juntunen phase ceramics and associated fiber industries are widespread across the Upper Great Lakes (Map 7.2). Continued evidence of contact with Blackduck ceramic-using populations is notable in the Bois Blanc phase, as are possible linkages to Glen Meyer and Pickering phase populations of Ontario and contemporaneous groups in Wisconsin (Brose 1978; Mason 1981; McPherron 1967a, 1967b; Wright 1966b).

Regional diversification as recognized by ceramic styles is still more evident by the time of the final Juntunen phase at the Juntunen site, although widespread contacts apparently persisted. Direct evidence of these contacts is documented by the presence of Middle Mississippian (Ramey Incised type) and Oneota ceramics in association with Juntunen phase deposits, as well as ceramics with close relationships to Mero ceramics of Wisconsin and Uren-Middleport Middle Ontario Iroquois ceramics (Brose 1978; Mason 1981; Wright 1966b). In point of fact, McPherron (1967a:279, 1967b) has hypothesized a shift from primarily westerly contacts during the earlier phases to closer relations with Iroquoians during the later Juntunen phase.

A recent ceramic compositional analysis using neutron activation was designed to test the apparent heterogeneity of Late Woodland period ceram-

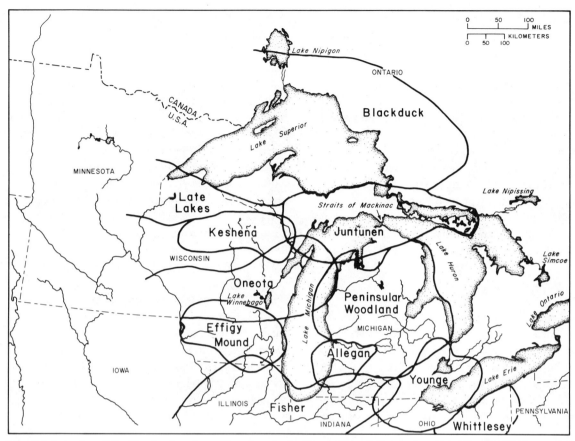

Map 7.2. Later Late Woodland cultural manifestations in the Upper Great Lakes region. (After Brose 1978:Figure 2b.)

ics in the Upper Great Lakes (Clark et al. 1992). Using a substantial sample of ceramics, including some from the Juntunen site, and geological clay samples, this analysis clearly established reference groups which "probably represent source zones rather than localized sources" for clay and temper materials. These groups generally reflect regionally distinctive ceramics, but also show broad-scale regional transport of ceramics, specifically including Straits of Mackinac Juntunen-related specimens, in various portions of the Lake Superior basin during late prehistory (Clark et al. 1992:263–265). Thus, a combination of local manufacture and regional transport may help account for the heterogeneity inherent in Late Woodland period ceramics in the Upper Great Lakes and, by extension, the fiber industries preserved as impressions on them.

In summary, fiber perishables employed as implements of decoration and surface finish on ceramics from the Juntunen site provide evidence of rather diverse fiber industries in this portion of the Upper Great Lakes during the Late Woodland period. Although incompletely analyzed and reported in most areas, the *Juntunen* fiber industries seem *generally* related to other contemporaneous specimens in the Northeast, but the Juntunen and Effigy Mound samples are apparently more complex than most other known fiber industries in the broad region. Moreover, the available samples provide data for a hitherto largely ignored form of material culture. The specific forms from the Juntunen site seemingly document that local craftspeople in the Straits of Mackinac area developed their own distinctive fiber industries in relation to other contemporaneous Late Woodland forms in the Upper Great Lakes.

Like the better understood ceramics on which they were preserved, the Juntunen fiber industries may be reflective of one or more related ethnic groups on the basis of the available data. These data suggest that a combination of local development *and* regional exchange and contact probably best accounts for the distribution of ceramics and associated fiber industries preserved thereon in the Upper Great Lakes (cf. Dawson 1977, 1979). Future research should be designed to correct the apparent bias against fiber industries and the data derived from them can be used then to help reconstruct regional prehistory. Broader anthropological issues concerning style and ethnicity inherent in material culture may be addressed then as well.

ACKNOWLEDGMENTS

Analysis of fiber industries from the Juntunen site has been facilitated by individuals at the University of Michigan, the University of Pittsburgh, and elsewhere. Richard Ford, director, and Michael Shott, then a research assistant, of the Museum of Anthropology, University of Michigan, kindly provided initial access to the collections and were patient in permitting an extended period of study. James M. Adovasio, then at the University of Pittsburgh, likewise provided critical assistance in the transport of the collections, as well as analytical advice. Jennifer Manifold, Karen Martin, Jack Wolford, Diana Thornton, and Jerry Corvino, all then students in the Department of Anthropology, University of Pittsburgh, undertook a variety of tasks which further aided our efforts. Thomas Bennett, Debbie Cutten, and John Mosher, graduate and undergraduate students at the University of Southern Maine, assisted with final production of this chapter, as did Shirley Thompson at the University of Maine at Farmington (UMF). Also at UMF, Belinda Cox drafted the two accompanying maps and Fred Dearnley produced some of the photographs.

Dwight Wallace offered a valuable critique of an earlier draft of this chapter. Hamilton and Petersen also acknowledge the support of James B. Richardson III, chief curator, Section of Anthropology, Carnegie Museum of Natural History, and Rea postdoctoral fellowships which made preparation and presentation of the first draft of this chapter possible. While sincere thanks are extended to each of these individuals, the authors accept full responsibility for any errors or omissions in this preliminary report.

APPENDIX 1. JUNTUNEN CERAMIC ANALYSIS CODING KEY

Attributes

Vessel Id No. (0001, 0002, etc.)   Phase (Mackinac = 1, Juntunen = 2, Bois Blanc = 3)   No. of sherds (001, 002, etc.)

Vessel Portion

01 = whole vessel
02 = rim & collar & castellation
03 = rim & collar
04 = rim & neck & shoulder & body
05 = rim & castellation
06 = rim & neck
07 = rim & shoulder
08 = rim & body
09 = neck
10 = neck & shoulder
11 = neck & body
12 = shoulder
13 = shoulder & body
14 = body
15 = base
16 = unknown

Continued on next page

Exterior Surface Finish	01 = smoothed
	02 = wiped
	03 = scraped
	04 = twined
	05 = cord-paddled
	06 = cord-rolled
	07 = other

Lip Surface Finish (As Above)
Interior Surface Finish (As Above)

Lip Form	01 = square
	02 = round
	03 = pointed
	04 = thickened
	05 = other

Lip or Rim Modification	01 = none
	02 = notched
	03 = scalloped
	04 = castellated
	05 = collared
	06 = other

Rim Eversion	01 = incurvate
	02 = straight
	03 = slight excurvate
	04 = moderate excurvate
	05 = severe excurvate
	06 = other

Vessel Form
Maximum Lip Thickness (in mm) (e.g., 01.15 = 1.15mm)
Maximum Thickness 1 cm below Lip (in mm) __.__
Maximum Neck Thickness (in mm) __.__
Maximum Body Thickness (in mm) __.__
Maximum Collar Thickness (in mm) __.__
Maximum Oral Diameter (in cm) __.__
Maximum Vessel Height (in cm) __.__

Carbon Deposits	01 = present
	02 = absent

Repair Hole	01 = present
	02 = absent

Manufacture Technique	01 = unknown
	02 = coiled
	03 = modeled
	04 = slab
	05 = other

Continued on next page

Temper Type
Maximum Temper Size (in mm) __.__
Minimum Temper Size (in mm) __.__
Temper Percentage ____%
Texture
Hardness
Exterior Color
Core Color
Interior Color

APPENDIX 2. JUNTUNEN FIBER PERISHABLE CODING KEY

Vessel Id. No. (0001, 0002, etc.)

Decoration/Surface Finish	01 = Decoration
	02 = Surface Finish
Location of Decoration	01 = Interior
(Pick One)	02 = Lip
	03 = Exterior
Type of Decoration	01 = Cordage
(Pick One)	02 = Cord-Wrapped Stick
	03 = Cord-Wrapped Cordage
	04 = Fabric/Basketry
	05 = Punctate
	06 = Other
Technique of Application	01 = Simple Stamped/Impressed
	02 = Drag Stamped
	03 = Paddled
	04 = Other

Design Sequence
First Design Unit
(Motif and Type)

01 = Right Oblique CWS
02 = Left Oblique CWS
03 = Horizontal CWS
04 = Vertical CWS
05 = Other CWS
06 = Right Oblique CWC
07 = Left Oblique CWC
08 = Horizontal CWC
09 = Vertical CWC
10 = Other CWC
11 = Right Oblique Cordage

Continued on next page

	12 = Left Oblique Cordage
	13 = Horizontal Cordage
	14 = Vertical Cordage
	15 = Other Cordage
	16 = Right Oblique Punctate
	17 = Left Oblique Punctate
	18 = Horizontal Punctate
	19 = Vertical Punctate
	20 = Other Punctate
	21–99 = Other combinations as necessary
Second Design Unit	Same as Above
Third Design Unit	Same as Above
Fourth Design Unit	Same as Above
Fifth Design Unit	Same as Above
Maximum Extent of Decoration (mm) (i.e., __.__)	0000 = Not available

Punctation

Punctate Shape	01 = Round
	02 = Rectangular
	03 = Elongate Rectangular
	04 = Irregular Rectangular
	05 = Crescent
	06 = Other
Punctate Type	01 = "Stick"
	02 = Split Wood
	03 = Fingernail
	04 = Carved Wood
	05 = Other
Maximum Punctate Length (mm) (i.e., __.__)	
Maximum Punctate width (mm) (i.e., __.__)	

Cordage

Cordage Use	01 = Simple
	02 = Complex Outer
	03 = Complex Foundation
	04 = Weft
	05 = Warp
Cordage Structural Type	01 = Two Ply, S-spun, Z-twist
	02 = Two Ply, Z-spun, S-twist
	03 = Three Ply, S-spun, Z-twist
	04 = Three Ply, Z-spun, S-twist
	05 = Compound Two Ply, S-spun, Z-twist
	06 = Compound Two Ply, Z-spun, Z-twist
	07 = Compound Two Ply, Z-spun, S-twist
	08 = Compound Two Ply, S-spun, S-twist
	09–99 = Other combinations as necessary

Continued on next page

Maximum Cordage Diameter (mm) (i.e., __.__)
Angle of Twist (in degrees) (i.e., __.__)
Segments/0.5 cm (i.e., __.__)

Complex Combination

Structural Type	01 = CWStick
	02 = CWCordage
	03 = CWPaddle

Maximum Foundation Diameter (mm) (i.e., __.__)
Wraps/1 cm) (__.__)
Maximum Element Diameter (mm) (i.e., __.__)

Basketry/Fabric

Structural Type	01 = Close Simple Twining
	02 = Open Simple Twining
	03–99 = Other combinations as necessary
Portion	01 = Body Fragment
	02 = Unknown Selvage
	03 = Side Selvage
	04 = End Selvage
	05 = Other
Wear	01 = Present
	02 = Not Present
Weft Type	01 = Single Strand Z-twist
	02 = Single Strand S-twist
	03 = Two Ply, Z-twist
	04 = Two Ply, S-twist

Maximum Weft Diameter (mm) (i.e., __.__)
Wefts/1 cm (i.e., __.__)

Warp Type	01 = Single Ply Z-twist
	02 = Single Ply S-twist
	03 = Two Ply, Z-twist
	04 = Two Ply, S-twist

Maximum Warp Diameter (mm) (i.e., __.__)
Warp/1 cm (i.e., __.__)

REFERENCES CITED

Adovasio, J. M.
1977 *Basketry Technology: A Guide to Identification and Analysis.* Aldine, Chicago.
1982 Basketry and Netting Impressions. In *The Prehistory of the Paintsville Reservoir, Johnson and Morgan Counties, Kentucky,* compiled by J. M. Adovasio, pp. 830–844. Ethnology Monographs 6. Dept. of Anthropology, Univ. of Pittsburgh, Pittsburgh.

Adovasio, J. M., and R. L. Andrews (with R. C. Carlisle)
1980 Basketry, Cordage and Bark Impressions from the Northern Thorn Mound (46Mg78), Monongalia County, West Virginia. *West Virginia Archeologist* 30:33–72.

Andrews, R. L., and J. M. Adovasio
1980 *Perishable Industries from Hinds Cave, Val Verde County, Texas.* Ethnology Monographs 5. Dept. of Anthropology, Univ. of Pittsburgh, Pittsburgh.

Anfinson, Scott (editor)
1979 *A Handbook of Minnesota Prehistoric Ceramics.* Occasional Publications in Minnesota Anthropology 5. Minnesota Archaeological Society, Fort Snelling.

Bisbing, Richard, and Susan Martin
1993 Analysis of Fibers and Textiles from 20KE20. *The Michigan Archaeologist* 39(3–4):170–174.

Brashler, Janet G.
1981 *Early Late Woodland Boundaries and Interaction: Indian Ceramics of Southern Lower Michigan.* Publications of the Museum, Anthropological Series 3(3). Michigan State Univ., East Lansing.

Brose, David S.
1978 Late Prehistory of the Upper Great Lakes Area. In *Northeast,* edited by Bruce G. Trigger, pp. 569–593. Handbook of North American Indians, vol. 15, William G. Sturtevant, general editor. Smithsonian Institution, Washington, D.C.

Clark, Caven P., Hector Neff, and Michael D. Glascock
1992 Neutron Activation Analysis of Late Woodland Ceramics from the Lake Superior Basin. In *Chemical Characterization of Ceramic Pastes in Archaeology,* edited by Hector Neff, pp. 255–267. Prehistory Press Monographs in World Archaeology 7. Madison.

Cleland, Charles E.
1966 *The Prehistoric Animal Ecology and Ethnozoology of the Upper Great Lakes Region.* Anthropological Papers 24. Museum of Anthropology, Univ. of Michigan, Ann Arbor.

Dawson, Kenneth C. A.
1977 An Application of the Direct Historical Approach to the Algonkians of Northern Ontario. *Canadian Journal of Archaeology* 1:151–181.
1979 Algonkian Huron-Petun Ceramics in Northern Ontario. *Man in the Northeast* 18:14–31.

Emery, Irene
1980 *The Primary Structure of Fabrics: An Illustrated Classification.* The Textile Museum, Washington, D.C.

Evans, G. E.
1961 Prehistoric Blackduck-Historic Assinboine: A Reassessment. *Plains Anthropologist* 6(14):271–275.

Finlayson, William D.
1977 *The Saugeen Culture.* Archaeological Survey of Canada Paper 61. National Museum of Man Mercury Series. Ottawa.

Fitting, James E.
1965 *Late Woodland Cultures of Southeastern Michigan.* Anthropological Papers 24. Museum of Anthropology, Univ. of Michigan, Ann Arbor.
1970 *The Archaeology of Michigan.* Natural History Press, Garden City.
1976 Patterns of Acculturation at the Straits of Mackinac. In *Culture Change and Continuity: Essays in Honor of James Bennett Griffin,* edited by Charles E. Cleland, pp. 321–344. Academic Press, New York.
1978 Regional Cultural Development, 300 B.C to A.D. 1000. In *Northeast,* edited by Bruce G. Trigger, pp. 28–43. Handbook of North American Indians, vol. 15, William G. Sturtevant, general editor. Smithsonian Institution, Washington, D.C.

Hamilton, Nathan D., and David R. Yesner
1985 Early, Middle and Late Woodland Ceramic Assemblages from the Great Diamond Island Site, Casco Bay, Maine. In *Ceramic Analyses in the Northeast: Contributions to Methodology and Culture History,* edited by James B. Petersen, pp. 39–72. Occasional Publications in Northeastern Anthropology 9(2).

Hurley, William M.
1974 *Silver Creek Woodland Sites, Southwestern Wisconsin.* Office of the State Archaeologist Report 6. Univ. of Iowa, Iowa City.
1975 *An Analysis of Effigy Mound Complexes in Wisconsin.* Anthropological Papers 59. Museum of Anthropology, Univ. of Michigan, Ann Arbor.
1979 *Prehistoric Cordage: Identification of Impressions on Pottery.* Taraxacum, Washington, D.C.

Kenyon, W. A.

1982   *The Grimsby Site, A Historic Neutral Cemetery.* Royal Ontario Museum, Toronto.

King, Mary E.

1968   Textile Fragments from the Riverside Site, Menominee, Michigan. *Verhandlungen des XXXVIII Internationalen Amerikanistenkongresses,* pp. 117–123.

Lugenbeal, Edward

1978   The Blackduck Ceramics of the Smith Site (21KC3) and Their Implications for the History of Blackduck Ceramics and Culture in Northern Minnesota. *Midcontinental Journal of Archaeology* 3(1):45–68.

MacNeish, Richard S.

1958   *An Introduction to the Archaeology of Southeast Manitoba.* National Museum of Canada Bulletin 157. Ottawa.

Mason, Ronald J.

1966   *Two Stratified Sites on the Door Peninsula of Wisconsin.* Anthropological Papers 26. Museum of Anthropology, Univ. of Michigan, Ann Arbor.

1981   *Great Lakes Archaeology.* Academic Press, New York.

McPherron, Alan L.

1967a   *The Juntunen Site and the Late Woodland Prehistory of the Upper Great Lakes.* Anthropological Papers 30. Museum of Anthropology, Univ. of Michigan, Ann Arbor.

1967b   On the Sociology of Ceramics: Pottery Style Clustering, Marital Residence, and Cultural Adaptations on an Algonkian–Iroquoian Border. In *Iroquois Culture, History, and Prehistory: Proceedings of the 1965 Conference on Iroquois Research,* edited by Elizabeth Tooker, pp. 101–107. New York State Museum and Science Service, Albany.

Michels, Joseph W., and Ira F. Smith (editors)

1967   *Archaeological Investigations of Sheep Rock Shelter, Huntingdon County, Pennsylvania.* Dept. of Anthropology, Pennsylvania State Univ., Univ. Park.

Nicholson, B. A.

1990   Ceramic Affiliation and the Case for Incipient Horticulture in Southwestern Manitoba. *Canadian Journal of Archaeology* 14:33–59.

Noble, Vergil E.

1983   In Dire Straits: Subsistence Patterns at Mackinac. *The Michigan Archaeologist* 29(3):29–48.

Pendergast, James F.

1973   *The Roebuck Prehistoric Village Site Rim Sherds—An Analysis.* Archaeological Survey of Canada Paper 8. National Museum of Man Mercury Series. Ottawa.

Petersen, James B.

1985   Ceramic Analysis in the Northeast: Resume and Prospect. In *Ceramic Analysis in the Northeast: Contributions to Methodology and Culture History,* edited by James B. Petersen, pp. 1–25. Occasional Publications in Northeast Anthropology 9(2).

Petersen, James B., Nathan D. Hamilton, James M. Adovasio, and Alan M. McPherron

1984   Netting Technology and the Antiquity of Fish Exploitation in Eastern North America. *Midcontinental Journal of Archaeology* 9(2):199–225.

Petersen, James B., and Marjory W. Power

1983   *The Winooski Site and the Middle Woodland Period in the Northeast.* Dept. of Anthropology, Univ. of Vermont. Submitted to Interagency Archeological Services, Mid-Atlantic Region, National Park Service, Philadelphia.

Prahl, Earl, David Brose, and David Stothers

1976   A Preliminary Synthesis of Late Prehistoric Phenomena in the Western Basin of Lake Erie. In *The Late Prehistory of the Lake Erie Drainage Basin,* edited by David Brose, pp. 251–282. Cleveland Museum of Natural History, Cleveland.

Rachlin, Carol K.

1960   The Historic Position of the Proto-Cree Textiles in the Eastern Fabric Complex, An Ethnological-Archaeological Correlation. *National Museum of Canada Bulletin* 167:80–89. Ottawa.

Ramsden, Peter G.

1977   *Refinement of Some Aspects of Huron Ceramic Analysis.* Archaeological Survey of Canada Paper 63. National Museum of Man Mercury Series. Ottawa.

Reid, C. S., and Grace Rajnovich

1980   Ash Rapids Corded: Newly Defined Late Woodland Ceramics from Northwestern Ontario. *Ontario Archaeology* 34:69–86.

Ritchie, William A.

1965   *The Archaeology of New York State.* Natural History Press, Garden City.

Ritchie, William A., and Robert E. Funk

1973   *Aboriginal Settlement Patterns in the Northeast.* New York State Museum and Science Service Memoir 20. Albany.

Salzer, Ronald J.

1974   The Wisconsin North Lakes Project: A Preliminary Report. In *Aspects of Upper Great Lakes Anthropology,* edited by Elden Johnson, pp. 40–54. Minnesota Archaeology Series II. Minnesota Historical Society, St. Paul.

Scholtz, Sandra Clements
1975   *Prehistoric Plies: A Structural and Comparative Analysis of Cordage, Netting, Basketry, and Fabric from Ozark Bluff Shelters.* Arkansas Archeological Survey Research Series 9. Univ. of Arkansas Museum, Fayetteville.

Stothers, David M.
1977   *The Princess Point Complex.* Archaeological Survey of Canada Paper 58. National Museum of Man Mercury Series. Ottawa.

Stothers, David M., and Gordon M. Pratt
1981   New Perspectives on the Late Woodland Cultures of the Western Lake Erie Region. *Midcontinental Journal of Archaeology* 6(1):91–121.

Wright, James V.
1966a The Pic River Site. *National Museum of Canada Bulletin* 206:54–99. Ottawa.
1966b *The Ontario Iroquois Tradition.* National Museum of Canada Bulletin 210. Ottawa.
1967   *The Laurel Tradition and the Middle Woodland Period.* National Museum of Canada Bulletin 217. Ottawa.
1969   Michipicoten Site. *National Museum of Canada Bulletin* 224:1–85. Ottawa.
1972   *Ontario Prehistory: An Eleven-Thousand-Year Archaeological Outline.* National Museums of Canada, Ottawa.
1980   The Role of Attribute Analysis in the Study of Iroquois Prehistory. In *Proceedings of the 1979 Iroquois Pottery Conference*, edited by Charles F. Hayes, pp. 21–26. Rochester Museum and Science Center Research Reports 13. Rochester.

Wright, James V., and James E. Anderson
1963   *The Donaldson Site.* National Museum of Canada Bulletin 184. Ottawa.

Yarnell, Richard A.
1964   *Aboriginal Relationships Between Culture and Plant Life in the Upper Great Lakes Region.* Anthropological Papers 23. Museum of Anthropology, Univ. of Michigan, Ann Arbor.

8

William C. Johnson

A New Twist to an Old Tale:

Analysis of Cordage Impressions on Late Woodland

Ceramics from the Potomac River Valley

In the Middle Atlantic region, researchers have postulated that the Potomac Creek complex represents a Late Woodland period intrusion of Montgomery complex people into the Potomac River Coastal Plain physiographic province at ca. A.D. 1350 or earlier. This study presents cordage twist data from the Potomac River Valley to enable testing of the presumed continuity between the Potomac and Montgomery complexes. Cordage impressions are examined as preserved on ceramics of the Potomac Creek Cord Impressed type[1] from the Patawomeke site in the Coastal Plain province and the Shepard Cord Marked type from five Montgomery complex sites in the Potomac River Piedmont and Ridge and Valley provinces.

Karl A. Schmitt (1952:68) was the first archaeologist to propose a relationship between Potomac Creek Cord Impressed ware from the Patawomeke site (44St2), located adjacent to the Potomac River estuary on Potomac Creek in Stafford County, Virginia, and Shepard Cord Marked ceramics, the pri-

mary diagnostic artifact of sites assigned to the Montgomery (focus) complex, ca. A.D. 1150–1350. The Montgomery complex villages and hamlets are situated upstream from the Patawomeke site, above the Fall Line, along the main stem of the Potomac River and the lower reaches of its major tributaries in the Piedmont and Ridge and Valley provinces of Maryland and Virginia (Map 8.1).

In 1944, Schmitt (1952, 1965:30) originally suggested that Potomac Creek Cord Impressed and Shepard Cord Marked ceramics might be related as the result of an intrusion of Montgomery complex people into the Coastal Plain province of the Potomac River Estuary from the Piedmont province, rather than as an example of the simple diffusion of ceramic styles and technology. This migration was seen as the result of military pressure, perhaps a reaction to Iroquois political influence or actual incursions late during the Late Woodland period, resulting in a coalescence of the Montgomery population in the Tidewater area and the construction of

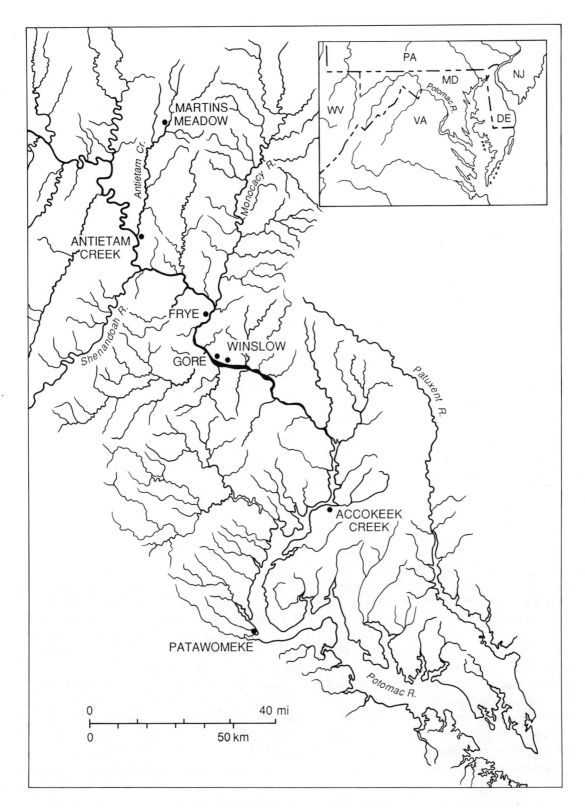

Map 8.1. Location of select archaeological sites in the Potomac River drainage.

large palisaded villages there. The resultant, possibly intrusive manifestation was defined as the Potomac Creek (focus) complex, ca. A.D. 1300–1650 or later, with the Patawomeke site as its type station. This theme has been subsequently reiterated by Howard MacCord (MacCord et al. 1957:25, 28), John Witthoft (1963:65–67), Richard Slattery and Douglas Woodward (1992:157–158), and most comprehensively by Wayne Clark (1980), among others.

Most recently, MacCord (1984; Manson and MacCord 1985) reported an analysis of the distribution of selected ceramic attributes and other artifacts derived from Carl Manson's and his own excavations in the deep midden associated with the stockade at the Patawomeke site. Manson excavated two ten-foot squares by natural levels and arbitrary six-inch increments within natural levels below the plow sole in 1957. MacCord's stratigraphic testing in 1983, four five-foot square units, also followed natural strata, but maintained tighter stratigraphic control; the midden was removed in two-inch levels (MacCord 1984:12). MacCord (1984:13–15, Tables 1–4; Manson and MacCord 1985:20, 38, Tables 2 and 8) presented select ceramic attributes derived from both excavations at Patawomeke by relative percentages of temper clast size and by type and frequency of chronologically sensitive vessel lip and rim profile modes.

These data generally indicate a temporal shift away from ceramic attributes characteristic of the Shepard Cord Marked type toward those more diagnostic of Potomac Creek Cord Impressed type at the Patawomeke site. MacCord has argued that these time/stratigraphic trends suggest a gradual evolution from the specific ceramic technological and stylistic attributes of the Montgomery complex to a new combination of attributes peculiar to ceramics of the Potomac Creek complex.

In light of these suggestions, the final twist direction for cordage preserved on ceramics from MacCord's testing at Patawomeke has been studied. Two issues are addressed in this study: 1) the degree of similarity between Shepard Cord Marked and Potomac Creek Cord Impressed ceramics and, therefore, the synonymy of the two populations of potters; and 2) the degree of certainty that the Potomac

Creek complex was indeed intrusive into the Tidewater Potomac River area. The Patawomeke cordage sample has been compared to cordage on ceramics from five sites of the Montgomery complex in the Potomac River Piedmont and Ridge and Valley provinces. These five sites include Winslow (18Mo9), Gore (18Mo20), Frye (44Ld10), Martins Meadow (18Wa23), and Antietam Creek (18Wa62) (see Map 8.1).

RESEARCH BACKGROUND

Cordage manufacture is one of the oldest perishable technologies documented in the archaeological record of North America. Cordage twist direction is a very stable attribute in textile technologies and was highly standardized and population specific among Native American groups. For example, Newton's (1974) study of two Gé-speaking Timbira tribes in central Brazil, the Krīkati and the Pukobye, demonstrates that these tribes retain distinct terms for one another, in spite of their temporary amalgamation in the 1920s, the close physical proximity of their villages, occasional intermarriage between them, and ongoing participation in each other's ceremonies. More importantly for the present research, the two tribes preserve distinct preferences in their manufacture of material culture and significantly, in their motor habits for hammock construction, the only item of native manufacture which both groups share. Although their hammocks are apparently similar in construction, the Krīkati favor counter twining, or alternating Z- and S-twined weft rows for construction of open simple twined mesh (OSS/Z) (78%), while the Pukobye prefer S-twist twining (58%) over counter twining (39%). More significantly, the Krīkati have a predilection for final Z-twist cordage production (68%), while the Pukobye favor predominantly final S-twist cordage production (64%) (Newton 1974:245–246, Tables 9.4 and 9.5).

Studies of dry cave and rockshelter sites in the Arid West, where extant and sometimes very large assemblages of perishables are preserved, have demonstrated that specific spin and twist patterns in cordage manufacture, as well as slant direction and splice and selvage techniques in basketry construction, are the results of highly standardized, culture-specific motor habits. These learned behavior patterns frequently demonstrate cultural continuity for considerable periods of time (e.g., Adovasio 1970, 1977, 1986a; Andrews and Adovasio 1980; Maslowski 1978). As Maslowski (1984:51, this volume) has argued, the motor habits involving the manufacture of cordage are learned at an early age by children from older family or group members and are transmitted from generation to generation within those same groups.

As modification in these basic motor habits generally has no adaptive value, they are more resistant to change than are predilections or behavior modes associated with other decorative, ceremonial, and subsistence-related technologies. In fact, most cultural groups probably are not fully conscious of the results of their patterned habits of cordage manufacture and the associated initial spin and final twist direction of the cords they produce. Newton (1974:238), in regard to the Krīkati and Pukobye, has similarly noted that "although individuals may change their location, they do not erase the cultural learning that has taken place during the first fifteen years of life."

Reversal of the prevailing cordage twist pattern in the archaeological record of a particular geographic or culture area signals either population replacement by a group with a different cordage production tradition or a major technological innovation, perhaps the introduction of a new raw material source for cord fibers, for example. A new raw material might be processed using a different manufacturing technique, such as the employment of a spindle, thus producing cordage which potentially exhibits the opposite twist. This latter scenario tentatively can be eliminated from case studies in the Eastern Woodlands since few, if any, examples of the use of a spindle are conclusively known ethnographically or archaeologically in the region. However, the fact that most ethnographic spindles are made from perishable materials, such as wood, may account for their absence in the regional archaeological record.

The presence of approximately equal frequencies of different final twists within a cordage sample may indicate population mixing, either by the influx of alien groups displaying different cordage manufacturing techniques or through proximity to a boundary between areas with different cordage and textile-manufacturing traditions. This scenario could result in a mixing of people through an agency such as marriage exchange, with an attendant blending of textile and other traditions. Finally, most cordage assemblages exhibit some minor variation in the prevailing twist pattern, probably due to handedness or to other idiosyncratic behavior manifested by the cordmakers.

Since the late 1960s, archaeologists have utilized cordage twist direction, along with other textile industry attributes, to demonstrate change or continuity within specific geographic areas in the Eastern Woodlands (e.g., Doyle et al. 1982; Johnson 1975, 1981:48, 1987a:534–536, 553–555, Tables 67 and 69; Johnson et al. 1989:20, 21, Table 6, Figure 5; Johnson and Speedy 1993; Maslowski 1973, 1984, this volume; Munson 1971:10–11; Petersen this volume; Petersen and Hamilton 1984; Winfree 1972). This is also the case in the Arid West (e.g., Adovasio 1985, 1986b; Andrews and Adovasio 1980:358–369; Andrews et al. 1988; Fry and Adovasio 1970; Maslowski 1978).

In the middle and upper Ohio River Valley, cordage twist direction, as preserved in negative impressions on aboriginal ceramics, is regularly reported in both published and unpublished site reports where it has become a standard concern. A large number of examples can be cited (e.g., Archaeological and Historical Consultants 1990:97; Boyce 1985:42; Dancey 1988:229; Fassler 1987:159; George 1983:29; George et al. 1990:50; Hemmings 1984:29; Henderson 1986:41, 1988:539, Table 12.2; Henderson and Pollack 1985:143, Table 1; Herbstritt 1981:36; Hughes and Kerr 1990:101–106; Johnson 1978:45, Table 6, 1982, 1987b:1021; Marwitt et al. 1986:12; Maslowski and Dawson 1980:21; Morton and Carskadden 1987:8; Moxley and Bloemker 1985:44, Table 4; NPW Consultants 1983:50, 70, 149, 161, Tables 6, 10, 24 and 28; Pollack and Henderson 1984:7; Railey 1984:74–75; R. Christopher Goodwin & Associates 1990: 89, Table 2; Seeman 1985:44, Table 4; Sharp and Turnbow 1987:143).

Closer to the present study area, Mounier (1974:34–35) noted the use of final S-twist cordage to wrap paddles used in construction of Union Lake Corded and Fralinger Corded ceramic wares along the tidal Maurice River in southernmost New Jersey. Egloff and Potter (1982:104) also recorded the association of S-twist cordage and Nomini Cord Marked ceramics in the Potomac River Estuary. Even earlier, Holland (1970:49–50, 55–56, 70) noted that particular cordage twists were associated with certain ceramic types, including Dan River Cordmarked, Grayson Cordmarked, Grayson Net and Knot Roughened, and Wythe Cordmarked in southwestern Virginia. Of further interest, Holland also recognized that the netting represented on Dan River Net Impressed ceramics was based on final S-twist cordage when derived from sites in the Piedmont province, but had a final Z-twist on comparable ceramics from Grayson and Floyd counties in the Ridge and Valley province of Virginia.

Holland's (1966:40) observation of a final Z-twist among cordage impressions on shell-tempered Keyser Cordmarked sherds from the Quicksburg site (44Sh3) is also potentially significant; located in the northern Shenandoah River Valley of Virginia, the Quicksburg site is attributable to the Luray complex. Herbstritt (1993) has recently indicated, however, that the twist direction on Keyser Cordmarked sherds from the Quicksburg site is final S, although the frequency and sample size were not presented. This report seemingly indicates that Holland recorded the cordage twist direction on sherds of Keyser Cordmarked and other Virginia wares as they appeared in the *negative* impressions on the sherds and *not* as the cordage would appear in the *positive*, as is the prevailing custom now in North America. Nonetheless, the distinction Holland recognized between different samples of Dan River Net Impressed ceramics still may well be valid.

Curry and Kavanagh (1991:7–8) have also commented on the differential association of Z-twist cordage with limestone-tempered Page ware and S-twist cordage with chert-tempered ceramics at the Brosius site (46Mn2), located on the Potomac River in the Ridge and Valley province of West Virginia. This observation was based on an analysis by Robert Maslowski.

In the Upper James River Estuary, Johnson and Speedy (1992) recently examined cordage impressions derived from late Middle Woodland period cord-marked and so-called "fabric-impressed" wares from three sites in Prince George County of southeastern Virginia. The cordage impressions displayed a predominant final S-twist across all three temper types and both surface finishes, suggesting population continuity in this area during the late Middle Woodland period. A final Z-twist was employed, however, in cordage used to plait together dowels which were utilized, in turn, to produce Late Woodland Townsend series ceramics at the same three sites, one of which is the historic location of Weyanoke Old Town. These data suggest a population replacement in this part of Prince George County sometime after the end of the Middle Woodland period at ca. A.D. 800.

Cordage impressions preserved on sherds of Potomac Creek Cord Impressed ceramics from the Patawomeke site have been previously analyzed by Falk (1983), although her analysis was limited to those represented as corded decoration on the sublips and collars of vessels. However, Falk, like Hurley (1979) and Wigglesworth (1986), treated the various cord-impressed designs as decoration per se and not as representations of other culture-specific attributes. Consequently, Falk (1983:19) only casually reported the cordage twist direction for Potomac Creek Cord Impressed ceramics and then only for specimens employed in direct cord-impressed decoration on rim sherds. She did not report the cordage twist direction for specimens used in the application of what she called "pseudo-cord-impressed" decoration, as displayed in the Patawomeke site rim sherd sample. Falk (1983:12, 14–15, 19) apparently felt that these specimens did not constitute two ply twisted elements, perhaps because she misinterpreted Hurley's (1979:5–6) definitions of cordage "bead" and "segment."

Falk (1983:3) did not observe any "bead" elements among the positive cordage casts for the "pseudo-cord-impressed" sherds. Therefore, she assumed that the fiber imprints in each "segment" of cordage among the "pseudo-cord-impressed" sherds were untwisted or unspun fibers. Beads, as defined by Hurley (1979:5), are present only in replied cordage, i.e., cords composed of multiple spun elements which are twisted together, usually opposite the direction of the initial spin, and then combined with similar cords and twisted together, again, in the opposite direction. Parenthetically, none of the cordage casts from the Potomac Creek Cord Impressed ceramics exhibited evidence of replied cords in the present study.

It was often difficult or impossible to determine the twist direction for the cordage used in application of the pseudo-cord decoration on the Potomac Creek Cord Impressed and Shepard Cord Marked ceramics analyzed herein. This problem is attributed to the fact that much of the cordage employed in this type of decoration had extremely fine diameters and was often loosely twisted. Not infrequently, these attributes produced only an incomplete series of isolated, parallel segments along the edge of the stamping implement. In such cases, the final twist of the cord could not be discerned since no two successive segments were preserved in the passage of the cord around the stamping tool. Typically, the initial spin of the component elements of these cords was not determinable either, since they were too fine and loosely spun to leave diagnostic impressions on the sherd surfaces.

METHODS

A combined total of 320 Potomac Creek Cord Impressed sherds, exhibiting a cord-marked surface finish and/or a direct corded or pseudo-cord decoration, were selected from all nine excavation levels in MacCord's Unit D strata test at the Patawomeke site. A minimum of 25 sherds were selected from each two-inch arbitrary excavation level within the midden. Care was exercised to avoid selecting multiple sherds derived from the same vessel so that the sample would not be skewed. A larger group of 70 sherds was selected from level 1 in Unit D, the plow zone, as it represented a larger volume of site sediment and, presumably, pot sherds. Additionally, a sample derived from the plow zone might be more representative of vessels broken and dumped in the immediate area of the stockade-related midden because subsequent plowing presumably would have distributed the sherds over a wider area. Casts were also obtained from eight sherds of Rappahannock Fabric Impressed ware, essentially all the examples from Unit D which exhibited relict impressions of the original plaited dowel-stamped surface finish.

Sherds were selected from Unit D since it represented the deepest excavation by MacCord. It should more precisely chronicle time/stratigraphic change in artifact attributes than would his other three test units, which were excavated in shallower midden deposits. In retrospect, a sample from a broader area might have been valuable since the ratio of final cordage twist directions in the plow zone sample deviates furthest from the mean for the entire sample. This fact probably reflects its derivation from a larger and more representative sample of ceramic vessels and associated cordage impressions.

For comparison, cordage preserved on smaller ceramic samples from five Montgomery complex sites in the Potomac River Piedmont and Ridge and Valley provinces were also examined. As noted above, these include the Winslow (18Mo9) (n = 32 sherds), Gore (18Mo20) (n = 18 sherds), and Frye (44Ld10) (n = 23 sherds) sites, all located along the floodplain of the Potomac River. The Winslow and Gore sites are located adjacent to and on Selden Island, respectively. The Frye site is located upstream, below the mouth of the Monocacy River.

Samples from two other sites, Martins Meadow (18Wa23) and Antietam Creek (18Wa62), were also included. Both of these sites are located upstream in the Hagerstown Valley portion of the Great Valley section, along the main stem of Antietam Creek and at its confluence with the Potomac River, respectively (Stewart 1982:78, 84–87). The sample from the Martins Meadow site included 105 sherds (of which 20 are grit-tempered), and the sample from the Antietam Creek site included 84 sherds.

The sample from the Winslow site consists of rim sherds loaned by Howard MacCord and derived from various excavations made by R. Gates Slattery. The two smaller samples from the Gore and Frye sites represent surface collections made by MacCord in 1983. The samples from the Martins Meadow and Antietam Creek sites were derived from excavations and various surface collections from several sources; these were loaned by R. Michael Stewart.

The exterior surfaces of the sherds in all six samples were dry scrubbed with a soft-bristle toothbrush and talcum powder, a mild abrasive. This process cleaned the negative impressions in the sherds without further distorting them, and thus enhanced the recordation of the finer detail of the cordage impressions. Latex positives of the preserved cordage impressions were then made. The casts of the cords were analyzed for initial spin and final twist direction, Z or S, as outlined in Maslowski (1973:4–6) and Hurley (1979:5–11). Initial spin and final twist direction were recorded as the cord appears in the positive, which, as noted above, is the prevailing convention in North America, rather than as it appears in the negative on the sherd. The cordage represented in the impressions appears to be generally two ply; that is, it seems to be composed of two spun elements twisted together in the opposite direction from the spin. No obvious examples of replied cordage were observed.

RESULTS

Of the 320 positive casts for the Potomac Creek Cord Impressed sherd sample from the Patawomeke site, 258 were sufficiently distinct or unambiguous enough for determination of the cordage twist direction. The balance of the casts are either too distorted—as the result of the potters' smoothing over the cord-marked surfaces—or not precise enough in delicate detail for accurate classification (i.e., the pseudo-cord-decorated examples). Other casts do not unequivocally represent cord marking and thus were not included either. Several of these latter casts suggest the presence of open simple or diagonal twined fabrics with obliquely applied tension (see Winfree 1972), and at least one example of a close, diagonal, Z-twist twined textile. The frequencies and percentages of the cordage final twist for the sample of the Potomac Creek Cord Impressed sherds from Unit D at the Patawomeke site

are presented by excavation level and surface finish and decorative technique (Table 8.1).

Regrettably, none of the Rappahannock Fabric Impressed sherds preserve impressions distinct enough to even guess at the final twist of the cordage used in plaiting together dowels used to malleate the vessel walls (see Lafferty 1981:316–317, 321, Plate 53; cf. Wigglesworth 1986:43, Figure 8). All sherds from the Winslow site yielded casts sufficiently distinct to determine the cordage twist, although a small number did not unequivocally represent cord marking. The sherds derived from the surface of the Gore and Frye sites were characteristically small and weathered, as would be expected from a plow zone sample. Only 11 and 16 casts from the Gore and Frye sites, respectively, were sufficiently distinct enough for determination of the final twist direction. Although the sample of grit-tempered sherds from the Martins Meadow site is small, all examples preserved clear cordage impressions. The only adequate sample of grit-tempered sherds was derived from the Antietam Creek site. Of the sample of 88 sherds examined, 84 yielded distinct cordage impressions. Preliminary analysis of the remaining examples suggests the presence of open twined fabrics which have not been included here.

The casts from the Gore, Frye, and Martins Meadow sites suitable for analysis are too few to be considered adequate samples per se. However, in conjunction with the larger samples from the Winslow and Antietam Creek sites, they document the cordage manufacture habits of the Montgomery complex populations in the Piedmont province and Great Valley section. The cordage final twist frequencies and percentages for each of the five Montgomery complex sites are presented by ceramic temper aplastic categories (Tables 8.2–8.4).

The overwhelming final twist exhibited in the Potomac Creek Cord Impressed sample from Patawomeke is initial S-spun, final Z-twist (92.6%). The slightly lower representation of final Z-twist cordage (87.3%) in the level 1 plow zone sample from Unit D may be more representative, as noted above, since it was likely derived from a larger number of vessels.

Table 8.1. Frequency and Percentage of Final Z-Twist and S-Twist Cordage on Potomac Creek Cord Impressed Ceramics from Excavation Unit D at the Patawomeke Site (44St2) by Excavation Level, Surface Finish, and Decorative Technique

Unit D	Cord-Marked Surface Finish				Corded Decoration				Pseudo-Corded Decoration				All Cordage				Total	
	Z-Twist		S-Twist		Z-Twist		S-Twist		Z-Twist		S-Twist		Z-Twist		S-Twist			
Level	N	%	N	%	N	%	N	%	N	%	N	%	N	%	N	%	N	%
Level 1	33	94.3	2	5.7	8	80.0	2	20.0	7	70.0	3	30.0	48	87.3	7	12.7	55	100.0
Level 2	17	89.5	2	10.5	4	100.0	0	0.0	5	100.0	0	0.0	26	92.9	2	7.1	28	100.0
Level 3	16	100.0	0	0.0	4	66.7	2	33.3	4	80.0	1	20.0	24	88.9	3	11.1	27	100.0
Level 4	14	100.0	0	0.0	2	100.0	0	0.0	6	100.0	0	0.0	22	100.0	0	0.0	22	100.0
Level 5	23	92.0	2	8.0	8	100.0	0	0.0	6	100.0	0	0.0	37	94.9	2	5.1	39	100.0
Level 6	21	100.0	0	0.0	—	—	—	—	—	—	—	—	21	100.0	0	0.0	21	100.0
Level 7	15	93.8	1	6.3	—	—	—	—	2	100.0	0	0.0	17	94.4	1	5.6	18	100.0
Level 8	22	91.7	2	8.3	—	—	—	—	—	—	—	—	22	91.7	2	8.3	24	100.0
Level 9	21	91.3	2	8.7	1	100.0	0	0.0	—	—	—	—	22	91.7	2	8.3	24	100.0
TOTAL	182	94.3	11	5.7	27	87.1	4	12.9	30	88.2	4	11.8	239	92.6	19	7.4	258	100.0

Table 8.2. Frequency and Percentage of Final Z-Twist and S-Twist Cordage on Ceramics from the Winslow Site (18Mo9) by Temper Type, Surface Finish, and Decorative Technique

| | Cord-Marked Surface Finish | | | | Pseudo-Corded Decoration | | | | All Cordage | | | | |
| | Z-Twist | | S-Twist | | Z-Twist | | S-Twist | | Z-Twist | | S-Twist | | Total |
Temper	N	%	N	%	N	%	N	%	N	%	N	%	N
Various Grits													
Granite	1	100.0	0	0.0	1	100.0	0	0.0	2	100.0	0	0.0	2
Quartz	8	80.0	2	20.0	7	77.8	2	22.2	15	79.0	4	21.1	19
Sand	2	100.0	0	0.0	3	100.0	0	0.0	5	100.0	0	0.0	5
Untempered/ Grit Inclusions	2	100.0	0	0.0	2	100.0	0	0.0	4	100.0	0	0.0	4
TOTAL Various Grits	13	86.7	2	13.3	13	86.7	2	13.3	26	86.7	4	13.3	30

Table 8.3. Frequency and Percentage of Final Z-Twist and S-Twist Cordage on Ceramics from the Gore (18Mo20) and Frye (44Ld4) Sites by Temper Type, Surface Finish, and Decorative Technique

	Gore (18Mo20)					Frye (44Ld10)				
	Cord-Marked Surface Finish					Cord-Marked Surface Finish				
	Z-Twist		S-Twist		Total	Z-Twist		S-Twist		Total
Temper	N	%	N	%	N	N	%	N	%	N
Various Grits										
Granite	3	100.0	0	0.0	3	1	100.0	0	0.0	1
Quartz	2	66.7	1	33.3	3	3	75.0	1	25.0	4
Sand	0	0.0	1	100.0	1	—	—	—	—	—
Limestone and Quartz	2	100.0	0	0.0	2	2	66.7	1	33.3	3
Limestone	1	100.0	0	0.0	1	5	100.0	0	0.0	5
Chert	1	100.0	0	0.0	1	—	—	—	—	—
TOTAL Various Grits	9	81.8	2	18.2	11	11	84.6	2	15.4	13
Mussel Shell	0	0.0	3	100.0	3	—	—	—	—	—

A possible underrepresentation of final S-twist cordage in the total Unit D sample at Patawomeke is also suggested by the final twist data evidenced in Falk's (1983:19) sample of 33 direct cord-impressed decorated rim sherds assigned to her Type I, Variety A decoration category. In this group, final Z-twist and S-twist examples were represented in "almost equal" frequencies. The cordage used in the direct cord decoration in Falk's Type I, Variety B, and Type I, Variety C apparently exhibited a pre-

dominant final Z-twist, which is more consonant with the pattern displayed by the total Unit D sample in this study.

The preferred final twist direction of the cordage represented among the sherds from the five Montgomery complex sites was also predominantly Z. It varied only slightly between them: 86.7% at the Winslow site, 84.6% at the Frye site, 81.8% at the Gore site, 80% at the Martins Meadow site, and 89.3% at the Antietam Creek site.

Table 8.4. Frequency and Percentage of Final Z-Twist and S-Twist Cordage on Ceramics from the Martins Meadow (18Wa23) and Antietam Creek (18Wa62) Sites by Temper Type and Surface Finish

	Martin Meadow (18Wa23)					Antietam Creek (18Wa62)				
	Cord-Marked Surface Finish					Cord-Marked Surface Finish				
	Z-Twist		S-Twist		Total	Z-Twist		S-Twist		Total
Temper	N	%	N	%	N	N	%	N	%	N
Various Grits										
Quartz	13	81.3	3	18.8	16	36	92.3	3	7.7	39
Quartz and										
Limestone	0	0.0	1	100.0	1	9	100.0	0	0.0	9
Limestone	3	100.0	0	0.0	3	30	83.3	6	16.7	36
TOTAL										
Various Grits	16	80.0	4	20.0	20	75	89.3	9	10.7	84
Mussel Shell	9	10.6	76	89.4	85	—	—	—	—	—

DISCUSSION

Analysis of the 258 cordage casts from a sample of Potomac Creek Cord Impressed sherds from MacCord's Unit D at the Patawomeke site indicates that the preferred final cordage twist direction was Z, as employed in wrapping both paddles for surface finish and tools for decoration. The final twist-direction ratio obtained for the sample from level 1, the plow Zone, in Unit D suggests that the overall pattern for the Patawomeke site may not be quite as overwhelmingly Z as is the Unit D sample at 92.6%, although the lesser percentage of 87.3% is not really much different. The ratio of final Z-twist to S-twist in this study is consistent with the less precisely documented predominant twist direction reported by Falk (1983:19) for her Patawomeke sample, derived exclusively from 68 rim sherds evidencing direct cord impressed decoration. It is noteworthy that the cordage employed in wrapping the paddles for surface finish of the Potomac Creek Cord Impressed vessels and the dowels utilized in their decoration was apparently constructed in the same fashion, that is, with an overwhelming preference for a final Z-twist.

No cordage twist information is available for the Potomac Creek Cord Impressed ceramics from the contemporary and culturally related Accokeek Creek site; Accokeek Creek lies across the Potomac River Estuary and upstream from the Patawomeke site. However, examination of photographs of Potomac Creek Cord Impressed ware published by Stephenson (1963:Plates 13–18) suggests that the majority of the depicted rim sherds exhibit final Z-twist cordage when the twist direction can be discerned. Although this is an unsatisfactory method for collecting cordage twist data, it does suggest that the prevailing final twist for the Potomac Creek complex as a whole may prove to be Z. This possibility needs to be confirmed by direct examination of positive casts derived from Potomac Creek Cord Impressed ceramics from other sites assigned to this complex, however.

Although the cordage samples derived from the Winslow, Gore, and Frye sites in the Piedmont province and the Martins Meadow and Antietam Creek sites in the Great Valley section are small, they do suggest that a final Z-twist was the preferred cordage configuration among Piedmont and Ridge and Valley groups attributable to the Montgomery complex. This does not "prove" that the Potomac Creek complex represents an intrusion of alien Montgomery complex people into the Tidewater Potomac River, but the presence of cordage with a predominant final S-twist in either complex would categorically eliminate the possibility that the two wares were the time-successive products of the same potters.

Finally, a larger and more completely preserved sample of Middle Woodland and earlier Late Woodland cord-marked, fabric-marked (read: plaited dowel-stamped), and cord-decorated ceramics from the vicinity of Potomac and Piscataway creeks needs to be examined to determine their predominant cordage twist directions. Unfortunately, none of the eight studied Rappahannock Fabric Impressed sherds from Unit D at the Patawomeke site produced impressions clear enough for analysis. A predilection for final S-twist cordage on Middle Woodland and/or early Late Woodland ceramics around either Potomac or Piscataway creeks would indicate that the Potomac Creek complex was indeed intrusive. Again, the presence of predominant final Z-twist cordage in either area would not obviate the possibility of an intrusion by a displaced Montgomery complex population.

Obviously, one Z-twist cordage-producing group could replace another. The presence of cordage impressions exhibiting the opposite final direction, S-twist, on earlier indigenous Mockley Cord Marked or Rappahannock Fabric Impressed ceramics would make that replacement unequivocal. Synonymy of cordage-manufacturing processes for the early and late Late Woodland/Protohistoric populations along the Tidewater Potomac River would suggest that group-specific cultural or biological attributes should be examined to confirm or reject Schmitt's (1952, 1965:30) original hypothesis about the connections between the Potomac and Montgomery complexes. Clearly, larger cordage samples from a greater number of sites attributable to both complexes are needed to verify the preliminary results of this study.

Parenthetically, the analysis of cordage twist on ceramics exhibiting various temper aplastics from the five Montgomery complex sites also provides evidence suggesting two additional cultural patterns in the Potomac River Piedmont and Ridge and Valley provinces that were not the subject of scrutiny in the original study. The first of these patterns is that the potters who manufactured the limestone-tempered vessels, traditionally referred to as Page Cord Marked ware as diagnostic of the Mason Island (focus) complex, employed cordage with the same predominant final twist as did the makers of the quartz and granite-tempered Shepard Cord Marked ware. The Mason Island complex has been traditionally taken to be successor to the Montgomery complex after ca. A.D. 1350–1450, and the Mason Island complex was followed by the Luray (focus) complex, characterized by shell-tempered ceramics (e.g., Slattery and Woodward 1992:158–159), after ca. A.D. 1450. In any case, the common twist on the Page Cord Marked and Shepard Cord Marked ceramics may indicate continuity between populations who have been typically differentiated by their use of either quartz and granite-tempered ceramic wares or limestone-tempered ceramic wares, at least in the Potomac River Ridge and Valley province. Thus, these differences may merely represent changes in ceramic technology over time and/or available aplastic temper sources without implying population replacement.

The implications of the second apparent pattern are perhaps more obvious and more significant. Among the artifacts from the Frye and Martins Meadow sites were a number of shell-tempered Keyser Cord Marked sherds. Keyser Cord Marked pottery is considered to be the primary diagnostic of the Luray complex, the terminal Late Woodland cultural manifestation in the Potomac River Piedmont and Ridge and Valley provinces.

Only three shell-tempered sherds in the available sample from the Frye site preserve cordage impressions distinct enough for determination of the final twist. However, a much larger sample (n = 85) is present in the Martins Meadow site sample (see Tables 8.2 and 8.3). The cordage final twist displayed by the depauperate shell-tempered Keyser Cord Marked sample from the Frye (S-twist = 100%) and Martins Meadow (S-twist = 89.4%) sites is opposite that for the grit-tempered wares from the five Montgomery complex sites.

If this pattern is documented in ceramic samples from other sites in the Potomac River drainage, as Curry and Kavanagh (1991) and Herbstritt (1993) seem to indicate, then two implications are inescapable. The first is that the Luray complex population is indeed intrusive and it apparently replaced the indigenous Montgomery and subsequent Mason Island groups, if, in fact, the latter two complexes represent two successive populations. The second implication is of equal importance for Potomac River culture history. Although the Luray complex people are intrusive, they are unequivocally *not* representatives of a Late Prehistoric period Monongahela intrusion from the upper Ohio River Valley. Elsewhere, I have argued for the exclusion of the Potomac River basin shell-tempered, cord-marked, and otherwise pedestrian pottery-making complexes, from the umbrella of the Monongahela culture (Johnson 1981:77–78). These objections were based on the presence of minor stylistic variations between Monongahela and Keyser ware and, more importantly, on the basis of the apparent absence of a catalyst for a migration of Monongahela populations across the high Allegheny Mountain section during the latter part of the Pacific climatic episode, ca. A.D. 1400–1500.

Today, the high Allegheny Mountain section, which is largely included in the Canadian biotic province (Dice 1943), displays a mean frost-free day growing season approximately seven weeks shorter than that characteristic of the lower and middle Monongahela River Valley, the Monongahela culture heartland (see Johnson et al. 1989:11, Figure 4). It is highly unlikely that the limited frost-free growing season in the Allegheny Mountain section could have supported one or more village removals of maize horticulturists during the climatic decline leading into the Neo-Boreal episode, although it is clear that this same area supported a number of Monongahela village removals during the previous, warmer Neo-Atlantic episode.

Limited cordage twist data for Keyser Cord Marked ceramic samples analyzed in this study offer the potential for rejecting a post–A.D. 1400 Monongahela intrusion into the Potomac River Valley and for rejecting the synonymy of the Monongahela and Luray populations. With the exception of a small pocket of final S-twist cordage makers situated along the main stem of the Ohio River at the confluence of the Beaver River, Monongahela ceramic samples uniformly exhibit predominant final Z-twist cordage (Maslowski 1984:54, Table 2; Johnson and Speedy 1995). Presuming that the putative final S-twist cordage pattern for Keyser Cord Marked ceramics can be further substantiated,[2] then the two populations—Monongahela and Luray—simply cannot be the same. The source of the donor population for the Luray complex folk must be sought elsewhere.

In summary, examination of positive cordage casts derived from Potomac Creek Cord Impressed ceramic sherds from the Patawomeke site in the Potomac River Tidewater area and various grit-tempered ware sherds from five Montgomery complex sites in the Potomac River Piedmont and Ridge and Valley provinces indicates a pattern of predominant final Z-twist cordage for both areas. Synonymy of the preferred cordage twist direction in the textiles of both areas indicates that the Montgomery complex could have supplied the donor population for the subsequent Potomac Creek complex, as has been repeatedly argued in the past. Examination of cordage preserved on the surfaces of earlier Middle Woodland and initial Late Woodland period cord-marked, fabric-marked, and cord-decorated ceramics from the vicinity of the later Potomac Creek sites is still necessary to conclusively determine if the Potomac Creek culture is itself intrusive, or if its ceramics merely represent the diffusion of an alien pottery-making tradition.

ACKNOWLEDGMENTS

This is a revised version of a paper delivered at the 1989 Middle Atlantic Archaeological Conference, Rehoboth Beach, Delaware. The author thanks Howard A. MacCord Sr. and R. Michael Stewart for the loan of the collections upon which this analysis is based. Howard MacCord is further acknowledged for his encouragement in this research, and thanks go to him, J. M. Adovasio, and James B. Petersen for reading and commenting on earlier drafts of this chapter. Dwight Wallace also offered useful comments. I would also like to thank Keith B. Egloff, Virginia Department of Historic Landmarks, for his last-minute help in clarifying the provenience of one of the site samples. Marie J. Zeidler drafted Map 8.1. This manuscript and tables were ably typed and composed by Tanna B. Torres.

NOTES

1. Ceramic type names have been used throughout this chapter in correspondence with their original definition. Thus, "Cord Impressed," "Cord Marked," "Cordmarked," and "Net Impressed," among others, have been cited as components of binomial type designations, while "cord-marked," "fabric-impressed," "cord-decorated," and other designations have been employed by the author as descriptive terms.

2. A recently reported putative Monongahela culture village site, Bedford Village (36Bd90), located on the Raystown Branch of the Juniata River in the Appalachian Mountain section of south-central Pennsylvania (Catton 1994), is more precisely an early Luray complex site. The recovered ceramics include diagnostic Keyser Cord Marked vessel rims. Cordage impressions on the associated shell-tempered ware are predominantly final S-twist (78.3%).

REFERENCES CITED

Adovasio, J. M.
1970 The Origin, Development and Distribution of Western Archaic Textiles. *Tebiwa* 13(2):1–40.
1977 *Basketry Technology: A Guide to Identification and Analysis.* Aldine, Chicago.
1985 Style, Basketry, and Basket Makers: Another Look. Paper presented at the 50th annual meeting of the Society for American Archaeology, Denver.
1986a Prehistoric Basketry. In *Great Basin,* edited by Warren L. d'Azevedo, pp. 194–205. Handbook of North American Indians, vol. 11, William G. Sturtevant, general editor. Smithsonian Institution, Washington, D.C.
1986b Artifacts and Ethnicity: Basketry as an Indicator of Territoriality and Population Movements in the Prehistoric Great Basin. In *Anthropology of the Desert West, Essays in Honor of Jesse D. Jennings,* edited by Carol J. Condie and Don D. Fowler, pp. 43–88. Univ. of Utah Anthropological Papers 110. Salt Lake City.

Andrews, R. L., and J. M. Adovasio
1980 *Perishable Industries from Hinds Cave, Val Verde County, Texas.* Ethnology Monographs 5. Dept. of Anthropology, Univ. of Pittsburgh, Pittsburgh.

Andrews, R. L., J. M. Adovasio, and T. G. Whitley
1988 Coiled Basketry and Cordage from Lakeside Cave (42BO385), Utah. Paper presented at the 21st annual Great Basin Anthropological Conference, Park City.

Archaeological and Historical Consultants, Inc.
1990 *Archaeological Data Recovery at Site 36Fa368, Grays Landing Lock and Dam, Fayette County, Pennsylvania.* Submitted to the Pittsburgh District, U.S. Army Corp[s] of Engineers under Contract No. DACW59-88-C-0006. Draft Final Report.

Boyce, Hettie L.
1985 The Novak Site: A Late Woodland Upland Monongahela Village. *Pennsylvania Archaeologist* 55(3):21–49.

Catton, Deborah K.
1994 Preliminary Report of the Bedford Village Site, 36Bd90. Paper presented at the 65th annual meeting of the Society for Pennsylvania Archaeology, Pittsburgh.

Clark, Wayne E.
1980 The Origins of the Piscataway and Related Indian Cultures. *Maryland Historical Magazine* 75(1):8–22.

Curry, Dennis C., and Maureen Kavanagh
1991 The Middle to Late Woodland Transition in Maryland. *North American Archaeologist* 12(1):3–28.

Dancey, William S.
1988 The Community Plan of an Early Late Woodland Village in the Middle Scioto River Valley. *Midcontinental Journal of Archaeology* 13(2):223–258.

Dice, Lee R.
1943 *The Biotic Provinces of North America.* Univ. of Michigan Press, Ann Arbor.

Doyle, Richard A., Nathan D. Hamilton, and James B. Petersen
1982 Early Woodland Ceramics and Associated Perishable Industries from Southwestern Maine. *Maine Archaeological Society Bulletin* 22(2):4–21.

Egloff, Keith T., and Stephen R. Potter
1982 Indian Ceramics from Coastal Plain Virginia. *Archaeology of Eastern North America* 20:95–117.

Falk, Carole Portugal
1983 Cordage Impressed on Potomac Creek Pottery: Decoding the Corded Style Motifs and the Methods of Pattern Manufacture. *Maryland Archeology* 19(2):1–20.

Fassler, Heidi
1987 Guilfoil: A Middle Fort Ancient Village in Fayette County. In *Current Archaeological Research in Kentucky,* edited by David Pollock, pp. 154–186. Kentucky Heritage Council, Frankfort.

Fry, G. F., and J. M. Adovasio
1970 Population Differentiation in Hogup and Danger Caves, Two Archaic Sites in the Eastern Great Basin. *Nevada State Museum Anthropological Papers* 15:208–215. Carson City.

George, Richard L.

1983   The Gnagney Site and the Monongahela Occupation of the Somerset Plateau. *Pennsylvania Archaeologist* 53(4):1–97.

George, Richard L., Jay Babish, and Christine E. Davis

1990   The Household Site: Results of a Partial Excavation of a Late Monongahela Village in Westmoreland County, Pennsylvania. *Pennsylvania Archaeologist* 60(2):40–70.

Hemmings, E. Thomas

1984   Fairchance Mound and Village: An Early Middle Woodland Settlement in the Upper Ohio Valley. *West Virginia Archeologist* 36(1):3–68.

Henderson, A. Gwynn

1986   Type Description for Armstrong and Lick Creek Series Ceramics. *West Virginia Archeologist* 38(2):40–47.

1988   Ceramic Analysis of Stratum 4/4A. In *Excavations at the Hansen Site (15GP14) in Northeastern Kentucky,* by Steven R. Ahler, pp. 535–570. Archaeological Report 173. Program for Cultural Resource Assessment, Dept. of Anthropology, Univ. of Kentucky. Submitted to Kentucky Transportation Cabinet, Division of Environmental Analysis, Frankfort.

Henderson, A. Gwynn, and David Pollock

1985   The Late Woodland Occupation of the Bentley Site. In *Woodland Period Research in Kentucky,* edited by David Pollack, Thomas N. Sanders, and Charles D. Hockensmith, pp. 140–164. Kentucky Heritage Council, Frankfort.

Herbstritt, James T.

1981   Bonnie Brook: A Multicomponent Aboriginal Locus in West Central Pennsylvania. *Pennsylvania Archaeologist* 51(3):1–59.

1993   A Late Prehistoric Social Boundary for the Susquehanna/Potomac Divide. Paper presented at the annual meeting of the Middle Atlantic Archaeological Conference, Ocean City.

Holland, C. G.

1966   The John Harter Collection from a Site in Southern Shenandoah County. *Archeological Society of Virginia Quarterly Bulletin* 21(2):40–41.

1970   *An Archeological Survey of Southwestern Virginia.* Smithsonian Contributions to Anthropology 12. Washington, D.C.

Hughes, Myra A., and Jonathan P. Kerr

1990   *A National Register Evaluation of Selected Archeological Sites in the Gallipolis Mitigation Site at Greenbottom, Cabell County, West Virginia.* Cultural Resource Analysts, Inc., Lexington. Submitted to the Huntington District Corps of Engineers, Huntington, and Commonwealth Technology, Lexington.

Hurley, William M.

1979   *Prehistoric Cordage: Identification of Impressions on Pottery.* Taraxacum, Washington, D.C.

Johnson, William C.

1975   The Late Woodland Period in Northwestern Pennsylvania: A Reappraisal and Update, 1975. Paper presented at the 42nd annual meeting of the Eastern States Archaeological Federation, Columbus.

1978   Ceramics. In 46SU3 Revisited, by Jan D. Applegarth, J. M. Adovasio, and Jack Donahue, pp. 41–65. *Pennsylvania Archaeologist* 48(1).

1981   The Campbell Farm Site (36FA26) and Monongahela: A Preliminary Examination and Assessment. Paper Presented at the 4th Monongahela Symposium, California State College, California, Pennsylvania.

1982   Ceramics from Meadowcroft Rockshelter: A Re-Evaluation and Interpretation. In *Meadowcroft: Collected Papers on the Archaeology of Meadowcroft Rockshelter and the Cross Creek Drainage,* edited by R. C. Carlisle and J. M. Adovasio, pp. 142–162. Dept. of Anthropology, Univ. of Pittsburgh, Pittsburgh.

1987a   Paintsville Ceramics. In *Paintsville Reservoir, Kentucky, Revisited: The 1982 Archaeological Investigations,* by J. M. Adovasio, W. C. Johnson, P. T. Fitzgibbons, R. C. Carlisle, J. Donahue, F. J. Vento, N. L. Yedlowski, and J. L. Yedlowski, pp. 449–582. Cultural Resource Management Program, Dept. of Anthropology, Univ. of Pittsburgh, Pittsburgh. Submitted to the U.S. Army Corps of Engineers Huntington District, Huntington, under Contract Number DACW69-82-C-0075.

1987b   Ceramics. In *Phase I Archaeological Investigations at Grays Landing, Fayette County, Pennsylvania,* by A. Quinn, J. M. Adovasio, W. C. Johnson, R. C. Carlisle, and D. R. Pedler, pp. 89–110. Cultural Resource Management Program, Dept. of Anthropology, Univ. of Pittsburgh, Pittsburgh. Submitted to Gannett Fleming Water Resources Engineering, Inc., Harrisburg, under Delivery Order No. 5, Contract DACW59-85-D-0005, U.S. Army Engineer District, Pittsburgh Corps of Engineers.

Johnson, William C., William P. Athens, Martin T. Fuess, Luis G. Jaramillo, Keith R. Bastianni, and Elizabeth Ramos

1989   *Late Prehistoric Period Monongahela Culture Site and Cultural Resource Inventory.* Cultural Resource Management Program, Dept. of Anthropology, Univ. of Pittsburgh. Submitted to the Pennsylvania Historical and Museum Commission, Bureau for Historic Preservation, Harrisburg.

Johnson, William C., and D. Scott Speedy
1992 Cultural Continuity and Change in the Middle and Late Woodland Periods in the Upper James River Estuary, Prince George County, Virginia. *Journal of Middle Atlantic Archaeology* 8:91–106.
1995 Cordage Twist Direction as a Tool in Delineating Territorial Boundaries and Demonstrating Population Continuity During the Late Woodland and Late Prehistoric Periods in the Upper Ohio River Valley. *West Virginia Archeologist*, in press.

Lafferty, Robert H.
1981 *The Phipps Bend Archaeological Project.* Univ. of Alabama Office of Archaeological Research, Research Series 4. Moundsville.

MacCord, Howard A.
1984 Evidence for a Late Woodland Migration from Piedmont to Tidewater in the Potomac Valley. *Maryland Archeology* 20(2):7–18.

MacCord, Howard A., Richard G. Slattery, and Karl Schmitt
1957 *The Shepard Site Study (18Mo3), Montgomery County, Maryland.* Archeological Society of Maryland Bulletin 1. Baltimore.

Manson, Carl P., and Howard A. MacCord
1985 The Stratigraphic Sequence at Patawomeke. In *Falls Zone Archeology in Virginia*, edited by Howard A. MacCord, pp. 13–40. Howard A. MacCord, Richmond.

Marwitt, John P., Kathleen Sauser, and Rebecca Sterling
1986 1980 Excavations at the Childers Site (46MS121), Mason County, West Virginia. *West Virginia Archeologist* 38(1):1–23.

Maslowski, Robert F.
1973 An Analysis of Cordmarked Watson Ware. *Pennsylvania Archaeologist* 43(2):1–12.
1978 Moorehead Cave Cordage Analysis: Its Cultural and Technological Implications. Paper presented at the 43rd annual meeting of the Society for American Archaeology, Tucson.
1984 The Significance of Cordage Attributes in the Analysis of Woodland Pottery. *Pennsylvania Archaeologist* 54(1–2):51–60.

Maslowski, Robert F., and David L. Dawson
1980 Childers (46-MS-121): A Terminal Late Woodland Village. *West Virginia Archeologist* 30:4–32.

Morton, James, and Jeff Carskadden
1987 Test Excavations at an Early Hopewellian Site near Dresden, Ohio. *The Ohio Archaeologist* 37 (1):8–12.

Mounier, R. Alan
1974 An Archaeological Investigation in the Maurice River Tidewater Area, New Jersey. *Man in the Northeast* 7:29–56.

Moxley, Ronald W., and James D. Bloemker
1985 The Man Site: A Preliminary Report on a Late Prehistoric Village Site in Logan County, West Virginia. *West Virginia Archeologist* 37(2):3–22.

Munson, Patrick J.
1971 An Archaeological Survey of the Wood River Terrace and Adjacent Bottoms and Bluffs in Madison County, Illinois, Part I. In *Archaeological Surveys of the American Bottoms and Adjacent Bluffs, Illinois*, by Patrick J. Munson and Alan D. Harn, pp. 3–17. Illinois State Museum Reports of Investigations 21. Springfield.

Newton, Dolores
1974 The Timbira Hammock as a Cultural Indicator of Social Boundaries. In *The Human Mirror, Material and Spatial Images of Man*, edited by Miles Richardson, pp. 231–251. Louisiana State Univ. Press, Baton Rouge.

NPW Consultants, Inc.
1983 *Excavation of Two Monongahela Sites: Late Woodland Gensler (36Gr63) and Proto-historic Throckmorton (36Gr160).* Submitted to Consolidated Coal Company, Pittsburgh.

Petersen, James B., and Nathan D. Hamilton
1984 Early Woodland Ceramic and Perishable Fiber Industries from the Northeast: A Summary and Interpretation. *Annals of Carnegie Museum* 53:413–445. Pittsburgh.

Pollack, David, and A. Gwynn Henderson
1984 A Mid-Eighteenth Century Historic Indian Occupation in Greenup County, Kentucky. In *Late Prehistoric Research in Kentucky*, edited by David Pollack, Charles D. Hockensmith, and Thomas N. Sanders, pp. 1–24. Kentucky Heritage Council, Frankfort.

Railey, Jimmy A. (editor)
1984 *The Pyles Site (15MS28), a Newtown Village in Mason County, Kentucky.* William S. Webb Archaeological Society Occasional Paper 1. Lexington.

R. Christopher Goodwin & Associates, Inc.
1990 *Archeological Data Recovery from Prehistoric Site 36FA363, Grays Landing Lock and Dam.* R. Christopher Goodwin & Associates, Inc., Frederick. Submitted to the U.S. Army Corps of Engineers, Pittsburgh District, Pittsburgh.

Schmitt, Karl, Jr.
1952 Archeological Chronology of the Middle Atlantic States. In *Archeology of Eastern United States*, edited by James B. Griffin, pp. 59–70. Univ. of Chicago Press, Chicago.

1965   Patawomeke: An Historic Algonkian Site. *Archeo-logical Society of Virginia Quarterly Bulletin* 20 (1):1–36.

Seeman, Mark F.

1985   *The Locust Site (33Mu160): The 1983 Test Excavation of a Multicomponent Workshop in East Central Ohio.* Kent State Research Papers in Archaeology 7. Kent.

Sharp, William E., and Christopher A. Turnbow

1987   The Muir Site: An Upland Fort Ancient Community in the Inner Bluegrass Region of Kentucky. In *Current Archaeological Research in Kentucky,* edited by David Pollock, pp. 137–152. Kentucky Heritage Council, Frankfort.

Slattery, Richard G., and Douglas R. Woodward

1992   *The Montgomery Focus: A Late Woodland Potomac River Culture.* Archeological Society of Maryland Bulletin 2.

Stephenson, Robert L.

1963   The Artifacts. In *The Accokeek Creek Site, A Middle Atlantic Seaboard Culture Sequence,* by Robert L. Stephenson and Alice L. Ferguson, pp. 82–168. Anthropological Papers 20. Museum of Anthropology, Univ. of Michigan, Ann Arbor.

Stewart, R. Michael

1982   Prehistoric Ceramics of the Great Valley of Maryland. *Archaeology of Eastern North America* 10:69–94.

Wigglesworth, Lynn

1986   Pottery from the Gravelley Run Site, Atlantic County, New Jersey. *Bulletin of the Archaeological Society of New Jersey* 40:39–45.

Winfree, R. Westwood

1972   A New Look at Cord-Marked Pottery. *Quarterly Bulletin of the Archaeological Society of Virginia* 26(4):179–189.

Witthoft, John

1963   General interpretations. In The Townsend Site near Lewes, Delaware, edited by H. Geiger Omwake and T. D. Stewart, pp. 59–69. *The Archeolog* 15 (1):1–72.

9

Jenna Tedrick Kuttruff

Carl Kuttruff

Mississippian Textile Evidence on Fabric-Impressed Ceramics from Mound Bottom, Tennessee

This chapter presents aspects of the manufacture and use of textiles by Mississippian period populations who lived at the Mound Bottom site in Tennessee, ca. A.D. 900–1250. It is based on an analysis of 345 identifiable fabric impressions on pottery sherds recovered during excavations at Mound Bottom in 1974 and 1975. Positive casts of the textiles were made from the negative impressions on at least 62 salt pan ceramic vessels. The textile casts were examined for textile structure and techniques of manufacture, as well as for their usage as tools in the manufacture of fabric-impressed pottery. Spaced or open weft twining of several types, considerably fewer examples of possible compact or close weft twining, and other complex structures consisting of multiple fabric structures were identified; S-twist weft twining strongly predominated. Another study previously applied an ordinal index of textile production complexity to these Mound Bottom sherds and examined intrasite and intersite variability (Kuttruff and Kuttruff 1992).

David Braun (1983:107) has interpreted midwestern pottery vessels as utilitarian implements or tools. In his perspective, pottery attributes are "evidence of the techniques used by potters to achieve particular characteristics of utility in the finished vessels" (Braun 1983:107). Some attributes such as paste composition may have resulted from both natural and cultural factors, but other ceramic attributes such as morphology, manufacturing techniques, decoration, and place of disposal may have resulted from cultural factors alone. Consequently, pottery has been used by archaeologists not only for culture-historical systematics but also to gain insight into aesthetics, the organization of social networks, and characteristics of economic networks, among other topics.

Whereas pottery may be considered an archaeologist's delight because of its frequent breakage and disposal, along with its generally excellent preservation in the archaeological record, textiles are not. Textiles and textile products may have been equally as common, if not more common, than pottery within particular cultural contexts in prehistory. However, textile use, wear, and discard patterns differ from those of ceramics, and their survival is certainly less typical. In spite of such biases, archaeological textiles, including those preserved as negative impressions on ceramics, should be systematically studied so that this potentially significant evidence can be used to enrich our understanding of populations known only through the archaeological record.

MOUND BOTTOM SITE DESCRIPTION

Mound Bottom (40CH8) is a large Mississippian period site located in middle Tennessee near the western edge of the Nashville Basin, approximately 33 km west of Nashville. It is situated in a horseshoe bend of the Harpeth River about 17 km above its confluence with the Cumberland River (Map 9.1). The site consists of a large civic-ceremonial and habitation center which covers an area of about 36.4 hectares (Map 9.2). One large platform mound is 10.5 meters high and covers an area of about 0.63 hectares at its base. A rectangular plaza lies to the east of this large mound and is surrounded by ten lesser platform mounds. One low mound is situated near the center of the plaza, and two small mounds lie to the east of the plaza area. Habitation areas are located to the east, south, and west of the mound group. Artifact cross-date comparisons and a series of nine radiocarbon dates from the site indicate a range of occupation ca. A.D. 900–1250 (Kuttruff 1979; O'Brien 1977).

MISSISSIPPIAN PERIOD
FABRIC-IMPRESSED CERAMICS

Description of Salt Pan Ceramics

A small number of the Mississippian ceramics from the Mound Bottom site are classifiable as fabric-impressed pottery pans. These pan forms are more commonly known as "salt pans," a term long established in the archaeological literature and derived from the recognized association of this type

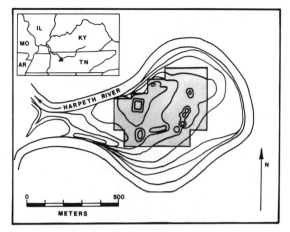

Map 9.1. Location of the Mound Bottom site in the Middle Mississippi–Lower Ohio region. (Kuttruff and Kuttruff 1992:2; adapted from Fisher 1926, Tennessee State Archives map CH 1370.) Shaded area is shown in Map 9.2.

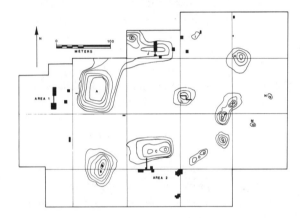

Map 9.2. The Mound Bottom site showing distribution of mounds and excavation units. (Kuttruff and Kuttruff 1992:3; adapted from O'Brien 1977:Figure 1.)

of ceramic ware with saline springs (e.g., Brown 1980:20; Phillips 1970:95). Salt pans are shell tempered, have a generally circular to oval bowl shape, and vary in size. They are often much larger than other classes of Mississippian period plates or bowls. The exterior surfaces of salt pans typically exhibit fabric impressions. Roughened or plain surfaces on salt pans are a minority, although this observation may be partially due to the difficulty of distinguishing most of these sherds from other Mississippian large vessel plain sherds unless they are exceptionally thick or include rim sherds. Reports of grass- and leaf-impressed surfaces have been made (e.g., Orr 1951:316, Figure 4; Phillips 1970:96; Walker and Adams 1946:91), but these are less common. Decorated pans are also rare, but some do occur. Salt pan decorations include punctations, grooves on flattened lips, and red-slipped or painted vessels (Brown 1980:24–25).

Distribution and Association of Salt Pan Ceramics

As noted by Ian Brown (1980:25–27), fabric-impressed salt pans are most commonly associated with the core area of Mississippian populations. The general distribution of fabric-impressed and smoothed-surface salt pans is concentrated in the middle Mississippi River drainage and tributary drainages. Their distribution among the Mississippian culture populations and related populations and their correlation with the distribution of known saline springs in the Midwest and upper Southeast have been discussed in detail by Brown (1980:11–19, 25–27, Figures 3 and 5). For the Mississippian culture, this distribution is confined to the Mississippi River drainage between St. Louis and northeastern Arkansas, the Ohio River drainage eastward to central Indiana, and to the Tennessee and Cumberland River drainages in Kentucky, Tennessee, and Alabama, as well as other drainages in the outlined area. Generally, the heaviest concentrations of salt pan sherds are found in proximity to salines or salt springs, but they are also found in other contexts at considerable distances from salt springs.

Obvious associations of salt pan sherds with known salt springs include those in the Kimmswick area of Jefferson County, Missouri (Brown 1980:15), in Gallatin County in southeastern Illinois (Brown 1980:15; Muller 1984) and the French Lick in Nashville, Tennessee (Brown 1980:15; Marshall 1916:31–34). Numerous excavations and other work have documented the occurrence of salt pans at considerable distances from salines in association with habitation areas and other site types that are not directly associated with salt springs. Examples of nonsaline associations for salt pan pottery are well documented from excavated sites in middle Tennessee and include habitation sites, cemeteries, and mound center sites (e.g., Benthall 1983; Dowd 1972; Kline 1979; Klippel et al. 1984).

Mound Bottom is also an example of the presence of salt pan pottery at a site type other than salines since there is no known salt spring in the immediate vicinity of the site. Extensive excavations at Mound Bottom have demonstrated the association of salt pan sherds with habitation areas and domestic structures. While the civic-ceremonial areas of the site were not extensively sampled, all of the salt pan sherds that were recovered from Mound Bottom came from habitation areas. These habitation areas included both domestic structures and associated midden deposits.

Utilization of Salt Pan Ceramics

When recovered at or near salines, the use of salt pans for the evaporation of salt brine has been postulated. However, additional uses for such ceramic vessels also have been proposed. These other uses include communal eating pans (Clay 1963:242), cooking vessels (Linton 1944:376; Thruston 1973:157–159; Webb 1952:90, 93), and ritual functions (Brown 1980:29). Webb (1952) and Thruston (1973) suggest that they were merely employed as large stationary cooking vessels; Linton (1944:376) saw their main use more specifically in "parching corn or toasting acorns in ashes to remove the tannic acid." Based upon historical references, it has also been suggested that salt pan ceramics may have been used as hearths to make bread (Brown 1980:29). Thus, the inferred utilization of salt pan ceramics goes well beyond their presumed association with the evaporation of salt brine.

MOUND BOTTOM FABRIC-IMPRESSED CERAMICS

This study is based on the fabric-impressed salt pan sherds that were recovered during excavations at the Mound Bottom site in 1974 and 1975. These excavations were sponsored by the Tennessee Department of Conservation and directed by Carl Kuttruff. The fabric-impressed salt pan sherds considered in this chapter were a minority ware in the total ceramic collection recovered from the site. The 510 salt pan sherds from surface collections and excavations constitute less than 3% of the total ceramic inventory. All of the pan forms from the Mound Bottom site were classified as either Kimmswick Plain or Kimmswick Fabric Impressed (O'Brien 1977:351–352). The Kimmswick Fabric Impressed type is only one classification of many for a basic pottery type that is found in association with the Mississippian period throughout the Midwest and upper Southeast. In his synthetic study, "Salt and the Eastern North American Indian," Brown (1980:20) listed some 14 different formal type names for ceramic salt pans. However, he concluded that there are only two basic types of salt pans: one is adorned with textile impressions on the exterior and sometimes on the interior surfaces, and the other has a smooth or merely roughened exterior surface. These two pan types are often found at the same site, as was the case at Mound Bottom.

The Kimmswick Fabric Impressed type was defined by Williams (1954:219–220). Phillips (1970:95) later suggested that all fabric-impressed salt pan sherds from the Southeast be classified as Kimmswick Fabric Impressed, and this interpretation was followed in the classification of the Mound Bottom ceramics. The pan sherds with plain surfaces were correspondingly classified as Kimmswick Plain. A minimum number of seven vessels of Kimmswick Plain from Mound Bottom were identified by O'Brien, as compared with a minimum number of 62 Kimmswick Fabric Impressed vessels (O'Brien 1977:374–378).

All of the pan forms from Mound Bottom, in conformance to the formal type descriptions, have a coarse shell temper and a contorted and porous texture with either plain or fabric-impressed surface finishes. Vessel shapes consist of large shallow pans which were low, wide vessels generally over 30 cm in diameter, ranging upward to greater than 50 cm in diameter. Measured wall angles of the pans average 60° to 70° from vertical, but may approach nearly 80°. In general, the shapes of the pans, varying from circular to oval, are quite irregular and uneven (O'Brien 1977:374–378).

Two types of rim forms were identified among the Mound Bottom salt pan vessels. One is a simple, direct rim that was often only rounded. Sherds from 17 vessels with this rim form were identified. Measured rim diameters for 10 of the 17 vessels range from 30 to 52 cm, with a mean of 43 cm. A second rim form has a slightly flaring or thickened rim. This portion of the sample includes sherds from at least 45 vessels, and estimated rim diameters range from 28 cm to 50 cm, with a mean of 41 cm. Although occasionally noted at other sites, there were no sherds in this collection that had fabric impressions on their interior surfaces.

TEXTILES AS TOOLS
IN POTTERY MANUFACTURE

William H. Holmes presented an early general discussion of the use of textiles in the modeling and embellishing of aboriginal pottery in the eastern United States. Holmes (1903:68) reported five classes of textile markings found on pottery: 1) impressions of rigid forms such as baskets; 2) impressions of pliable fabrics; 3) impressions of textiles used over the hand or some other suitable implement; 4) impressions of cords wrapped around modeling paddles or rocking tools; and 5) impressions of pieces of cordage or other textile units specifically applied for decoration. He also indicated that in many cases textile effects were mechanically imitated in impressions and markings on pottery. Pliable fabrics, according to Holmes (1903:71), were used as exterior supports in holding or handling vessels that were in a plastic condition. In this way, textiles facilitated the removal of partially dried clay vessels from molds and supported them during subsequent stages of the shaping and finishing processes. Moreover, textiles wrapped around the surface of plastic pottery walls also would have prevented rapid drying and consequent cracking.

Since the time of Holmes, analysts have debated whether the fabric impressions on salt pans were decorative or functional (e.g., Brown 1980:30–31). Holmes (1896:45) believed that they were decorative in nature since not all salt pans were fabric-impressed. Linton (1944:373) considered modeled and incised decoration, cord marking, and fabric impressions as a better means of decorating cooking pots than the use of painted designs, because the paint would be obscured by smoke blackening. In Linton's view, fabric impressions provided one outlet for aesthetic expression that could withstand a good deal of smoke blackening without being obscured.

Currently, many archaeologists accept a functional explanation for the fabric impressions and believe that the fabrics served to facilitate molding the pans. It has been generally accepted that salt pans were constructed using some form of a mold. Baskets, earthen basins, and wooden or clay molds have all been proposed as aids in salt pan manufacture (e.g., Brown 1980:31–36; Orr 1951:316–317). Brown suggests that some form of technological advance made the use of textiles unnecessary in the production of smooth-surfaced salt pans, but this matter remains unresolved. However, various construction techniques for salt pan ceramics can be proposed (see Brown 1980:Figure 6).

One inferred method of manufacture (or a variation thereof) is used in the following discussion of Mound Bottom textiles, as derived from Keslin (1964:50):

A basin-shaped pit was prepared in the soil and its concave surface was compacted either by tamping or puddling. A portion of twined cloth was then placed over the pit and clay was spread over the surface of the cloth. It is probable that the clay was first malleated and then smoothed with the hand. When the clay had dried sufficiently, the vessel was removed from the mold and separated from the fabric which had facilitated removal. After an additional drying period the vessel was fired.

Textiles could have been used repeatedly in this manner of pottery manufacture. Since the manufacture of textiles is more time and labor intensive than the manufacture of pottery, such reuse would have been desirable. The stresses placed upon the textiles during the handling of large plastic ceramic vessels would have been considerable, but this technique would have minimized the stresses on the ceramics. The textile attributes that were necessary or desirable for usage in such a technique of ceramic manufacture are discussed below.

TEXTILE MANUFACTURE

Textile manufacture requires at least three levels of decision making. Each level affects the others and ultimately affects the resulting fabric characteristics, which, in turn, determine performance in various final uses. These three levels of decision making include: 1) fiber selection and processing; 2) yarn construction or structure; and 3) fabric construction or structure.

Fiber Selection and Processing

Textile impressions on pottery do not provide a good source of information relating to fiber selection and processing. The fibers represented in the Mound Bottom sample are most probably vegetal or cellulosic, as opposed to animal or protein. This supposition is based on information from similar Mississippian textile remains that are extant, rather than on direct evidence found in negative impressions or positive cast reconstructions. However, the use of protein fibers of animal hair and feathers also has been documented in Mississippian textiles (e.g., Holmes 1896; King and Gardner 1981; Kuttruff 1988, 1993; Sibley et al. this volume; Willoughby 1952). Animal fibers were sometimes used in combination with vegetal fibers.

Either soft (bast) fibers, which are elongated strands from the stem structure or inner bark of plants, or hard (leaf) fibers of plants, which are comparatively stiff elongated strands from leaves and leaf stems, may have been utilized (Emery 1966:5; Hurley 1979:3–4; Scholtz 1975:10). The use of bast fibers would have produced a more flexible textile than the use of leaf fibers. Evidence of extensive fiber shredding and/or separation, such as protruding fiber ends, was not observed in the impressions or in the positive casts. However, it may not be possible to see evidence on this scale due to the coarseness of the paste of the pottery and the subsequent use and wear of the vessels. The fibers observed in the positive casts looked very similar throughout the sample in any case.

Yarn Construction or Structure

Following Emery (1966:9), three classifications of yarn structure, or fabric elements, were observed. These all can be classified under the head-ing of fibers of limited length and include combined unspun, single spun, and plied spun yarns (Table 9.1). Only one example of a combined unspun fabric element was represented in the sample (Figure 9.1A). The passive elements of this spaced twined fabric apparently consisted of multiple strands of fibrous material used as a unit, but the strands were not twisted together. It was one of the coarser fabrics in the total sample, with the passive combined elements measuring 4.0 mm and the active spun single elements measuring 3.0 mm. Because they were not spun, the fibers of the combined elements were free to spread out or open up, and thus there were no spaces between the inactive elements. Other spaced twined fabrics with spun singles or plies exhibited at least a small opening or space between passive elements.

The most commonly occurring yarn structure is spun single yarn (Figure 9.1B). Spinning is the process of drawing out and twisting together fibers of limited length into a continuous strand. Length, size, strength, and texture of the yarn can be controlled during the spinning process. A single yarn is the simplest continuous assemblage of spun fibers that is suitable for fabric construction. These yarns are present in the Mound Bottom sample both as active and passive elements of twined fabrics and range in diameter from 1.0 to 3.0 mm. Of the identifiable active twining elements, 97.7% are spun single yarns, and 87% of the passive elements are of this type.

Plied yarns are formed by twisting together two or more spun single yarns. All of the examples identified appear to be two ply, that is, composed of two single yarns twisted together (Figure 9.1C).

Table 9.1. Classification of Yarn Structures from the Mound Bottom Site

	Active Elements		Passive Elements	
	No.	%	No.	%
Unspun				
Combined	0	0.0	1	0.3
Spun				
Single	338	97.7	301	87.0
Plied	8	2.3	44	12.7
TOTAL	346	100.0	346	100.0

These plied yarns are present both as active (n = 8) and as passive (n = 44) elements of twined fabrics. They are present in 45, or 13%, of the identifiable fabric structures.

Both the direction and the angle of the ply twist were recorded. In all instances, the yarns were S-plied, or twisted in such a fashion to produce a slant down to the right (\) when held in the vertical position. The angle of twist ranges from 15° to 35° from the vertical axis of the yarn. Emery (1966:12) designated a yarn of "medium" twist as having an angle between 10° and 25°, and a "tight" twist as having an angle between 25° and 45°. Using these designations, 41% of the plied passive elements have a medium twist and 59% have a tight twist. Among the plied active elements, 87.5% have a medium twist and 12.5% have a tight twist.

Fabric Construction or Structure

The most common form of fabric structure in the sample is twining. In a twined fabric, at least two active elements spiral or turn about each other and enclose the opposite set of passive elements. According to Emery (1966:196), twined fabrics can vary from one another in the following ways: 1) the direction of the twining twist; 2) the number and succession of non-twining elements; 3) the amount or degree of twining twist between passages of non-twining elements; and 4) the number of components of each twining group. Another variation in twined fabrics is whether the active or twining elements are in the warp (lengthwise) or weft (crosswise) direction of the fabric.

Because the textile evidence preserved as negative impressions on pottery sherds is fragmentary, it is usually impossible to determine the direction of the warp and the weft elements of the fabric structure. In spaced twining, the weft is generally assumed to be the active, or twining set, of elements. This is based on Emery's statement that warp twining is consistently compact or close twined and weft twining can be either compact or spaced. Examples of complete or nearly complete Mississippian period twined textiles seem to support this assumption (e.g., Kuttruff 1988; Scholtz 1975). However, it cannot be taken as a conclusive statement.

Figure 9.1. Mound Bottom site yarn construction with sherd on the left and cast on the right: A) combined unspun yarn; B) spun single yarn; C) spun plied yarn.

Of the total of 510 sherds examined, fabric structures could be identified for 346, or 67.8%. Three basic twined fabric structures are identifiable in the Mound Bottom sample using Emery's classification. These include: 1) spaced (open) two strand S-twist weft twining; 2) spaced (open) two strand S-twist alternate-pair weft twining; and 3) possibly compact (close) two strand twining. A fourth category was also used to include complex structures, or combinations of two or more fabric structures (Table 9.2).

Spaced two strand S-twist weft twining (Figure 9.2A) is present on 76.8% of the identifiable sherds. An S-twining twist slants down to the right (\) when the active elements are held in the vertical direction, but slants down to the left when the passive elements are held in the vertical position. In every case where the direction of the twining twist is discernible, it is an S-twist. The spacing between twining rows varies from less than 3 mm to more than 20 mm.

Spaced two strand S-twist alternate-pair weft twining (Figure 9.2B) is the second most frequently occurring fabric structure and constitutes 17.1% of the identifiable sample. In this structure, the twining elements enclose the passive, or warp, units in pairs and repeatedly form new pairs by splitting those in the previous row. This results in a zigzagging of the deflected warps.

The third category of possibly compact two strand twining (Figure 9.2C) is questionable because it was difficult to determine its true structure due to the closeness of the yarns. Impressions made by compact warp or weft twining and warp or weft faced plain weave would have been almost identical. Without the actual fabric, a positive identification is not typically possible. There are only five examples, or 1.5% of the sample, in this category. The distance between centers of the obscured elements ranges from 7 mm to 13 mm.

There are 16 examples in the fourth category of complex structures, or combinations of two or more fabric structures (Figure 9.3). They constitute 4.6% of the identifiable sample. This category includes combinations of compact and spaced twining, spaced and alternate-pair twining, twining and 1/1 interlacing, twining and irregular interlacing, and areas of grouped yarns. Most of the pottery sherds are too small to give a clear indication of overall patterning which would have resulted from the combinations of fabric structures. One example of spaced and alternate-pair twining forms an obvious diagonal design line in the fabric structure (Figure 9.3B). The combinations of compact and spaced twining form horizontal design lines.

Textile Attributes and Pottery Manufacture

Textile attributes can reveal information about variation in textile use. Specimen morphology and composition affect the performance of a textile under varying conditions, and the costs involved in both labor and materials may reflect the importance or value placed upon a particular textile specimen. Since this study deals only with textiles used in the manufacture of large, utilitarian ceramic vessels, certain textile attributes likely would be desirable and others likely would be avoided. Therefore, a rather narrow view of the total Mississippian period textile complex might be obtained if this were the only source of textile information.

There remains the question of whether the textiles used in pottery manufacture were made solely for that purpose, or were originally made with other uses in mind. In the latter case, the usage of textiles in pottery manufacture would be a secondary rather than a primary function, and their particular utilitarian characteristics would be determined by different criteria. However, these textiles were at least selected to function in pottery manufacture and, therefore, certain characteristics would have been considered in their selection. If the textiles were created specifically for pottery manufacture and were purely functional, a limited variety of textiles might be expected. However, if the textiles were created for other purposes, or were considered as a means of decoration, then a greater degree of textile variation might be expected. Drooker (1989, 1990, 1992) attempted to classify the textiles utilized on fabric-impressed pottery from the Wickliffe Mounds site in Kentucky according to functional categories. She concluded that the textiles most likely represented the range of utilitarian large-sized textile items made and used in the village, such as garments, blankets, hunting and fishing nets, and possibly large bags.

Table 9.2. Classification of Fabric Structures from the Mound Bottom Site

	No.	%
Spaced twining	266	76.8
Spaced alternate-pair twining	59	17.1
Compact structures	5	1.5
Complex structures	16	4.6
TOTAL	346	100.0

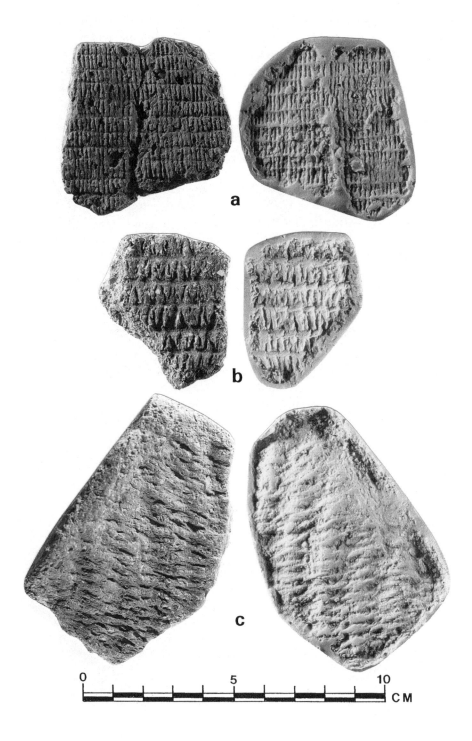

Figure 9.2. Mound Bottom site fabric structure with sherd on the left and cast on the right: A) spaced two strand, S-twist twining; B) spaced two strand S-twist alternate-pair twining; C) compact two strand twining.

Figure 9.3. Mound Bottom site complex or combined fabric structures with sherd on the left and cast on the right: A) compact and spaced twining; B) spaced and alternate-pair twining; C) grouped yarns.

Fabric Characteristics

Specific characteristics of fabrics used in pottery manufacture would include relatively high levels of flexibility, strength, and durability. These characteristics would be desirable because of the stresses placed upon the fabric when used as described above. Each of these characteristics is related to choices made during the manufacture of the textile. These choices ultimately determine fiber content, yarn structure, and fabric structure.

Yarns made of longer fibers, such as bast or leaf fibers, generally have more strength than yarns made of shorter fibers. The longer the fibers, the lesser the twist (or spin) necessary to make a cohesive yarn. As noted above, in some instances twist is not even necessary. The angle of twist in the single yarns was not discernible in the pottery impressions. However, it was fairly obvious that some degree of twist was employed. Up to a point of diminishing return, an increase in the amount of twist in a yarn will increase its strength.

The number of fibers spun together also affects the strength of a yarn and will be reflected in yarn diameter. The Mound Bottom yarn diameters range from 1.0 to 4.0 mm. Only 1.1% of the yarns are 4.0 mm in diameter, 69.6% range from 2.0 to 3.9 mm, and 29.3% range from 1.0 to 1.9 mm in diameter. In combination with the fiber type, the diameter of the yarns also affects the stiffness of the fabric. A fabric made with large yarns composed of stiff fibers is less flexible than one made with smaller yarns of comparable fibers. A plied yarn is generally stronger and more even in diameter than a single yarn, but plying also adds to the labor cost involved. This added strength and evenness may not have been necessary, however, since in the Mound Bottom sample plied yarns are present in only 13% of the fabric structures.

More than 95% of the identified Mound Bottom fabric structures are fairly simple. The labor costs involved in making these fabrics would be lower than if the fabric structures were more complex and intricate. In the spaced two twined structures, increasing the distance between the rows of twining elements would decrease time necessary for their construction. The spacing between twining rows also affects the flexibility of the fabric, with increasingly open constructions being more flexible and more easily manipulated.

The stability of fabric structure also may have been an important factor in relation to its usage in pottery manufacture. An open twined fabric would be much more stable and would have less yarn slippage than a comparably open interlaced fabric. It should be noted that no open interlaced fabric structures were identified, even though a fabric of this type could have been made more quickly than the structures represented in the sample.

Fabric Wear and Manipulation

Some evidence of fabric wear was identified from the pottery impressions (Figure 9.4). This evidence included missing or broken active and/or passive elements, and fabric distortion (see Figure 9.4A). Fabric distortion was evidenced by overly irregular twining rows that may have been forced out of their original position by stress applied during use of the textile in ceramic manufacture. Fabric distortion also was noted when the angle of intersection between active and passive elements was considerably different than a 90° angle (see Figure 9.4B).

Layering of fabric was noted in the impressions (see Figure 9.4C). This layering may have been the result of folds in a textile as it was placed in the mold or the result of the use of more than one textile to fill the mold. Only one-third of the instances of layering were noted on rim sherds; the remaining two-thirds were on body sherds. If the layering resulted from a single flat textile being placed into a curved, basin-shaped mold, then one would expect more layering near the outer edges of the vessel. However, other factors affecting these observations include indistinguishable fabric impressions near the rims due to smearing or smoothing and difficulty in determining the position of a body sherd in most pan vessel forms. Consequently, those body sherds exhibiting fabric layering actually may have been from a position fairly close to the outer edge of the vessel.

Figure 9.4. Mound Bottom site fabric wear and manipulation with sherd on the left and cast on the right: A) missing/broken elements and distortion of twining rows; B) distortion of angle of intersection of warp and weft; C) layering.

In summary, the antiquity of textiles predates the antiquity of ceramics in the eastern United States, and the ceramic arts have been intimately associated with the textile arts. Holmes (1903:68) considered textile forms and markings to be characteristic of the initial stages of the ceramic arts in this portion of North America. Many Early Woodland period ceramics illustrate these associations, and they are also evident in Mississippian period fabric-impressed ceramics as demonstrated here and elsewhere (e.g., Drooker 1992; Wilder 1951).

Attributes of textiles as evidenced on fabric-impressed Mississippian pottery have been analyzed and related to characteristics of their utility. The decisions made during textile manufacture determine specific textile attributes and, ultimately, fabric characteristics and end-use performance. Fiber type attributes result from both natural and cultural factors; attributes such as fiber processing, yarn construction, fabric structure, and decoration result more from cultural factors. The combinations of these attributes determine the characteristics of utility in finished textiles. In this study, the final twist in all plied yarns was in the S-direction and all discernible twining twist or weft slant was also in the S-direction. Similar findings have been reported by Drooker (1989, 1990, 1992) for a larger sample of textile impressions from the Wickliffe site in Kentucky. This pattern may indicate broad-scale cultural preferences for both yarn construction and twining twist among Mississippian textiles, at least as represented in ceramic impressions.

The use of textiles in the manufacture of Mississippian ceramics served both decorative and functional purposes. The textiles facilitated removal of ceramic vessels from their molds and minimized stresses on them during handling and drying. Textiles used in the process of pottery manufacture were subjected to considerable stress, and therefore strength and durability along with flexibility would have been important fabric characteristics. Textile attributes represented on the fabric-impressed ceramics from the Mound Bottom site in Tennessee reflect the decisions and techniques used to achieve the necessary textile characteristics in the finished structures. If the textiles were made

solely to be used in pottery manufacture, then these decisions reflect an effort to create fabrics strictly suitable for that purpose. However, if the use of the fabrics in pottery production was a secondary use, as may well have been the case, then the preserved attributes more likely reflect the selection of specific fabrics that were suitable for the manufacture of pottery.

REFERENCES CITED

Benthall, Joseph L.
1983 Archaeological Investigation at the Noel Cemetery Site. Unpublished ms. on file, Tennessee Division of Archaeology, Dept. of Conservation, Nashville.

Braun, David P.
1983 Pots as Tools. In *Archaeological Hammers and Theories,* edited by James A. Moore and Arthur S. Keene, pp. 107–134. Academic Press, New York.

Brown, Ian W.
1980 *Salt and the Eastern North American Indian, An Archaeological Study.* Lower Mississippi Survey Bulletin 6. Peabody Museum, Harvard Univ., Cambridge.

Clay, R. Berle
1963 *Ceramic Complexes of the Tennessee–Cumberland Region in Western Kentucky.* Unpublished M.A. thesis, Dept. of Anthropology, Univ. of Kentucky, Lexington.

Dowd, John T.
1972 *The West Site: A Stone Box Cemetery in Middle Tennessee.* Tennessee Archaeological Society Miscellaneous Paper 10.

Drooker, Penelope Ballard
1989 *Textile Impressions on Mississippian Pottery at the Wickliffe Mounds Site (15Ba4), Ballard County, Kentucky.* Unpublished M.A. thesis, Harvard Univ., Cambridge.
1990 Textile Production and Use at Wickliffe Mounds (15Ba4), Kentucky. *Midcontinental Journal of Archaeology* 15(2):163–220.
1992 *Mississippian Village Textiles at Wickliffe.* Univ. of Alabama Press, Tuscaloosa.

Emery, Irene
1966 *The Primary Structure of Fabrics: An Illustrated Classification.* The Textile Museum, Washington, D.C.

Holmes, William H.
1896 Prehistoric Textile Art of the Eastern United States. *Annual Report of the Bureau of American Ethnology, 1891–1892,* pp. 3–46. Smithsonian Institution, Washington, D.C.

1903   Aboriginal Pottery of the Eastern United States. *Annual Report of the Bureau of American Ethnology, 1898–1899*, pp. 1–237. Smithsonian Institution, Washington, D.C.

Hurley, William M.
1979   *Prehistoric Cordage: Identification of Impressions on Pottery*. Taraxacum, Washington, D.C.

Keslin, Richard O.
1964   Archaeological Implications of the Role of Salt as an Element of Cultural Diffusion. *The Missouri Archaeologist* 26:1–174.

King, Mary E., and Joan Gardner
1981   The Analysis of Textiles from Spiro Mound, Oklahoma. In *The Research Potential of Anthropological Museum Collections*, edited by Anne-Marie E. Cantwell, James B. Griffin, and Nan A. Rothschild, pp. 123–139. Annals of New York Academy of Sciences 736. New York.

Kline, Gerald W.
1979   *Fall/Winter 1977 Phase II Archaeological Testing at the Ducks Nest Site (40WR4)—Proposed State Route 55 Bypass Highway Construction Project, Warren County, Tennessee*. Dept. of Anthropology, Univ. of Tennessee, Knoxville. Submitted to the Tennessee Dept. of Transportation.

Klippel, Walter E., and William M. Bass (editors)
1984   *Averbuch: A Late Mississippian Manifestation in the Nashville Basin*. Dept. of Anthropology, Univ. of Tennessee, Knoxville. Submitted to the National Park Service, Atlanta.

Kuttruff, Carl
1979   Mound Bottom and Pack Sites, Tennessee. Unpublished ms. on file, Tennessee Division of Archaeology, Dept. of Conservation, Nashville.

Kuttruff, Jenna Tedrick
1988   *Textile Attributes and Production Complexity as Indicators of Caddoan Status Differentiation in the Arkansas Valley and Southern Ozark Regions*. Unpublished Ph.D. dissertation, Dept. of Clothing and Textiles, Ohio State Univ., Columbus.
1993   Mississippian Period Status Differentiation through Textile Analysis: A Caddoan Example. *American Antiquity* 58(1):125–145.

Kuttruff, Jenna Tedrick, and Carl Kuttruff
1992   Textile Production and Use as Revealed in Fabric Impressed Pottery from Mound Bottom (40CH8), Tennessee. *Mississippi Archaeology* 27(2):1–27.

Linton, Ralph
1944   North American Cooking Pots. *American Antiquity* 9:369–380.

Marshall, Park
1916   The Topographical Beginnings of Nashville. *Tennessee Historical Magazine* 2(1):31–39.

Muller, Jon
1984   Mississippian Specialization and Salt. *American Antiquity* 49(3):489–507.

O'Brien, Michael J.
1977   *Intrasite Variability in a Middle Mississippian Community*. Unpublished Ph.D. dissertation, Dept. of Anthropology, Univ. of Texas, Austin.

Orr, Kenneth G.
1951   Change at Kincaid: A Study of Cultural Dynamics. In *Kincaid, A Prehistoric Illinois Metropolis*, by Faye-Cooper Cole and others, pp. 293–359. Univ. of Chicago Press, Chicago.

Phillips, Philip
1970   *Archaeological Survey in the Lower Yazoo Basin, Mississippi, 1949–1955*. Papers of the Peabody Museum of Archaeology and Ethnology 60(1). Harvard Univ., Cambridge.

Scholtz, Sandra Clements
1975   *Prehistoric Plies: A Structural and Comparative Analysis of Cordage, Netting, Basketry, and Fabric from Ozark Bluff Shelters*. Arkansas Archeological Survey Research Series 9. Univ. of Arkansas Museum, Fayetteville.

Thruston, Gates P.
1973   Antiquities of Tennessee and the Adjacent States . . . In *Antiquities of the New World, Early Explorations in Archaeology* 11. AMS Press, New York. (Orig. pub. 1890.)

Walker, Winslow M., and Robert McCormick Adams
1946   Excavations in the Mathews Site, New Madrid County, Missouri. *Transactions of the Academy of Science of St. Louis* 31(4):75–120.

Webb, William S.
1952   *The Jonathan Creek Village, Site 4, Marshall County, Kentucky*. Univ. of Kentucky Reports on Anthropology 8(1). Lexington.

Wilder, Charles G.
1951   Kincaid Textiles. In *Kincaid, A Prehistoric Illinois Metropolis*, by Faye-Cooper Cole and others, pp. 366–376. Univ. of Chicago Press, Chicago.

Williams, Stephen
1954   *An Archaeological Study of the Mississippian Culture in Southeast Missouri*. Unpublished Ph.D. dissertation, Dept. of Anthropology, Yale Univ., New Haven.

Willoughby, Charles B.
1952   Textile Fabrics from the Spiro Mound. *The Missouri Archaeologist* 14:107–118.

10

Joan S. Gardner

The Role of Storage and Handling
in the Preservation of Fibrous Materials
in Museums and Other Repositories

Proper storage and handling of fragile fibrous specimens in museums and other repositories is essential for their survival. Variations in the type of fiber raw materials and their state of preservation may necessitate corresponding differences in their conservation. This chapter presents basic information about appropriate methods of storage and handling of such specimens, particularly the very fragile remnants of prehistoric fibrous industries from eastern North America and elsewhere.

The treatment of fibrous materials should be left to trained conservators whenever possible, although conservation techniques have been developed which are useful to professional conservators and researchers alike (e.g., Florian 1977; Gardner 1979, 1980, 1988; Kronkright 1981; Schaffer 1976). The sheer multitude of plants available to native craftsmen in the East and elsewhere can make conservation treatment complicated. Other complications result from cellular differences between different plant parts, such as root, stem, inner and outer bark, etc., utilized in an object's construction, as well as preservation biases inherent in the archaeological record and factors of recovery and curation.

In the past, overly stringent or inappropriate cleaning and mending methods have stripped away the natural patina of different fibrous materials which once protected them and/or have caused other problems leading to their deterioration. Even the seemingly innocuous cleaning technique of vacuuming (with a muslin screen over the nozzle of the vacuum) can be damaging if incorrectly administered (see Wolf 1977 and Florian et al. 1990 for discussion of basketry cleaning methods and associated problems). Likewise, the storage of fibrous specimens often has been haphazard, with little concern for protection from heat, humidity, dust, air movements, and insect pests, among other threats. Inappropriate cleaning, mending, and storage have contributed to the deterioration of fragile fibrous specimens in many cases (Florian et al. 1990:216–226).

Proper storage has become an important aspect of conservation that personnel in museums and other repositories may now address with great success. Through proper storage and handling techniques, fragile specimens may be curated under conditions which will greatly improve their long-term stability and thus will help ensure their survival.

STORAGE AND HANDLING RECOMMENDATIONS

Museums and other repositories can help preserve fibrous specimens in their collections in several different ways. These include: 1) retention of detritus from fibrous objects to be used for fiber identification and analysis of suitable conservation treatments; 2) analysis of plant fibers and constituents by botanists since specific conservation procedures then can be designed for the whole structure of an individual specimen; and 3) proper storage and handling of such specimens, whether whole or fragmentary. Proper storage requires that only chemically inert or acid-free materials be in direct contact with the fibers, that proper supports be fashioned to prevent breakage or warpage and, finally, that environmentally controlled storage areas be established for their housing. If environmentally controlled storage is impossible, creation of favorable micro-environments for the stored fibrous objects should be instituted.

Various chemically inert or acid-free materials are used at the Carnegie Museum of Natural History (CMNH) to support or enclose fibrous materials. These include acid-free tissue and matboard, expanded polyethylene foam (e.g., Ethafoam and Jiffyfoam trade names), and polyester batting, muslin, and polyethylene in sheet form. Acid-free tissue can be either alkaline buffered (with a pH range of 7.0 to 8.5), or unbuffered (usually near neutral, or 7.0 pH). Unbuffered tissue is generally preferred if the storage area is subject to humidity problems. Before purchasing these or other supplies, the specific properties of each material should be investigated so that they can be used most beneficially. For example, catalogs and other information can be obtained directly from suppliers that cater to conservation-minded institutions; these suppliers often provide invaluable advice as well.

Most of the archaeological fiber specimens from eastern North America are fragmentary with brittle extremities that need protection. All too often specimens from some of the most significant archaeological sites in the region have been allowed to languish in containers that are too large, too tight, or otherwise incorrectly packed. The fragments become more degraded with each opening of the drawer and/or container that holds them. Poor storage and uninformed handling thus take their toll.

Each fibrous specimen should have acid-free tissue folded or nestled closely around it however it is stored. This acid-free enclosure can then be nestled in a box with polyethylene foam, cotton, or other supportive material underneath and around it. Cotton, however, should not be in direct contact with the fiber specimens as they may become embedded in the cotton and damaged. Stacking of specimens on top of one another is not recommended. It is also important that each specimen rests on a piece of acid-free matboard so that upon examination it can be lifted by the matboard rather than by the fiber specimen itself.

Inversion of flat fragments can be accomplished by placing another piece of matboard atop the specimen, immobilizing it with inert materials, and by carefully and deftly turning it over. This prevents manipulation of brittle or delicate binding stitches, etc., that might break if the specimen is lifted or flexed.

It should be emphasized that creativity is paramount in designing supportive and chemically stable containers to accommodate fragmentary fibrous specimens and whole specimens of varying shapes and sizes. It is important that attention be paid also to whether or not toxic materials (such as arsenic or DDT) have been used on them. A particulate face mask and plastic gloves should be used to handle items so treated, and they should be handled as little as possible.

Various techniques can be used to anchor flat fibrous objects such as sandals or matting so that they are stored safely, but the specific techniques depend on their condition. If a fibrous object is tightly woven and in good condition, it may be anchored to acid-free, lignin-free matboard with cotton twill tape. Carefully placed slits in the matboard will allow for secure placement of the object.

Other storage techniques may be more appropriate (e.g., Johnson and Horgan 1979; Ward 1978). An acid-free container designed for storage of archaeological fabrics (Piechota 1978) may be modified for storage of fragile fiber fragments as well. Storage containers may be easily constructed from polyethylene foam, which comes in various thicknesses and, recently, in a flexible rod form that can be formed into rings. For example, flat mat fragments from Craig Mound at the Spiro site have been stored by using bubblepack and polyethylene cut-out layers placed around the fragments to hold

them securely within alkaline-buffered, tissue-lined boxes (Gardner 1980:18–23). Polyethylene foam cut-outs and acid-free matboard and tissue also provide safe storage for fiber specimens (Figure 10.1). As noted above, fiber specimens should be surrounded with acid-free tissue so that the tissue can be used to lift them and to prevent the fibers from becoming embedded in the surrounding bubblepack or polyethylene foam.

Three-dimensional and/or curved fibrous objects, such as sandals, baskets, net bags, etc., may need interior support to prevent warping or collapse over time. These may be padded with acid-free buffered or unbuffered tissue (Figure 10.2) or with "pillows" made from unbleached muslin filled with polyester batting. Complete baskets

Figure 10.1. Basketry fragment from Utah curated at the Carnegie Museum of Natural History. Cut polyethylene foam supports a curved portion of the basket (toward right) which has been placed on acid-free, lignin-free matboard. The matboard has been cut to the shape of the specimen and placed on acid-free tissue to enable it to be lifted from the foam support. The foam support rests on a second piece of matboard.

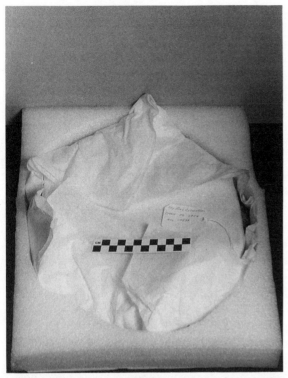

Figure 10.2. Basketry fragment from Utah curated at the Carnegie Museum of Natural History. Note tissue folded over specimen for long-term storage.

may be stored with an interior support of polyethylene foam or acid-free matboard cut to the appropriate diameter to preclude the use of large amounts of wadded tissue. However, a section should be removed from the interior support to allow its removal from the specimen when necessary. Interior supports should be acid-free and should be separated from the specimens so they will not become embedded in them. Acid-free tissue, cotton muslin (natural color and properly washed), or thin polyethylene foam sheeting can be used to separate the supporting structure from the specimen (Figure 10.3). Polyethylene foam comes in different thicknesses and is appropriate for interior support for tall objects such as Haida or Tlingit hats, for example (see Govier 1980 for illustration of such a support structure). Appropriate pads and exterior coil supports are further discussed by Odegaard (1986) and Clark (1988). Although these authors discuss ethnographic basketry, their storage support ideas are obviously also appropriate for archaeological fiber specimens. A recent publication edited by Rose and de Torres (1992) presents many creative solutions for problems related to proper curation of museum collections.

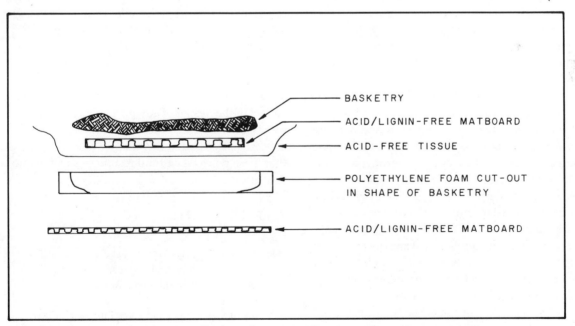

Figure 10.3. Schematic representation of basketry fragment and storage components.

If at all possible, fibrous specimens should be stored in facilities that have climate control—ideally 70°F at 50% relative humidity. Fluorescent lights should have ultraviolet light filtering sleeves and the room should be free of rodents and insect pests. If the storage room cannot have climate control for one reason or another, somewhat stable micro-environments can be created inside a "tight" container or storage case. Such cases or containers will slow down fluctuations in temperature and humidity (Piechota 1978) and provide a less deleterious situation than leaving objects on an open shelf. Steel, rather than wood, cabinets are preferred for storage of museum specimens. If fiber specimens must remain in wooden drawers, then the latter should be lined with acid-free tissue, matboard, or polyethylene foam.

When fibrous specimens must remain on open shelves, they should be enclosed in plastic boxes (shirt or shoe size), or in containers made from polyethylene foam. Large objects, or those with protruding feathers, for example, may need to be covered using supported "tent" structures made from polyethylene sheeting. Plastic boxes should be polyethylene, polypropylene, or styrene. Acid-free, lignin-free boxes of varying heights are available from suppliers that cater to museums. If a protective "tent" structure is necessary, the plastic should not touch the specimen since trapped humidity can cause mold where they are in contact (Wendrich 1991). An interior support is again necessary to prevent deformation of pliable basketry or other structures. Fabrication of these kinds of enclosures certainly requires ingenuity and patience.

When oversized fiber objects do not fit into cabinets or on regular shelving, they are often placed on top of storage cases where heat, dust, and air movements may be deleterious. Again, these objects can be containerized on individual wooden platforms with a superstructure or "tent" arrangement built over them so that air movement and dust are kept off. Such covered structures are also useful when the object must be moved since the platform can be lifted rather than the specimen itself.

If the specimen is unstable or has a curved shape, a "nest" of acid-free tissue, or a ring of poly-

ethylene foam can be placed around its base to steady it (Odegaard 1986). The "nest" or ring can be tied onto the platform with cotton twill tape or cotton twine through perforations in the platform. Hot-melt glue also has been used to anchor such rings (Schlichting 1994). It should be emphasized that corrugated cardboard is highly acidic and should never contact any specimen. If corrugated cardboard must be used, it should be covered with polyethylene sheeting, polyethylene foam, or acid-free alkaline-buffered tissue to prevent direct contact.

To facilitate movement and/or inversion of fibrous specimens, particularly flat and fragmentary ones, extra platforms of various sizes should be available in the storage area so that an object can be carefully and securely held while being inverted. When curation personnel are not available to transport and handle fragile fibrous specimens, researchers should be instructed on how to do so properly. Proper handling procedures are largely common sense, but curators can provide useful tips which will minimize risk to such specimens. Researchers often express concern about handling fragile objects, and conservators and other museum personnel should cooperate toward this end.

In summary, fibrous perishables from archaeological sites are quite rare in eastern North America and elsewhere. Likewise, ethnographic fiber artifacts are often rare and somewhat fragile. Consequently, archaeologists and museum curators should cooperate with conservators and other personnel in the design of adequate storage environments and handling procedures. Attention to the concerns discussed in this chapter will help ensure that these precious cultural resources survive into the future.

REFERENCES CITED

Clark, Thurid
1988 Storage Supports for a Basket Collection: A Preventive Conservation Approach. *Journal of the American Institute for Conservation* 27:87–99.
Florian, Mary-Lou E.
1977 Plant Material Used in Some Ethnological Artifacts, Structure, Fabrication and Deterioration Re-

lated to Conservation Treatment. *American Institute for Conservation Preprints*, pp. 51–55. Boston.

Florian, Mary-Lou E., Dale P. Kronkright, and Ruth E. Norton
1990 *The Conservation of Artifacts Made from Plant Materials*. J. Paul Getty Trust, Los Angeles.

Gardner, Joan S.
1979 Pre-Columbian Textiles from Ecuador: Conservation Procedures and Preliminary Study. *Technology and Conservation* 4(1):24–30.
1980 *The Conservation of Fragile Specimens from the Spiro Mound, LeFlore County, Oklahoma*. Contributions from the Stovall Museum 5. Univ. of Oklahoma, Norman.
1988 Conservation of the Windover Fabrics and Wood. Paper presented at the 53rd annual meeting of the Society for American Archaeology, Phoenix.

Govier, Tom
1980 Conservation of an 1899 Basketry Rain Hat. *Canadian Conservation Institute* 4:12–13. Ottawa.

Johnson, E. Verner, and Joanne C. Horgan
1979 *Museum Collection Storage*. Protection of the Cultural Heritage Technical Handbooks for Museums and Monuments 2. UNESCO.

Kronkright, Dale P.
1981 New Directions in Native American Basketry Conservation. *American Institute of Conservation Preprints*, pp. 95–108.

Odegaard, Nancy
1986 *The Care of Basketry Collections*. Materials Conservation Laboratory. Texas Memorial Museum, Univ. of Texas at Austin, Austin.

Piechota, Dennis
1978 Storage Containerization: Archaeological Textile Collections. *Journal of American Institute for Conservation* 18:10–18.

Rose, Carolyn L., and Amparo E. de Torres (editors)
1992 *Storage of Natural History Collections: Ideas and Practical Solutions*. Society for the Preservation of Natural History Collections, Pittsburgh.

Schaffer, Erika
1976 The Preservation and Restoration of Canadian Ethnographic Basketry. *Studies in Conservation* 21:129–133.

Schlichting, Carl
1994 *Working with Polyethylene Foam and Fluted Plastic Sheet*. Canadian Conservation Institute Technical Bulletin 14. Ottawa.

Ward, Philip R.
1978 *In Support of Difficult Shapes*. British Columbia Provincial Museum Methods Manual 6. Victoria.

Wendrich, Willemina
1991 *Who Is Afraid of Basketry?: A Guide to Recording Basketry and Cordage for Archaeologists and Ethnographers*. Centre for Non-Western Studies Publications 6. Leiden Univ., Leiden.

Wolf, Sara J.
1977 A Survey of Basketry Cleaning Methods. *American Indian Art* 2(3):24–25.

11

Catherine S. Fowler

Eastern North American Textiles:
A Western Perspective

Using "textiles" to refer to a broad range of fiber perishables (e.g., Adovasio 1970; Holmes 1896; King 1979, 1986; Mason 1904), the great antiquity of this major class of artifacts has been documented for western North America, or the West, almost since radiometric dating was developed over 45 years ago. In 1951, an excavation level at Fort Rock Cave in southeastern Oregon containing woven sandals was radiocarbon dated to 8200 B.C. ±230 (Cressman 1951). Later during the 1950s, this date was followed by several more nearly as old in association with baskets and other textile artifacts from Danger Cave in Utah, and younger dates from Lovelock Cave in Nevada and Ventana Cave in Arizona. Due to the often remarkable state of organic preservation in the deep, dry caves of the Great Basin and Southwest, textiles have been commonly recovered over a long period and have been usually analyzed and reported. This is not to say that textile reporting has been always of the highest caliber, however, nor have these textiles

been utilized to the fullest degree in chronological reconstructions and other interpretations.

With a few notable exceptions (e.g., Cressman et al. 1942; Kent 1957; Morris and Burgh 1941, etc.), at least some of the real potential of textiles has been realized in the West only over the last 20 years or so, largely on the basis of work initiated by James Adovasio and carried forward by him and Rhonda Andrews. This brief renew is most obviously designed to comment on aspects of the volume chapters concerning fiber industries from eastern North America, or the East. Emphasis is given to connections in research methods and findings between the East and the West. Various perspectives about the western North American chronology for fiber perishables as presently understood are also discussed, along with some of the problems still pertinent in western textile research (see appendix to this chapter).

Given the size of the data base for the West, the focus of the review on western textiles is primarily on basketry. Comments about other textile types are included too as they are pertinent to the different volume chapters. In all aspects, one will note the centrality of the research done by Andrews and Adovasio. The untimely death of Andrews leaves a void in textile analysis in the West and the East alike that will not soon be filled.

COMMENTS ON THE VOLUME CHAPTERS

The contributions to this volume focus on a number of aspects of prehistoric perishable technologies in the East, bringing together for the first time a collection devoted exclusively to these materials. As pointed out by Petersen in his introductory essay, fiber industries and other perishables are not commonly found in archaeological sites in eastern North America, but rather occur only under unusual circumstances. For the most part, environmental conditions in the East mitigate against good preservation of fiber (and other) perishables, except when in contact with certain materials such as copper, when recovered from dry caves or rockshelters, or when found in water-saturated settings. Often, evidence of eastern perishables is indirect, as for example when impressed into clay on ceramics. Thus, as opposed to much of the West, where textile fragments and even whole items are relatively common, eastern counterparts are rare. Yet, as this collection of essays amply demonstrates, research on fiber perishables in the East has now reached such a point and enough materials have been recovered, either directly or indirectly, that statements about them are worthwhile. The contributions presented here provide data on textile chronologies, methods of analysis, and certain aspects of theoretical inquiry that are timely and should prove useful to other researchers.

For purposes of discussion and comparison with the western data, the individual chapters have been grouped into general categories by theme or topic—although some chapters obviously include data and approaches which fall into more than one category. The first set of chapters are primarily chronological, or deal wholly or partially with developmental sequences or textiles from a specific temporal period. These chapters include Andrews and Adovasio's treatment, which summarizes sequences for the entire East through the Late Archaic period, as well as the contributions by Heckenberger and others, and to a lesser degree, Petersen, Hamilton and others, and Kuttruff and Kuttruff, describing specific sequences or textile types from sites of the Early Woodland, later Woodland, and Mississippian periods. Each of these contributes to our overall knowledge of North American developmental sequences in general and allows for the integration of some specific sets of western and eastern data.

Discussion of these developmental chapters is followed by four chapters that focus on the more theoretical issue of using fiber perishables to infer possible prehistoric group boundaries or ethnicity. These contributions include treatments by Maslowski and also Johnson of cordage, and by Hamilton and others and Petersen of cordage and other materials. These four chapters have parallels in principle to certain studies attempted in the West, where findings have been similar but where the data base differs from the East.

The chapters by Kuttruff and Kuttruff on a particular Mississippian period fabric-impressed ware and Johnson on Mid-Atlantic cordage-impressed wares have only indirect parallels in the textile (and ceramic) literature in the West. The principles of analysis they describe are broadly important, however. One other chapter, by Sibley and others, attempts to reconstruct the full range of behavior related to a particular Mississippian textile on the basis of technological and contextual data. This contribution has indirect counterparts in the western literature, but it describes a type of textile not found there.

Finally, Gardner's chapter reminds us, westerners and easterners alike, of some of the proper methods for caring for fragile fiber perishables, while Petersen's introduction provides a plan of action equally applicable in the East and West, particularly for areas in both regions where the data base is poor and/or possibly can be reworked from new perspectives. More specific comments on the chapters follow.

Andrews and Adovasio

Andrews and Adovasio divide the data for their treatment of the developmental sequence of the East into four temporal periods: Paleoindian (?–8000 B.C.), Early Archaic (8000–6000 B.C.), Middle Archaic (6000–4000 B.C.), and Late Archaic (4000–1000 B.C.). They review the data for each period as represented in eastern sites, along with some of the attendant problems of dating and interpretation. This is a pioneering effort since no one to this time has attempted such a reconstruction using data from the East, although brief comments about the region were included in an earlier overview (Adovasio 1974:122–124). Adovasio and Andrews have previously undertaken broad regional syntheses for various portions of the West, as well as for the western region generally (e.g., Adovasio 1970, 1974, 1986; Andrews and Adovasio 1980; Andrews et al. 1986, etc.). The types reconstructed for each temporal period are nicely summarized in their Table 2.1, and some invite comments from a western perspective.

Regarding the earliest basketry type (in fact the *only* type) documented for the Paleoindian period before 8000 B.C., simple and twill plaiting as found at Meadowcroft Rockshelter and perhaps other locations, little can be added from a western perspective. Plaiting is not present in any of the early archaeological sequences in the West as presently known. Instead, in the West, temporal priority goes to twining as a construction technique; twining showed up in the form of sandals, bags, mats, and perhaps baskets in the Great Basin, Lower Pecos and Trans-Pecos Texas, and the Southwest by ca. 8000–7500 B.C. (Adovasio 1986; Andrews and Adovasio 1980; Hewitt 1980; see also the appendix to this chapter for a discussion of the Great Basin, Lower Pecos and Trans-Pecos Texas, and the Southwest). The early contexts in these western settings would be characterized as Early Archaic, however, since the Paleoindian period is ill-defined or of shorter duration in most of these areas.

Plaiting did become an important component of Early Archaic sequences in at least one portion of the West: the Lower Pecos and Trans-Pecos Texas region. It is reportedly present in Hinds Cave by ca. 6000 B.C., and was certainly well represented by 4000 B.C. (Andrews and Adovasio 1980). It has similar dates in Coahuila, Mexico, and seemingly nearly so in the Tehuacan Valley of Mexico, leading Adovasio (1974) to argue for a Mexican source for plaiting to the north. Perhaps, in light of the early finds in the East, that suggestion may require revision. Thus far, the finds of early plaiting are far to the north and east of Texas and Coahuila, urging caution in designating the source area. The possibility nonetheless remains that the East may be more important to this issue than previously thought.

Interesting evidence of open plain twined bags with *cordage* warps is present in eastern Early Archaic contexts, especially in Tennessee. Cordage warps are a common feature of one of the widely distributed basketry and bag techniques in the Desert West, especially in the northern and western Great Basin, but also perhaps (but thus far much later) in California (see appendix to this chapter). In the early 1900s, Otis T. Mason pointed out the similarities between eastern and western bag-making techniques, including the finishing features, citing a published report (Holmes 1896) on finds near Mammoth Cave, Kentucky (Mason 1904:263).

Lawrence E. Dawson (personal communication 1989) has followed up on these similarities in the East, West, and certain portions of Asia to suggest that this technology may have been one of the earliest to enter the New World with the Native Americans (also see Adovasio, various references). Although Dawson's arguments are still unpublished, the linkages he proposes are very convincing and the details to support them are impressive. The better dated finds reported by Andrews and Adovasio should lend additional support to Dawson's position. Andrews and Adovasio also point to an additional parallel between the East and the West in twining techniques during this early period: the presence of wrapped twining. This rare technique is found ethnographically and also archaeologically (by ca. 500 B.C.) on the Northwest Coast (Croes and Blinman 1980) and in Lower Pecos and Trans-Pecos Texas, but at this point it would be premature to suggest any sort of connection between these areas.

Andrews and Adovasio's lengthy discussion of the extensive and significant collection of Middle Archaic period textiles from the Windover Bog Cemetery in Florida, ca. 5500 B.C., is very welcome. This collection apparently includes fabric garments, which are rarely recovered archaeologically in the region, among other forms. Certainly nothing in the West rivals these finds, including the Southwest, where fabric garments and later loom-woven ones are well known. The complexity of techniques is likewise unparalleled, especially in the twining.

Of particular interest are the apparently equal percentages of S-twist and Z-twist cordage warps in the Windover twining, while S-twist plied wefts are typical. These data apparently have much broader (and confusing) implications for suggesting standardized or ethnically defined technological preferences in particular populations, assumptions upon which many interpretations in prehistoric textile analysis are based. The continuation of plaited forms, which are well dated for this period (as well as the Late Archaic period) at Meadowcroft Rockshelter, adds evidence to counter the argument advanced by Brasser (1975) that ethnographic traditions of plaiting in the Northeast were derived from contact between the Natives and Europeans (but some type of alteration due to contact may not be ruled out).

Although Andrews and Adovasio document several new types of twining for the Late Archaic period, it is the appearance of coiling in the Ozark Bluff region that is of most interest (although these specimens are not well dated). Andrews and Adovasio already draw certain parallels between the types recovered in the Ozark Bluffs—one rod, two rod stacked, and bundle foundations—and types from Lower Pecos and Trans-Pecos Texas, as well as the Plains. Coiling in Texas seems to date much earlier than suggested for the Ozark Bluffs, between 7000–6000 B.C. at the earliest in Texas in contrast with ca. 4000–1000 B.C. in the Ozark Bluffs, but until the Ozark Bluff samples can be reliably dated, their relation to a possible Texas source is premature. Nonetheless, both the Texas and adjacent Mexican sequences show additional developments and refinements in coiling, and thus they may well have

been the source for eastern coiling. Coiling in much of the West may have been derived from these areas as well (see appendix to this chapter).

Andrews and Adovasio conclude with several cogent points, but probably the most important of these has to do with the seeming complexity of eastern fiber technologies, even though the frequencies of known specimens are not nearly as great as those from the West. They note that the East was in no way impoverished technologically and that, in fact, it displayed a richness at least equal to that of the West. The historical picture that Andrews and Adovasio reconstruct is certainly interesting in spite of the low specimen counts. It should cause everyone interested in these important classes of artifacts to rethink the role of eastern textiles in the overall development of textile industries in North America.

Heckenberger and Others

This chapter describes a unique collection of textile artifacts from an Early Woodland period cemetery, the Boucher site, in northwestern Vermont. The Boucher collection is unique in that it is relatively large (n = 155 specimens), well preserved because of the proximity of most pieces to copper, and has a narrow time frame, ca. 800–100 B.C. Heckenberger and others also present data for other Early Woodland and later Woodland periods in the East, thereby continuing the developmental discussions of Andrews and Adovasio beyond the Late Archaic. This contribution largely utilizes the terminology and analytical methods suggested by Adovasio (1977), making it even more complementary.

Several types of twining and one form of braiding are included in the Boucher collection. Both open and close twining have predominant cordage warps, which is interesting in terms of the above discussion of the occurrence of earlier cordage warp fabrics. Although some of the forms are clearly bags, others apparently included actual garments (e.g., shirts, shrouds, etc.) interred with the dead. Adovasio and Andrews (this volume) have described apparent garments from the Middle Archaic Windover Bog Cemetery, and certainly others are known from later periods, but the Boucher collection is an important one because of its antiquity and the variation therein. Garments began to appear in western sites roughly 2000–2500 years ago, in Basketmaker sites of the Southwest (robes, girdles, sashes) and in the Lovelock culture of the Great Basin (aprons), but in both of these latter areas such finds are not particularly common at quite such an early date as at Boucher.

Also of interest within the Boucher collection is the marked preference for a particular spin and twist in both twining warps and wefts, as well as cordage. Unlike what is apparent at Windover, standardization at the Boucher site suggests good possibilities for using these data to suggest broader ethnic and/or cultural affiliations (e.g., the Adena). The Boucher decorative techniques, including one element wrapped twining, lattice work, and color variations, may eventually prove to be good subcultural points of definition. Some of these attributes apparently had continuity into historic times, as the authors suggest.

One interesting aspect of the Boucher collection (and of those from most other eastern contexts) not often seen in the West is the bias created by differential preservation. As the authors note, the preserved fiber structures (garments, bags, and cordage) are largely all associated with copper, usually in the form of adornment beads. The preserved fiber perishables were typically in direct contact with copper. Thus, the fragmentary specimens represent structures which were located in areas where necklaces or perhaps arm bands or bracelets were worn. There is no preservation of footwear or garments from the lower body.

In western sites where there is good preservation because of dryness, a much broader range of functional types is usually found, or at least there is no obvious reason to suspect a systematic preservation bias. It is unfortunate, however, that there is no agent of preservation comparable to that of copper as seen at Boucher and various other eastern sites in the wetter environments of the West, such as northern California and the Northwest Coast. Ceramics and thus ceramic impressions are also lacking in these latter areas and many other portions of the West, further limiting opportunities for the preservation of fiber perishables. The East is fortunate to have had both copper-working and ceramic technologies in areas where perishables preservation is otherwise poor. As with Andrews and Adovasio's chapter, this study appropriately emphasizes the sophistication of twining techniques, including decoration elements, present early in the East.

Petersen, Hamilton and Others, Kuttruff and Kuttruff

Although the focus of these three chapters is not strictly chronological (see other comments below), each of them contributes to knowledge of eastern developmental sequences, and thus they follow the previous chapters. Petersen's chapter on fiber industries during the Woodland period in general carefully documents apparent changes in cordage twist and spin preferences for coastal versus interior groups in New England for several thousand years. Particularly important is the transition that occurred between Ceramic periods 4 and 5, that is, ca. A.D. 1000. Up until that time, the cordage twist preference for the coastal areas was Z-twist, while the interior areas (primarily along waterways) were characterized by an S-twist preference. After that date, Z-twist cordage and twining began to dominate in the interior as well. Although it is uncertain whether or not there is a single, easily explained cause for this change, it does obviously reflect a discontinuity which needs further study (see additional comments about this endeavor below).

The contribution by Hamilton and others documents unequal samples of a variety of fiber perishables during three phases of Late Woodland–period occupation at the Juntunen site in the Great Lakes. Dated ca. A.D. 800–1400, these too establish the different structural forms of cordage and more complicated forms of fiber construction characteristic of the East during the Woodland period. Moreover, they suggest the importance of studying fiber perishables as preserved on ceramics. Likewise, the chapter by Kuttruff and Kuttruff discusses a particular type of fiber perishable-impressed ceramic ware that is common in the heartland of the Mississippian period in the Midwest and adjacent areas during later prehistory. It thus appears to be a chronological as well as a technological marker in this region. Some of the previous interpretations of the functions of this ceramic ware in salt preparation are also questioned, based on distributional data that no longer allow its strict correlation with sites at saline springs. Although none of the chronological aspects of these chapters invites further comments from a western perspective, they are important to the overall sense of chronology in eastern fiber industries that one gets from the volume as a whole.

Maslowski, Johnson, Hamilton and Others, Petersen

These four contributions treat similar topics in different portions of the East: the Ohio Valley (Maslowski), the Potomac Valley (Johnson), the Upper Great Lakes (Hamilton and others) and northern New England (Petersen). All examine cordage spin and twist and twining weft slant as represented primarily on cordage-marked and fabric-paddled ceramic vessels. All similarly conclude that there is considerable value in viewing this feature independently of other ceramic attributes since it helps to define aspects of the textile technological system, as well as that of ceramics. They are further convinced that textile attributes can be used successfully in the definition of ethnic and/or cultural group boundaries.

Maslowski devotes some consideration to instances where cordage spin and twist (or ply) do seem to have been standardized in archaeological and ethnographic contexts. Some of the examples he cites are from the West, including his own work in the western Texas area, where two ply, S-spun, Z-twist cordage was the dominant pattern for certain fiber materials for nearly 8000 years, as it was at nearby sites in Mexico. Similarly, he notes, Lovelock Cave in Nevada produced a standard cordage twist, approximating 99% S-twist over a long period. However, at Danger Cave in the Utah portion of the Great Basin, both S-twist and Z-twist cordage persisted in roughly equal proportions for nearly 10,000 years (see Maslowski references). Although he does not fully explain how cases such as this (and Windover Bog Cemetery) should be inter-

preted, or whether they only appear to contradict arguments about the importance of standardization, the data he provides are thought provoking. He then goes on to discuss some possible subgroupings of Ohio Valley sites based on differences in cordage impressions on ceramics that may have culture-historical value.

The chapter by Hamilton and others and the chapter by Johnson address more geographically restricted areas. Again, they seek to characterize these areas in terms of cordage twist and twining weft slant preferences. The chapter by Hamilton and others provides some sense of the difficulty of doing so. Great care must be taken to isolate the full range of structural complexity in a particular sample such as that from the Juntunen site, given the apparently confounding results of the craftpeople's manipulation of two ply cords into compound cordage, thereby reversing the final twist preference in the compound structures. Johnson's analysis is more problem oriented in that he seeks and tentatively establishes linkages between two late prehistoric manifestations in the Potomac Valley on the basis of cordage twist data from six sites.

Finally, Petersen's chapter is more geographically broad based and more detailed in terms of cordage twist/weft slant correlations, site distributions, and chronological periods. Nonetheless, it reaches conclusions similar to those of Maslowski and Johnson. The cordage and twining data provide additional clues about possible shifts in ethnic boundaries, social networks, or spheres of interaction that remain to be fully explained.

Although various researchers in the past have argued that textile technologies and particularly basketry are among the best markers of ethnic groups, not nearly as many as might be expected have put these suggestions into practice for the interpretation of fiber perishables data in the East or the West. Often, and especially where the archaeological data on perishables seem to fit those for ethnographically resident groups, western researchers have called attention to these similarities (e.g., Adovasio and Andrews 1985; Andrews et al. 1986; Haury 1950; Jennings 1957; Morris and Burgh 1941, etc.). But as the past deepens and the archaeological record becomes less clear, few expand the arguments to identify ethnic groups and boundaries, or potential population movements in the more distant past (but see Adovasio 1980a; Hattori 1982).

Recently, a few researchers have ventured further into this topic using data from the West in an attempt to better understand some of the geographically broad-based archaeological cultures. For example, Hayes and Webster (1992) have noted differences in technical and decorative aspects of Basketmaker II and III textiles of all categories between a Kayenta core area and others on the periphery; these differences may have ethnic as well as chronological implications. Andrews and others (1986) have also summarized arguments for textiles and ethnicity in the northern and central Great Basin, including in their discussion basketry, cordage, and sandals. However, much more needs to be done in the West and the East alike toward understanding variation in ethnographic technologies, especially in cordage, sandals, netting, and knot manufacture. Likewise, cases in which major variation apparently occurs in a single group need further discussion and interpretation.

For example, I recently observed exact opposites in cordage twist in Klamath ethnographic collections at the Hearst Museum, University of California, Berkeley, correlated with *Juncus/Scirpus/Typha* cordage versus that used in fishing gear (nets and lines) of *Urtica/Apocynum/Linum* and other fine fibers. A similar difference based on raw material (and also perhaps function) is observable in the cordage from Lovelock Cave, Nevada (Loud and Harrington 1929), and is paralleled in archaeological sites in Warner Valley, Oregon (Fowler and Cannon 1990; see also Magers 1986, etc.). Interestingly, Spier (1930:145, 152, 174) reported that among the Klamath, women made cordage and rope, and men "and a few women" made fish nets and lines. But, unfortunately, we do not know how or why this division of labor developed, why it should correlate so well with material types, or why one sex should seemingly prefer the opposite fiber twist and ply to the other. Given that technologies such as net making, cordage manufacture, basket coiling, etc., often have

different histories within each ethnic group, this latter aspect needs to be explicitly considered, among other possibilities (L. Dawson, personal communication 1989). Such problems aside, however, the chapters concerned with cordage/twining and ethnicity in this volume offer good incentive for western and other eastern researchers to try similar applications.

Kuttruff and Kuttruff

The essay by Kuttruff and Kuttruff is a study of ceramic manufacture and decoration using textiles. It also contributes to analytical methods. To my knowledge, there is no exact parallel in manufacture techniques between the textile-impressed shallow ceramic vessels from Mississippian sites, as described by Kuttruff and Kuttruff, and any ceramics known in the West. However, there is ample evidence that it was not uncommon for some of the earliest Basketmaker II unfired, fiber-tempered pottery to have been started by impressing clay into either coiled or plaited baskets (e.g., Morris 1980:65, Figures 32 and 33). In the 1920s, Earl Morris (1927) and others discussed the issue of whether or not pottery making began using this procedure, as well as its role in pottery decoration. Their discussions have many parallels with that presented by Kuttruff and Kuttruff, as well as with discussions by other colleagues that they cite.

Sibley, Jakes, and Larson

This chapter describes various aspects of a complex fabric fragment recovered from the Mississippian period Etowah site in Georgia; they report its technology (studied through microscopy), its function, perhaps as part of a garment marking high status, and its ultimate discard in a burial context. The fabric is composed of complex yarns involving hair, feathers, some type of bast fiber core, and perhaps other decorative elements. Although the fabric fragment may have some more or less unique attributes, it has certain parallels to other Mississippian textile fragments from the Southeast and elsewhere. It also has general parallels in western textiles, particularly in terms of its complexity, something also seen in some Anasazi and Hohokam garments from the Southwest. Nonloom and loom textiles from this latter area of this vintage, as well as earlier specimens, can have complex yarn structures that incorporate hair and feathers. Space dying, tie-dye, painting, and other complex forms of decoration produced by the weave structure are also known in the Southwest. A number of these have been comparably recovered from burials, but other contexts are also known. Fewer can be interpreted as high-status burial goods, although some may have been. The range of known fabric types is definitely greater in the Southwest than in the Southeast and elsewhere in the East generally, perhaps due to preservation factors. But the few available fragments of Mississippian cloth definitely indicate a high level of technical skill, in much the same way as do more common basketry and other fiber technologies from the East.

Gardner

Given the state of preservation of many fiber perishables from the East, guidance certainly should be sought and given concerning their proper care and handling. Gardner's chapter sets out some preliminary considerations in this regard, but undoubtedly can be expanded to include a broader range of materials. For example, a series of "don'ts" might be just as useful as a list of "do's" for archaeologists and ethnographers untrained in the handling and conservation of fiber perishables. Conservation methods and principles are sometimes difficult to keep current, however, and therefore anyone who ends up with responsibility for such materials should seek out the latest information, as well as advice and perhaps the help of a trained conservator, as Gardner notes. A recent guide, *The Conservation of Artifacts Made from Plant Materials*, by Florian, Kronkright, and Norton (1990) offers valuable advice about handling various problems, as do some of the other references cited by Gardner.

Petersen

Petersen's chapter introducing this volume summarizes well the history of textile research in eastern North America and to a lesser degree that

in western North America. Through that history one can see a series of problems emerge, such as a lack of standardization in terminology, analytical methods (including which attributes are recorded), presentation format, theoretical underpinnings, integrative orientation, and more complete anthropological interpretation. These problems he sets out as challenges for the future of textile research in eastern North America, but they should be heeded in the West as well. Western studies often suffer from many of the same faults, although many also display various virtues. This is characteristic of some research done long ago as well as some done today. If textile analysis is to move positively forward and take its rightful place alongside other useful types of archaeological (and ethnological) research, as argued by Adovasio and Andrews, as well as others, it must take heed of these suggestions.

In summary, the series of contributions included in this volume represent several notable firsts. They constitute a first in terms of attempting a broad, topical synthesis of eastern North American fiber perishables, a first in their description of new data from previously known and newly reported sites, and a first in setting out some theoretical parameters within which perishables analyses might progress in the future. Each of the chapters, although complete in itself, calls for additional data and more research. The accompanying appendix attached here discusses the status of textile research in various portions of the West, and it too suggests where more data and new syntheses are needed. As can be seen, western North America has produced a larger number of samples than have been found and reported in the East, but research there has just as many problems. Numerous western (and some additional eastern) textiles are curated in museums and other collections which can be studied and restudied from one or another fresh perspective, perhaps reaching new or more complete interpretations as a result. One hopes that a volume such as this written 10 or 20 years hence will reflect some of these new directions.

Given that the other chapters in this volume address fiber industries east of the Rocky Mountains with the exclusion of western Texas, or the Lower Pecos and Trans-Pecos areas, this coverage will include the region west of the Rockies and western Texas. Environmental considerations, as well as what are apparently actual areal and chronological relationships, suggest the placement of at least the drier portions of southern and western Texas and adjacent areas of Mexico with the Desert West (Andrews and Adovasio 1980). The other portions of the West to be covered in this review include the Great Basin, Southwest, California, and the Northwest Coast. Although textile chronologies are best developed for the Great Basin and western Texas, some statements also can be offered for the other areas.

Unfortunately, as in eastern North America, no area in the West is yet thoroughly documented and all have interpretation problems left to be resolved. Some areas that have produced rich collections of ethnographic textiles, such as California and the Northwest Coast, are relatively little known from the standpoint of well-documented archaeological specimens. Environmental conditions not unlike those encountered in much of the East have mitigated against favorable preservation of archaeological textiles in much of the nonarid West, with a few notable exceptions. Recent finds in water-logged settings (e.g., Croes 1976, 1977, 1992, 1993; Croes and Blinman 1980) and even a few negative molds in clay (e.g., Pettigrew and Lebow 1987) have made some of the recovery techniques used in the East also characteristic in the West. In contrast with the East, the presence of long-standing and active ethnographic basketry traditions in much of the West often aids in the interpretation of western textiles in terms of a historic baseline, but this same knowledge of historic and modern materials sometimes also confuses and confounds interpretations.

Subregions of the West

The Great Basin

As noted above, it was the Desert West and more specifically the western and northern Great Basin that produced some of the first and still some of the earliest textiles to be directly dated in the Western Hemisphere (e.g., Cressman 1951). However, long before the development of radiocarbon dating, it was suggested by various researchers that textiles found in the region were old and therefore merited considerable attention. In 1929, Lewellyn L. Loud and Mark R. Harrington, working in the Humboldt Basin of western Nevada, suggested that matting, bags, baskets, sandals, and cordage commonly preserved in Lovelock Cave were at least as old as—if not older than—Basketmaker textiles from the Southwest, then thought to be about 3500 to 4000 years old (Loud and Harrington 1929:120f., citing Kidder 1924:119). It was believed that these western Great Basin specimens might even be a "Sub-Basket-Maker" representation of pre-agricultural development, but at the least they were thought to be contemporaneous with the Basketmaker culture.

Luther S. Cressman (1939; Cressman et al. 1942), working in the Fort Rock Basin and other areas of southeastern Oregon, found sandals and other perishables *below* layers of ash thought to be associated with the eruption of Mt. Mazama (at modern Crater Lake). Based on these finds, he argued for an even greater antiquity for these northern Great Basin materials, perhaps predating the Basketmaker sequence by 1000 years. The earliest materials in the northern Great Basin appeared to be twined sandals, bags, and mats, as well as both twined and coiled baskets, the latter an important feature of the Basketmaker sequences in the Southwest as then understood (Harrington in Loud and Harrington 1929:26).

Radiocarbon dating helped to establish absolute dates for Lovelock Cave and the Fort Rock Basin in the early 1950s. Cressman (1951) was able to vindicate his claims for the antiquity of the Oregon textiles with dates on layers containing sandals and possibly basketry as old as 8200 B.C. ± 230. The Lovelock Cave sequence, ultimately combined by

Robert Heizer and colleagues with sequences from other nearby caves and rockshelters, indicated that the basal dates for these textiles were considerably younger, 1218 B.C. ±260 and 531 B.C. ±260 (Cressman 1956; Heizer 1956), although other finds in the area went back as far as 9000 B.C.

In particular, excavations at Danger Cave on the Nevada–Utah border in the early 1950s helped to substantiate the antiquity of basketry and other textiles in that region, with the level bearing these materials going back to roughly 7000 B.C. (Jennings 1957:64). The work done at Danger Cave also lead Jennings (1957) to develop a new interpretive model for Great Basin prehistory, one not based on the previously prevalent sequence of the Southwest. Jennings's Desert Culture model, later synthesized into a broader Desert Archaic, then became the interpretive framework for a much larger region.

In the late 1960s, Adovasio began systematically re-examining *all* of the extant textile collections from the Great Basin and other western areas to synthesize these data for use in regional and broader reconstructions (e.g., Adovasio 1970, 1974). Since that time, he and Andrews have continued to analyze new data as they have become available, and they have periodically offered revised syntheses (e.g., Adovasio 1986; Adovasio and Andrews 1983; Andrews et al. 1986). Through this work it has been possible to establish subregional variations and chronologies for regional collections. The present perspective on Great Basin textiles can be summarized as follows (see Adovasio 1986):

1) Early in the whole of the region, beginning about 9000 B.C. or so, simple or plain twining in both open and close varieties appeared, as preserved in deep, dry sites. The twining characteristically had Z-twist wefts, except in the eastern Great Basin, where an early preference for S-twist weft twining was shown. Common items made by these methods include sandals, bags, mats, and, in some areas, burden baskets and other containers. In the north, close plain twining over two ply, Z-twist cordage warps was also early, ca. 8000 B.C. (Hattori 1982:90).

2) At ca. 6500 B.C., coiling made its appearance in the eastern Great Basin, particularly at Hogup Cave. This early coiling, of which few specimens are known, was made over single rod foundations with interlocking stitches and probably had ties to areas to the south (e.g., Lower Pecos and Trans-Pecos Texas). The most common artifact type among the coiled specimens is the flat tray, a useful tool for various types of seed processing, including parching. Coiling did not displace twining, and, in fact, it took roughly 2000 years for it to become as common as twining in the eastern Great Basin. Coiling did not appear in the western Great Basin until about ca. 4500 B.C., when it began to show up in small amounts, again in the form of flat trays. Unlike the earliest eastern Great Basin coiling, in the western Great Basin it was made using a multiple rod foundation. However, by the time it was present in the western Basin, the eastern Basin also had multiple rod foundation coiling, along with some unique and localized types (e.g., one rod and bundle stacked). Coiling was absent in the northern Great Basin until much later, although twining types had been elaborated in the north, with the cordage warp variety very common. Mats, sandals, and bags also exhibited some subregional patterning and were far more diverse than earlier. Both coiled and twined wares from the whole region were first decorated during this period, with inlaid feathers in the western coiling, as well as overlays, wrappings, and false embroidery in twining over a larger area.

3) By 2000 B.C., coiling had come to dominate both the western and eastern Great Basin areas, while twining definitely declined. In the eastern area, one rod and bundle foundations became dominant, signaling the development of the Fremont Culture in association with cultigens and village living. Fremont basketry forms are found in eastern and southern Utah, southern Nevada, and portions of southern Idaho and western Colorado. However, this localized basketry tradition disappeared around A.D. 1200 without leaving traces in any ethnographic population. Beyond its distribution, other subregions also developed some unique textile attributes during later prehistory. In the western area, a distinctive type of

plaiting appeared by perhaps 2000 B.C., but certainly by 1000 B.C. Designated Lovelock Wicker, this technique involved the use of split but doubled weft elements plaited with rigid whole twig elements. The most common container made using this technique was a large, conical burden basket. These baskets also featured elaborate twined and plaited selvages, as well as twined starts, and were often elaborately decorated. This tradition disappeared by around A.D. 1000.

4) In the northern Great Basin, coiling finally emerged around A.D. 1000, but probably largely as bowls rather than as large, flat trays. Other forms in twining were also present, including some made on rigid warps with semi-rigid wefts. The cordage warp twining of this area may have emerged historically in the ethnographic traditions of the Klamath and Modoc on the western edge of the area, and/or perhaps among the groups farther north. The source of the coiling may have been the western Great Basin, but that is uncertain. Basket forms then produced in coiling were not unlike those of the historic Northern Paiute or Northern Shoshone (Fowler and Dawson 1986), but also may have been influenced by Plateau groups to the north. Other Great Basin areas also witnessed the transition toward the types of baskets identified with the historic ethnographic occupants of the region, mostly having begun ca. A.D. 1000–1200.

Although the overall sequence seems reasonably clear and concise in this presentation (some details have been omitted for the sake of brevity), there are still problems with it. For example, the exact dating and distribution of the cordage warp twining in the western and northern areas is unclear. Some feel that it was very early, as early as any aspect of the perishables sequence for the overall region. Others have argued previously that it was much later, and, at least in the western subregional area, it may be no older than ca. A.D. 400–500 (Heizer and Krieger 1956). A concerted effort needs to be made to better establish its chronology and placement and, perhaps more importantly, the significance of its distribution. This tradition of cordage warp twining was recognized early (Mason 1904) as having had links to eastern North America

(e.g., Kentucky), but, as reported above, it was even more widespread than previously known.

Other remaining questions include the as yet enigmatic origins of the Fremont culture and the distinctive basketry which it produced, as well as the sources and routes of the dispersion and elaboration of coiling in the region. Coiling is certainly older in the eastern Basin subregion than elsewhere in the Great Basin, but exact linkages to older complexes to the south have not been fully established. Additional questions also remain about the ultimate source of coiling in the northern subregion, as well as about the fate of Lovelock Wicker. Likewise, there are numerous gaps in the distribution of subregional types and styles of Great Basin basketry due, at least in part, to the paucity of deep, dry sites in various locations. Linkages to California, the Southwest, and western Texas have all been proposed for the Great Basin. While these remain plausible, the details of such linkages need to be worked out.

Lower Pecos and Trans-Pecos Texas and Northern Mexico

The fact that a number of deep, dry caves in the Chihuahuan Desert area of western Texas and northern Mexico contain extensive textile assemblages has been known for many years. Unfortunately, a number of such sites were excavated in the 1930s, primarily for their textile artifacts and without much concern for the provenience of these and other finds; a few early notable exceptions are known (e.g., Taylor 1966). In recent years, however, additional sites have been excavated in the region with proper contextual controls (e.g., Story and Bryant 1966; see also Andrews and Adovasio 1980) and a good chronology has been defined for the region. It also has been possible and fruitful to reanalyze some of the previously excavated collections and thereby relate them to the regional sequence (e.g., McGregor 1992).

By far the best reported site-specific sequences come from Hinds Cave (Andrews and Adovasio 1980), the lower Pecos River (e.g., McGregor 1992), and Coahuila, Mexico (e.g., Johnson 1977; Taylor 1966, 1988). Based on these data, Andrews and Adovasio

(1980:366–367) were able to offer summaries for these areas (especially for the basketry) that can be combined into an overall sequence. An outline of this sequence follows (see also Adovasio 1980b):

1) The earliest dated basketry from the region occurred roughly at ca. 7500 B.C. and is twined (at Hinds Cave, an untypable "handle" is dated to about that date). Although twining was relatively uncommon (perhaps it was waning in popularity even by this time, according to Andrews and Adovasio), types represented by ca. 6000 B.C. were open simple twining with S-twist wefts and open diagonal twining with S-twist wefts. Coiling entered the regional record sometime between 7500 and 6050 B.C., as, in all likelihood, did plaiting. Early coiling had a single rod foundation, with stitches split on the nonwork surface. The only form certainly represented was the parching tray, and some of these were constructed with a rightward work direction, while others had a leftward work direction. By roughly 5000–4000 B.C., bundle foundations had been introduced, presumably from farther south in Mexico, as discussed further below. Local areas began to exhibit preferences for one or another foundation type, including whole rod or bundle forms in western Texas and some half rod types in Mexico. However, like twining, coiling remained a minority type in the regional record relative to plaiting. Twill plaiting became favored in the Coahuila area.

2) Plaiting in the form of mats became very common in the western Texas area beginning ca. 4000 B.C., as did coiling on a bundle foundation in both areas. The Coahuila sequence elaborated on single rod types of coiling, although both areas retained the basic single rod form as well. Work direction in the western Texas area was primarily leftward, while Coahuila retained an approximately equal mixture of both directions. Twill plaiting continued to be the dominant construction type, and by ca. 2000 B.C. the type showed various elaborations in pattern as well as finishing techniques. Simple baskets of varying shapes were made, along with mats and sandals (Taylor 1988).

3) By roughly 2000 B.C., coiling on a single rod had become rare in both areas—perhaps absent in Coahuila—and preferences for bundle foundations in western Texas and half rod foundations in Coahuila were characteristic. False braid rims occurred on coiling in both areas, although self rims were also common. Plaiting continued to be elaborated, and some of the Texas sites have produced twilled varieties which, in some cases, had painted geometric decoration. Some coiled baskets in Mexico contained small, woven geometric patterns by at least A.D. 1, or a bit later. Twining became more common in the Coahuila area, although it was never totally lost in either area before that. Textiles from the El Paso portion of Trans-Pecos Texas began to exhibit some influences from the Mogollon of the Southwest by ca. A.D. 700–800, especially the well-known two rod and bundle bunched foundation type in the coiling.

4) The period from roughly A.D. 1000 to European contact in western Texas and A.D. 500 to contact in Coahuila was dominated by plaited types, both elaborately twilled and simple forms. Elaborate plaited patterns diminished in western Texas before European contact, but some persisted in Coahuila. Both coiling and twining also persisted, with the Texas coiling exhibiting additional southwestern influences, at least until the twelfth century. The Coahuila area exhibited some subareal preferences for either bundle foundation coiling or single rod types. But, in all, the sequences for both areas remained similar to each other; at least they were close enough for Andrews and Adovasio (1980:368) to suggest that they were technologically linked, if not linked linguistically, to Coahuiltecan speakers. Adovasio (1980b:97) has further suggested that the Coahuila sequence is just enough earlier in most respects for it to have served as the point of derivation for the western Texas area. McGregor (1992:103) echoes this point, affirming Adovasio's (1980b) suggestion of affinity, but she also points out some differences worth further investigation. For example, the greater similarity between coiling in the Big Bend region and that of Coahuila when contrasted with the Lower Pecos deserves additional study.

The question of origins for the Coahuila textile forms and perhaps some of the other influences on the western Texas forms remain unanswered. In the 1970s, Adovasio (1974:117–119) argued in favor of general affinities for this coiling and plaiting with other areas farther south in Mexico. In particular, he noted that the Tehuacan Valley textiles reported by MacNeish and others (1967) suggested the presence of bundle foundation coiling there by roughly 6800–5000 B.C., perhaps 1000 years earlier than their presence in the north by ca. 5000–4000 B.C. (see also King 1979, 1986). At the time, given the apparent lack of significant antiquity for plaiting in eastern North America, Adovasio felt that its sources in the Coahuila and western Texas areas also were probably to the south in Mexico, but perhaps farther north than the Tehuacan Valley. However, since the Tehuacan Valley seems to have lacked twining, that left the Great Basin or the Southwest as the source(s) for this, the earliest technique in both Coahuila and western Texas. The early single rod coiling, although not precisely like its Great Basin counterparts (e.g., split stitch versus interlocking stitch), was again more northerly than Mexican in appearance. In short, there were and still are many questions to be answered for the region.

McGregor (1992) recently attempted to rectify one other problem pertinent to the textile sequences for this region: the attribution of form and function using the often fragmentary textile record. Using what she refers to as "functional sets" (a concept at least in part derived from Croes [1977]), McGregor applied these to the record for western Texas through the use of ethnographic analogy. In addition to the coiled circular tray forms previously identified, she also suggests the use of circular twined trays, perhaps occasionally for parching, along with the use of coiled bowls (with a somewhat open stitch) for food collecting and perhaps storage, netted carrying baskets/frames similar to those used by the historic O'odham (the *kiaha*) and others, twined gathering/storage bags and baskets, plaited and twined pouches for storing valuables, and a wide array of plaited, twined, and sewn mats. Although some of the forms and functions are speculative, her analysis minimally points toward a research agenda not fully realized through the analysis of textile fragments alone.

The Southwest

Southwestern prehistory has long been studied, to the point that some of its aspects are among the best known worldwide. However, in spite of this long-term productive research, other aspects of prehistory in this region are still poorly documented. One such aspect is the origin and development of the rather complex textile traditions that ultimately emerged in the Southwest. In 1941, Earl Morris and Robert Burgh produced a classic monograph on Anasazi basketry using substantial samples and including valuable details about technology and design. Kate Peck Kent (1957) expanded the coverage to other textiles, particularly fabrics made from cotton for clothing, blankets, footwear, bags, quivers, and various types of netting. Like Morris and Burgh's data base, Kent used a large, relatively late sample, mainly attributable to the period ca. A.D. 300–1550.

In 1950, Emil Haury described over 100 specimens of coiled basketry, a few specimens of plaiting, and two twined bag fragments from Ventana Cave in the Hohokam region of southwestern Arizona, again attributing them to later prehistory, ca. A.D. 800–1400 (Haury 1950:411; see also Sayles 1938). Tularosa and Cordova caves (Martin et al. 1952) produced basketry and sandals from preceramic Mogollon contexts, with dates somewhat earlier at ca. 800–900 B.C. (Matson 1991:228). A similar situation obtained at Bat Cave, also within the Mogollon area (Dick 1965). However, even with these samples, southwestern textile sequences are best documented only for the last 2000 years or so.

This situation has not changed much in recent years. There is still a notable deficit of documented textiles for most of the Archaic period in the Southwest (B. Huckell, personal communication 1992). Finds in the northernmost portion of the region in the Colorado Plateau area provide notable exceptions. In 1968, Lindsey and others published the results of cave excavations immediately north of Navajo Mountain in northeastern Arizona (Lindsey et al. 1968:96). Dates of 5750 B.C. ±120 and 5200 B.C. ±150 were associated with open twined sandals in early levels at Dust Devil Cave. These finds have been matched since by comparable types and dates at Cowboy Cave roughly 166 kilometers (100 miles) to the north in Utah (Hewitt 1980; Jennings 1980). Still more recently, an open twined sandal was dated to 5490 B.C. at Old Man Cave near Blanding, Utah (Geib 1992).

Several specimens of one rod interlocking stitch coiled basketry were also recovered from Sand Dune Cave in a pre-Basketmaker context, of which Adovasio (1974:119) has said: "In all particulars, including splices, this basketry is identical to the earliest one rod coiling from northern Utah, and it is my hypothesis that it diffused southward from the Eastern Great Basin." Basketry at Cowboy Cave includes several one rod types such as one rod with interlocking stitch, one rod and welt with noninterlocking stitch, one rod with split stitch, and one rod with bundle noninterlocking stitch. All of these types date from between 6000 B.C. and 4600 B.C., although they also persisted into later phases at Cowboy Cave. Rather than the one rod with interlocking stitch type being the oldest there, that claim apparently goes to the one rod with welt and noninterlocking stitch type (Hewitt 1980:50).

Later occupations at these various sites produced classic Basketmaker II basketry types, as originally defined by Morris and Burgh (1941) in northern Arizona. These types most commonly include two rod and bundle foundation coiling, one or one-half rod and bundle, and one rod spaced coiling. The Cowboy Cave sample also contains other types that reflect continued interaction with the Great Basin. However, Cowboy Cave, like various other sites in the northern Southwest, has a 2000-year occupational hiatus in its cultural deposits during the middle portion of the Archaic period, which further complicates the sequence. This gap in the local record, combined with the complete absence of Archaic textile data from the central and southern Southwest, leaves the developmental record incomplete at best.

The number of sites and corresponding textile samples increase dramatically for the period after the introduction of cultigens into the Southwest by ca. 1000 B.C. This period from 1000 B.C. until the advent of the Spanish in the 1500s (ca. A.D. 1550) has been the subject of the most intensive textile inves-

tigation in the region, with literally thousands of sites reported and a lesser number excavated. The regional farming cultures, Anasazi, Hohokam, and Mogollon, began to differentiate from one another by ca. 300 B.C., if not earlier. Their textile complexes also reflect something of this differentiation, with different proportions of twined to coiled to plaited basketry in each case, as well as varieties of finger-woven sandals and belts, and later loom-woven blankets, dresses, shirts, and other garments (e.g., Adovasio 1974; Adovasio and Gunn 1986; Kent 1983; Magers 1986; Morris 1980; Whiteford 1988).

Basketmaker (BM) Anasazi (ca. 1000 B.C.–A.D. 500) twining traditions produced some of the finest textiles ever made in the Southwest. These include finely made bags and sandals, as well as basketry, mats, turkey feather robes, etc. Many specimens were elaborately decorated with dyed banded patterns, space dyed geometric motifs, and multiple weft patterns (e.g., Hayes and Webster 1992; Kent 1983; Morris 1980). Twining began to wane in BM II times, having been replaced by coiling for basketry, including several varieties with complex stitches and patterns. Most common among the coiling types was the two rod and bundle foundation with noninterlocking or split stitches. It was present in the transitional Archaic complexes at Sand Dune Cave, Bat Cave, and Tularosa and Cordova caves (Matson 1991). Open coiling with intricate stitches was also an attribute of BM II and BM III, and pieces of this type are occasionally found northward into northern Utah, Wyoming, and Idaho, where they may have represented trade items (Adovasio 1974:121).

In the Mogollon area, two rod and bundle non-interlocking or split stitch coiled basketry was also important, and this type also appeared fairly late in the western Texas sequence, as noted above. Bundle with rod core coiling also occurred in the Mogollon area, as did bundle foundations, and half rod and bundle foundations; however, none of these latter forms were particularly popular (Adovasio 1974:120). Twining and plaiting were present there as well, with the latter becoming more popular over time while the former waned. Plaiting probably continued to link the Mogollon area with Mexico.

The Hohokam area likewise showed linkages to Mexico in its plaiting, but plaiting was not common there overall. Coiling was more common, especially the bundle foundation type, a type seen in northern Mexico and also among historic groups in the region such as the O'odham. One rod coiling similar to that from Sand Dune Cave was also present (Adovasio 1974:120), along with some minority types. One rod coiling, although late in the Hohokam area (like all other basketry evidence), may provide a link to the eastern Great Basin (Adovasio 1974:120).

As noted above, the developmental sequence in the Southwest remains unclear for much of its duration in most areas, given the scarcity of specimens attributable to the Archaic period. In the far northern portion, the incomplete record may never be filled in because of what was apparently an occupational hiatus (Matson 1991). Elsewhere in the Southwest, however, more research in dry caves and rockshelters may be fruitful for elucidation of relationships to the Great Basin, northern Mexico, western Texas, and California, as well as better definition of its own distinctive textile history.

California

Although California certainly has a rich diversity of basketry traditions in its historic ethnographic record, a similar situation does not pertain to the archaeological record there. In fact, with the exception of a few late finds (see Moratto 1984) and the wealth of ethnographic materials, little can be said about the prehistoric basketry of California except through inference. Undoubtedly, this limited record is largely due to environmental conditions which do not favor preservation of perishables in most cases.

In the historic period, California was about equally divided among groups that almost exclusively used twining (the northern area), those that exclusively used coiling (the southern area), and those in between who used both construction techniques (the central area) (Elsasser 1978). Much of the twining in the northern area reflects affinities with northern Great Basin forms, and, while archaeological specimens are almost totally lacking,

it can be assumed that twining either diffused from the northern Basin or the Northwest Coast. Most basketmakers employed close simple (plain) twining over rigid warps, with either an S-twist or Z-twist twining weft slant. They also used overlay and wrapped twining techniques found to the north and east. One small archaeological specimen of twining with S-twist plied wefts was found at the Thomas site in Marin County, but it probably dates no older than A.D. 1200 (Baumhoff 1953).

As one moves farther south, actual specimens of cordage warp basketry, attributable to the Catlow Twine type in the northern Great Basin, have been recovered from a small number of sites in central California. Baumhoff (1957) recorded eight such sites, but again none is older than ca. A.D. 1200. Cordage warp basketry was rare among ethnographic groups in California; thus, the presence of this form in the archaeological record suggests either a near complete loss or abandonment by the onset of the historic period and/or some sort of population replacement. Twined basketry is also known from impressions on baked clay in sites attributable to the Windmiller complex in the Central Valley, where it may be as old as ca. 2000 B.C. (Ragir 1972). Baked clay balls, supposedly used for "stone boiling" food in basketry containers, are also known from Windmiller sites of this antiquity, providing further indirect evidence of basketry to this reconstruction (Elsasser 1978:634; Moratto 1984:201).

Most researchers assume that coiling came to California from the east, that is, from the western Great Basin (e.g., Dawson 1989; Hattori 1982; Heizer 1949). However, again, only indirect evidence of coiling is available until late in the regional record. Heizer (1949) argued for the presence of coiling in the Central Valley during the Middle Horizon, beginning ca. 1500 B.C., given the increased number of bone awls and their sophistication. More recently, Dawson (1989) proposed an interesting hypothesis based on the characteristics of coiling technology and decoration among ethnographic groups; it supports Heizer's suggested origin and time of arrival. Otherwise, actual archaeological specimens of coiled basketry are limited to much later contexts. For example, 16 fragments from a single

coiled basket of the one rod foundation and interlocking stitch type were dated ca. A.D. 1200 at the
Thomas site in Marin County (Baumhoff 1953).

Information about prehistoric basketry from
southern California is not much more common,
although preservation conditions are certainly
more favorable in a number of interior desert settings and other areas. Warren and True (1961) suggested on the basis of the presence of bone awls
that coiled basketry may have been present as
early as late San Dieguito times, ca. 9000–6000 B.C.,
in coastal and immediately adjacent interior areas.
Actual specimens of coiled basketry, apparently
with a multiple rod foundation, are present in the
same region by Encinitas times, ca. 6000–2000 B.C.,
along with diagonal twining with S-twist plied
wefts. Other scattered finds of both coiling and
twining are known from the area, but these have
not been well synthesized. For example, Coville
Rockshelter in Inyo County produced both coiling
and twining from contexts dated roughly ca. A.D.
1–1200. Types reported there include three rod
bunched foundation coiling with split stitches, a
type known in western Nevada to the east, and
two rod and bundle coiling, a type known from the
Southwest (Adovasio 1974:122). The twining includes both open and close forms, and specimens
have either S-twist or Z-twist wefts. Other even
later finds are known as well, but most of these are
poorly dated and/or related to ethnographic
groups (e.g., Elsasser 1978:634; Mohr and Sample
1955; Moratto 1984; Sutton and Yohe 1988).

The Northwest Coast

Prior to the 1970s, little was known of early fiber
perishables in the Northwest Coast region, although the richness of the ethnographic traditions
again suggested a long period of development
prior to contact with Europeans. Twined, plaited,
and coiled basketry forms were all present among
ethnographic populations (Holm 1990:623–629),
but the archaeological record had yielded few examples due in large part to environmental conditions there. However, since the mid-1970s, reports
on water-saturated sites in the Puget Sound area
and coastal British Columbia have revealed some

very remarkable artifacts in near perfect states of
preservation (e.g., Bernick 1983, 1987; Croes 1976,
1977, 1989, 1992, 1993; Croes and Blinman 1980),
rivaling in various ways the finds from the
Windover Bog Cemetery in Florida (Andrews and
Adovasio this volume). Unfortunately, the finds in
these areas are not quite as old as the Windover
specimens, but they nonetheless instruct about the
record of cordage and basketry manufacture in this
region over a time span about 4000 years long.

Croes (in Croes and Blinman 1980:188) describes
72 specimens of basketry and matting from the
Hoko River site dated ca. 600–500 B.C. Hoko River
is a fishing camp on the Olympic Peninsula of
Washington. This fiber assemblage includes twining, plaiting, wrapping (which is a combination of
twining and plaiting), and sewing (mat) forms.
Twining techniques include both open and close S-
twist plied wefts, sometimes with the inclusion of
three strand and wrapped twining. Plaiting includes plain or checker weave, as well as twill
types, while the wrapping specimens involve the
use of an additional weft wrapped between elements in openwork plain plaiting. Tule mats sewn
with cordage are also associated.

Forms in the Hoko River assemblage include
the common burden basket, bands, truncated
cone-shaped baskets, knobbed and cone-shaped
hats, bags, mats, and possibly skirts and/or capes.
All of these techniques and forms are known at
one or more of the other water-saturated sites
around Puget Sound, dated ca. 1000 B.C.–A.D. 1000
(e.g., Croes 1976, 1989, 1992), and all are known in
the large sample from the Ozette site, a prehistoric
early Makah village also on the Olympic Peninsula (Croes 1977). All of these techniques and
forms are further known among Makah, Nootka,
and Salishan ethnographic populations in the
broader region. Of some interest, coiling, which is
known among the coastal and interior Salishan
ethnographic groups, is not present in the archaeological samples, suggesting perhaps its late
arrival on the coast from the interior. Stylistic
analyses of basketry and cordage from other Puget
Sound/Gulf of Georgia sites, as well as from farther
north in British Columbia, are now suggesting the

development of regional styles with at least 2000–3000 years of continuity (Bernick 1987; Croes 1992, 1993).

Elsewhere in the southern Northwest Coast and adjoining Plateau region, the textile record is much more meager. For example, Fowler (1989) reported on six twined basketry fragments, as well as other perishables, from Times Square Rockshelter, located east of the Cascade Mountains in Oregon. This small sample, which may date ca. 1500 B.C.–A.D. 500, reveals Great Basin affiliations, in addition to correlations with ethnographically known coastal groups in Oregon. Interior riverine samples also seem to reflect both Great Basin and coastal influences, but remain poorly dated (e.g., Caldwell and Mallory 1967; Mills and Osborne 1952; Osborne 1957).

Clay impressions of basketry, possibly close simple (plain) twining with S-twist plied wefts, were also recently recovered in Jackson County, Oregon (Pettigrew and Lebow 1987:7.51), as were two small fragments of the same type in another site west of the Cascades in Oregon (Baxter et al. 1983:57). The latter two finds are again poorly dated, but both are likely quite recent. They also fit well with ethnographic materials from the broader region.

The Northwest Coast is now beginning to contribute excellent information to the early textile prehistory of the West. Ethnographically, it was a complex of predominantly twined forms, but with plaiting and coiling also present among a number of groups. Archaeological sites in the region, especially water-saturated ones, have produced some of the most impressive samples of prehistoric fiber perishables known anywhere in the West and broader North America, but few as yet have produced specimens of great antiquity. One can only hope that this will change in the future.

REFERENCES CITED

Adovasio, J. M.
1970   The Origin, Development and Distribution of Western Archaic Textiles. *Tebiwa* 13(2):1-40.
1974   Prehistoric North American Basketry. In *Collected Papers on Aboriginal Basketry*, edited by Donald R. Tuohy and Doris L. Rendall, pp. 133-153. Nevada State Museum Anthropological Papers 16. Carson City.
1977   *Basketry Technology: A Guide to Identification and Analysis.* Aldine, Chicago.
1980a Fremont: An Artifactual Perspective. In *Fremont Perspectives,* edited by David B. Madsen, pp. 35-40. Utah State Historical Society, Antiquities Section Selected Papers 16. Salt Lake City.
1980b The Evolution of Basketry Manufacture in Northeastern Mexico, Lower and Trans-Pecos Texas. In *Papers on the Prehistory of Northeastern Mexico and Adjacent Texas,* edited by Jeremiah F. Epstein, Thomas R. Hester, and Carol Graves, pp. 93-102. Univ. of Texas at San Antonio Center for Archaeological Research Special Report 9. San Antonio.
1986   Prehistoric Basketry. In *Great Basin,* edited by Warren L. d'Azevedo, pp. 194-205. Handbook of North American Indians, vol. 11, William G. Sturtevant, general editor. Smithsonian Institution, Washington, D.C.

Adovasio, J. M., and R. L. Andrews
1983   Material Culture of Gatecliff Shelter: Basketry, Cordage and Miscellaneous Fiber Constructions. In *The Archaeology of Monitor Valley 2. Gatecliff Shelter,* by David H. Thomas, pp. 279-289. Anthropological Papers of the American Museum of Natural History 59(1). New York.
1985   *Basketry and Miscellaneous Perishable Artifacts from Walpi Pueblo, Arizona.* Ethnology Monographs 7. Dept. of Anthropology, Univ. of Pittsburgh, Pittsburgh.

Adovasio, J. M., and Joel D. Gunn
1986   The Antelope House Basketry Industry. In *Archeological Investigations at Antelope House,* edited by Don P. Morris, pp. 306-397. National Park Service, U.S. Dept. of the Interior, Washington, D.C.

Andrews, R. L., and J. M. Adovasio
1980   *Perishable Industries from Hinds Cave, Val Verde County, Texas.* Ethnology Monographs 5. Dept. of Anthropology, Univ. of Pittsburgh, Pittsburgh.

Andrews, R. L., J. M. Adovasio, and R. C. Carlisle
1986   *Perishable Industries from Dirty Shame Rockshelter, Malheur County, Oregon.* Ethnology Monographs 9. Dept. of Anthropology, Univ. of Pittsburgh, Pittsburgh.

Baumhoff, Martin A.
1953   Carbonized Basketry from the Texas Site. *University of California Archaeological Survey Reports* 19:9-11. Berkeley.
1957   Catlow Twine from Central California. *University of California Archaeological Survey Reports* 38:1-5. Berkeley.

Baxter, P. W., R. D. Cheatham, T. J. Connolly, and J. A. Willig
1983   *Rigdon's Horse Pasture Cave: An Upland Hunting Camp in the Western Cascades.* Univ. of Oregon Anthropological Papers 28. Eugene.

Bernick, Kathryn

1983 *A Site Catchment Analysis of the Little Qualicum River Site, DiSc1: A Wet Site on the East Coast of Vancouver Island, B.C.* Archaeological Survey of Canada Paper 118. National Museum of Man Mercury Series. Ottawa.

1987 The Potential of Basketry for Reconstructing Cultural Diversity on the Northwest Coast. In *Ethnicity and Culture*, edited by Reginald Auger, Margaret F. Glass, Scott MacEachern, and Peter H. McCartney, pp. 251-257. Univ. of Calgary Archaeology Association, Calgary.

Brasser, Ted J.

1975 *A Basketful of Indian Culture Change.* Canadian Ethnology Service Paper 22. National Museum of Man, Ottawa.

Caldwell, Warren W., and Oscar L. Mallory

1967 *Hells Canyon Archeology.* Smithsonian Institution River Basin Surveys Publications in Salvage Archeology 6. Lincoln.

Cressman, Luther S.

1939 Early Man and Culture in the Northern Great Basin Region and South-Central Oregon. *Carnegie Institution of Washington Yearbook* 38:314-317. Washington, D.C.

1951 Western Prehistory in the Light of Carbon-14 Dating. *Southwest Journal of Anthropology* 7(3):289-313.

1956 Additional Radiocarbon Dates, Lovelock Cave, Nevada. *American Antiquity* 21(3):311-312.

Cressman, L. S., F. C. Baker, H. P. Hansen, P. Conger, and R. F. Heizer

1942 *Archaeological Researches in the Northern Great Basin.* Carnegie Institution of Washington Publication 538. Washington, D.C.

Croes, Dale R.

1977 *Basketry from the Ozette Village Archaeological Site: A Technological, Functional and Comparative Study.* Unpublished Ph.D. dissertation, Dept. of Anthropology, Washington State Univ., Pullman.

1989 Lachane Basketry and Cordage: A Technological, Functional and Comparative Study. *Canadian Journal of Archaeology* 13:165-205.

1992 An Evolving Revolution in Wet Site Research on the Northwest Coast of North America. In *The Wetland Revolution in Prehistory*, edited by Byrony Coles, pp. 99-111. Wetland Archaeology Research Project Occasional Paper 6. Dept. of History and Archaeology, Univ. of Exeter, Exeter.

1993 Prehistoric Hoko River Cordage: A New Line on Northwest Coast Prehistory. In *A Spirit of Enquiry, Essays for Ted Wright*, edited by John Coles, Valerie Fenwick, and Gillian Hutchinson, pp. 32-38. Wetland Archaeology Research Project Occasional Paper 7. Dept. of History and Archaeology, Univ. of Exeter, Exeter.

Croes, Dale R. (editor)

1976 *The Excavation of Water-Saturated Archaeological Sites (Wet Sites) on the Northwest Coast of North America.* Archaeological Survey of Canada Paper 50. National Museum of Man Mercury Series. Ottawa.

Croes, Dale R., and Eric Blinman (editors)

1980 *Hoko River: A 2500 Year Old Fishing Camp on the Northwest Coast of North America.* Reports of Investigations 58. Laboratory of Anthropology, Washington State Univ., Pullman.

Dawson, Lawrence E.

1989 Fields of Clover: Larry Dawson's Thirty-Eight Years with the Lowie Museum Collections. The Spread of Coiled Basketry in California. Exhibition pamphlet, Lowie Museum of Anthropology, Univ. of California, Berkeley.

Dick, Herbert W.

1965 *Bat Cave.* Monographs of the School of American Research 27. Santa Fe.

Elsasser, Albert B.

1978 Basketry. In *California*, edited by Robert F. Heizer, pp. 626-641. Handbook of North American Indians, vol. 8, William G. Sturtevant, general editor. Smithsonian Institution, Washington, D.C.

Florian, Mary-Lou E., Dale P. Kronkright, and Ruth E. Norton

1990 *The Conservation of Artifacts Made from Plant Materials.* J. Paul Getty Trust, Los Angeles.

Fowler, Catherine S.

1989 Perishables. In *Times Square Rockshelter (35Do212): A Stratified Dry Rockshelter in the Western Cascades, Douglas County, Oregon*, by Lee Spencer, pp. 397-443. Lee Spencer Archaeology. Submitted to U.S. Forest Service, Roseburg.

Fowler, Catherine S., and W. Cannon

1990 Perishable Artifacts from Warner Valley Caves. Paper presented at the 23rd annual meeting of the Great Basin Anthropological Conference, Reno.

Fowler, Catherine S., and Lawrence E. Dawson

1986 Ethnographic Basketry. In *Great Basin*, edited by Warren L. d'Azevedo, pp. 705-737. Handbook of North American Indians, vol. 11, William G. Sturtevant, general editor. Smithsonian Institution, Washington, D.C.

Geib, P. R.

1992 Anasazi Origins: A Perspective from Preliminary Work at Old Man Cave. Paper presented at the 57th annual meeting of the Society for American Archaeology, Pittsburgh.

Hattori, Eugene M.

1982 *The Archaeology of Falcon Hill, Winnemucca Lake, Washoe County, Nevada.* Nevada State Museum Anthropological Papers 18. Carson City.

Haury, Emil W.

1950 *The Stratigraphy and Archaeology of Ventana Cave, Arizona.* Univ. of Arizona Press, Tucson.

Hayes, Kelley Ann, and Laurie D. Webster

1992 New Trials for Old Shoes: Sandals, Textiles, and Baskets in Basketmaker II. Paper presented at the 57th annual meeting of the Society for American Archaeology, Pittsburgh.

Heizer, Robert F.

1949 The Archaeology of Central California, I: The Early Horizon. *University of California Anthropological Records* 12(1):1-84. Berkeley.

1956 Recent Cave Explorations in the Lower Humboldt Valley, Nevada. *University of California Archaeological Survey Reports* 33(42):50-57. Berkeley.

Heizer, Robert F., and Alex D. Krieger

1956 *The Archaeology of Humboldt Cave, Churchill County, Nevada.* Univ. of California Publications in American Archaeology and Ethnology 47(1). Berkeley.

Hewitt, Nancy J.

1980 Fiber Artifacts. In *Cowboy Cave,* by Jesse D. Jennings, pp. 49-74. Univ. of Utah Anthropological Papers 104. Salt Lake City.

Holm, Bill

1990 Art. In *Northwest Coast,* edited by Wayne Suttles, pp. 602-632. Handbook of North American Indians, vol. 7, William G. Sturtevant, general editor. Smithsonian Institution, Washington, D.C.

Holmes, William H.

1896 Prehistoric Textile Art of the Eastern United States. In *Annual Report of the Bureau of American Ethnology, 1891-1892,* pp. 3-46. Smithsonian Institution, Washington, D.C.

Jennings, Jesse D.

1957 *Danger Cave.* Univ. of Utah Anthropological Papers 27. Salt Lake City.

1980 *Cowboy Cave.* Univ. of Utah Anthropological Papers 104. Salt Lake City.

Johnson, Irmgard W.

1977 *Los Textiles de la Cueva de la Candelaria, Coahuila.* Instituto Nacional de Antropologia e Historia, Dept. de Monumentos Prehispanicos, Coleccion Cientifica 51. Mexico City.

Kent, Kate Peck

1957 *The Cultivation and Weaving of Cotton in the Prehistoric Southwestern United States.* Transactions of the American Philosophical Society 47(2). Philadelphia.

1983 *Prehistoric Textiles of the Southwest.* Univ. of New Mexico Press, Albuquerque.

Kidder, Alfred V.

1924 *An Introduction to the Study of Southwestern Archaeology, with a Preliminary Account of the Excavations at Pecos.* Phillips Academy and Yale Univ. Press, New Haven.

King, Mary E.

1979 The Prehistoric Textile Industry of Mesoamerica. In *The Junius B. Bird Pre-Columbian Textile Conference,* edited by Ann P. Rowe, Elizabeth P. Benson, and Ann-Louise Schaffer, pp. 265-278. The Textile Museum, Washington, D.C.

1986 Preceramic Cordage and Basketry from Guilá Naquitz. In *Guilá Naquitz: Archaic Foraging and Early Agriculture in Oaxaca, Mexico,* edited by Kent V. Flannery, pp. 157-161. Academic Press, New York.

Lindsay, A. J., J. R. Ambler, M. A. Stein, and P. M. Hobler

1968 *Survey and Excavations North and East of Navajo Mountain, Utah, 1959-1962.* Museum of Northern Arizona Bulletin 45. Flagstaff.

Loud, Lewellyn L., and Mark R. Harrington

1929 *Lovelock Cave.* Univ. of California Publications in American Archaeology and Ethnology 25(1). Berkeley.

MacNeish, R. S., Antoinette Nelken-Terner, and Irmgard W. Johnson

1967 *The Non-ceramic Artifacts,* edited by Douglas S. Byers, pp. 3-258. The Prehistory of the Tehuacan Valley, vol. 2. Univ. of Texas Press, Austin.

Magers, Pamela C.

1986 Weaving and Miscellaneous Wooden and Vegetal Artifacts. In *Archeological Investigations at Antelope House,* edited by Don P. Morris, pp. 224-305. National Park Service, U.S. Dept. of the Interior, Washington, D.C.

Martin, P. S., J. B. Rinaldo, E. Bluhm, H. D. Cutler, and R. Grange

1952 *Mogollon Cultural Continuity and Change: A Stratigraphic Analysis of Tularosa and Cordova Caves.* Fieldiana: Anthropology 40. Field Museum of Natural History, Chicago.

Mason, Otis T.

1904 Aboriginal American Basketry: Studies in a Textile Art Without Machinery. *Annual Report of the U.S. National Museum, 1902,* pp. 171-548. Washington, D.C.

Matson, R. G.

1991 *The Origins of Southwestern Agriculture.* Univ. of Arizona Press, Tucson.

McGregor, Roberta

1992 *Prehistoric Basketry of the Lower Pecos, Texas.* Prehistory Press Monographs in World Archaeology 6. Madison.

Mills, John E., and Carolyn Osborne
1952 Material Culture of an Upper Coulee Rockshelter. *American Antiquity* 17(4):352-359.

Mohr, Albert, and L. L. Sample
1955 Twined Water Bottles of the Cuyama Area, Southern California. *American Antiquity* 29(4):345-354.

Moratto, Michael J.
1984 *California Archaeology.* Academic Press, New York.

Morris, Earl H.
1927 The Beginnings of Pottery Making in the San Juan Area: Unfired Prototypes and the Wares of the Earliest Ceramic Period. *Anthropological Papers of the American Museum of Natural History* 28(2):125-198. New York.

Morris, Earl H., and Robert F. Burgh
1941 *Anasazi Basketry: Basket Maker II through Pueblo III: A Study Based on Specimens from the San Juan River Country.* Carnegie Institution of Washington Publication 533. Washington, D.C.

Morris, Elizabeth A.
1980 *Basketmaker Caves in the Prayer Rock District, Northeastern Arizona.* Anthropological Papers of the Univ. of Arizona 35. Tucson.

Osborne, Douglas
1957 *Excavations in the McNary Reservoir Basin Near Umatilla, Oregon.* Smithsonian Institution Bureau of American Ethnology Bulletin 166. Washington, D.C.

Pettigrew, R. M., and C. G. Lebow
1987 *Data Recovery at Sites 35JA27, 35JA59, and 35JA100, Elk Creek Lake Project, Jackson County, Oregon.* Infotec Research, Eugene.

Ragir, S. R.
1972 *The Early Horizon in Central California Prehistory.* Contributions of the Univ. of California Archaeological Research Facility 15. Berkeley.

Sayles, E. B.
1938 Perishable Materials. In *Excavations at Snaketown, Material Culture,* by Harold S. Gladwin, Emil W. Haury, E. B. Sayles, and Nora Gladwin, pp. 159-162. Arizona State Museum, Tucson.

Spier, Leslie
1930 *Klamath Ethnography.* Univ. of California Publications in American Archaeology and Ethnology 30. Berkeley.

Story, Dee A., and Vaughn Bryant Jr. (assemblers)
1966 *A Preliminary Study of the Paleoecology of the Amistad Reservoir Area.* Final Report of Research Under the Auspices of the National Science Foundation (GS-667).

Sutton, Mark Q., and Robert M. Yohe
1988 Perishable Artifacts from Cave No. 5, Providence Mountains, California. *Journal of California and Great Basin Anthropology* 10(1):117-123.

Taylor, Walter W.
1966 Archaic Cultures Adjacent to the Northeastern Frontiers of Mesoamerica. In *Archaeological Frontiers and External Connections,* edited by Gordon F. Ekholm and Gordon R. Willey, pp. 59-94. Handbook of Middle American Indians, vol. 4. Univ. of Texas Press, Austin.

1988 *Contributions to Coahuila Archaeology, with an Introduction to the Coahuila Project.* Southern Illinois Univ. at Carbondale Center for Archaeological Investigations Research Paper 52. Carbondale.

Warren, Claude N., and David L. True
1961 The San Dieguito Complex and Its Place in California Prehistory. *University of California, Los Angeles, Archaeological Survey Report,* 1960-1961:246-338. Los Angeles.

Whiteford, Andrew
1988 *Southwestern Indian Baskets: Their History and Their Makers.* School of American Research Press, Santa Fe.

Contributors

J. M. Adovasio is an authority on archaeological basketry and other fiber industries in national and international contexts. He is the author of *Basketry Technology: A Guide to Identification and Analysis,* among many other publications on the subject. Jim holds a Ph.D. in anthropology from the University of Utah. He is currently a Professor and Chair of the Departments of Anthropology and Geology, and Director of the Mercyhurst Archaeological Institute at Mercyhurst College.

The late R. L. Andrews was the former Director of the Perishables Analysis Facility at the University of Pittsburgh and later the Director of the Perishables Analysis Facility in the Mercyhurst Archaeological Institute at Mercyhurst College.

Louise A. Basa is the Chief of the Cultural Resources Section, Division of Construction Management in the New York State Department of Environmental Conservation (NYSDEC). After graduate work at the University of Pennsylvania, she taught at the University of Vermont and elsewhere before joining the NYSDEC.

Catherine S. Fowler is an ethnographer working primarily in the Great Basin of western North America. She has specific interests in archaeological and ethnographic textiles. Catherine holds a Ph.D. from the University of Pittsburgh and is a Professor in the Department of Anthropology at the University of Nevada at Reno.

JOAN S. GARDNER is the Conservator in the Section of Anthropology at the Carnegie Museum of Natural History. She holds a M.A. and has extensive experience in the conservation of archaeological and ethnographic collections, including significant specimens from Spiro Mound and the Windover site.

NATHAN D. HAMILTON is an Associate Professor in the Department of Geography/Anthropology at the University of Southern Maine. Nathan's Ph.D. in anthropology was awarded by the University of Pittsburgh, and he is currently a Research Associate at the R.S. Peabody Museum of Archaeology at Phillips Academy. His interests include maritime adaptations and prehistoric technologies in northeastern North America, Japan, and Peru.

MICHAEL J. HECKENBERGER recently completed his Ph.D. in the Department of Anthropology at the University of Pittsburgh where his dissertation research involved ethnoarchaeology in the Brazilian Amazon. Michael is currently coordinating the South American component of a permanent Native American exhibit at the Carnegie Museum of Natural History.

KATHRYN A. JAKES is a Professor at The Ohio State University and current chair of the Department of Textile and Consumer Sciences. A polymer chemist, she examines the chemical and physical changes in fibers which are the result of aging. Kathryn's most recent research involves identification and characterization of fibers used by native people in eastern North America and the microspectroscopic identification of dyes on fibers. She collaborated with the late Lucy R. Sibley on research investigating pseudomorphs after fibers and Etowah textiles.

WILLIAM C. JOHNSON was awarded a Ph.D. in anthropology by the University of Pittsburgh. Bill's long-term interests include ceramic and fiber perishables analyses, among others, especially as they pertain to Ohio Valley and Mid-Atlantic topics. He is currently employed as a Senior Environmental Scientist by the Cultural Resources Section of the Transportation Group of Michael Baker Jr., Incorporated.

FRANCES B. KING is Director of the Paleoethnobotanical Laboratory at the Center for Cultural Resource Research at the University of Pittsburgh. Fran received a Ph.D. from the Department of Agronomy, University of Illinois. Her interests include the prehistoric and historic use of plants, as well as the evolution of domesticated plants.

CARL KUTTRUFF is a consulting archaeologist and an Adjunct Professor of Anthropology at Louisiana State University. Carl has conducted extensive archaeological research in the eastern United States, as well as in Mexico, the Philippines, and the Marshall Islands. His research encompasses both prehistoric and historic periods.

JENNA TEDRICK KUTTRUFF received her Ph.D. from Ohio State University and is an Associate Professor of Human Ecology at Louisiana State University. Her research interests are directed toward the analysis and interpretation of prehistoric and historic archaeological textile remains.

LEWIS H. LARSON has been involved in archaeological research at the Etowah site in Georgia for over three decades. He holds a Ph.D. in anthropology from the University of Michigan and is currently Professor of Anthropology in the Department of Sociology and Anthropology at West Georgia College. He is the State Archaeologist for Georgia.

ROBERT F. MASLOWSKI holds a Ph.D. in anthropology from the University of Pittsburgh and is Staff Archaeologist for the Huntington District, U.S. Army Corps of Engineers. Bob has studied textile and cordage collections from Peru, Yugoslavia, Trans-Pecos Texas, and the western United States, and he currently specializes in Ohio Valley archaeology.

ALAN L. MCPHERRON received a Ph.D. in anthropology from the University of Michigan, where he conducted a landmark analysis of collections from the Juntunen site. More recently, he published an edited volume on his collaborative research at the Divostin Neolithic site in Yugoslavia. Alan is an Associate Professor in the Department of Anthropology at the University of Pittsburgh.

JAMES B. PETERSEN is an Associate Research Professor in the Department of Social Sciences and Business and Director of the Archaeology Research Center at the University of Maine at Farmington. He holds a Ph.D. in anthropology from the University of Pittsburgh and is a Research Associate in the Section of Anthropology at the Carnegie Museum of Natural History and at the R. S. Peabody Museum of Archaeology.

The late LUCY R. SIBLEY was a Professor in what was then the Department of Textiles and Clothing at The Ohio State University. A textile historian, she had a special interest in archaeological textiles and collaborated with Kathryn A. Jakes over a long period in the study of Etowah textiles.

Index

Coahuila, 88–91, 182–83, 190–92; fiber industries developmental sequence, 190–92
Cognitive map, 74–76, 80–86
Coiling, 8, 10, 102, 113, 186, 188, 192; antiquity of, 33, 44–45, 183, 188–94; definition of, 31; feather decoration, 189, 194; structural decoration, 191, 194
Coiling types: close, bundle foundation, 33, 44, 183, 191–94; close, half rod foundation, 191; close, half rod and bundle foundation, 193; close, one rod foundation, 33, 44, 183, 189, 191–95; close, one rod and bundle foundation, 189, 193; close, one rod and welt foundation, 193; close, two rod stacked foundation, 33, 44, 183, 195; close, two rod and bundle foundation, 191, 193, 195; close, three rod bunched foundation, 195; open (spaced), one rod foundation, 193
Cole complex, 91–93, 96
Cole site, Ohio, 91, 93
College of the Atlantic, 7
Colorado, 189
Colorado Plateau, 192
Columbus, Ohio, 96
Complex cordage constructions, 2, 9, 37, 42, 123, 128, 131; cord-wrapped cord, 102–4, 121–23, 126, 128–31; cord-wrapped paddle, 102–4, 122–23, 128–31; cord-wrapped stick, 102–6, 122–23, 128–31; definitions of, 123
Connecticut River drainage, 102, 114, 155n
The Conservation of Artifacts Made from Plant Materials (Florian and others), 187
Contact period, 7–8, 69; dating, 100–102; fiber industries, 7–8, 66–68, 103–4, 110, 112, 114, 133
Containers, 31, 34, 36, 42–43, 45, 102–3, 132, 189, 194; *see also* Basketry, and Boxes
Context: archaeological, 80, 84–85; systemic, 80, 82–85
Copper artifacts, 3, 44, 52–53, 56, 64–66, 73, 79–80, 84–85, 107, 183–84
Cord-marked ceramics, 5, 88–96, 148–55, 156n, 164, 185
Cord-paddled ceramics. *See* Cord-marked ceramics
Cordage, 2, 5, 8–11, 14, 30–31, 50, 53–56, 81–82, 96, 102, 104, 120, 122, 128, 130, 163, 181–84, 186, 188, 195; antiquity of, 32, 45, 67; attributes, 5, 9, 13, 37, 56, 148; definition of, 31, 53, 56, 102; dyed decoration, 57
Cordage spin and twist, 5, 9, 13; definition of, 89–90; direction of, 13, 56, 89–91, 105; frequency of, 14, 36–38, 41–44, 53, 56–57, 60, 62–64, 66, 70n, 74–75, 89–96, 103–12, 123–24, 128–30, 132, 146–47, 150–55, 156n, 165, 172, 181, 183, 185, 189; indicating cultural relationship, 13–15, 64, 111–15, 146–47, 153–55, 172, 184–85; raw material determinants, 13–15, 90–91; *see also* Twining weft slant (or twist), and Twist
Cordage types: braided, 33, 37, 42–43, 53–55, 103; four ply, simple, 56–57; one ply, simple, 36, 42, 56; three ply, compound, 123, 129; three ply, simple, 56–57, 68, 123, 125–26, 129; two ply, compound, 123, 125, 129, 132; two ply, simple, 33, 36–38, 41–45, 56–57, 89–91, 103–5, 123, 125–26, 129–32, 185
Cordillera, 31; *see also* Rocky Mountains
Cordova Cave, N. Mex., 192–93
Cornelius, Reverend Elias, 79
Coville Rockshelter, Calif., 195
Cowboy Cave, Utah, 193

Cowls, 66; *see also* Clothing, and Garments
Cradle, 31, 102
Craig Mound, Okla. *See* Spiro Mound, Oklahoma
Crater Lake, 188
Cressman, Luther S., 188
Croes, Dale R., 96, 192, 195
Cumberland River, 161–62
Curry, Dennis C., 148, 154
Cuyahoga County, Ohio, 42
Czech Republic, 32

Dameron Rockshelter, Ky., 91, 93–95
Danger Cave, Utah, 89, 180, 185, 188
Dawson, Lawrence E., 182, 194
Decco site, Ohio, 91, 93
Desert Archaic. *See* Jennings, Jesse D.
Desert Culture. *See* Jennings, Jesse D.
Desert West, 5, 13–14, 16n, 182, 188; *see also* Arid West
"Dilly bag," 13
Door Peninsula, Wis., 133–35
Dream Time, 12
Dresses, 193; *see also* Clothing, and Garments
Driver, Harold, 2, 30–31
Drooker, Penelope Ballard, 167, 172
Dust Devil Cave, Ariz., 192
Duvall site, W. Va., 92–93, 95

Early Archaic period: dating, 33–34, 36; fiber industries, 33–34, 36, 67, 182; location of sites, 35
Early Lakes phase, 133; distribution of, 134
Early Woodland period, 3, 5, 50–69, 113; dating, 50, 54–55, 67, 101–2; fiber industries, 3, 5, 50, 53–69, 103–5, 107–8, 111, 113–14, 133, 172, 181, 183–84
East Creek site, Vt., 51
Eastern Woodlands, 147; *see also* North America, eastern
Eckstorm, Fanny Hardy, 6
Economics, role of fiber industries in, 130–32; economic exchange, 10–11, 14, 80; market economy, 7, 12–13
Effigy Mound tradition, 133; distribution of, 134–35
Egloff, Keith T., 148
El Paso, Tex., 191
Embroidery, 13; false, 189
Emery, Irene, fabric classification of, 9, 36–37, 56, 81–82, 164–65
Encinitas period, 195
Ethnicity, role of fiber industries in, 3, 10–15, 64, 88–91, 96–97, 111–15, 136, 146–47, 181, 183–86
Etowah River, 74
Etowah site, Ga., 3, 73–86, 186–87; burial association, 79–80, 83–85; compositional analyses, 76–79, 85; dating, 74, 79, 85; fabric systems, 75, 80–82; matting, 75, 84–85; Mound C, 73–74, 79–80, 83; yarn systems, 75–76, 80–82
Europeans, 2, 7–8, 32, 66, 82, 183, 191, 195; fiber industries, 82

Fabric-paddled ceramics, 4, 5, 69, 88, 103–4, 106, 108–10, 121, 124, 127–28, 148, 154–55, 156n, 160–72, 185
Fabrics, 2–3, 5, 10, 31, 41, 45, 57, 59–66, 73–86, 96, 102–4, 123–24, 132, 150, 160–72, 183, 186–87, 192; definition of, 8; differentiation from cordage in impressions, 9, 102; *see also* Basketry, Cloth, Textiles, and Woven

Fairchance complex, 93–95
Fairchance site, W. Va., 93–95
Falk, Carole Portugal, 89, 148–49, 152–53
Feurt phase, 91–92, 96
Fiber artifacts, 1–3, 5, 8–9, 11, 50, 53, 64, 67, 69, 96, 101–2, 112, 121–22; *see also* Fiber industries, Fiber perishables, Perishables, and Textiles
Fiber industries: analytical methods, 9, 37, 53, 56–57, 59, 121–23; attributes for classification of, 5, 8–10, 13–14, 37, 56–57, 59, 90–91, 102–10, 122–23, 138–40, 148, 164–65; cleaning, 9, 174; conservation, 9, 174, 186; culturally diagnostic nature of, 3, 10–15, 64, 88–91, 111–15, 135–36, 146–47, 172, 185–86; definition of, 2, 30–31, 102; determinants of variability, 13–15, 90–91, 111–15, 135–36, 146–47, 185–86; dyed decoration, 3, 6, 7, 187; feather constituents, 3, 73, 75–85, 86n, 164, 186–87, 193; goals of research, 10–16, 181; hair constituents, 3, 63, 65–68, 73, 78, 80–81, 84–85, 164, 186–87, 189; history of research, 2–8, 31–32, 53, 67–69, 81–82, 100, 180–81, 188–96; quill constituents, 6; raw materials, identification, 5, 10, 34, 37–43, 56, 59, 76–82, 90–91, 114, 123, 132, 174; raw materials, structural determinants, 8, 13–15, 90–91, 147, 186–87; reflection of social status, 11, 73–75, 79–86, 186–87; storage, 174–78; structural decoration, 45, 59, 66–67, 167, 186, 189
Fiber industries, archaeological: antiquity of, 3, 5, 8, 30, 32–45, 67–68, 100–102, 114, 133, 146, 172, 182–83, 188–96; behavioral reconstruction of, 73–86; casting, 122, 150; ceramic negative impressions, 2–3, 5–6, 9, 31, 67–68, 88, 90–96, 100–15, 120–36, 144–56, 160–72, 181, 184, 188; limitations of negative impressions, 2, 5, 9, 101, 108, 123, 133, 149–53, 164–65, 167, 170; nonceramic negative impressions, 2, 31–32, 34, 36, 65, 67, 101, 181, 194, 196; preservation bias against, 2, 64, 69, 102, 114, 160–61, 167, 172, 183, 188, 194; preservation conditions for, 2–3, 31, 37, 39, 42, 44, 53, 64, 73, 76, 79–80, 84, 101, 114, 180–81, 183–84, 188, 195–96
Fiber industries, ethnographic, 6–8, 11–16, 96, 112–13, 146–47, 177–78, 182, 186
Fiber industries of eastern North America: archaeological, 2–8, 13–14, 30–45, 50–69, 73–86, 91–97, 100–15, 120–36, 144–55, 160–72, 175–78, 180–88, 190, 192; ethnographic, 2–3, 6–8, 183
Fiber industries of western North America: archaeological, 1–3, 6, 13–14, 30, 32, 45, 88–91, 146–47, 176–77, 180–96; ethnographic, 1–3, 112, 182, 185, 188, 190, 192, 194–96
Fiber perishables, 2, 32, 36, 42, 44–45, 67, 122, 129, 133, 135, 180–81, 184–85, 195; *see also* Fiber artifacts, Fiber industries, Perishables, and Textiles
Fiber rings, 31
Finishing. *See* Rim Finishing and Selvages
"Fish sandwiches," 31
Fish traps, 31, 102
Florian, Mary-Lou E., 187
Florida, 36–42, 68, 182–85, 195
Florida State University, 36
Floyd County, Va., 148
Foley Farm phase, 95
Footwear. *See* Sandals

Form of fiber industries, 2–3, 8–16, 30–32, 34, 36–37, 41–45, 59, 64–65, 73–86, 102–3, 128–32, 160–61, 167, 184, 192, 195
Fort Ancient culture, 91–93, 96
Fort Rock Basin, 188
Fort Rock Cave, Oreg., 180
Fowler, Catherine S., 196
Franklin County, Vt., 50, 105, 107
Fremont culture, 189–90; distribution of, 189; fiber industries, 189–90
French Farm site, W. Va., 91–92
French Lick, Tenn., 162
Fringe, 14
Frye site, Md., 146, 149–50, 152–55; cordage, 152; location of, 145

Gallatin County, Ill., 162
Gambling trays, 44
Gardner, Joan S., 81, 181, 187
Garments, 11, 12, 41, 57, 64–66, 73, 82–85, 107, 167, 182–84, 193; *see also* Aprons, Belts, Breechcloths, Capes, Clothing, Cowls, Hats, Hoods, Kilts, Mantles, Robes, Sashes, Shirts, Shrouds, and Skirts
Gender roles, fiber industries as reflective of, 11–12, 90, 186
Gensler site, Pa., 91–92, 95
Georgia, 73–86, 186–87
Georgia Historical Commission, 79
Glacial Kame complex, 44
Glaciated Allegheny Plateau, 91–93, 95
Glade Branch site, Ky., 94–95
Glen Meyer phase, 134
Gnagey site, Pa., 91–92
Goldcamp site, Ohio, 91, 93
Gore site, Md., 146, 149–50, 152–55; cordage, 152; location of, 145
Graham Cave, Mo.: dating, 33; location of, 35; twining, 33
Grayson County, Va., 148
Grayson, J. E. *See* D. Catling
Great Basin, 31, 89, 180, 182, 184–86, 188–90, 192–96; fiber industries developmental sequence, 188–90; subregion, eastern, 189–90, 193–94; subregion, northern, 188–90, 194; subregion, western, 188–90, 194–95
Great Lakes, 8, 122, 133, 184; *see also* Upper Great Lakes
Great Plains, 43, 133; *see also* Plains
Great Valley section, 148, 150, 153
Gue Farm site, W. Va., 91, 93
Gulf of Georgia, 195–96
Gulf of Mexico, 34

Hagerstown Valley, 149
Hamilton, Nathan D., 181, 184–85
Hammocks, 11, 146
Handedness, as explanation for spin/twist variability, 14, 90, 147
Handsman, Russell G., 10
Hannan, Frank, 7
Harding, Deborah G., 37
Harpeth River, 160; location of, 160
Harrington, Mark R., 188

Lovelock Wicker type plaiting, 188–89
Lower Pecos (Texas), 5, 16n, 36, 44, 97n, 182–83, 188–91; influence on Ozark Bluffs, 43–44; *see also* Texas, western, and Trans-Pecos (Texas)
Luray (focus) complex, 148, 154–55, 156n

MacCord, Howard A., 146, 149–50
Mackinac ceramic ware. *See* Mackinac phase
Mackinac phase, 120–21, 124, 126, 128–30, 133; distribution of, 134
MacNeish, Richard S., 192
Madison ceramic ware, 133
Maine, 7, 43, 52, 67, 100–104, 106, 108–15
Maine Indian Basketmakers Alliance, 7
Mammoth Cave, Ky., 182
Mann site, W. Va., 91, 93
Manson, Carl P., 146
Mantles, 82–85; *see also* Clothing, and Garments
Marin County, Calif., 194–95
Maritime Provinces, 6, 66–68, 114
Marmet Bluffs site, W. Va., 91–92
Marmet Village site, W. Va., 91–92
Martins Meadow site, Md., 146, 149–50, 152–55; cordage, 153; location of, 145
Maryland, 144–56
Maslowski, Robert F., 146, 148, 150, 181, 185
Mason Island (focus) complex, 154–55
Mason, Otis T., 3, 182; classification of North American basketry, 3
Mason site, Maine: dating, 67; twining, 67
Massachusetts, 68
Material culture, 1, 10–16, 69, 89, 120, 135; criticism of materialist research, 11, 14–15, 112–13; research goals, 10–16, 181
Mato Grosso, Brazil, 11
Mats, 10, 32, 34, 45, 84, 102–3, 132, 182, 188–89, 191–95; *see also* Matting
Matting, 8, 31, 34, 36, 41, 75, 84–85, 188, 195; definition of, 30; *see also* Basketry, and Mats
Maurice River, 148
McFate complex, 95
McGregor, Roberta L., 191–92
McMullen, Ann, 10
McPherron, Alan L., 120, 122, 133–34
Meadowcroft Rockshelter, Pa.: cordage, 43; dating, 33–34, 42–43, 94; location of, 35, 95; plaiting, 33–34, 42–43, 182; raw materials, 34, 42–43
Mechanical alteration, 37, 40–42, 80–81, 164, 172
Mending, 37, 39, 42, 59, 123; *see also* Repairs
Mero ceramic ware, 134
Mesoamerica, archaeological fiber industries, 6, 32; *see also* Mexico, and New World
Metric attributes for fiber industries, 5, 9, 37, 56–59, 63–64, 138–40
Mexico, 32, 88–91, 182–83, 185, 188, 190–93; *see also* Coahuila, and Mesoamerica
Mezhirich site, Ukraine, 32
Michigan, 43–44, 67–69, 120–36
Mid-Atlantic. *See* Middle Atlantic

Middle Archaic period: dating, 33, 36–37, 42; fiber industries, 33, 36–42, 45, 67, 182–83; location of sites, 35
Middle Atlantic, 144–56, 181
Middle Horizon period, 194
Middle Mississippian ceramics, 134; *see also* Mississippian period
Middle Woodland period, 68, 73, 88, 113; dating, 100–102; distribution of sites, 95; fiber industries, 68, 73, 88, 93–95, 103–4, 109, 111, 113, 133, 148, 154–55, 181, 183
Middlesex (phase) complex, definition of, 53; diagnostic artifacts, 53; fiber industries, 50–69
Midwest, 3, 52–53, 88–97, 160, 162–63, 184
Milo, Maine, 108
Miscellaneous fiber constructions, 30–31; definition of, 31
Missisquoi River, 50; location of, 51
Mississippi River, 162
Mississippian period, 3, 5; core area, 162; fiber industries, 73–86, 160–72, 181, 184–87; nonfiber artifacts, 79–80, 83–84
Missouri, 34, 42, 162
Mogollon, fiber industries, 191–93
Moldavia, 32
Monocacy River, 149; area of, 145
Monongahela ceramic ware, 155
Monongahela culture, 91–95, 155–56n
Monongahela River drainage, 91, 155; area of, 91, 95
Monroe County, Tenn., 36
Montgomery complex, 144, 146, 154–55; ceramics, 144, 146, 149; cordage, 150, 152–55; dating, 144; distribution of, 144
Montgomery County, Mo., 34
Moorehead Cave, Tex., 90–91
Moorehead complex, 43, 101–2
Moorehead, Warren K., 74, 79, 83
Morphology. *See* Form
Morris, Earl H., 186, 192–93
Morrison Shelter, W. Va., 94–95
Morrow site, N.Y., 67; dating, 67; twining, 67
Mound Bottom site, Tenn., 160–72; ceramics, 162–63; dating, 160–61; location of, 161; twining, 160, 164–71
Mound C. *See* Etowah site
Mounier, R. Alan, 148
Mt. Horeb Mound, Ky., 68; dating, 68; twining, 68
Mt. Mazama, 188
Munsungan Lake, 106, 109
Museum of Anthropology, University of Michigan, 120–21
Muskingum Island site, W. Va., 93–95
Mythological beliefs, role of fiber industries in, 12

Nashville Basin, 161
Nashville, Tenn., 161–62
Native American contact with Europeans/Euroamericans, effects of, 2, 7–8, 32, 66, 183
Native Americans, 2, 182–83; Cherokee, 79; Cheyenne, 112; Coahuiltecan speakers, 88–91, 191; Gé speakers, 146; Haida, 177; Iroquoian speakers, 113–14, 134, 144; Karok, 112; Kayabi, 12; Klamath, 186, 190; Kwakiutl, 112; Maidu, 81–82; Makah, 195; Mehinaku, 11; Micmac, 6–7; Modoc, 190; Nootka, 195; Northern Paiute, 190; Northern Shoshone, 190; O'odham, 192, 194; Paiute, 112; Passamaquoddy, 7; Pima, 112; Salishan speakers, 96,

Webb, William S., 68, 162
Webster, Laurie D., 186
Weed Shelter, W. Va., 94–95
Wefts, 8–9, 36–39, 43–45, 53–64, 67, 69, 88–89, 102, 122–24, 128, 165, 184, 189–90, 194–96; cordage used as, 45, 54–56, 60, 67, 124, 126; definition of, 31; fixed, 36; rows, 36; "running," 36; types of weft (or stitch) slant, 13, 105; *see also* Twining
West Virginia, 91–96, 148
Western Hemisphere, 188; *see also* New World
Weyanoke Old Town site, Va., 148
Wickliffe Mounds site, Ky., 167, 172
Wiessner, Polly, 112
Wigglesworth, Lynn, 148
Williams, Stephen, 163
Willoughby, Charles C., 3, 81–83
Wilson, Thomas, 34
Windmiller complex, 194
Windover Bog Cemetery, Fla., 182, 184–85, 195; basketry, 37; burial associations, 40; composite construction, 42; cordage, 33, 41–42; dating, 33, 36–37; functional types of fiber artifacts, 41; human age/sex associations, 40; location of, 35; mechanical alteration, 40; other artifact associations, 41; plaiting, 33, 41; pollen associations, 41; raw material processing, 40; raw materials, 39–42; repairs, 39; residue, 40–41; sel-vages, 38; splices, 38–39; subsistence associations, 41; textiles, 37, 41; twining, 33, 37–41; warps, 37–38; wear, 39; wefts, 38
Windsor County, Vt., 105
Winslow site, Md., 146, 149–50, 152–55; cordage, 152; location of, 145
Wisconsin, 133–34
Witthoff, John, 146
Wooden artifacts, 2, 6–7, 40–42, 53
Woodland period, 31, 45; dating, 67, 100–102; fiber industries, 31–32, 42, 45, 67–69, 100–14, 120–36, 144–56, 172, 181, 183–84
Woodside phase, 96
Woodward, Douglas R., 146
Work direction, 38, 112–13, 191
Works Progress Administration (W.P.A.), 5
Woven, 8–9, 41, 45, 63, 82, 96, 112–13; loom woven, 8, 10–11, 183, 186, 193; nonloom woven, 3, 8, 10–11, 31–32, 41, 43, 57, 64–66, 68, 102–3, 180, 186, 193; *see also* Interlacing, and Weaves
Wright, James V., 133
Wyoming, 193

Yanomamo, twined basketry, 14; twined pesimak woman's apron, 11–12, 14
Yarn, 9, 73–78, 80–82, 85, 164–66, 170, 172, 186–87; *see also* Ply